The KABBALAH *of the* SOUL

The Transformative Psychology and Practices of Jewish Mysticism

LEONORA LEET

Inner Traditions
Rochester, Vermont

Inner Traditions International
One Park Street
Rochester, Vermont 05767
www.InnerTraditions.com

Library of Congress Cataloging-in-Publication Data

Leet, Leonora.
  The kabbalah of the soul : the transformative psychology and practices
of Jewish mysticism / Leonora Leet.
      p. cm.
Includes bibliographical references and index.
  ISBN 0-89281-957-X
  1. Soul (Judaism) 2. Transmigration—Judaism. 3.
Cabala—Psychological aspects. 4. Spiritual life—Judaism. 5. Conduct
of life. I. Title.
  BM645.S6L44 2003
  296.1'6—dc21
                                        2003001830

Printed and bound in the United States at Lake Book Manufacturing, Inc.

10 9 8 7 6 5 4 3 2 1

Text design and layout by Virginia Scott Bowman
This book was typeset in Bembo, with Schneidler and Avenir as display typefaces

"*The Kabbalah of the Soul: The Transformative Psychology and Practices of Jewish Mysticism* is a daring and innovative exposition of the secret doctrines and practices of the Jewish mystical tradition. Writing in a lively and lucid manner, Leonora Leet guides the reader through the intricate nooks and crannies of the Kabbalah, focusing particularly on the intersection of cosmological teaching and psychological healing. As with her other books on Kabbalah, Leet has produced a volume that both engages ancient wisdom and translates it into an idiom that is uniquely applicable to the present."

Elliot R. Wolfson, Abraham Lieberman Professor of Hebrew and Judaic Studies at New York University, author of *Through a Speculum That Shines*

"This is a work of astounding erudition and truly amazing variety and originality. *The Kabbalah of the Soul* is an illuminating 'guide for the perplexed' for our time through the labyrinth of the Jewish mystical tradition. By way of dazzling excursions into psychology, religious history, consciousness expansion, Eastern and Western meditative methods, musical theory, literature and many other arts and sciences, it is also very much of a masterly and wise bildungsroman—doing for the soul what once Hegel did for the mind so awesomely in his *Phenomenology;* for here Leonora Leet recounts the stages of a soul's progress and ascent through 'temptations of a fallen culture' to the hope for a transformed life on Earth."

Philip Beitchman, Ph.D., author of *Alchemy of the Word: Cabala of the Renaissance* and *The View From Nowhere: Essays in Mysticism, Literature and Philosophy*

"The ongoing process of reclaiming the rich and complex soul of the Kabbalah requires not only recounting the past, but pushing into unknown territory to find Light. Leet's words, continuing the Zoharic and Lurianic traditions, build a new and inclusive model of personal transformation that will be of great interest to anyone concerned with finding the Divine on Earth."

Jason Shulman, Director, A Society of Souls, a school of Integrated Kabbalistic Healing

To my granddaughter
Sarah Goodman
And to her parents,
My daughter Tamar and son-in-law Keith,
For this most wondrous gift of life

Numberless are the wonders of this world
From crimson sunsets coloring still waters
Or morning glories greeting the sun's return
To all the elegant patterning at each level
Of complexity the mind can pierce,
A wonder baffling physicists who seek
To bottom the infinite depths of cosmic creation.

But of all the wonders of this world,
The marvel that most astonishes my heart
Is the precious perfection of my granddaughter Sarah,
Smiling right from her birth with the infinite
Potential of her consciousness to give
To this whole cosmic parade that special meaning
Already filling my newly connected life.

CONTENTS

Appendices

1

THE SCALE
OF THE SOUL

INTRODUCTION TO A NEW COSMIC MODEL FOR
KABBALISTIC SOUL PSYCHOLOGY

Throughout the history of the Jewish mystical tradition that culminates in the Kabbalah, humanity has been understood to play a pivotal role in the perfection of the cosmos, transforming its original emanations of ever more materialized individuality into such purification of identity as can finally unite the finite with the infinite in the full realization of divine personality. To explicate how humankind can be so centrally involved in the cosmic process, this tradition has developed complex theories of the multidimensional nature both of the human soul and of the cosmos, but it has not been as successful in integrating these two inseparable aspects of experienced reality. This chapter will attempt to synthesize the main traditions of Jewish esoteric cosmology as a framework for the following studies of the human soul and of the mechanisms of transformative spiritual work that, at each of its psycho-cosmological levels, can enable it to reach ever higher dimensions of consciousness.

Before turning to the complex subject of kabbalistic cosmology, we should briefly review the understanding of the soul appearing in the *Zohar*, the most important work of the Kabbalah, which surfaced in thirteenth-century Spain. This seminal work presents a theory of three soul levels based on the three words used in the Bible to signify the soul: *nefesh*, *ruach*, and *neshamah*. In a discussion of the afterlife, they are hierarchically arranged, "one within the other," on the two levels of the lower and higher selves:

> Three names has the soul of man: *nefesh*, *ruah*, *neshamah*. They are all comprised one within the other, yet they have three distinct abodes. *Nefesh* remains in the grave until the body is decomposed and turned into dust, during which time it flits about in this world. . . . *Ruah* enters the earthly Garden (of Eden) and there dons a likeness which is in the semblance of the body it tenanted in this world. . . . *Neshamah* ascends at once to her place, the region from whence she emanated, and for her sake the light is kindled to shine above. She never again descends to earth. In her is consummated the One who combines all sides, the upper and the lower. And as long as she has not ascended to be united with the Throne, the *ruah* cannot crown itself in the lower Garden, nor can the *nefesh* be at ease in its place. . . . Once this is accomplished, however, both the others are united each with its sphere; for all three are one, forming one whole, united in a mystical bond, according to the prototype above, in which *nefesh*, *ruah*, and *neshamah* constitute together one totality.[1]

The Nefesh is the lowest level and represents the birthright animal or vital soul that cannot by itself survive the decomposition of the body. The higher two levels are personal achievements of soul growth that can survive the disintegration of the vital soul after death, the Ruach apparently subject to the process of reincarnation, which the Kabbalah calls *gilgul*, while the Neshamah can retain its identity in the divine realm of spirit from which it emanated and, unlike the Ruach, "never again descends to earth." For, as we are further told: "in her is consummated the One." Where the Neshamah is the divine element in the human soul, the Ruach represents the fully realized human level on which mankind is supposed to be functioning. Isaac Luria, who developed the most influential reformulation of the Zoharic Kabbalah in sixteenth-century Safed, then in Palestine, was later to stress this point. In the words of his foremost interpreter, Chayyim Vital: "for, as we know, it is the *ruach* that is called 'human.' Understand this well!"[2] Not only is the Neshamah deemed necessary to complete the human soul and fulfill the potential of its lower levels, but it is also essential for the illumination of the higher realms from which it emanated, and, as we shall later see, its final ascension "to be united with the Throne" illuminates the very purpose of the cosmos.

To understand the important distinction made here between the Neshamah and the lower levels of the soul as well as the different structure of these Nefesh and Ruach levels, we should turn to the treatment of the soul in the *Midrash ha-Ne'elam on Ruth*, thought to be in the earliest stratum of the *Zohar*:[3]

> The Holy One, blessed be He, gave two fine crowns to man, for him to use in this world, namely, *nefesh* and *ruaḥ*. . . . [T]he *nefesh* cannot survive in the body without being stimulated by the *ruaḥ*, which rests above it.
>
> When man begins to serve and worship his Creator with these two, he is stimulated by a holy stimulus from above, which rests upon man and surrounds him on every side. . . . And what is its name? *Neshamah.* The *neshamah* is a higher power than that which is called *ruaḥ*, because the *ruaḥ* was provided by the Holy One, blessed be He, for service in this world, while the *neshamah* always acts as a stimulus for service in the upper realms. . . .
>
> Just as there is a *ruaḥ* and a *nefesh* on the right-hand side, on the side of the good inclination, so there is a *ruaḥ* and a *nefesh* on the left-hand side, on the side of the evil inclination.[4]

The vital Nefesh soul is meant in man to function as part of a conjoined Nefesh/Ruach soul "for service in this world," and when such human activity is intended as a form of divine "service," it draws down the holy Neshamah soul "for service in the upper realms."

In the first treatment in this passage, the dual forms of "service" by the human and divine elements of the multileveled soul are both recognized to be good, however opposite they may be in orientation. But in the final treatment there is a reversion to the talmudic understanding of the soul as subject to the opposing influences of the Yetzer ha-Tov (the good inclination) and the Yetzer ha-Ra (the evil inclination), an understanding the *Zohar* synthesizes with its new view of the soul as so divided at each of its levels. This is not the simpler understanding of the conflict in the soul as one between its divine and so good element, the Neshamah, and its animal and so bad element, the Nefesh, an understanding whose vitality has persisted well into the hasidic period.[5] It is rather one that recognizes each of the earth-oriented soul levels as being, like the cosmic worlds with which we shall soon see they may be correlated, essentially double aspected. In chapters 2 and 3 on the Nefesh and Ruach soul levels, respectively, we shall see how this double aspecting, while subjecting the soul to such temptation as may finally be symbolized by the myth of the Fall, is necessary for the soul's final perfection. But to understand how this can be, we must first come to an initial understanding of kabbalistic cosmology.

There are three main approaches to the questions of cosmic origins and processes that have dominated Jewish cosmological thinking—those of the Bible, of the *Zohar*, and of the Lurianic writings—and these have ever been in conflict. First there is the Bible's account of the creation of the heavens and earth in seven "days," which has had a long subsequent development in the Merkabah-Hekhalot conception of seven halls or heavens, in the talmudic understanding of the symbolic nature of the Genesis account, and in the fourteenth-century development of the further talmudic concept of the Shemitot, or cosmic eras, that informs the *Sefer ha-Temunah*. Turning now to the most influential work of the Kabbalah, the *Zohar*, we find a cosmos emanating from a central point in spheres upon spheres, originally without number. In later fourteenth-century additions this process of emanation is seen to produce four cosmic worlds, given the names of Atzilut (Emanation), Beriah (Creation), Yetzirah (Formation), and Asiyah (Action); and each of these cosmic spheres is understood to have two opposing aspects, an inner, purer half, comparable to its brain, and an outer, denser half, comparable to its skull or shell. Finally, in the cosmology developed by Isaac Luria, who was called the Ari, there is the new conception of a Tzimtzum, the contraction of the divine Ein Sof, the Unlimited One, first to define a centering point to the Limitless Light and then the withdrawal of most of this light from that point in all directions, leaving a spherical vacuum in which the four worlds of the Spanish Kabbalah could be emanated from the outside inward in descending levels of spiritual purity and in both circular and linear forms. For the initial processes of the Tzimtzum are followed by the insertion of a linear ray of light containing the ten Sefirot of the Tree of Life, the central diagram of the Kabbalah, in the form of the primordial cosmic man, Adam Kadmon. Each of these worlds is further understood to be composed of the ten subspheres of its Tree of Sefirot, the circular aspect of the worlds that develops at each stage in the penetration of the inserted line of light. So there is first the conflict between seven and four cosmic worlds, eras, or dimensions, then the conflict between whether these cosmic worlds were emanated from the center outward or from the periphery of a cosmic circle inward, and finally the question of whether each cosmic world is composed of two or ten subdivisions.

What primarily distinguishes Zoharic and Lurianic cosmology is that the former is strictly emanationist, bringing the cosmic process through past stages of increasing materiality only up to this fallen world of Asiyah, while the latter is future oriented. In the Lurianic cosmology elaborated in the most important text of the Lurianic Kabbalah, the *Eitz Chayyim* of Chayyim Vital, there are two stages that follow the initial Tzimtzum, those of the Shevirah, or shattering of the vessels, and of that Tikkun through which those shattered vessels are to be reconfigured. As we have seen, the first act following the divine withdrawal is the reinsertion into the vacated space within the cosmic sphere of a line of light containing the ten Sefirot, the divine attributes, in the form of a primordial cosmic man. It is the vessels of these Sefirot that shatter,[6] that prove inadequate to contain the power of the Limitless Light, the Or Ein Sof, and that thus require repair. In this work of Tikkun the cosmic process becomes transformed from a past to a future orientation, the original form of the single anthropocosm being reconfigured into the multiple forms of the divine personalities, the Partzufim, through the spiritual development of humanity. It is, moreover, such a transformation of the divine unity into multiple divine personalities that would seem, for Luria, to be the whole purpose of the cosmic process. With this brief review of the elements that will here be synthesized into the more coherent model of kabbalistic cosmology that can also be correlated with kabbalistic soul psychology, let us look more closely at each of the three main sources of Jewish cosmology.

THE TRADITION OF BIBLICAL COSMOLOGY

We can begin to synthesize the creation account in Genesis 1 with the four worlds of kabbalistic cosmology by recognizing its symbolic character, as suggested already in the Talmud. In Eruvin 18a and Berakhot 61a, the contradictions between the creation accounts in Genesis 1 and 2 are resolved by understanding that the first refers to the creation "in thought" and the second to the creation "in deed."[7] With such a view of Genesis 1 as providing not the actuality but the ideal plan for cosmic evolution, we can understand the seven "days" of creation to provide an archetypal model of the whole progress of cosmic development.

Such an approach also appears in the Lurianic tradition, in the thoughts of Israel Sarug concerning events that occurred before the Tzimtzum, as summarized by Gershom Scholem:

> In the beginning *Ein-Sof* took pleasure in his own autarkic self-sufficiency, and this "pleasure" produced a kind of "shaking"

(*ni'anu'a*). . . . As a result of this "shaking," "primordial points" were "engraved" in the power of *Din*, thus becoming the first forms to leave their markings in the essence of *Ein-Sof* . . . and the primordial Torah, the ideal world woven in the substance of *Ein-Sof* itself, came into being. . . . [T]he hidden law of the whole of creation that is inscribed within the "engraving" of *Ein-Sof* is henceforward active and expresses itself throughout all subsequent processes. . . .[8]

Thus both biblical and Lurianic cosmology can be understood to contain an initial plan of ideal cosmic evolution that "expresses itself throughout all subsequent processes."

If we look at Genesis 1 from this perspective, we can see how its seven "days" can be made coherent with the four worlds of the Kabbalah. Elsewhere I have shown both how this biblical creation account is informed by the esoteric keys of geometry and music, the keys of the hexagram and of the harmonic series, and how it can be made coherent with the four-worlds doctrine of kabbalistic cosmology.[9] I shall now summarize some of this earlier analysis, beginning with the issue of coherence.

There is no problem about associating the first world of Atzilut (Emanation) with the creation of light on the first day since both may be understood to represent a divine emanation not separable from its divine source. From the kabbalistic perspective, creation really begins with the second world of Beriah (Creation), and the firmament created on the second day would seem to fulfill this same function of separating the Creator from the Creation. So too may the garden world of the third day be related to the third world of Yetzirah (Formation) since the Kabbalah associates this world with the Garden of Eden and the transgression of Adam that led to the materialization of the fourth world of Asiyah (Action), our own solid world.

It is with the fourth day that a problem may be thought to arise since the creation of the sun and moon on this day does not seem to include the earth created on the third day. But this problem may perhaps be resolved by a comment made on this verse in the *Zohar:* "Observe that stars and planets exist through a covenant that is the firmament of the heaven, in which they are inscribed and engraved."[10] For if the sun and moon can be identified with the "stars and planets," which is just what they are, then we can understand them to represent all the physical constituents of the cosmos, including the earth with the totality of its natural elements. In any case, such a limited correlation of the days of creation with cosmological stages does appear in the Kabbalah. As Scholem has shown, in discussing the relation of the seven days of creation to the lower seven Sefirot, "The correlation of the 'Sefirot of the building' [the lower seven Sefirot] with the days of creation became extremely complex. Many kabbalists, including the author of the bulk of the Zohar . . . regarded creation, which from the mystical viewpoint was the completion of 'the building' of emanation, as having been already completed by the fourth day.[11]

If we can consider the vegetative earth of the third day to represent a more spiritual level of creation and the astronomical features of the fourth day to represent all the material components of the cosmos, then we can make a full correspondence between the first four days of creation and the four cosmic worlds of the Kabbalah. On this basis, we can go on to chart the more virtual, still to be manifested, higher dimensions of consciousness figured in the remaining three days of creation, dimensions that may be thought, with Sarug, to have been inscribed in the "space" of Ein Sof that is to become the locus of the finite cosmos. This location will, in turn, contain the residual light, called the Reshimu, that is to be left in the primordial space, called Tehiru, after the withdrawal of the light of Ein Sof during the Tzimtzum.

Unlike the biblical source of all Jewish sevenfold cosmological modeling, the four worlds that entered kabbalistic cosmology in the fourteenth century and supplanted the competing Sabbatical cosmology of the fourteenth-century *Temunah* by the time of the Safed Kabbalists, some two hundred years later, would seem to have been a product of Pythagorean influence. Pythagorean cosmology is encoded in the figure of the Tetractys, which requires some examination. This is a figure of ten dots or pebbles arranged in the form of an equilateral triangle on four descending lines of one, two, three, and four dots, respectively, as shown in figure 1.1.

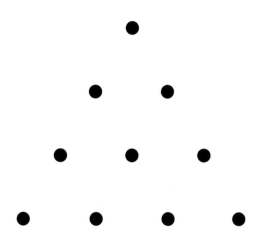

Figure 1.1. The Tetractys

Geometrically the four descending rows of dots in the Tetractys represent the progression through the dimensions: the single dot represents the nondimensional point; the two dots the one-dimensional line, which requires two points to define it; the three dots the two-dimensional plane, which requires three dots to define its minimal form of the triangle; and the four dots the three-dimensional solid, which requires four dots to define its minimal form of the tetrahedron, the solid composed of four equilateral triangles.

The four lines of the Tetractys also define the ratios of the major harmonics, understood as the sequential, partial expressions of the first or fundamental tone: the ratio of 2:1 of the upper two lines represents the interval of the octave between the second harmonic and the first, the generating tone or fundamental; that of 3:2 the interval of the musical fifth between the third and second harmonics; and that of 4:3

the interval of the musical fourth between the fourth and third harmonics, that is, the interval between the fifth above the first octave and the second octave. As we shall later see, it is the inversion of these ratios into fractions that defines the geometric relationship of string length to harmonic tone, the relationship that contains the central Pythagorean insight into cosmic functioning. The Tetractys, then, neatly defines the relationship, mediated by number, of the geometry of form to the harmonic structure of sound, of space to time, the finite to the infinite, that is the essential gnosis of sacred science;[12] and its union of four worlds with ten elements has had a pervasive influence upon kabbalistic cosmology.

As previously noted, I have elsewhere shown that this same knowledge informs the Genesis creation account, the order and nature of the days being determined by the harmonic series and the geometric form of the hexagram, the Star of David. Briefly summarizing my argument for this musical correspondence, it should initially be noted that the first seven notes in the harmonic series may be represented in the familiar terminology of solfeggio and the notes in the key of C as follows: (1) Do/C; (2) Do^1/C; (3) Sol/G; (4) Do^2/C; (5) Mi/E; (6) Sol^1/G; (7) Tay/Bb. Now, in Genesis 1, the first, second, and fourth days—corresponding to the tone of Do and its first two octaves, which appear in the first, second, and fourth positions of the harmonic series—are those concerned with heavenly creation: with the creation of the supernal light on the first day, of the firmament called "heaven" on the second day, and of the sun and moon on the fourth day. Likewise, the third and sixth days—corresponding to the tone of Sol and its first octave, which appear in the third and sixth positions in the order of the harmonic series—are those concerned with earthly creation, the third-day creation of the dry land with its vegetation and the sixth-day creation of the animals and humankind. Next, the fifth day—corresponding to the harmonizing tone of Mi, which appears fifth in the harmonic series—is concerned with the creation of what might be called the "flowing" animals, the fish in the flowing element of water and the birds in the flowing element of air. And finally the seventh day of suspended work—corresponding to the "septimal seventh," the harmonic seventh that is a slightly flatter version of the well-tempered minor seventh (Bb in the key of C) and whose suspension demands a modulation to the new key of the subdominant—is reflective of the transformative nature of the Sabbath.

As can be seen, it is only the esoteric key of the harmonic series that can explain the curious inversion of the third and fourth days, in which the progression through the creation of heavenly elements is suddenly interrupted by the earthly creation of the third day. For the heavenly creation of the first, second, and fourth days corresponds to the positions in the harmonic series in which the tonic tone of Do appears, as the earthly creation of the third and sixth days corresponds to the positions in which the dominant tone of Sol appears in this series, the fifth and seventh days corresponding to neither of these harmonic categories while representing qualities corresponding with their musical harmonic tones.

I have rehearsed this material at such length because these harmonic correspondences will further help us to understand Genesis 1 as a creation "in thought," as the ideal plan of cosmic evolution virtually inscribed in the fabric of existence. How the geometric coordinates of the hexagram may similarly explain aspects of the Genesis account that are otherwise incomprehensible—as in the stipulation for the third day, "Let the waters under the heaven be gathered together unto one place and let the dry land appear" (Gen. 1:9)—can be gleaned from figure 1.2, which illustrates both the harmonic and geometric coordinates of the days of creation.

The geometric coordinates of the Tetractys symbol may also explain why Kabbalists knowledgeable about sacred science, implicit in such a reference to what "we know from the science of geometry"[13] by Chayyim Vital in the *Eitz Chayyim*, may have felt they could not go beyond the four worlds clearly correlated with the progression through the geometric dimensions from the point to the solid.

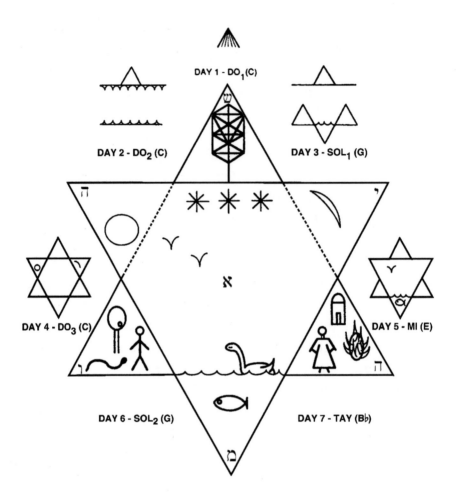

Figure 1.2. The Hexagram of Creation

But the basis for such an extension of the dimensions beyond the three of space already existed at the very beginning of the kabbalistic tradition, in the *Sefer Yetzirah*. In verse 5 of chapter 1, we may find the key to a seven-dimensional cosmos: "Ten Sefirot of Nothingness: Their measure is ten which have no end. A depth of beginning, a depth of end; a depth of good, a depth of evil; a depth above, a depth below; a depth east, a depth west; a depth north, a depth south. The singular Master, God faithful King, dominates them all from His Holy dwelling until eternity of eternities."[14] In this remarkable passage, we are taken from the three dimensions of space ("a depth above, a depth below; a depth east, a depth west; a depth north, a depth south") to an Einsteinian fourth dimension of time ("A depth of beginning, a depth of end") and from there still further to a fifth dimension, a moral dimension ("a depth of good, a depth of evil") woven into the fabric of existence that ensures that as we sow so shall we reap, a dimension of purposive causality that may be called Providential. But the passage does not stop there; it gives us yet another dimension, the knowledge that the justice working itself out within the frame of space-time cannot be reduced simply to a mechanism, however marvelous, but is itself controlled by a higher power ("The singular Master, God faithful King, dominates them all from His Holy dwelling"), a dimension that invests the cosmic mechanism with meaningfulness. And beyond this sixth dimension, itself one of eternity, is the final dimension of Sabbatical rest, the "eternity of eternities" that sums up and contains these endless measurements.[15] With this new key in hand, let us now return to our prior model of a seven-dimensional cosmos, the Genesis creation account.

Our earlier attempt to synthesize the creation account in Genesis 1 with the four cosmic worlds of the Kabbalah brought us to the fourth day, which may be correlated with the world of the present. If we can accept this identification of the fourth day with the fourth cosmic world of Asiyah, and so with the present world of solid matter and all it is capable of generating, then we should also be able to identify it with the soul level that is native to the spiritually undeveloped person, the Nefesh soul, and view the remaining three days as defining the virtual higher dimensions of consciousness, dimensions whose characteristics might be thought, with Sarug, to have been inscribed in the Reshimu but which require human soul development for their actualization.

The biblical account gives us clues as to the nature of these soul levels. As the fourth day contributes a level of creation under "rule" (Gen. 1:16), it suggests that the Nefesh soul is or should be ruled, whether by a Torah internalized in the heart or one externalized in codified laws. In contrast, the fifth and sixth days bring us to creation levels that are both termed "blessed" in the Genesis text (1:22, 28). We have seen that the fifth day is one involving the flowing elements of water and air, and so the Ruach soul level, which can be understood to correspond to it, would represent the spiritual dimension that can enter the divine flow. The sixth day would similarly correspond to the Neshamah soul level and define it as that which not only no longer needs to be ruled but is also above the flow in the higher state of spiritual "dominion" (Gen. 1:26).

Further qualities of the basic three soul levels have been derived from the triadic structure of the Tree of Life Diagram, whose ten Sefirot are represented in the three columns of the Lurianic version of this central kabbalistic diagram shown in figure 1.3. The divine attributes represented by the ten Sefirot are named in descending order: Keter (Crown); Chokhmah (Wisdom); Binah (Understanding); Chesed (Mercy); Gevurah (Judgment); Tiferet (Beauty); Netzach (Eternity); Hod (Splendor); Yesod (Foundation); and Malkhut (Kingdom). In the Adam Kadmon form of the Tree of Life Diagram, the first three are associated with his head, Keter above his crown, Chokhmah on the right side of his brain, and Binah on its left side; the next three are associated with his upper torso, Chesed on his right arm, Gevurah on his left arm, and Tiferet directly on his heart; the next three are associated with his lower torso and limbs, Netzach on his right knee, Hod on his left knee, and Yesod back up at his genitals (which suggests a crossed leg rather than the traditional standing posture);[16] finally, Malkhut is associated either with both the female genitalia and the head of the male organ or with the feet.

These placements have been interpreted to define three levels of psychic functioning, the upper triad associated with the mental faculties,

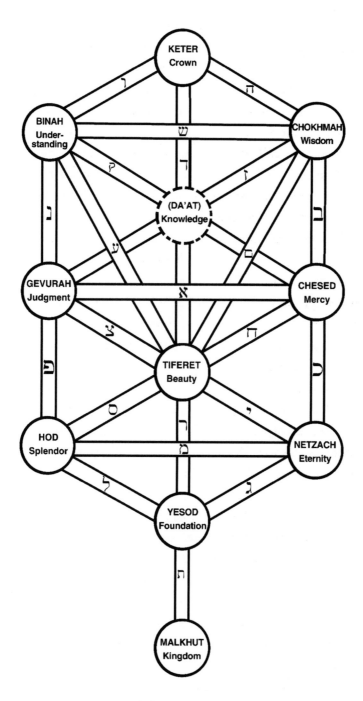

Figure 1.3. The Tree of Life Diagram

the middle triad with the emotional faculties, and the lower triad with the sensual faculties, and these levels of psychological experience have often been further transferred to the three main soul levels, defining the Neshamah soul as the mental, the Ruach soul as the emotional, and the Nefesh soul as the sensual level of conscious experience. Each triad also features an opposition of qualities that are harmoniously balanced by the middle member of each, those of the right column representing the more spiritually expansive, more merciful pole and those of the left column the more egotistically constricted and judgmental pole. It is this structure of the Tree that has been the focus of most attempts to apply the Kabbalah to human psychology, from Moses Cordovero's *Tomer Devorah* (The Palm Tree of Deborah) to contemporary forms of New Age spirituality, and aspects of the Tree, particularly in its reconfiguration of the Sefirot into Partzufim, will be featured in the following chapters, which will generally understand the soul to be composed of two similarly opposed aspects at each of its levels.

Such discussions will also place these soul levels within a larger cosmic structure than that normally employed in the Kabbalah but consistent with the Bible. As we have seen, the fourth cosmic world of the material present, corresponding to the fourth "day" of the "creation in thought," has been identified with the Nefesh soul. And we can now further elaborate the coordinates to the fifth and sixth cosmic days and worlds in terms of the two future stages appearing in traditional Jewish eschatology, understanding the fifth such cosmic world to correspond not only to the Ruach soul but also to the future Messianic Age and the sixth cosmic world not only to the Neshamah soul but also to the World to Come, the Olam ha-Ba.

We have thus far only considered the three levels of the soul that take their names from the three terms for soul found in the Bible, terms traditionally combined in the acronym Naran. But to the Nefesh, Ruach, and Neshamah levels of the soul with which the *Zohar* is concerned, we now must consider the two soul levels that the

Talmud added to the biblical three,[17] those named Chayah and Yechidah, which are further developed in the later Lurianic Kabbalah. We shall later see that in the final Sabbatical day and world, these highest two soul levels are uplifted into the condition of holiness that invests all Sabbatical experience, the experience of unification, on the Chayah level of a unification with its unconscious shadow self and finally, on the Yechidah level, of the lower finite self with its higher infinite form. The seventh dimension is that in which all opposites are brought into a generative unification, generative of the highest level of the soul, the Yechidah or unified soul, and this holy being, the goal of creation, is that fully developed soul able to combine in its own nature the finite and the infinite.

The seven cosmic worlds that can be correlated with the seven days of Genesis can finally be seen to represent seven dimensions of available experience: the four dimensions of space-time that inform Nefesh consciousness; the fifth dimension of Providential causation, whose workings the Ruach consciousness can comprehend and master; the still higher level of Neshamah consciousness, whose comprehension of the purpose of creation invests all experience in which it participates with the sixth dimension of meaningfulness; and the final levels of Chayah and Yechidah consciousness, in whose unifications of opposites, ultimately of the finite with the infinite, the seventh dimension of holiness is generated. We shall soon understand why the seventh dimension can uniquely be assigned two soul levels, but now need only understand this archetypal model of a seven-dimensional cosmos as one already virtually present whose highest levels can be touched in exalted moments of understanding and lead the soul into communion with the Holy.

Our focus has thus far been upon biblical cosmology, and we have seen how this ancient Hebraic formulation can be made coherent with the Hellenically inspired four-worlds doctrine of later kabbalistic cosmology while allowing a larger frame for the future coevolution of the human and the Divine. But before turning to the Zoharic and Lurianic forms of kabbalistic cosmology, we should conclude this study of biblical cosmology by considering its further history.

The application of a sevenfold division to cosmology is first carried from Genesis into the Merkabah-Hekhalot texts of seven palaces or heavens through which the soul must journey to achieve the highest of mystical experiences, the Throne vision. But from the Talmud through the fourteenth-century *Temunah* to the seventeenth-century Sabbatians (the followers of the false Messiah, Sabbatai Tz'vi), it was the biblically derived concept of the Shemitot, of seven cosmic eras, that continued to exert an influence on Jewish cosmological thought, particularly in periods of Messianic tension.

The theory of the Shemitot derives most immediately from such talmudic statements as that of Rav Katina, itself derived from the creation account, as Scholem shows, "that the world would last for 6,000 years and be destroyed in the seventh millennium, in which a parallel is drawn between the days of creation and those of the world, seen as a great cosmic week."[18] As elaborated in the *Temunah*, each cosmic world or cycle endures for a Shemitah of 7,000 years dominated by a particular Sefirah and the reading of the Torah appropriate to it, our Shemitah being under the dominance of the Sefirah of Gevurah or Din, the Sefirah that signifies rigorous judgment. This basic Sabbatical concept of cosmic time, of six world cycles followed by a seventh period of consummation, is one that can be assimilated, with some qualification, to the more standard kabbalistic concept of the four cosmic worlds.

The translations of Shemitot into cosmic worlds is clearest with regard to the Olam ha-Ba, the World to Come, Kabbalists having speculated that "the world to come would be the creation of another link in the chain of 'creations,' or *shemitot* ('sabbaticals': according to the view of the author of the *Sefer ha-Temunah*)."[19] As the Olam ha-Ba was considered to be a Shemitah, a cosmic cycle or world in a series of such worlds, so are there strong reasons to argue the same for the Messianic

Age. Perhaps the chief reason relates to the important Messianic concept of a new Torah to be then revealed. Since in the concept of the Shemitot each Shemitah is accorded its own revelation of the Torah, the antinomian view of the Messianic Age as containing such a revelation implies that it must be considered a separate Shemitah. This Messianic understanding was, in fact, the reason for the wide acceptance of the Shemitot concept by the Sabbatians, among other Kabbalists.

As the Messianic future was treated, for all intents and purposes, as a separate Shemitah, a cosmic world with its own Torah, so was the Edenic past, as Scholem shows in his discussion of the changing Torah:

> The accepted position was that of the *Sefer ha-Temunah*, namely, that we are now in the *shemittah* of judgment, dominated by the sefirah Gevurah, and the principle of strict justice. Consequently, this must have been preceded by the *shemittah* of *Hesed* or loving-kindness, which is described as a kind of "golden age.". . . [I]n the previous *shemittah* the Torah was read completely differently and did not contain the prohibitions which are the product of the power of judgment; similarly, it will be read differently in the *shemittot* to come. The *Sefer ha-Temunah* and other sources contain descriptions of the final *shemittah* which are of a distinctly utopian character. . . . [This is] among the main reasons why the doctrine of shemittot was accepted so widely in kabbalistic circles.[20]

If the golden past and utopian future are granted the status of separate Shemitot, and we can identify the Shemitah of the present with the cosmic world similarly identified with the present, the fourth, then we can establish the same coherence between these two competing kabbalistic concepts of cosmic time as we earlier did with the biblical creation account.

But this can only be done by separating the Sabbatical cosmology of the Shemitot from that of the Sefirot, not as radical as it might seem since their incorporation in the Shemitot doctrine appears to have been primarily serving a hidden Messianic agenda, the emergence of a more lenient reading of the Torah, rather than aiding cosmological understanding. Such a separation of Shemitot from Sefirot is necessary for our synthesis since the Shemitot are generally understood to proceed through just the seven Sefirot from Chesed to Malkhut, and this would place us in the *second* Shemitah of Gevurah in a seven-week cosmic Jubilee cycle, a position inconsistent with our placement in the *fourth* world of the four worlds doctrine. Accepting this separation, however, we can simply equate the concept of cosmic worlds with the Sabbatical number of the Shemitot and so extend this concept to include future worlds. It is best, then, to separate the concept of the Shemitot from that of the Sefirot and focus simply on its numerical definition of seven world eras, whether these be understood to occupy one or seven cosmic weeks. Identifying the present with the fourth cosmic world of Asiyah and placing this within the larger cosmic structure of seven worlds would thus allow us to extend the concept of cosmic worlds to include three such additional worlds. Such a projection of seven rather than four cosmic worlds will have the further effect of placing the particular development of Jewish esoteric mysticism that developed between the twelfth and sixteenth centuries, and is most narrowly termed the Kabbalah, within the context of the larger Jewish mysticical tradition. But we should finally consider how this model of seven worlds can be related to both Zoharic and Lurianic cosmology, beginning with the *Zohar*.

THE CONFLICT BETWEEN ZOHARIC AND LURIANIC COSMOLOGY

The central cosmological text of the *Zohar* presents an emanationist process that is at all its levels double aspected:

> The Holy One, blessed be He, found it necessary to create all these things in the world to ensure its permanence, so that there should be, as it were, a brain with many membranes encircling it. The

whole world is constructed on this principle, upper and lower, from the first mystic point up to the furthest removed of all the stages. They are all coverings one to another, brain within brain and spirit within spirit, so that one is a shell to another. The primal point is the innermost light of a translucency, tenuity, and purity passing comprehension. The extension of that point becomes a "palace" *(Hekal),* which forms a vestment for that point with a radiance which is still unknowable on account of its translucency. The "palace" which is the vestment for that unknowable point is also a radiance which cannot be comprehended, yet withal less subtle and translucent than the primal mystic point. This "palace" extends into the primal Light, which is a vestment for it. From this point there is extension after extension, each one forming a vestment to the other, being in the relation of membrane and brain to one another. Although at first a vestment, each stage becomes a brain to the next stage. The same process takes place below, so that on this model man in this world combines brain and shell, spirit and body, all for the better ordering of the world.[21]

In this model there is an original "primal Light" in which a "primal mystic point" is defined that becomes the brain of the whole cosmos. This now "extends into the primal Light," emanating outward to form a surrounding circle or sphere of "less subtle" light that provides a "vestment" for it, a process that continues without apparent end and in which each subsequent circle or sphere may be considered the less "translucent" garment of the preceding one, as that can be considered the more radiant "brain" of the subsequent covering, but in which each extension is, nonetheless, composed of the dual halves of "brain" and "vestment." This model already has much that will be incorporated by Luria into his fuller, but different, model. There is something like the later Lurianic distinction between the "inner light" and the "surrounding light" in the *Zohar's* "primal point" and the "primal Light" into which it extends, the former becoming the immanent form of the

Divine and the latter its transcendent form, always surrounding the expanding spheres of ever denser light that constitute the cosmos.

But there are a few major differences between the Zoharic and Lurianic models. The most important involves the Tzimtzum, which produces both a central point and a circumference *within which* all subsequent worlds will be located:

> You should know that at the beginning of everything . . . there was no empty or open space; the light of the Infinite was everywhere. . . . So the infinite contracted itself in the middle of its light, at its very central point, withdrawing to the circumference and the sides, leaving an open space in between. . . . This empty space is circular, the same on all sides, and the World of Emanation and all the other worlds are to be found inside that circle, with the light of the Infinite uniformly surrounding it.[22]

The next stage is the insertion into this empty space of a line of light from the surrounding light of Ein Sof, a linear ray that also expands into circular spheres of ever increasing density as they approach the center. It is the outermost sphere that is here the purest and alone connected to the Infinite: "From the first, the Infinite, blessed be He, both surrounded all the worlds and was surrounded by them, enclothed within them up to the end of the World of Emanation. However, it touched and attached itself only to the World of Emanation and not to the worlds of Creation, Formation, and Action."[23]

If the light at the center may be associated with the divine immanence and that with the feminine Shekhinah, while the light beyond the periphery is associated with the divine transcendence either of Ein Sof or the Holy One, blessed be He, then the Zoharic version would seem to identify the Emanator with the divine feminine, as in its understanding of the third Sefirah of Binah (also the Partzuf of Imma-Mother) as the womb from which flow the seven lower Sefirot that are identified with the seven days of creation, while the Lurianic version identifies this Emanator with the divine masculinity. Whether or not this consideration motivated Luria to make such a shift of creative power from the center to the periphery, he or his disciple Chayyim Vital was clearly disturbed by its conflict with the cosmic genesis appearing in the *Zohar* and sought to minimize it by identifying the movement from the periphery to the center only with the lesser circular aspect and prescribing an opposite understanding of the linear progression. "Each world, and every single detail of each world, has these two aspects—circular and linear. One of the characteristics of the circles is that the higher-quality circles encompass and surround those of lower quality. . . . The linear aspect is just the opposite, for what is innermost is the highest and best quality of all, while the outermost layer is the worst of them all."[24] How this can be when the Sefirot of Adam Kadmon, with which this line is initially identified, place Keter just within the outer circumference and Malkhut at the lower central point cannot be explained. Indeed, Vital might well apply to himself what he says about the *Zohar*: "Examination of the words of Rabbi Shimon bar Yochai in the *Zohar* . . . yield evidence of varying and contradictory expressions. . . . The later kabbalists tried in vain to investigate this but were unable to do so. Because it is a very great and difficult question. . . ."[25]

The problem becomes most acute in discussing the physical world: "As for this world—our physical universe—it is the middle point inside all of the circles in that open, void, and empty place. . . . It is the greatest possible distance from the Infinite. . . . That is why it is so utterly physical and material, even though it is the innermost point of all the circles. Understand this well!"[26] For students of the *Zohar* this was, indeed, the point most difficult to understand. And Vital's attempt to explain the very Zoharic passage quoted earlier does not help:

> This proves that all the worlds surround one another. Even though from this passage it might seem to be the opposite, since the innermost one is the brain, and its container—the skull—is of

lesser quality. If, however, you open the eyes of your understanding you will see that this quotation is speaking from our point of view. . . . The sphere that is closest to us is the most external of all, and is called the "shell" over all the rest. With regard to the worlds themselves, however, this is not so. Rather, the innermost one is the "shell," and what encircles all the others is the "brain."[27]

If the only way to make the Lurianic cosmos coherent with that of the *Zohar* is to put us in the place of the Zoharic Emanator and reverse the *Zohar's* clear positioning of the "brain" and "shell," placing the "shell" at the center rather than the periphery where a "shell" surely belongs, then we must recognize the failure of Vital's attempt to make these two kabbalistic cosmologies coherent and face the inherent conflict between them.

Although the unsystematic nature of the *Zohar* and the oversystematized quality of the *Eitz Chayyim* pose different obstacles to understanding the cosmologies they present—except for the fact that they are clearly in conflict with each other—they can each contribute to the new model for kabbalistic cosmology that I am here trying to develop from the main traditional sources of Jewish esoteric cosmology. As the cosmology of the main body of the *Zohar* does not limit the cosmic expansion to four worlds, it is the Lurianic version that must finally be compared with the other numerical concept of creation, that of the biblical seven days.

There is no doubt that Luria embraced the newer kabbalistic cosmology of four worlds, each comprising the ten concentric spheres identified with the ten Sefirot of that world, though there are various inconsistencies. He first posits that between Ein Sof and the four worlds there was originally a cosmos-filling figure in the form of a man, called Adam Kadmon, who is later given his own world of ten Sefirotic spheres above those of the other four worlds, thus bringing the number of worlds up to five. Then there is the correlation of each of the five Partzufim—Arikh Anpin (Long Face), Abba (Father), Imma (Mother),

Ze'ir Anpin (Short Face, the son), and the Nukvah (Female, the sister and bride of Ze'ir Anpin)—with its own world composed of ten Sefirot, bringing the total number of worlds again to five, and with the addition of Adam Kadmon to six. Finally, there is the further insertion between Adam Kadmon and Arikh Anpin of another Partzuf, one figuring as well in the Zoharic Idrot, that of Atik Yoman, the "Ancient of Days" of early apocalyptic literature, bringing the total number of named figures who each are assigned a cosmic world to the biblical seven! But it is not on the basis of such inconsistencies that I would argue for the coherence of Lurianic cosmology with a structure of seven cosmic worlds, rather on the very nature of its cosmic history.

As we have seen, the Lurianic cosmic drama does not end with the Tzimtzum and the insertion into the cosmic sphere of the line of ten Sefirot constituting the body of Adam Kadmon. The second act of this drama involves the shattering of these Sefirotic vessels, which proved inadequate to contain the influx emanating from the surrounding light of Ein Sof. This Shevirah, the Lurianic version of the Fall, separated the coarser light of the broken vessels from the purer light of the Ein Sof they were supposed to contain and so to endow with individuated form. Then, when most of this more spiritual light rebounded upward, the fragments of the broken vessels, the Kelipot, served to trap the remaining spiritual light in the evil of a soulless materialism. It is this realm, identified with the now fallen fourth world of Asiyah, that Lurianic cosmology places at the coarse center of the cosmic sphere. The remaining stage, which can only be fulfilled by man, is that Tikkun or reconstruction of the broken vessels into new forms better than those of the original cosmic manifestation. As Scholem has noted: "In a sense the *tikkun* is not so much a restoration of Creation—which though planned was never fully carried out—as its first complete fulfillment."[28] What the Tikkun ultimately effects is the transformation of the single Adam Kadmon into the multiple Partzufim, a transformation in which man is both to contribute and share.

Now, the greatest problem with Luria's theory is that its primary cosmology of four worlds leaves no room for, the future Tikkun that is such an essential feature of Lurianic cosmic history. The way in which this is usually addressed is to understand the Shevirah as having caused each of the four worlds to "fall" to the position of the world beneath it, with the formerly spiritual fourth world of Asiyah now becoming completely materialized, and that the work of Tikkun is to raise each successively up both to its former position and former wholeness. Understood in this way, there is no need for any additional worlds. The process of emanation may be viewed as proceeding downward through the four worlds from the periphery to the center and that of Tikkun as reversing the direction of movement at the lowest fourth world into an upward progress through the same now-reconstructed upper three worlds. But to understand the course of cosmic history in this way is to allow for no cosmic gain. If the Sefirotic vessels were inadequate in their first manifestation, the exact reconstruction of their broken fragments to their former wholeness would leave them as defective as in their original emanation and give no value to their subsequent, and sure to be repeated, catastrophe. The true power of Luria's reformulation of kabbalistic cosmology lies precisely in its projection of a cosmic recon-figuration that results in a more perfect product than that originally produced, which makes of the Shevirah, in the words of Augustine, a "fortunate fall."

But if the worlds of Tikkun are to be essentially different from the worlds of emanation, then they cannot be modeled by the same three upper worlds. Use of the same four-worlds model to represent both the downward process of emanation and the upward process of recon-figuration, when that latter is understood to signify a perfecting of the upper worlds that changes their essential nature, rather implies a switch to a covert seven-worlds model, the three original upper worlds, the transformative fourth world, which reverses the direction of move-ment, and the upward progress through three upper worlds so changed that they can more accurately be termed the fifth through seventh worlds. Such an awareness can be seen when the Tree of Life Diagram is used to model Lurianic cosmic history, a modeling in which the original course of emanation is understood to proceed downward through the left column of the Tree and that of Tikkun to proceed upward through the right column of the Tree, after reversing directions at Malkhut, often identified with the fourth world. But there is, of course, no comparable way of indicating the before and after of such progress through the spheres of the upper three worlds in the Lurianic Tzimtzum model.

What is required, then, is a spherical model that contains not four but seven differentiated spheres, these seven proceeding either outward, as in the Zoharic model, or inward, as in the model of Luria. Given such a choice, there is no question that the Zoharic model is superior. When the *Eitz Chayyim* records that "it arose in His simple will to create worlds and to emanate emanations,"[29] the implication is that the creative process involves a progression from simpler to more complex forms of organization, simplicity requiring less compass for its definition than complexity. Thus a model of successively enclosed spheres that proceeds from its tiny center to its larger circumference, as with the Zoharic version, will better model the progression from simplicity to complexity than the reverse Lurianic model.

Though both versions begin with an infinite light in which a central point is first defined and then becomes the center of an expansion into that primal light, there is, nonetheless, an advantage to the fixed circumference of the Lurianic Tzimtzum, especially with Sarug's further elaboration, which understands the residual light, Reshimu, within the space, Tehiru, of this fixed cosmic sphere to be "engraved" with the laws of each dimension of cosmic totality, thus permitting the future worlds of the Tikkun to be virtually present for those individuals and communities with sufficient spiritual development to access and shape these levels. I have, indeed, elsewhere argued that the mechanism of Luria's Tzimtzum is not only coherent with the quantum cosmology of modern science but provides a more intellectually satisfying model for cosmic origins.[30]

It is in the further filling of this vacated finite space that the problem of the cosmic future arises, a problem that can best be resolved by synthesizing the form of the cosmic space produced in the Lurianic Tzimtzum with elements of the other two persisting traditions of kabbalistic cosmology, that ultimately deriving from the Bible, which would raise the number of cosmic worlds, eras, or dimensions to seven, and that deriving primarily from the *Zohar*, which would locate the source of emanation at the center of the cosmic sphere and understand its seven spherical "worlds" to extend outward toward the circumference of the finite cosmos fixed by the prior action of the Tzimtzum. A final reason for preferring to locate the source of emanation at the center, as in the Zoharic contribution to our model, is that it also makes this final model coherent with the big bang theory of quantum cosmology, an advantage for any modern spiritual model of the cosmos.

A NEW MODEL FOR KABBALISTIC COSMOLOGY

There are two main reasons for developing models to explain any otherwise disorganized realm of data. The primary reason is that only such an imaginative grasp of the material allows the mind to comprehend it. A second reason has been suggested that not only allows us to recognize how isomorphic the model is to its domain but also enriches our understanding of this domain: "A promising model is one with implications rich enough to suggest novel hypotheses and speculations in the primary field of investigation—in short, to see *new connections*."[31] In what follows we shall see that this is, indeed, true of the new synthesized model for kabbalistic cosmology I am proposing.

Cosmic models have traditionally drawn their metaphors from the prevailing scientific theories of their times. As Newtonian physics supported the metaphor of a clockwork universe, so has the computer revolution supplied the latest metaphors for cosmic systems. To paraphrase John: "In the beginning was the program, and the program was with the programmer, and the program was the programmer." But for the

Kabbalah the programming of the programmer begins before the cosmic beginning, in the unlimited being of Ein Sof. To requote the pertinent points of Israel Sarug's understanding of Lurianic cosmology, as summarized by Scholem: "'primordial points' were 'engraved' in the power of Din, thus becoming the first forms to leave their markings in the essence of *Ein-Sof* . . . and the primordial Torah, the ideal world woven in the substance of Ein-Sof itself, came into being. . . . [T]he hidden law of the whole of creation . . ." In this view, the infrastructure weaving through the substance or light of Ein Sof already contains the program for all possibilities, though in the implicit form of its still undisturbed unity.

But the more standard Lurianic tradition tells us that a beginning is finally made with the establishment of a point at the very center of Ein Sof, a point that already expresses the whole point of creation! If we can return to John's reworking of Genesis in its traditional English translation—"In the beginning was the Word"—then this word would surely be *ani*, the first person pronoun "I" that begins the divine proclamation of the Ten Commandments with the self-definition: "I [am] the Lord thy God" (Exod. 20:2). In contrast to the utter transcendence of the impersonal Ein Sof, this divine "I" defines itself in terms of a personal capacity for relatedness to the humanity yet to be generated in the evolution of the cosmic program. This is the aspect of divine Presence the Kabbalah will ultimately characterize as the "feminine" Shekhinah. In appendix B, I summarize the kabbalistic understanding of the Sh'ma as proclaiming, in its final word *echod,* not the divine *unity* but rather a *unification.* This is the unification of the unqualified form of the Tetragrammaton with the form of this Name qualified by the term for "thy God," *Elohaynu,* that expresses the personal aspect of the divine Presence within the cosmos. As the former signifies the divine transcendence also symbolized as male, so does the latter signify the symbolically female form of the divine immanence. The process of the Tzimtzum that follows further distinguishes these two divine aspects, whose reunification in and through the cosmic development of spiritually purified human personality represents the ultimate fulfillment of the cosmic process now beginning.

For what follows the fundamental vocal tone or vibratory establishment of an individuating point in the Lurianic model is the withdrawal of almost all of the Or Ein Sof, the Limitless Light, equally around this point to leave a spherical vacuum, the process known as the Tzimtzum. We can better understand this next stage in what will become the process of forming cosmic worlds by considering another aspect of the authentic Lurianic doctrine, that a primary purpose of the Tzimtzum was the effort of Ein Sof to purge itself of the roots of Din, that constrictive, judgmental aspect that will later be identified with the Sefirah of Gevurah. For Scholem has shown that, in the beginning, "*Ein-Sof* gathered together the roots of *Din*, which had been previously concealed within Him, to one place. . . . [T]he power of *Din* . . . left in primordial space . . . intermingled in a confused fashion with the remnants of the light of *Ein-Sof* that had remained behind even after *zimzum*, like the drops of oil that remain in a vessel after it has been emptied. This residue was called *reshimu*."[32] If we apply our program metaphor to this view of Ein Sof, the Unlimited One would be trying to purge itself of the constraining program that has infiltrated its being as well as immediately distancing itself from all that the Din-concentrated centering point has begun to represent.

But from another perspective, the Reshimu, or residual light, would seem to represent those elements of the original program of Ein Sof that resonated to the self-definition of the newly established point and clung to the energy vibrating from this center. These would be the aspects of the original program designed to order the development of ever more conscious particular systems, subprograms that form the infrastructure of the residual light and cohere into the new program defining the course of cosmic evolution. This more particular and particularizing program at the cosmic center from its beginning would order the elements from what we shall soon see to be two separate sources of light in an evolution marked by seven discrete phases.

In this model, the fourth world of our material present would occupy the median layer of a seven-layered finite cosmos. It may, indeed, be considered the only fully material layer, enclosing the three prior layers of ever more corporeal cosmic evolution immanently within it and being enveloped by the three ever more etherealized dimensions of spirit that are both to guide and fulfill man's spiritual destiny. The reason that the first and seventh worlds can be equally pure though differing in complexity is that each is directly attached to a form of the Infinite. For unlike the Lurianic model, which views the central point not as a source of the Limitless Light but only as a position on which the fixed end of a divine compass may be placed to begin the definition of a finite space, the Zoharic model understands the central point to be the infinite source of all the subsequent emanations, that "The primal point is the innermost light of a translucency, tenuity, and purity passing comprehension." But as in the Lurianic model, the Zoharic world that would complete the expanding cosmic progress and reach its Tzimtzum circumference, here the seventh, would be attached to the infinite light beyond and surrounding it.

In our synthesized model, then, there would be two sources of the Limitless Light, these being the "inner light" at the central point and the "surrounding light" beyond but touching the translucent cosmic circumference. Thus the worlds extending from the center of immanent light to the median layer would become progressively less spiritual and more corporeal, while those extending from this median layer to the circumference of transcendent light would become the ever more etherealized embodiments of spiritually purified individuality. Let us try to understand this waning and waxing of the infinite light more precisely by first contemplating figure 1.4 that offers a graphic model of this cosmos and its dual sources of illumination; its seven worlds, each divided into inner and outer stages, are further pictured as within a hexagram cut-out of the Limitless Light and show a still more defined division of the seventh world.[33] The relationship of the hexagram to this cosmic model will be featured in the discussions of chapter 5, the chapter also culminating in a vision of the seventh world, that whose strongly

Figure 1.4. The Seven-World Cosmos

marked division in our model will become understandable in the immediately following sections. Figure 1.4 shows an image of the seven-dimensional cosmos that synthesizes the different traditions of the Kabbalah into a new model for kabbalistic cosmology.

We have seen that in our synthesized model, "the primal point is the innermost light of a . . . purity passing comprehension," that is, it contains an infinite light, the light that is to illumine all the worlds successively within the Lurianic circle of the Tzimtzum. But where in the Zoharic model each emanation from that central point of light "extends into the primal Light," in the Tzimtzum model the sphere of cosmic space that comes to surround this primal point would cut its "innermost light" off from "the primal Light."

Before proceeding further, it should be noted that the light that is to fill the first cosmic vessel is thus still the unfiltered pure light of Ein Sof. Here our model agrees with the traditional understanding of the first world of Atzilut (Emanation) as still one with the Emanator, the division between Creator and Creation being kabbalistically understood to occur between the first and second worlds, as in the biblical account that assigns such a dividing firmament to the second day.

But if the outermost sphere of the Tzimtzum is to cut off the innermost light from contact with the primal light, then the light into which it would have to extend in the process of vessel formation would rather have to be that of the "residual light" we have already encountered. Called the Reshimu, this is the light that was left after the withdrawal of the Or Ein Sof, the Limitless Light, from the vacated space produced during the process of Tzimtzum that begins, in this version, with the definition of a primal point of *light*. And since we earlier saw that the light of the Reshimu intermingled with the roots of Din or judgment, this residual light would be defined as not only informed by the program for such finite or limited development as would necessarily constrict the intensity of the innermost light but also as having such a capacity for formal containment as would be particularly suited to its required role as vessel for this inner light, another and more positive reason that the roots of Din were placed within the realm of the finite.

Later we shall see that the Reshimu also contains significant chaotic elements, but at this point we just need to recognize that we are looking at a bounded cosmos containing only the primal light at its center and the surrounding residual light, the outermost elements of the Reshimu being further lit by the Limitless Light beyond the translucent cosmic sphere and that this added illumination progressively decreases as the Reshimu approaches the cosmic center. With this understanding, we can now consider the process by which the central light extends into this residual light in the next stage of vessel formation, beginning with a further application of the "program" paradigm.

We have seen that this residual light is composed of such a constrictive or particularizing program as can be identified with the kabbalistic concept of "Din," the judgmental, discriminating aspect of the divine also known as the fifth Sefirah of Gevurah. We can thus view this residual light as having an infrastructure composed of the implicit program for all aspects of cosmic development, and that when the particular components of the inner light extend into the Reshimu, their various localized combinations will immediately cause the appropriate aspect of the implicit cosmic program to become explicit and organize these components in the one way—whether stable or unstable, complex or simple—that is consistent with the universal laws of the cosmic program. It is not that these components are "self-organizing," as so many complexity theorists have maintained, but that *they are organized* by the unique program for how the cosmos works in their case, the case that their particular combination of components has caused to become manifest. All systems are characterized by a higher level of deterministic rules and a lower level of indeterministic members, of program and initial components, and the running of their programs when truly complex will be both unpredictable and yet repeatable. This is the law for everything that was, is, and will become in all the phases of cosmic development, an evolution that is marked in our model by seven discrete phases and the more chaotic transitions briefly appearing at the phase shifts between the completion of one pattern of organization and the reestablishment of a pattern of organization on a yet more complex level, a shift of complex patterning that seems to occur when a particular magnitude in the evolution of the program has been reached. This is, finally, an evolution that will favor those systems whose stable complexity can both generate and recognize meaning.[34]

Let us return from this theoretical consideration of the program model to a more visually imaginative attempt to understand such an interaction of the inner and residual lights. We may begin by conceiving of this Reshimu as dispersed thinly throughout the cosmic space, the Tehiru, and that the first effect of the extension into it of the inner infinite light would be to displace the residual light immediately surrounding it, concentrating it at the periphery of its first magnitude of expansion. There it would be shaped into its vessel of darker light in a manner later to be made more fully comprehensible. But though darker, this vessel of residual light would still be translucent enough to allow much of the inner light to penetrate beyond it into the further stretch of residual light that is to define a second such space or world enclosed within its own spherically formed portion of this Reshimu. And as this process proceeds through yet a third and fourth formation of the residual light into containing spherical vessels, less and less of the innermost light would be able to penetrate through the successive containing spheres of grosser light until, with the fourth world, little of the inner light would be able to penetrate its darkness. But we must assume that enough light is yet able to pierce its density to produce the vessels of the remaining three worlds reaching to the cosmic boundary. From this fourth world on, however, the Reshimu would become progressively more illuminated by the surrounding infinite light, becoming ever more brilliant than the inner light its vessels are enclosing. The Or Ein Sof, penetrating the translucent spheres from the periphery inward, would thus light the seventh world with a brightness almost comparable to that of the first, less such light penetrating the sixth sphere, and still less the fifth, until almost none is again able to penetrate the median fourth sphere of our material world. These differing sources and degrees of illumination give a different character to the earlier and later worlds; in the worlds closer to the central light, the inner portion would be dominant, while in those closer to the periphery, the outer portion would dominate. How this cosmic model may further illuminate the nature of the soul we are now to see.

In our model of concentric spheres, and still focusing on the sphere of the fourth world, the space between the containing vessel of the previous world sphere and that of its own world sphere should now be understood to be filled with the soul proper. Such a soul would have two sources of orientation. Its inner half would mold itself to the form of the third-world spherical vessel, that closer to the center, while its outer half would nest within and be molded by its own containing vessel, that closer to the periphery. Not only would these inner and outer spherical boundaries exert an influence on the orientation of the soul stuff within, the inner half becoming more responsive to the influence of the center, which can also be identified with the past, and the outer half to the influence of the periphery, which is also that of the future, but its predominant light would derive from that direction. For the light from the center would first irradiate the inner half of a world soul as that from the surrounding light would first irradiate its outer half. So the soul would, from its very spatially imagined circumstances, develop two opposing natures with two opposing orientations. As their opposing natures develop from the stronger source of light illuminating them, so do their opposing orientations derive from the shapes of the boundaries to which they must mold themselves, orientations that are consistent with, and thus reinforce, the inherent nature of the aspect of the soul touching these boundaries.

It was stated earlier that, with respect to the median fourth world, all three of the worlds it encloses can be considered as immanent within it and all three of the outer worlds as transcendently surrounding it. But now we see another way in which the cosmic worlds are connected. Since the character of the soul is determined by the vessels of both its own world and of the world immediately before or within it, we may say that this most immediate prior world has a special relationship of influence on a present world. In the case of the fourth world, we may identify such influences from the third world of Yetzirah with the Yetzer ha-Tov, the good inclination, and the Yetzer ha-Ra, the evil inclination. We shall continue this discussion primarily at the conclusion of this section, when the future worlds have been more fully defined, but must now return to complete our analysis of the dual-aspected soul.

For as both soul halves approach the median point of their world, each would necessarily become less susceptible to the direction of the light reaching it and the form defining it. And this, in turn, would permit a transition to be made from that which is more central and so collective to that which is more outer and so individualized. It is at this median point of each soul level that the principle of balance would have to operate to bring the two potentially conflicting halves of the soul, as of all aspects of the cosmos, into complementarity.

We have already seen this principle expressed in the triadic structure of the Tree of Life Diagram, in whose every level the more expansive right line of Sefirot and the more constrictive left line of Sefirot are brought into balance by the mediating line of Sefirot at the center. Such balance is understood in the *Zohar* to be the original principle informing the mystery of existence. At the very beginning of the most recondite portion of the *Zohar,* the "Sifra de-Tzeni'uta" (The Book of Concealment), this is expressed as follows:

> It is taught: the Book of Concealment is the book that describes the balancing of the scale. For before there was balance one face did not behold the other. The primordial kings were dead, their crowns were lost, and the earth was desolate until from the head of the desire of desires precious garments came forth and were communicated. This scale hangs in the place that cannot be found or weighed. The point of equilibrium exists through itself; it cannot be grasped or seen. By it has been weighed and are weighed that which never was, that

which is, and that which will be. This most concealed mystery is
formed and prepared in the skull, filled with crystalline dew.[35]

Here we are told that the balancing point, the fulcrum of the scale,
existed before the manifestation of its two pans, a manifestation that
marks the turning point from something like the derived Lurianic concept of the Shevirah (the death of the primordial kings) to something
like the derived Lurianic concept of the Tikkun (the ability of the
"faces," or Partzufim, to interact with one another). It was at this turning point that the "precious garments" constituting the scale mechanism emerged from the deepest will (lodged in Keter, the Partzuf of
Arikh Anpin), a scale whose balance is implicitly present in its two pans.
One pan would seem to hold the emerging principle of inner essence
(the "crystalline dew," *tala de-bededulcha* in Aramaic) and the other the
emerging principle of outer form (the "skull"), the same duality we had
earlier seen expressed in the account of the emanation of worlds
appearing in the main body of the *Zohar*, though now provided with a
pre-existent mechanism of balance (*matkela* in Aramaic). Before applying this primordial principle of balance to the soul, there are other
aspects of the "Sifra de-Tzeni'uta" that can illuminate the cosmic model
here being developed.

Looking first at the reference to the kings—"The primordial kings
were dead, their crowns were lost"—we may recognize a reference to the
seven kings of Moab (Gen. 36:31–39), whose successive deaths were generally taken in the Kabbalah to refer to imperfect and destroyed earlier
worlds and were further identified by Luria with the primordial "world
of points" he called "the world of Tohu," chaos, a world where the
Sefirotic vessels were isolated in their own individualized attributes and
unable to interact or join with others in more complex forms of stability. To include such vessels in our model, we would have to regard the
Lurianic line of light containing the Sefirot to have entered the sphere of
the Tzimtzum from the surrounding Limitless Light before the point of
primal light, already present at the center, had begun to emanate worlds.

These finally shattered vessels may now be considered to join the roots of Din, earlier considered, in intermingling with the residual light left within the cosmic circle in the process of Tzimtzum.

Such a further mingling would give to this Reshimu a dual character. For it has been thought, on the one hand, to be inscribed with the laws involving each stage in the cosmic process and, on the other, to be in the state of chaos produced by the failure of the noninteracting original vessels to contain the divine light. This apparent conflict in Lurianic theory can be resolved, however, in terms of both chronology and consequence. Clearly the inscription of the Reshimu with the laws governing the cosmos was a product of the very first stage of the Tzimtzum, Ein Sof's concentration of the constrictive roots of Din in the location that is to become the finite space of the cosmos and whose finiteness their power of discrimination is meant to serve, and it would seem to represent the ideal plan or program for cosmic evolution. But the next effort of Ein Sof to determine the character of the cosmic sphere, the penetration of a line of its light for the purpose of producing separated individual natures resulted rather in the second stage of the Shevirah, the shattering of the originally emanated Sefirot, whose fragmented shells produced a world of chaos (Tohu) as they mingled with the previously law-inscribed residual light.

Since it is from this Reshimu that the soul is to form the Tzelemim, the soul bodies, of its ever higher levels, its opposing potentialities provide alternative pathways for the equally dual-aspected soul. We earlier saw that the opposing inclinations of the soul could be identified with the influences coming to the fourth world from the two halves of the still manifest third world of Yetzirah, the inner half of which can be further identified with the angels and the outer half with the demons (*shedim*). Applying these identifications, we may say that when the Nefesh soul follows the Yetzer ha-Tov, the good inclination, it will proceed in a disciplined way to construct from the surrounding Reshimu the Tzelem that will permit it to function optimally in a higher world. But when it follows the Yetzer ha-Ra, the evil inclination, it will rush precipitously into a disorganized medley of apparent powers, powers that cannot be properly used because of their disorganization and so only offer a seeming good, and become stuck in its chaos. The initial work of the evolving soul at each of its levels, then, is to distinguish the path of Tikkun from that of Tohu and to build its Tzelem from the constructive elements of the residual light that can properly illuminate its path to higher consciousness.

In the description of the first biblical day, a further correlation may be possible both for the soul's two opposing tendencies and its dual-aspected cosmic environment: "In the beginning God created the heaven and the earth. And the earth was without form, and void; and darkness was upon the face of the deep. And the Spirit of God moved upon the face of the waters. And God said, Let there be light: and there was light. And God saw the light, that it was good; and God divided the light from the darkness. And God called the light Day, and the darkness he called Night. And the evening and the morning were the first day" (Gen. 1: 1-5). In the original creation of Genesis, the earth was "without form" (*tohu*) and "void" (*bohu*). As its formless contents could not express their natures with any consistency, so were its forms empty of meaning. In the remainder of verse 2 we have a parallelism characteristic of Hebrew poetic style and generally signifying an equation of meaning. In the first half there is mention of "the face of the deep" and in the second of "the face of the waters," with the clear suggestion that "the deep" is that of "the waters." If we now take the word for face, *panai,* not in its secondary meaning as "surface" but more literal meaning of "face," then such a face upon the waters would have to be a reflection of what is above it.

But what is above it in the first half of the parallel passages is "darkness," *chosekh,* and in the second half is "the spirit of God," *ruach elohim.* If we do not equate them, then we can understand the hovering spirit of Elohim to be unable to see the reflection of His face in the waters because it is obscured by the darkness. But if they are to be equated, then the darkness would represent not an external barrier to vision but the very consciousness of the Ruach Elohim during the earliest phase of the cosmos, a darkened consciousness that cannot perceive its reflection in the meaninglessness of separated contents and forms, of such unconnected particulars as Luria would later assign to his world of Tohu. But then Elohim becomes enlightened in the very act of uniting the matter and form of the first substance, light, with the implication that in this condition of higher consciousness He can see all such unifications as true revelations of His face. This light, while divided from the darkness and called "good," does not, however, completely supplant the darkness, which is allotted its own half of time and given the primacy of this alternating sequence: "And the evening and the morning were the first day." Thus is initiated that duality of creation between the particulate and the collective permeating all aspects of the finite and finally judged to be "very good" (Gen. 1:31). And as above, so below. There would seem to be a coherence between the Creator and the Creation, the duality that can thus be understood to characterize the consciousness of the biblical Creator also having been seen to characterize both the inner light of the soul and the residual light that is to provide its body.

In order to gain a still better understanding of this process of Tzelem construction, we should return to our prior consideration of the beginning of the "Sifra de-Tzeni'uta" and further observe the action of the "crystalline" (a reference to the biblical "bdellium"), light-enhancing purity of the "dew," considering it now is to be the "brain" or soul of a world sphere, as it extends into the chaotic/ordering realm of the Reshimu to form the vessel of its "skull." But we should first briefly explore the relationship of the bdellium and dew given in the "Sifra de-Tzeni'uta" passage above, a relationship that goes back to the biblical story of the manna.

We are first told: "And when the dew that lay was gone up, behold, upon the face of the wilderness there lay a small round thing, as small as the hoar frost on the ground. And when the children of Israel saw it, they said one to another, It is manna" (Exod. 16:14–15). This "small

round thing," crystalline as hoarfrost, that was produced or delivered by
the dew, is then further defined: "And the manna was as coriander seed,
and the color thereof as the color of bdellium. And the people went
about . . . and made cakes of it: and the taste of it was as the taste of fresh
oil" (Num. 11:7–8). The divine source and life-sustaining quality of this
manna is further underscored in the later metaphorical references to the
dew from which it is derived, the former in the statement of the divine
figure, "my head is filled with dew" (Song of Sol. 5:2), and the latter in
the image of resurrection: "Awake and sing, ye that dwell in dust: for thy
dew is as the dew of herbs, and the earth shall cast out the dead" (Isa.
26:19). The divinely redemptive quality attributed to the symbol of dew
accords with the first biblical reference to the bdellium that modifies it,
which places it in the still unfallen land of Havilah: "And the gold of
that land is good: there is bdellium and the onyx stone" (Gen. 2:12). If
the bdellium is as translucently white as "hoarfrost," then in Havilah the
spectrum from white to gold to black is all "good." Finally, we are told
that the bdellium-resembling manna had "the taste of fresh oil." This
oily stickiness is, for my purpose, the most important quality of the
bdellium that is here qualifying the dew, for it permits us to imagine
more clearly the next stage in the cosmic process being defined in the
"Sifra de-Tzeni-uta."[36]

If we can thus attribute a still greater viscosity to this "dew" than
that found in the early morning droplets on opening petals, then we can
imagine this process as proceeding through the adhesive quality of this
translucent "dew" under the force of the flow that is propelling it from
the bounded world within into the chaotic/ordering residual light
without. This quality would be expressed by both halves of the soul and
further serve to differentiate them. For as the last portion to flow
through the vessel of a prior world would adhere to that inner boundary, so would the first portion, its most creative and adventurous element, stick to its outward environment and cause it to curl back around
it in the typical force-flow pattern that produces those mushroom
shapes ranging from the plant of this name to the cloud formed by an

atomic blast. What the forward-moving element of the soul would thus be accomplishing, when successful, is no less than the conversion of Tohu, the negative aspect of the realm into which it is extending, into Tikkun, that which it is forming through the very process of bringing the discords of individuality into harmony. But though it is only this creative aspect of the soul that can generate its still higher dimensions, its adventurousness can sometimes, particularly in the fourth world, cause it to get prematurely stuck in the surrounding chaos before it has been formed into a firm instrument for the higher expression of the soul. Where the inner aspect of the soul is subject to no such danger, its clinging to the past can nonetheless leave it stagnant if it is not refreshed by ever new sources of creative vitality derived from and helping to realize future possibilities. The soul needs both its individualizing and collectivizing tendencies to realize its highest potential, but since these may conflict as well as complement each other, what it needs even more is that balancing mechanism which "exists through itself . . . formed and prepared in the skull, filled with crystalline dew."

If we now apply this principle of balance to the dual-aspected soul, we may say that in the scale of the soul the opposing orientations of its aspects are ideally balanced. But we may further say that in the earlier worlds of emanation, in which the innermost light is stronger, the balance will be one that allows for such a dominance of the collective aspect as can still nurture the development of its individualizing aspect while in the worlds of the Tikkun, in which the illumination from the surrounding light is stronger, its balance will allow for such a dominance of the increasingly purified individuality as can still maintain a spiritual contact with its collective aspect, a distinction between the earlier and later worlds that will receive a further justification in the next section.

Finally, this is a balance that will also be transformative, not simply one going from a past to a future modeling, but one whose unification of the opposites of inner and outer, past and future, is generative of the new level of soul that can lift it to a higher-dimensional world. Though this balance should act transformatively in all the worlds, this function is nowhere more essential than in the fourth world of the cosmic present. For lying midway between the poles of divine immanence and divine transcendence is this fallen world of matter whose transformative purpose it is to convert the divine simplicity at the origin of the cosmic process into the multiple divine personalities that alone can fulfill the purpose for which the uniformly simple spiritual source entered the space-time specificity of matter, that personalizing process through which the cosmic child of fully developed humanity can finally unify the finite with the infinite through its own purified and empowered personality.

There is yet another way in which the median nature of the fourth world may be viewed. It can be viewed as the realm of the *personal*, understanding the prior or inner three levels to be the realm of the *impersonal* and the future or surrounding three levels to be the realm of the *transpersonal*. Viewed in this way, we can recognize our material realm to constitute an engine of transformation of the cosmos from the impersonal to the transpersonal, a transformation that only the development of personal uniqueness through the space-time specificity of matter has made possible.

We have thus far considered our cosmic model primarily in terms of the higher soul levels that may be associated with the ever larger spheres enveloping its material median level. As already suggested, however, this median level is to be equated not only with its spatial position but also with its temporal position between the past worlds of emanation and the future worlds of Tikkun. In these terms we can define the fourth through sixth worlds not only with reference to their soul levels but also their historical eras, understood as cosmic aeons. The fourth world would thus be identified not only with the Nefesh soul but also the cosmic present. Similarly the fifth world would be identified not only with the Ruach soul but also the most immediate cosmic future consistent with Jewish traditional sources, that of the Messianic Age, which we saw to be treated by the Shemitot cosmology, for all intents and purposes, as a separate cosmic era. In that earlier discussion we also saw that a separate Shemitah was accorded to the earlier legends of a

Garden of Eden, and we can now identify it with the third world of Yetzirah, where many Kabbalists have, in fact, placed it. This not only is the world of the angels and demons but also the world in which the pre-incarnate Nefesh soul first becomes manifest. Finally, we can identify the sixth world both with the Neshamah soul and the next cosmic phase recognized in these same traditional Jewish sources, that of the wholly spiritual World to Come, the Olam ha-Ba. If we wish a kabbalistic name for the seventh world—which we shall have reason in the final section of this chapter to correlate with the two remaining Lurianic soul levels, those of the Chayah and Yechidah souls—there is a Lurianic term that seems appropriate, that of the Olam ha-Matkela, the World of Balance, a term that we have already encountered in our consideration of the Zoharic "Sifra de-Tzeni'uta" and that sometimes replaced Atzilut, the standard name of the kabbalistic first world, in Lurianic writings.[37] As the seventh world may be viewed as complementary to the first, even as constituting its Tikkun, and as we shall shortly see it to be characterized by just such a balancing of opposites as is implied by this name, the Olam ha-Matkela would seem a perfect choice for the ultimate seventh world of cosmic history.

Now that the fifth and sixth worlds have again been defined, we can further develop our understanding of the relationship of the soul not only to the level of its own cosmic world but also to the world just prior to it, dual relationships based on the modeling of the outer half of the soul to the form of its own spherical vessel and that of its inner half on the vessel of the prior world. We can thus distinguish between the still independent functioning of the world immediately prior to the world to which the soul has developed and the worlds before that. These earlier worlds may be understood to be returned to the cosmic infrastructure of space-time and to constitute the updating of its program for each combination of possibilities.

We have already seen that at the level of the fourth world this means that the third world of Yetzirah will still maintain its influences on the fourth. What it implies for the fifth world is that the Messianic

Age of the redeemed Ruach soul will still inhabit a material world that superficially will seem unchanged and that this Ruach soul will also be able to function on its contained Nefesh level when necessary. But the soul's special relationship of worlds is most significant at the level of the sixth world. For this World to Come is available only to the Neshamah soul native to it and the Ruach soul of the prior world. The implication of this is that a Nefesh soul that has not evolved to the Ruach level while on Earth will not be assured of an individual afterlife but be returned to its collective source, a subject to be further developed at the close of chapter 2. As the nature of the seventh world will be developed more fully in the next two sections of the present chapter, we need only know now that its special relationship to the sixth world, primarily that of its inner half, implies that it may be considered a further level in a series of Worlds to Come, infinite not only in continuity but in entering the realm of the infinite Ein Sof.

THE MUSIC OF THE SPHERES

The cosmic model being proposed here is one consisting of seven concentric spheres suspended within the infinite light of Ein Sof and defining its center. But once the cosmos is so envisioned, it invites comparison with the geocentric cosmologies of the ancient world, cosmologies surely known to, and presumably influencing, the kabbalistic cosmologies we have been exploring. I bring this up because of one ancient elaboration of such cosmic models of concentric crystalline spheres that has particularly rich implications for our model. This is the Pythagorean tuning of the cosmic spheres that, legend has it, Pythagoras could actually hear, a power that most people are thought to have lost but that Pythagoras's spiritual development had enabled him to regain. This cosmic model of concentric spheres tuned to the Pythagorean diatonic scale remained an essential aspect of the Western esoteric tradition, as can be seen in an illustration by the seventeenth-century esotericist, Robert Fludd, shown in figure 1.5.

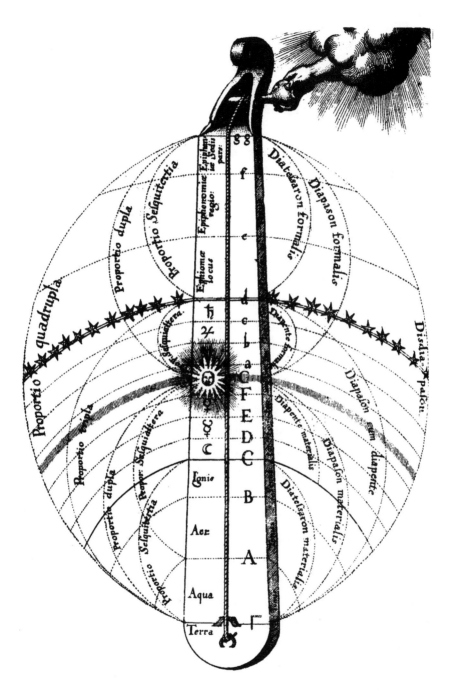

Figure 1.5. The Diatonic Cosmos of Robert Fludd

Though I have argued that the sevenfold Hebraic cosmology is preferable to the fourfold Pythagorean-Platonic cosmology, or should at least be integrated with it, I have elsewhere more fully presented my discovery of the harmonic key to the Genesis creation account, a discovery that reveals the Hebraic priesthood to have had a sacred science comparable to and possibly conversant with Pythagorean sacred science.[38] But in its acoustic science, the Pythagorean tradition not only defined the harmonic series; it also gave new definition to the musical scales, the most important of which, the diatonic major scale, became a central element in Plato's cosmology, particularly in defining the harmony of the world soul.[39] Because it will provide a major key for interpreting the seven spherical worlds of our new kabbalistic model, I shall briefly define this major scale of Western music.

Pythagoras appears to have used two side-by-side tetrachords, instruments with four strings, to define his scale. The eighth of these strings was tuned to the octave above the fundamental tone of the first string, the octave being the second harmonic or partial above the first, fundamental tone and the tone that sounds when a string, lightly depressed at its midpoint, is plucked. The fifth string was tuned to the third such harmonic, that of the musical fifth, sounded when the plucked string is lightly depressed at its two-thirds point. The fourth string was tuned to the fourth above the fundamental tone (which is also the interval between the third and fourth harmonics, that is, the interval between the fifth above the first octave and the second octave), sounded when the string is lightly depressed at its three-quarters point. In sum, the 2:1 harmonic ratio of the octave, the ratio of the order in which the harmonics or partials appear in the harmonic series, is the inverse of the $^{1}/_{2}$ fractioning of the string length; the 3:2 ratio of the fifth is the inverse of the $^{2}/_{3}$ fractioning of the string; and the 4:3 ratio of the fourth is the inverse of the $^{3}/_{4}$ fractioning of the string. The inverse numerical relationship between the ratios of these infinite harmonic sound waves in time and the finite geometrical fractioning of the string in space is also encoded in the Tetractys, and, as I have discussed elsewhere,[40] becomes the central gnosis of sacred science, of the necessary relationship of the finite to the infinite mediated by number.

But to return to the genesis of the diatonic scale, the four strings that have thus far been tuned provide the four tones of Do, Fa, Sol, and the octave of Do, the Fa tone also defining the harmonic mean between the fundamental tone and its octave and the Sol tone the arithmetic mean between them.[41] The problem now is how to tune the remaining four strings, the second and third, and the sixth and seventh. The "diatonic" solution is to use the interval of the whole tone appearing between the fourth and fifth strings, that between Fa and Sol, for each of the remaining strings. When whole tones are so inserted between the first and fourth tones and between the fifth and eighth, this process will yield just two tones (the meaning of "diatonic") plus a harmonic "limma," a remainder approximated in the well-tempered semitone. Thus between Do and Fa we get the two whole tones of Re and Mi plus the approximate half tone between Mi and Fa; and between Sol and Do we get the two whole tones of La and Ti plus the similarly approximate half tone between Ti and Do. Let us now turn to our seven world spheres and see what meanings may arise by tuning them to the tones of the diatonic scale.

We begin with the central feature of these spheres in Zoharic cosmology, the fact that each is double faceted, with an interior brain and an exterior skull, an essence and a form or vestment. Each of these aspects would thus seem comparable to the more inclusive form of tonality provided by the twelve-tone or "chromatic" scale. Giving these twelve tones (really half tones) their ascending chromatic solfeggio names, we have Do-Di, Re-Ri, Mi-Fa, Fi-Sol, Si-La, Li-Ti, Do. Now, when we lay the seven separate tones of the diatonic scale on the twelve separate tones of the chromatic scale and then compare this with the seven double-aspected spheres of our cosmic model, we get some remarkable correspondences that can further help us to define the qualitative nature of these cosmic stages.

When placed on the twelve-tone or chromatic scale, the seven tones of the diatonic scale define a most significant pattern. In the first four semitones of the chromatic scale, those whose solfeggio names are Do-Di and Re-Ri, the diatonic tones, Do and Re, are in the first halves of the first two whole tones. Now, if these whole tones can be regarded as corresponding to the kabbalistic cosmic worlds and are taken to illuminate these worlds, then what they are telling us about the first two worlds of Atzilut and Beriah is that they are characterized by the quality that may be attributed to just these first halves or semitones, the second halves having no more than a virtual status insofar as they are not manifested by the diatonic selection of tones. The qualities we can most simply associate with the two halves of the Zoharically expanded cosmic worlds would be that the first half manifests its soul essence in the more collective nature that can be associated with its closeness to the center, and the second half manifests that more individual soul covering whose form may be associated with the periphery. Thus in the first two worlds the soul cannot yet be distinguished from the collective spirituality of the whole, with perhaps the difference that such potential individuality is not capable of being manifested in Atzilut and is simply unmanifest in Beriah, which is similar to the difference in Pythagorean numerology between the monad, which is incapable of division, and the number 1, which is so capable. With the third whole tone of Mi-Fa, on the other hand, the diatonic scale marks the shift to what may be said to characterize the second half of the whole tone, that of individuality, though it is here held in balance with collective unity. When we turn, however, to the semitones of the fourth through sixth whole tones of the chromatic scale—those whose solfeggio names are Fi-Sol, Si-La, and Li-Ti—it is now the first halves that have a virtual status in the diatonic scale, with the second halves—the diatonic tones of Sol, La, and Ti—here achieving dominance. The implication of the first tonal switch from whole tones to a semitone, that from Mi to Fa, is that the corresponding fourth through sixth worlds of the Nefesh, Ruach, and Neshamah soul levels will be characterized not by collective unity but by a progressively more perfected individuality.

It is this development of the soul that permits it to be finally united, without loss of self, with the unifying energy of the Sabbatical world in the second semitone shift of the diatonic scale, this time to the octave, the upper Do marking the first half of the seventh world. And here we arrive at the most persuasive reason to employ the diatonic scale as a key to esoteric cosmology, that is, the character it allows us to posit for the seventh world. For if we can view the higher octave as signifying a completion of the cosmic process, then it would seem appropriate to place the sphere of the Tzimtzum around it. The implication of such a placement of the cosmic circle at the midpoint of the seventh world is that this world may thus be precisely defined as that which unifies the finite within the cosmic circle with the infinity surrounding it, and the characteristic of holiness that we can assign to this world, as to all sevenths, would seem to derive precisely from this unification. The correlative of the diatonic scale, therefore, proves as illuminating to kabbalistic cosmology as it has been to its Platonic counterpart, particularly in the support it gives to the kabbalistic understanding of a third-world Fall and of the source of Sabbatical holiness. But the prominence given to the first half of the seventh world by its correlation with the octave is the most meaningful result of the cosmological information that for thousands of years has been esoterically understood to be conveyed by the structure of the diatonic scale.

THE SEVENTH WORLD AND THE
SECRET DOCTRINE OF THE KABBALAH

We have seen that acceptance of the proposed musical-mathematical key to our cosmological model enables us to understand its culminating seventh world as split by the circle of the original Tzimtzum into a finite half and an infinite half. And it is this split that can further allow us to relate the remaining two Lurianic soul levels with this one cosmic world, the Chayah soul identified with just the octave half of the seventh world and the Yechidah level with the whole seventh world. Both halves may be associated with the same unifying purpose of the seventh world but at different levels. The Chayah soul is, indeed, double aspected in this modeling. As the culminating stage of the cosmic octave, its concern would be with cosmic unification, but as the lower finite half of the full Yechidah soul, it can engage in Devekut, the "clinging" that is a form of mystic communion, with its higher infinite self.

In trying to understand what kind of cosmic unification might be associated with the Chayah soul, we would do well to investigate an aspect of kabbalistic speculation that has long been considered dangerous because of the historical use made of it by the false Messiah Sabbatai Tz'vi. But it is time that the speculations of the Sabbatian theorist Nathan of Gaza be readmitted to kabbalistic discourse because of their cosmological insights. It is best to begin this investigation, however, with a central concern of the Lurianic Kabbalah, the redemption of the holy sparks that have fallen into the power of the Kelipot as a result of the Shevirah. As Chayyim Vital presents this doctrine: "Know that through Adam's sin all souls fell into the depths of the *qelippoth*. . . . Therefore the Shekhinah . . . descended among them in order to gather in the soul-sparks . . . to sift them [from the *qelippoth*], to raise them to the sphere of holiness, and to renew them. . . . [T]his is the work of God, until He shall have ended His work of gathering all the souls that have fallen into the *qelippoth* of the Anti-Adam of Belial and mingled with him from his head to his feet."[42] The need to raise the sparks from the Kelipot, a necessary condition for the fulfillment of the Lurianic Tikkun, was understood by the followers of Sabbatai Tz'vi to require a passage to the Other Side.

At this point it will be necessary to trace some further ramifications of Sabbatian theory. This is not to say that the Sabbatians or Sabbatai himself fulfilled or properly understood this theory. Indeed, Sabbatai is an exemplar of the false Messiah who crosses prematurely to the Other Side. Tz'vi Hirsch of Zhidachov, a great hasidic Kabbalist, has explained the error of the Sabbatians in terms given by his teacher, the Seer of Lublin: "It [i.e., Sabbatian antinomianism] happened because they desired to achieve the revelation of Elijah and to prophesy by the Holy Spirit . . . without troubling to discipline their natures or their material selves; and so, being unworthy and without caution, they overreached themselves by attempting to probe the Unity [of God] without [first] purifying their material natures."[43]

As expounded by Sabbatai and his leading exponents, Nathan of Gaza and Abraham Cardozo, the Sabbatian doctrine of redemption introduces a new element into the Jewish concept of the Messiah. Scholem summarizes this concept as follows:

> As long as the last divine sparks (*nitzotzot*) of holiness and good which fell at the time of Adam's primordial sin into the impure realm of the *kelipot* . . . have not been gathered back again to their source . . . the process of redemption is incomplete. It is therefore left to the Redeemer, the holiest of men, to accomplish what not even the most righteous souls in the past have been able to do: to descend through the gates of impurity into the realm of the *kelipot* and to rescue the divine sparks still imprisoned there. As soon as this task is performed the Kingdom of Evil will collapse of itself, for its existence is made possible only by the divine sparks in its midst. . . . The Messiah must go his lonely way into the kingdom of impurity and "the other side" *(sitra ahra)* and dwell there in the realm of a "strange god" whom he would yet refuse to worship.[44]

As expressed by Jacob Frank, the final nihilistic product of the Sabbatian movement, "we must descend and be cast down to the bottom rung, for only then can we climb to the infinite."[45] The apostasy of Sabbatai to Islam, and later of Frank to Catholicism, which this doctrine can so well explain, is not, however, crucial to the understanding of a Messiah whose primary task it is to enter the Other Side and rescue the souls imprisoned there. Indeed, Nathan of Gaza had developed its main tenets in a significant work of Sabbatian theology written before the apostasy, part of which is summarized as follows by Scholem:

When the light substance of *En-Sof* entered the *tehiru* in a straight line, the divine forms crystallized, and even the *qelippoth* and *dinim* deriving from the thought-less light found their appropriate, positive place in the emergent structures. However, not the whole *tehiru* was affected by the irruption of the ray of light from En-Sof. The "straight line" penetrated only the upper half of the primordial space (which should be pictured as a sphere), and there built the world of its "thought"; it did not reach the lower half, described by Nathan as "the deep of the great abyss." The great work of cosmic *tiqqun*, which Israel has to accomplish through the strength of the Law and the divine commandments, relates to the upper part of the *tehiru* only. The lower part persists in its unformed and chaotic condition *(golem)*, dominated by the *qelippah* until the advent of the messiah, who alone can perfect it. As a matter of fact, the thought-less lights too built worlds unto themselves, to wit the demonic worlds of the *qelippah*. . . . In the context of this doctrine, the Zoharic designation of the sphere of evil as the "other side" takes on a startlingly novel meaning. It refers to the "other side" of *En-Sof* itself, that is, to that half of it which resists the process of differentiation and organization.[46]

Nathan's cosmology distinguishes between the "thought-some" light of creative evolution and the "thought-less" light that resists the differentiating process of creation, the former also more closely associated with the upper half of the Tehiru, the space within the Tzimtzum, and the latter with its lower half. But application of this to our model requires a major revision of its character. We must now understand it to be divided into upper and lower hemispheres and that the conscious experience of the Nefesh, Ruach, and Neshamah soul levels pertains only to the upper hemisphere of these cosmic layers. This would leave an Other Side that can only be safely entered at the Chayah level and is the spiritual work proper to this level both to complete its own development and to redeem the weaker souls imprisoned there.

Nathan of Gaza's "thought-some" and "thought-less" light may perhaps be related to the modern psychological categories of the conscious and the unconscious self, the latter further understood to include the Jungian concept of the shadow. For Jung, the development of the "whole man" requires his "realization of the shadow,"[47] that part of him he had not previously cared to know about himself and therefore repressed, with grave consequences to his psychic health and spiritual evolution. At some point, because of either psychological distress or spiritual stagnation, the individual will need to confront this shadow if he or she is to progress to a greater sense of wholeness, both with him- or herself and with the cosmos. And what our model seems now to be telling us is that the point at which this confrontation becomes imperative is exactly at the point of entrance into the seventh heavenly sphere of Aravot.

But continuing its progress simultaneously through what can be considered both hemispheres of Chayah consciousness does not mean that the soul's behavior in the lower hemisphere must be opposite to that commanded in its earlier positive path, that "the old rabbinic concept of *mitzvah ha-ba'ah ba-averah,* literally, 'a commandment which is fulfilled by means of a transgression,'"[48] need be interpreted, with the Sabbatians, as commanding such transgression. The backward path would rather seem to involve the "undoing" of whatever was earlier inscribed by the soul in its unconscious half.

If we can consider this lower hemisphere to be the shadow of its positive mate and to contain a living record of whatever was repressed by the soul in its upward spiritual journey, then the downward passage through the lower hemisphere would have occurred as a mirror reflection of the soul's similar passage through its upward journey. But this mirror would be more like that picture kept by Dorian Grey in his closet, which Oscar Wilde imagined as visually recording all of Dorian's corruption. All such hidden corruption or repressed desires retain their potency as long as they are not confronted, and they exercise a power to tie the soul to the earth as with knots. Before the soul can be released from such desires, it must untie each of these knots. It is for this reason that, in the language of our revised model, the redeemed soul has to proceed from what was open to the light of consciousness to what was hidden in the unconscious, that it could undo all that still captivates the soul and release itself from its chaos of unresolved confusion. It is this redeemed self that can now engage in the highest of cosmic consummations, its further unification with its infinite divine self.

To comprehend this ultimate stage in the evolution of the soul, as of the cosmos, we should review "the secret doctrine of the Kabbalah," the doctrine whose source I have elsewhere attributed to the Zadokite priesthood[49] and whose first biblical expression is in the vision of the one prophet who was also a Zadokite priest, a vision that is to become, in turn, the source of the entire Jewish mystical tradition—Ezekiel's Throne vision:

> Now it came to pass . . . that the heavens were opened, and I saw visions of God. . . . [O]ut of the midst thereof came the likeness of four living creatures. . . . Now as I beheld the living creatures, behold one wheel upon the earth by the living creatures, with his four faces. . . . And above the firmament that was over their heads was the likeness of a throne, as the appearance of a sapphire stone: and upon the likeness of the throne was the likeness as the appearance of a man above upon it. . . . This was the appearance of the likeness of the glory of the Lord. And when I saw it, I fell upon my face, and I heard a voice of one that spake. And he said unto me, Son of man, stand upon thy feet, and I will speak unto thee. And the spirit entered into me when he spake unto me, and set me upon my feet. . . . (Ezek. 1:1, 5, 15, 26, 28; 5:1, 2)[50]

What has been understood to represent a chariot (Merkabah) has four levels, later correlated with the four worlds of the Kabbalah, the wheels, the living creatures (Chayot), the firmament, and the Throne, on which sits the divine glory (Kavod) in "the likeness as the appearance of a man." Of equal importance are the seer, called "son of man" (Ben Adam) many times in his book, and his vision of glorified man on the Throne.

The name "son of man" given the prophet implies God's adoption of the human Ezekiel as His son, a name that is to have a long and significant history in relation to the prophet Daniel, the legendary Enoch, and finally Jesus. Indeed, Jesus' adoption of this term places him directly in the central tradition of Jewish mysticism deriving from Ezekiel. In this revolutionary vision, what Ezekiel beholds on the divine Throne is quite simply the figure of glorified man. But the deepest meaning of this vision of deified man by a divine son is of their identity, that Ezekiel is recognizing the man on the divine Throne to be his own higher self, that there is an identity between the seer and the seen. Thus the term "son of man" would seem to signify he who has achieved the stage of enlightenment at which he can recognize the divine nature of his higher self.

There is a kabbalistic tradition that at the highest level of mystical ascent the face one sees on the Throne will be his own. Thus Abraham Abulafia, the great Kabbalah master of meditation, writes: "When an individual completely enters the mystery of prophecy, he suddenly sees his own image standing before him." And he proceeds to support this claim by quoting from a work of Moshe of Narbonne that refers to this earlier tradition: "When the sages teach that the prophets 'liken a form to its Creator,' they mean that they liken the form which is in the prophet's own soul . . . to its Creator, that is, to God. It is thus written, 'Over the form of the Throne there was a form like an image of a Man' (Ezek. 1:26). These forms and images exist in the soul of the prophet. . . ."[51] This understanding of Ezekiel's vision was already clear in the derivative visions of the prophet Daniel and the nonbiblical Book of Enoch, fairly contemporaneous with Daniel, to which we shall now briefly turn.

Written some four hundred years after Ezekiel, in the second century B.C.E., and thus suggesting an ongoing mystical tradition, Daniel's Throne vision contains two supernal figures, one of which is called by the same term, son of man, addressed by an angel to Daniel, himself, thus making clear the covert implication of Ezekiel's vision, the identity of seer and seen:

> The Ancient of days did sit . . . the hair of his head like the pure wool: his throne was like the fiery flame, and his wheels as burning fire. . . . [A]nd, behold, one like the Son of man came with the clouds of heaven, and came to the Ancient of days, and they brought him near before him. And there was given him dominion, and glory, and a kingdom. . . . And it came to pass, when I, *even* I Daniel, had seen the vision, and sought for the meaning, then, behold, there stood before me as the appearance of a man. . . . [H]e said unto me, Understand, O son of man: for at the time of the end shall be the vision. (Dan., 7:9, 13–14; 8:15, 17)

Such an identification of the prophetic and envisioned sons of man is made still clearer in a nonbiblical apocalyptic work, the Ethiopic Book of Enoch, now known as 1 Enoch. This is in the parables section, written some one hundred to two hundred years after the rest of this book, and dated by one scholar to the years 94–79 B.C.E.[52] Again there is a vision of two supernal beings, one older and the other younger:

> And there I saw one who had a head of days, and his head (was) white like wool; and with him (there was) another, whose face had the appearance of a man, and his face (was) full of grace, like one of the holy angels. And I asked one of the holy angels who went with me, and showed me all the secrets, about that Son of Man. . . . And he answered me and said to me: "This is the Son of Man who has righteousness. . . . And this Son of Man . . . will cast down the kings from their throne." (chap. 46)
>
> And it came to pass after this that my spirit was carried off, and it

went up into the heavens. . . . And that angel came to me, and greeted me with his voice, and said to me: "You are the Son of Man who was born to righteousness, and righteousness remains over you, and the righteousness of the Head of Days will not leave you. . . . He proclaims peace to you in the name of the world which is to come. . . . And all . . . will walk according to your way. . . ." (chap. 71)[53]

In Enoch's vision the son of man sitting on the Throne of Glory with the "head of days" is recognized to be his own final transfiguration in the World to Come, as it is of all the righteous who have followed his path to divine sonship, in keeping with the divine proclamation: "Israel is my son, even my firstborn" (Exod. 4:22).

The further development in the postbiblical period of what I have called the secret doctrine of the son occurs in such Merkabah-Hekhalot texts as 3 Enoch and the *Shi'ur Komah,* possibly dated between the second and fourth centuries C.E., though both have separately been dated as late as the seventh century C.E. The main difference of these works from Daniel and 1 Enoch is the substitute name of Metatron now given to the supernal figure earlier called the son of man, who is called both the angelic Prince of the Presence and "Youth" (Na'ar). The work now known as 3 Enoch brings the parallel traditions related to Enoch and Metatron into a higher synthesis that clarifies the deepest implications of Merkabah mysticism. In this text it is Rabbi Ishmael, who introduces himself as a descendant of the priestly lineage of Aaron and who is further identified in the title of his book with the unlikely title of "High Priest," that converses mystically with Metatron:

[I] (3) "Lord of the Universe, I pray thee, that the merit of Aaron . . . who received the crown of priesthood from Thy Glory on the mount of Sinai, be valid for me in this hour. . . ."

(7) I fell down and was benumbed by the radiant image of their eyes . . . until the Holy One, blessed be He, rebuked them, saying:

(8) "My servants, my *Seraphim,* my *Kerubim,* and my *'Ophannim!*

Cover ye your eyes before Ishmael, my son . . . and my glory, that he tremble not nor shudder!"

(9) Forthwith Metatron the Prince of the Presence, came and restored my spirit and put me upon my feet.

[IV] (1) I asked Metatron and said to him: "Why art thou called by the name of thy Creator, by seventy names? Thou art greater than all the princes, higher than all the angels, beloved more than all the servants, honoured above all the mighty ones in kingship, greatness and glory: why do they call thee 'Youth' in the high heavens?"

(2) He answered and said to me: "Because I am Enoch, the son of Jared. . . .

(10) And because I am small and a youth among them in days, months and years, therefore they call me "Youth" (*Na'ar*).

[VII] (1) . . . When the Holy One, blessed be He, took me away from the generation of the Flood, he lifted me on the wings of the wind of Shekina to the highest heaven. . . .

[IX] (2) And I was raised and enlarged to the size of the length and width of the world. . . .

[X] (1) All these things the Holy One, blessed be He, made for me: He made me a Throne, similar to the Throne of Glory. . . .

[XII] (5) And He called me THE LESSER YHVH in the presence of all His heavenly household; as it is written (Ex. XXIII. 21): "For my name is in him."

[XV] (1) As soon as the Holy One, blessed be He, took me in (His) service to attend the Throne of Glory . . . forthwith my flesh was changed into flames. . . .[54]

Though subservient to the Holy One, blessed be He, and seated upon a throne only "similar to the Throne of Glory," Metatron is yet called "THE LESSER YHVH" and rules as prince over all the other heavenly hosts. Most significantly, this intermediary between God and the creation, whose size is that of the whole created world, is not simply a supernatural being but the transfigured form of the biblical figure Enoch. Seated on a heavenly "throne," then, is the formerly human body of fire that has become a "lesser" form of the deity, both of these factors being represented in his designation as "Youth," a covert suggestion of his sonship to that king he serves as prince, since the son of a king is a prince.

Metatron is also called Youth in the *Shi'ur Komah*: "The Youth [*na'ar*] Metatron appears and prostrates himself before the Holy One, blessed be He."[55] Though he is not here associated with a human son figure, his own divine sonship is suggested, as in 3 Enoch, by use of the term *Na'ar*, Youth. But the *Shi'ur Komah* does introduce another form of what I have defined as the secret doctrine of the son, that adept who has secret knowledge of the Shi'ur Komah, "the measure of the [divine] body": "It is said that he who knows this mystery, is assured of his portion in the world to come (is assured to be a son of the world to come). . . . I [Rabbi Yishmael] and Rabbi Aquiba vouch for this, that whoever knows this measure of our Creator, and the praise of the Holy One, blessed be He, he will surely be a son of the world to come. . . ."[56] Though the translators here indicate the equation of the phrase "son of the world to come" with the concept of the portion reserved for and to be inherited by the righteous in the World to Come, and this connotation has been substituted for the more literal rendering "son of the world to come" in some translations, the phrase "*ben haolam haba*" does appear in almost all of the known manuscripts of the *Shi'ur Komah*.[57] Both here and in 3 Enoch, Rabbi Ishmael's association with the concept of divine sonship goes back to the understanding, suggested in Ezekiel, that one who has achieved the Throne vision, the recognition of the envisioned Glory as one's higher self, is a divine son, the central mystery of the Jewish mystical tradition deriving from the Hebraic priesthood.

As the Merkabah texts go back to Ezekiel's Throne vision, so does this tradition continue into the later Kabbalah, the two main Partzufim (divine personalities) of the *Zohar* being Arikh Anpin, the white-haired higher figure, and Ze'ir Anpin, the young lower figure. The name Ze'ir Anpin literally means "short face," as that of Arikh Anpin means "long face," the former traditionally taken to suggest short temper as the latter does long suffering. The Fall of man is also kabbalistically explained by human impatience, by a premature eating of the fruit on the sixth rather than the seventh day, and it is Ze'ir Anpin's characteristic short temper that allows him to be a paradigm of man both in his Fall and in his redemption, as we shall soon see.

In the further sexualized development of this concept of the Partzufim, in the Idrot sections of the *Zohar,* Ze'ir Anpin is understood to be the son of the sexualized derivatives of Arikh Anpin, who are Abba (Father) and Imma (Mother), as the Nukvah (Female) is the sister-bride figure finally separated from the originally androgynous son Partzuf of Ze'ir Anpin. But the centrality of this son figure is shown when these five Partzufim are placed on the reconfigured form of the Tree of Life Diagram. For while the other Partzufim occupy the positions of just one of the Sefirot—Arikh Anpin that of Keter, Abba that of Chokhmah, Imma, that of Binah, and the Nukvah that of Malkhut—Ze'ir Anpin occupies six of the ten Sefirot on the reconfigured Tree, those from Chesed to Yesod. And in the "Sha'ar ha-Kelalim" (Gate of General Principles) introductory section to the *Eitz Chayyim,* appearing in all Hebrew editions of Chayyim Vital's major work of Lurianic Kabbalah, it is only his Sefirot that both shatter and undergo a most remarkable rebirth.

In this important Lurianic treatment of the Shevirah, the Sefirotic vessel of Arikh Anpin is completely able to contain the Limitless Light, though at a distance, and that of Abba to receive it from Arikh Anpin face-to-face. While Imma can only receive it by turning her back to Abba, a condition that the Tikkun is dedicated to reverse, her vessel also does not break. We come finally to the contrasting fates of the Sefirot of Ze'ir Anpin and the Nukvah. As with the upper Partzufim, the vessel of the Nukvah, while partially damaged, does not break, and it is thus only the Sefirot of Ze'ir Anpin that are completely shattered: "And it [the Sefirah of Malkhut] does not completely [break] like the previous [Sefirot of Ze'ir Anpin] but it becomes a single Partzuf after the Tikkun, meaning that she [Malkhut] was now worthy to be made into a complete Partzuf despite being only one point [Nekudah], which the six Sefirot [of Ze'ir Anpin] did not merit to become."[58]

But the still conjoined Ze'ir Anpin and the Nukvah have a most symbolically interesting history after the reconfiguration of their Sefirot into Partzufim that defines the Tikkun. Lurianic cosmology assigns three very curious stages to the growth process of Ze'ir Anpin. There is a first gestation in the womb of Imma, a period after birth of nursing, and then a return to the womb of Imma for a second gestation. As explained in the "Sha'ar ha-Kelalim" section of the *Eitz Chayyim*:

> And now we will explain what the *Zohar* says in chapter Acharei Mot, p. 65: "After he [Ze'ir Anpin] has finished nursing, he enters a second period of gestation.". . . He [Ze'ir Anpin] becomes a fetus again in [the womb of] Imma, a second gestation, in order to acquire consciousness [*mochin*] for himself, even though he had already completed for himself a whole Partzuf of six Sefirot in the days of his nursing. And in order that you shall not be astonished by this, how there could be a second pregnancy [of Imma] after the [period of] nursing, does it not [say]: "From my flesh will I see God." . . . So is it with the supernal Imma, who becomes pregnant a second time with the souls of Ze'ir Anpin and the Nukvah, who are renewed in the mystery of the new consciousness that was given to them.[59]

Though even the author[60] feels called upon to express our amazement at the thought of such a return to the womb, its symbolic implication would seem to be that Ze'ir Anpin is "twice-born." Since the still conjoined Ze'ir Anpin and the Nukvah together consist of the lower seven

Sefirot, it seems that the consciousness they acquire during their second gestation would be that of the upper three Sefirot of Kether, Chokhmah, and Binah, the mental Sefirot that they need both to complete the Sefirot number of their mature Partzufim and their cognitive capacity for higher knowledge.

Thus the innermost mystery of the "Sha'ar ha-Kelalim" would seem to be its special understanding of the Partzuf of the son as he who, alone of the Partzufim, suffered the Shevirah or Fall that man is destined to repeat and whose rebirth can also provide the model for a similar human rebirth of the spirit through the development of higher consciousness. So too is the central mystery of the Kabbalah the same as that deriving from Ezekiel, the apotheosis of the earth-born divine son into that "son of the world to come" who can take the cosmic measure of the angelic Prince of the Presence because he is one with him in size and glory.

Achievement of the cosmic evolutionary goal of divine personality, particularly as formulated in the secret doctrine of the son I have defined and posited as the acme of Jewish mysticism, is essentially opposed to what adherents of the "perennial philosophy" have understood to be the goal of spiritual development, that of return to an undifferentiated One, a distinction essentially temporal in character. If we can correlate such spiritual goals with the temporal difference between the origin and fulfillment of the cosmos, between its Alpha and Omega, then this distinction can further illuminate the two main directions of mystical understanding and practice in human history: that which understands its goal as a return to a past state of undifferentiated Being and that which sees it as a process of Becoming, of a movement forward to the future perfection of multiple divine personalities. Where the former may be more identified with Eastern forms of mysticism, so can the latter be identified more with its Western forms. These differences may also be said to characterize the two main forms of human personality that our cosmic model has shown to define the two complementary centers of consciousness at each level of the soul, one having a more collective and the other a more individualized character, characteristics comparable to the two main classes that William James has distinguished in *The Varieties of Religious Experience*.[61]

If I am right that these differing orientations of consciousness, with their differing weights in individual cases, define the two essential classes of human personality as of religious experience, then it is not surprising to find evidences of both in any great spiritual tradition. Thus Eastern mysticism is noted for cultivating such practices as can bring the soul to that state of *nirvana* in which cosmic individuality is overcome in an acosmic return to undifferentiated Being. But the Krishna tradition in Hinduism and the Amitabha tradition in Buddhism express understandings similar to the goal of the Jewish mystical tradition I have emphasized, the human-divine co-creation of a more perfect spiritual realization than had existed before the cosmic beginning. In the Western traditions as well, there are currents of practitioners who would prefer the annihilation of individuality in such a *unio mystica* as cultivated by some Christian saints, preferring to annihilate rather than preserve the individual consciousness that can enclothe the divine in that "communion" of still distinguishable members called *devekut* in the Kabbalah.

But even in the Kabbalah, there are two opposing understandings of the Lurianic concept of Tikkun. There is that interpretation which understands the goal of Tikkun to be a simple return or restoration of the cosmic worlds to the positions they held before the Shevirah and of the soul as ascending back up through the same four worlds it is helping to restore to achieve a final *unio mystica* with Ein Sof that represents no cosmic gain. And then there is that which I have emphasized in all my books, the way forward from the world of Tohu—of the single divine embodiment of Adam Kadmon, whose inadequate Sefirot were unable to contain the light of Ein Sof and shattered—to that world of Tikkun understood to consist of the reconstitution of the shattered Sefirot not in the original form of Adam Kadmon but of multiple divine personalities. Most important is that median, six-Sefirot Partzuf of the son, Ze'ir Anpin, whose unification of the finite and infinite in the perfection of divine personality defines as well the path available to humanity that the human soul can choose to "enact," the path the remainder of this book will be charting.[62]

In the following chapters we shall explore the ascending levels of the soul, emphasizing the nearer worlds of fallen and redeemed man. Chapter 2 will take us from the pre-incarnate Nefesh soul in the third world of Yetzirah and the dual nature it there develops upon acquiring its Tzelem, spiritual body, to the sources for its fourth-world Fall, in an extended study of the false temptations of worldly power and pleasure, as well as the means available for transforming itself from the past to the future orientation that will begin its redemptive process. It is the position in our model of the fourth world upon the cusp of past and future that allows for the meditative technique I have called "The Transformative Moment," a technique that will be further developed in the third and fourth chapters on the Ruach and Neshamah levels of the soul as well as being featured in the guided meditation offered in appendix A.

In chapter 3 the stages within the Ruach soul level will be related both to the traditional chronology of the future Messianic Age, correlated with the fifth cosmic world, and to such levels of spiritual power—from creative thought, through the mastery of synchronicity and the more miraculous transformations and new creations of substance—as are reflected in the legends of the greatest of religious figures, access to all such levels being provided by a more fully developed model of transformative meditation based on an analysis of the structure of the combined Nefesh and Ruach souls. Chapter 4 will then apply this model of the Transformative Moment to an understanding of Neshamah consciousness in an analysis of the Patriarchs that finally relates such development of the Neshamah soul to the divine personalities, particularly Ze'ir Anpin, who also inhabit the World to Come, the sixth of the cosmic worlds.

In chapter 5 we finally reach the seventh world in a culminating analysis of what is, in effect, the six soul levels of the *Zohar* defined in the opening quotation of the present chapter, an analysis that also reviews as it traverses the various paths the soul may travel to ultimate self-realization. These are the lower Nefesh path of sex, the lower Ruach path of love, the lower Neshamah path of power, the upper Nefesh path of knowledge, the upper Ruach path of holiness, and the upper Neshamah path of unification. In this model, the upper Nefesh path is also synthesized with the Lurianic Chayah soul, and the highest two paths are further identified with the Lurianic Yechidah soul, distinguished into the two levels personified by Enoch and Metatron. It is the salvific relationship between the once human Enoch and his own divinized higher self, the mystical knowledge of their unity experienced archetypally as the Throne vision, that is the ultimate truth enshrined in the Jewish mystical tradition.[63] Finally, appendix B will show the relationship of the Throne vision to the prayer service, the way in which this highest form of Jewish spiritual practice both encodes and serves to realize this ultimate truth.

The imaginative grasp of this truth is further facilitated by the unique application of the diatonic scale to our unified kabbalistic model of the cosmos. For the graphic revelation of this secret doctrine through a unique feature of the seventh world of this cosmic model, the splitting of this world by the circumference of the Tzimtzum into finite and infinite halves, is one that only emerges from this cosmic model with the Pythagorean tuning of its concentric crystalline spheres to the diatonic scale.[64] It is this tuning, which correlates the cosmic consummation of the octave with the first half of the seventh-world sphere, that permits us to divide this holy seventh world into the finite and infinite halves, personified by Enoch and Metatron, that it is the special grace of the Yechidah soul to unify.

Such a synthesis of the Hebraic with the Hellenic is given voice in Milton's fantasy of the music of the spheres synthesized with the angelic music sung to the divine figure on the Throne, a fantasy that he invites us to share:

. . . to our high-rais'd fantasy present
That undisturbed Song of pure concent,
Aye sung before the sapphire-color'd throne
To him who sits thereon . . .

. . . .

That we on Earth with undiscording voice
May rightly answer that melodious noise;
As once we did, till disproportion'd sin
Jarr'd against nature's chime, and with harsh din
Broke the fair music that all creatures made
To their great Lord . . .

. . . .

O may we soon again renew that Song,
And keep in tune with Heav'n . . .[65]

In the following chapters, as we imaginatively explore the ever more rarefied reaches of the cosmos, resounding with the music of its spheres, it should become ever more apparent how truly vast, yet balanced, is the scale of the soul—and diatonic!

2

THE FOURTH-WORLD TRANSFORMATIONS OF NEFESH CONSCIOUSNESS

A REVIEW OF THE COSMIC MODEL

Chapter 1 developed a simple cosmic model that synthesized the main cosmological contributions of the various strands of the Jewish esoteric tradition: the seven "days" or dimensions of the Genesis creation account, the Zoharic emanation of dual-aspected cosmic worlds from a central point, and the inclusion of seven of such worlds within the enclosing sphere produced in the Lurianic Tzimtzum. In this chapter we shall follow the course of the lowest-level Nefesh soul from its first appearance in the third of the four kabbalistic worlds, that of Yetzirah, to its final fourth-world embodiment in man, and in both of these kabbalistic worlds we shall see this vital soul to be characterized by an essential polarity.

In the Yetziric origins assigned to this lowest soul level by the Kabbalah, its principal activity will be shown to be the acquirement of its Tzelem, the soul body that endows it with individuality and through which it further develops the polarity that pervades all aspects of kabbalistic cosmology. In the *Zohar* the cosmological understanding is of worlds upon worlds, each world progressively composed of a finer brain and grosser skull. And what is true of each dimension of divine reality is also true of the soul level inhabiting that dimension. But in acquiring its Tzelem, the soul makes a momentous shift from the more collective mode of consciousness that had earlier characterized the world spheres of the expanding cosmos to the more individuated mode that is to characterize the fourth to sixth spheres of the Nefesh through Neshamah levels of the soul.

As the first halves of these worlds are always closer to the center and the second half to the periphery, this provides a second way of understanding the essential polarity within the soul. Earlier defined as the polarity between the collective and the individual, we can now consider it more abstractly as the polarity between what can be called the "central" and the "lateral" tendencies of consciousness, "lateral" being preferred to the perhaps more precise "peripheral" because of the pejorative connotation of the latter.

Once we extend the number of concentric cosmic world spheres to seven, the fourth can be recognized to occupy a unique position in the cosmos, that of its middle layer. And if the inner half of the total cosmic sphere is further identified with the past, then the fourth world not only constitutes the median spatial layer but is situated on the cusp between past and future. In fact, we can view the fourth level of a seven-dimensional cosmos as its only material layer, containing the prior three worlds immanently within it and being enveloped by the three progressively more transcendent higher dimensions of consciousness.

It is, however, in the third world of Yetzirah that the Kabbalah places the Garden of Eden and the Fall, a Fall of the pre-incarnate Nefesh soul that both precipitates the manifestation of the world of matter and may also be correlated with the soul's acquirement of its Tzelem, its soul body. This third world switch from collective to individuated consciousness has an intriguing correlative in the structure of the diatonic scale. For as suggested in chapter 1, it is to this diatonic scale that the seven spheres of the adapted Lurianic cosmos may, on the

Pythagorean model, be tuned. It will be remembered from this earlier discussion that, when placed on the twelve-tone or chromatic scale, the seven tones of the diatonic scale define a most significant pattern. In the first four semitones of the chromatic scale, those whose solfeggio names are Do-Di and Re-Ri, the diatonic tones of Do and Re are in the first halves of the first two whole tones, which can be correlated to the first two kabbalistic worlds. If this correlation may be taken to illuminate the kabbalistic concept of cosmic worlds, then what it is telling us about the first two worlds of Atzilut and Beriah is that they are characterized by the quality that may be attributed to these first halves, a quality of collective unity, the second halves having no more than a virtual status. With the third whole tone of Mi-Fa, however, the diatonic scale marks the shift to what may be said to characterize the second half of the whole tone, that of individuality, though it is here held in balance with collective unity. When we turn to the semitones of the fourth through sixth whole tones of the chromatic scale—those whose solfeggio names are Fi-Sol, Si-La, and Li-Ti—it is now the first halves that have a virtual status in the diatonic scale, the second halves, correlated to the diatonic tones of Sol, La, and Ti, here achieving dominance. The third-world balance between the first and second semitones of the whole-tone correlative to the third world of Yetzirah, those whose solfeggio names are Mi and Fa, and the shift to the second half of the tone in the fourth world, thus give us keys to understanding the progress of the Nefesh soul in the kabbalistic worlds of Yetzirah and Asiyah.

But the geometric correlative of encircling spheres is as illuminating to the more traditional assignment of the Fall to the world of consensus reality that may be identified with the kabbalistic fourth world. For the unique position of the fourth world on the transformative point between past and future provides exactly the circumstances permitting a second fall, now in the choice of the fully free will of the humanly embodied Nefesh soul to model itself prematurely on the individualized possibilities of the future rather than the collective endowment of the past. Given the unique attribute of free will that makes man the image of God, man now has a conflict between his good inclination, the Yetzer ha-Tov that will aid his proper spiritual development, and his evil inclination, the Yetzer ha-Ra that is only too ready to follow the lure of such material gratifications as will forestall or entirely prevent his development of higher consciousness, that in which his true fulfillment, as that of the whole cosmic process, consists. The section of this chapter called "Temptations of a Fallen Culture" will be largely devoted to depicting the various paths of temptation to which the undeveloped Nefesh soul is prone.

But this will be followed by a model of transformative meditation that can begin the process that Luria called "Tikkun," the cosmic reconstruction that will fulfill the purpose of the spirit's descent into matter with its development of divine personality, lifting it higher than it was in that beginning which had first to be catastrophically shattered, the Lurianic second cosmic stage of Shevirah, before it could be perfected. Thus whether the movement of the Nefesh soul to the future modeling of its behavior is regarded as constituting its Fall or the beginning of its development of higher consciousness depends on the *intention* of that movement, its Kavanah, to use another Lurianic term. From Tzimtzum through Shevirah to Tikkun, Lurianic cosmic history can provide a guide to the cosmic voyage of the soul on which we are now embarking.

THE EARLY HISTORY OF THE SOUL

We begin the study of the soul by again considering the all-pervasive principle of cosmic construction defined in the *Zohar:*

> The Holy One, blessed be He, found it necessary to create all these things in the world to ensure its permanence, so that there should be, as it were, a brain with many membranes encircling it. The whole world is constructed on this principle, upper and lower, from the first mystic point to the furthest removed of all the stages.

They are all coverings one to another, brain within brain and spirit within spirit, so that one is a shell to another. . . . The same process takes place below, so that on this model man in this world combines brain and shell, a spirit and body, all for the better ordering of the world.[1]

The Zoharic understanding is that all levels of the macrocosm have the same arrangement of spirit to body reflected in the human microcosm. The cosmic relationship of soul to body at all stages of emanation is particularly pertinent at this point, for it seems to be defining the primary process by which the soul becomes embodied, acquires its Tzelem.

This the *Zohar* understands to occur before the soul has descended to this world. As Isaiah Tishby explains:

The actual belief in the preexistence of the soul is not questioned at all in the Zohar. The author describes in some detail the life and enjoyment of the soul in the Garden of Eden before it descends to the terrestrial world. . . . At this stage, the lowest stage in the divine realm, the souls become more crystallized as independent entities, for each soul's "formation is completed". . . in the storehouse in the Garden of Eden. . . . In the storehouse the souls are clothed in a celestial garment of light, in which the individual lineaments of their corporeal garments in this world can already be discerned.[2]

In terms of the later developed concept of the four cosmic worlds, the "lowest stage in the divine realm," that in which "formation is completed," may be identified with the third world of Yetzirah, Formation, and it is in this Garden of Eden world, which can also be correlated with the third "day" of biblical creation, that the soul becomes clothed in its "celestial garment of light," its subtle body or Tzelem, a term derived from the concept of "image" as this term was used in the central biblical text: "Let us make man in our image, after our likeness" (Gen. 1:26). We shall later consider the way in which man can be considered the image of God; but to speak in more general terms, the Tzelem is ordinarily understood to mean the form in which a spiritual essence can be reflected.

An analogous illustration that may clarify this meaning is the mysterious spatial pattern that can be "formed" by the temporal vibration of a sound. It can be easily demonstrated that if a thin layer of sand is placed on the skin of a drum and a sound is produced at its edge, the sand will form itself into a geometric pattern with infinite shadings to reflect the exact tone and timbre of the formative sound. That is, a particular sound contains a unique spatial form potentially within it that the right circumstances can permit it to manifest.[3] In the same way, it is thought that a spiritual entity can manifest itself in a form that uniquely reflects its essence and that can thus be considered its image or likeness. This understanding may even explain the relationship of Adam Kadmon, the original emanation, to Ein Sof, the Emanator, the relationship of image or form to vibratory source or essence. As the spatial pattern cannot exist without the generative sound, so is the subtle body dependent for its form and subsistence on the spiritual vibration informing it. Such a causative sequence can also be seen in the commonplace of esoteric cosmology that the first activity in the actual process of manifest creation was the production of a cosmic sound or vibration, in the West known as the Marmor (Saying) or the Word and in the East as the sound AUM, space and form being later developments in the process of manifestation.

It seems likely, therefore, that the Tzelem the Nefesh develops in the third world should also signify the quality that, for Gershom Scholem, is the definitive attribute of the Tzelem, individuality. This can be seen in the fuller context of his discussion of the Tzelem:

> The *zelem* is the principle of individuality with which every single human being is endowed, the spiritual configuration or essence that is unique to him and to him alone. Two notions are combined

in this concept, one relating to the idea of human individuation and the other to man's ethereal garment or ethereal (subtle) body which serves as an intermediary between his material body and his soul. Because of their spiritual nature, the *neshamah* and *nefesh* are unable to form a direct bond with the body, and it is the *zelem* which serves as the "catalyst" between them. It is also the garment with which the souls clothe themselves in the celestial paradise before descending to the lower world and which they don once again after their reascent following physical death; during their sojourn on earth it is hidden within man's psycho-physical system.

. . . In Lurianic Kabbalah the *nefesh*, *ru'ah*, and *neshamah* were each assigned a *zelem* of their own which made it possible for them to function in the human body.[4]

In addition to giving the soul an instrument through which it can exercise its inherent free will, the Tzelem also gives the soul a power it did not previously possess, its individuality, and it is precisely this acquirement of the soul through the Tzelem that appears to be necessary for it to fulfill its purpose. In creating its individual image through some alchemical transmutation of still subtle matter into ethereal substance, a process that can be associated with the locale of Eden, the Nefesh thus gains an instrument through which it can manifest its personal will in the progressively more material worlds, finally through the human body. The Tzelem gives the soul a near-focus lens that permits it to perceive reality under the aspect of concrete particularity. It adds a power of precise delineation that the soul did not previously possess. It is this capacity for the individuation both of the spiritual nature and of its perceptions given to the soul through its Tzelem that would seem to be the whole purpose of the angelic cosmic organism in producing the still subtle materialization of the third world out of which the soul could create its stable, subtle body.

This function of the Tzelem seems to be suggested in a passage from the *Ha-Nefesh ha-Chokhmah* (1290) of Moses de Leon, the

Geronese Kabbalist to whom primary authorship of the *Zohar* is generally attributed:

> The purpose of the soul in entering the body is to exhibit its powers and abilities in the world . . . and to undergo a *tikkun* above and below, for it is of high rank, [being] composed of all things, and were it not composed in a mystic manner of what is above and below, it would not be complete. . . . And when it is in this world, it perfects itself and completes itself from this lower world. . . . And then it is in a state of perfection, which was not the case in the beginning before its descent.[5]

The passage is primarily concerned to show that the soul's ultimate function in bringing about the Tikkun, or cosmic reconstruction, depends upon the elements of which it is composed, elements combining "what is above and below." Though we will often use the conventional vocabulary of descent in the remainder of this discussion, it must be understood that this usage is metaphorical, "above" being identified simply with a more spiritual state and "below" with one more material. This caveat is necessary since our spherical model defines the cosmic process primarily in terms of horizontal expansion rather than vertical descent. With this understanding we can now return to a further consideration of de Leon's passage, expanding its meaning to define a two-stage process, the first involving the acquirement of its subtle body from what is below and the second its final embodiment in man.

Reading this text both in this expanded sense and in the context of the cosmological model earlier proposed, it seems clear that this first process is one that concerns the two manifest stages of Yetzirah identified with the diatonic tones of Mi and Fa. If we can now identify the Mi stage with the newly descended Nefesh soul in an Edenic paradise, then the Fa stage might be understood to represent a grosser form of subtle Edenic matter. Applying de Leon's statement to this earlier phase, we may say that the soul, in some "mystic manner," draws upon this subtle matter to construct for itself its subtle image. The comparison is exact to the formative sound discussed above, which cannot produce its unique spatial pattern without the medium of the sand. Since it is thought that Nefesh souls still congregate in a Yetziric *gan eden* where they clothe themselves in the Tzelem they will continue to wear once they have achieved the further stage of physical embodiment, this would seem to be an ongoing process, the soul completing itself before such embodiment with a Tzelem composed in a "mystic manner" of what is "below," the Fa stage of Yetzirah, combined with the soul essence that is "above," the Yetziric Mi stage. It is only after it has completed itself with a Tzelem capable of bonding the soul essence to the physical body, that the soul can achieve the final perfection of its human embodiment. The radical conclusion of de Leon is that in its final physical body, the soul achieves a perfection it did not possess before its descent and that seems to incorporate the whole purpose of cosmic manifestation.

In so forming its Tzelem the Nefesh soul seems to be endowed with the unique capacity for free will, but this freedom, like that of unfallen Adam, may exist only in potential, the actualization of this potential immediately causing a two-stage process leading through a Yetziric to an Asiyic Fall. The first stage of this process would seem to involve a necessitated contraction of its formerly unconstrained soul essence into the Tzelem required to bond this essence to the physical body. In the comparison I have made between the kabbalistic cosmic worlds and the tones of the diatonic scale, the first two worlds of Atzilut and Beriah are not divided into the comparable halves of the chromatic semitones, but feature only the dominant first halves of these tones appearing in the diatonic scale, whose solfeggio names are Do and Re. As the correlatives of the first halves of these tones, the first two worlds can thus be spatially defined as centrally oriented. Thus the consciousness of the first two worlds would not only be collective but would fill the whole space of its world. The third-world correlative, however, is divided into the two diatonic half tones of Mi and Fa, and if they may be identified, respectively, with the Nefesh soul and its Tzelem, then the soul essence would be contracted from its former collective inhabiting of all the space of the first two worlds to its individual inhabiting of just the first half of the third world. If the soul may be said to first become manifest in Yetzirah, it is because it there becomes vested with the individuality conferred by the denser specificities of its Tzelem. But since its function is directed toward ever more material embodiment, so is it through the Tzelem that the Nefesh soul may be said to begin its purposeful exercise of freedom, freely choosing now to complete its progressive course into material form that will accomplish the fuller realization of its individuality.

The two different terms that were earlier applied to the stages of the individualizing process, the "fall" and "embodiment," contain two opposite ways of perceiving the material world, either as unfortunate or as desirable. As the myth of Adam incorporates the former vision, so the soul's free choice to embody itself in man is seen as a positive fulfillment of the purpose for which it was created, a purpose that requires the cosmic stage of materialization. The first completion of the soul, which has just been equated to formation of the Nefesh Tzelem, would seem, then, to define the capacity for freely willed action, though its only available choice is downward toward the acquirement of a physical animal body. But it is only in its human embodiment that this capacity becomes fully effective and the soul perfected, for as we shall soon see, man now develops the capacity to choose between two paths, either to continue the course into ever grosser material forms that has thus far characterized the Nefesh soul or to redirect this course toward such purification of its materially acquired individuality as can render it a fit vessel for the Limitless Light. The perfection that, according to de Leon, the soul achieves in its human embodiment can only be, then, this true freedom to exercise its will that distinguishes man from all other aspects and levels of creation.

Though the soul reveals the quality of will by the time it has descended to Yetzirah that allows it to form a spiritual body or Tzelem out of the sublimed substance of a grosser form of spirit and then to embody itself in the physical forms of the higher animals and man, its exercise of freedom seems to entail the requirement, or to be devoted to the acquirement, of bodies of ever greater density. This freedom seems to be a product of an even more intrinsic characteristic of the Nefesh soul, that of permanent identity. It is by this permanent identity that Nefesh souls can most clearly be distinguished from the angels who also inhabit Yetzirah. For the individual angels are generally thought to emerge, as it were, from the energy field of Yetzirah to accomplish a particular function or mission and then to lose forever their temporary individuality upon return to this field. It may be this permanent identity on the part of the Nefesh soul that accounts for its manifestation of free will, its will being liberated from collective response by its ability to sustain individual identity. But the freedom of the Nefesh soul seems to be wholly directed toward the acquirement of ever denser bodies of sense in which to function. It is only when the Nefesh has acquired both its Tzelem and its human physical body that the downward tendency of its will seems capable of being arrested. The freedom of the pre-Asiyic Nefesh, then, while devoted to the ever greater particularization and enhancement of its identity, seems to be more closely related to an instinctual process than to the deliberative process involved in true choice. And all of this accords with the standard definition of the Nefesh as the soul of the instinctive, animal body.

It is only with man, then, that true free will, based upon a choice of direction, becomes possible. The standard explanation of this from the time of the Talmud is that man was created with two opposing urges, a good urge, Yetzer ha-Tov, and an evil urge, Yetzer ha-Ra, as well as with the power to choose which of these inclinations to follow. We have seen that our model supports this understanding insofar as these inclinations may be precisely identified in verbal terms as "Yetziric" influences and associated with the Mi and Fa stages of the third world further understood to survive throughout the period of the fourth world. Man, however, is endowed with the capacity to counter any such influence through the power of his inherent free will and that other power distinguishing him from the animals, his capacity to name them, to use language. The trouble is that the very power to negate, which gives man the freedom to redirect the downward trend that has thus far characterized the process of divine manifestation, is, itself, tied to what can and has been called the Sitre Achra, the Other Side. If the angels can be identified with the Mi stage of Yetzirah, then this supposedly demonic "other side" can be identified with its Fa stage, and both may be thought to continue to shed their influences on the receptive soul of man.

But it is only because man has such a powerful Yetzer ha-Ra to counter and complement his Yetzer ha-Tov that he can become the fit instrument of the Tikkun, his generation from both elements of Yetzirah providing the creative tension within his will that is the foundation for the exercise of his freedom. Whether we speak of the left side of the Tree of Life Diagram or of the second-half stages of the cosmic spheres, we are speaking of the aspect of reality that gradually manifests ever more individuality of form, identity, and will. And it can also provide the power of just discrimination that can enable the will of man freely to choose the more balanced expression of self that seeks its enhancement in a heightened sense of spiritual communion. Harkening to his angelic rather than demonic impulses, man can start to build his Ruach Tzelem, which can then purify and uplift the Nefesh soul to the more refined and exquisite pleasures that can further rather than retard his spiritual development. If humankind is to be considered the goal of creation and its purposes to lead to greater good, then that "other side" to which man is part native cannot finally be considered to be an independent power of darkness but rather to play an integral part in a larger pattern of good, that balance of contraction and expansion shining in all the manifest stars. This is not to deny the power of human free will to introduce genuine evil into the cosmos. It is to deny that such evil is *caused* rather than *corrected* by the cosmic structure.

By examining this archetype of human nature, we have seen that man is not only endowed with free will but that the derivation of his sense of identity from his soul Tzelem places him in a special condition of resonance to the first flowering of the Yetzir ha-Ra that can also be identified with the second stage of Yetzirah. This combination would seem to promise the misinformed exercise of the will that can be correlated with the Fall, though it by no means requires it. But it is precisely this propensity, arising from his cosmically unique freedom, that makes man the true Tzelem, or image, of God. Of all forms of the inverse, this is surely the most startling. For it is the supreme paradox of creation that the being seemingly at cross purposes to the divine harmony should, from this very circumstance, develop that individuality of will through which it alone can truly image its Creator. In the *Derekh ha-Shem,* the Way of God, Moshe Chayyim Luzzatto shows that this is the very purpose of creation:

> I:2:i. God's purpose in creation was to bestow of his Good to another . . . the true perfect good that exists in His intrinsic essence. . . .

> I:2:ii. God's wisdom, however, decreed that for such good to be perfect, the one enjoying it must be its master. He must be one who has earned it for himself, and not associated with it accidentally [and without reason]. In a way, this can be said to partially resemble God's own perfection, at least to the degree that this is possible. . . .

> I:2:v. This primary, essential creature is man. All other created things, whether above or below man, only exist for his sake. . . .[6]

God's whole purpose in creation, then, was the creation of "another," another being like Him in the individuality that comes from mastering his own will, a mastery that not only involves freedom but also a purification of spirit. To this end, God began a deterministic process that would result in that progressive materialization from which man could develop the spiritual Tzelem that would make him the Tzelem of God, a purified but still free individual. Luzzatto speaks of this paradoxical inversion that makes for resemblance:

> I:5:iv . . . The world therefore contains two opposite general influences. The first is that of natural determinism, while the second is indeterministic. . . .
>
> The deterministic influence is directed downward from on high, while the indeterministic is directed upward from below. This is because the deterministic is the influence that stems from the highest Forces, and therefore, when it is directed toward the physical world, it is directed downward. The indeterministic influence, on the other hand, is the result of man's free will here in the physical world.[7]

Man's free will provides a way of return, or Tikkun, inverse to the deterministic forces that reflect the divine will. But if man's ability to exercise his will free of divine determination is essential to his cosmic contribution, then we can begin to understand the paradox of resemblance through inversion, that man can only become a divine Tzelem through his ability to contend victoriously with the power of the divine will, the very ability enshrined in the name Israel by which such a striver can become a Prince of God.[8] If we can further see man as standing in the pivotal fourth world between the prior worlds of divine determinism and the future worlds of human mastery, then all conditions that keep man within the bounds of such psychic determinism may be viewed as retarding his progress toward the truly free will by which he can become that Other whose resemblance to "the true perfect good that exists in His intrinsic essence" fulfills "God's purpose in creation." Where such retardation may be associated with the attempt to return to earlier cosmic conditions, that which furthers the liberation of the will may also be associated with the indeterminate possibilities arising in the future, with an intuited model of future perfection. Let us now proceed to construct a further chronological scenario for the evolution of human consciousness from the earliest human cultures, an evolution whose beginnings in an Adam-like state can finally bring us to the stage of true human freedom.

There is first the stage of unfallen Adam, that Nefesh Chayah, living soul, whose consciousness is still hormonally attuned to its solar-regulated environment and in harmony with it. The consciousness of such an unfallen man is further developed by R. A. Schwaller de Lubicz in his study of the significance of the crown of the skull in ancient Egyptian figurations, particularly the fact that the line drawn around the human crown separates the lower brain from the two hemispheres of the cerebrum that are responsible for what he calls "cerebral intelligence."[9] As he goes on to explain:

> If, in the figuration of man, we symbolically separate this *crown of the skull*, it leaves us only the *Divine Man*, Adamic Man (*Kadmon*, the prenatural *Adam* of the Kaballah) before his fall into Nature. . . . in detaching the crown when the intention so requires, they separate the organ, which is the symbol of the fall from divine, direct Intelligence into transitory nature; and this double brain (right and left) becomes the principle of the sexualization and of the intelligence of the Created World. . . . Thus, "Divine" man (without this part of the brain) represents the Principle or Neter, capable of living and acting, but only as the executant of an impulse that he receives; hence, he plays the role of an intermediary between the abstract impulse, outside of Nature, and its execution in Nature, without actual choice. In this regard, this entity has a primitive, and "prenatural" character.[10]

In this analysis of ancient Egyptian iconography, Schwaller de Lubicz has brought us back to the earliest understanding of precultural or Adamic man as a being acting not on the basis of its double brain but rather through a "direct Intelligence" of the divine received through compelling impulses. For this most ancient culture, as for its modern interpreter, such impulses are understood to originate not within the primitive neurological structure of the Adamic brain but beyond it, this Adamic lower brain serving as both the receiver and executor of these nonverbal impulses, whether in man's unfallen or rectified forms. For as Schwaller de Lubicz further shows of such a rectified human consciousness: "The life of this 'superman' (in pure contemplation and ecstasy) will again be that of 'Divine' man, but in *consciousness*—that is to say, no longer as a blind Neter, but as a being carrying within itself all knowledge, the sum of all possible experiences."[11]

In contrast to this "prenatural model," a further possibility can chart the progress of the human mind away from such unitive intelligence as may have been manifested in the earliest stage of human civilization. This stage would seem to manifest an unusual influence of the angelic dimension of Yetzirah, one that also allows it to be correlated with the colonizing insects, which seem to be ruled by some, perhaps emergent, form of group intelligence, and by extension to all the wholly instinctual reptiles and other lower animals. In the case of man, the suggestion would be of an internalized angelic presence, not simply of an angelic influence capable of being countered by the human will, but itself inhabiting that will.

The idea of man as inhabited by an internal angelic presence is supported by the interesting thesis of Julian Jaynes that man, from approximately 10,000 B.C.E. to 700 B.C.E., was governed by what he calls the "bicameral mind," "that at one time human nature was split into two, an executive part called a god, and a follower part called a man."[12] It is Jaynes's thesis that "bicameral man" was ruled by internal voices, to which he gave divine status and obedience, voices that guided him directly whenever decision making was required. Unlike the mythological ideal defined by Schwaller de Lubicz, the "bicameral man" of Jaynes is a product of the early development of the double brain, and the archaeological evidence he has amassed in support of his thesis is most persuasive that a form of human mentality something like what he describes must have existed in the early stages of civilization, stages defined by the movement out of the tribe into "towns of such size that everyone does not know everyone else."[13]

The boldest part of his thesis is the conjecture that brain structure is culturally rather than genetically determined and that at the earliest stage of civilization the portions of the right brain corresponding to the speech area of the left brain, most notably Wernicke's area, had its own form of speech capability:

> In ancient times, what corresponds to Wernicke's area on the right hemisphere may have organized admonitory experience and coded it into 'voices' which were then 'heard' over the anterior commissure by the left or dominant hemisphere. . . . auditory hallucinations exist as such in a linguistic manner because that is the most efficient method of getting complicated cortical processing from one side of the brain to the other. . . . it was excitation in what corresponds to Wernicke's area on the right hemisphere that occasioned the voices of the gods.[14]

Though for Jaynes "the voices of the gods" are simply "auditory hallucinations" produced by the peculiar neurological organization of the early "bicameral" mind that makes language the "most efficient method" of cortical coding, the evidence he presents from early texts shows that such voices were experienced as arising not from within the self but from a higher source both associated with but also beyond that self:

> cuneiform texts state that a man lived in the shadow of his personal god, his *ili*. So inextricably were a man and his personal god bound together that the composition of his personal name usually included the name of the personal god, thus making obvious the

bicameral nature of the man. . . . The evidence from hieratic texts is confusing. Each person has his ka and speaks of it as we might of our will power. Yet when one dies, one goes to one's ka. . . . The Egyptians' attitude toward the ka is entirely passive. Just as in the case of the Greek gods, hearing it is tantamount to obeying it. It empowers what it commands. . . . Another observation I would like to make concerns that very important word which governs the whole first chapter of Genesis, *elohim*. It is usually incorrectly translated in the singular as God. "Elohim" is a plural form . . . and better translations of "elohim" might be the great ones. . . . From the point of view of the present theory, it is clear that elohim is a general term referring to the voice-visions of the bicameral mind.[15]

Though Jaynes may be right that the divine voices were actually heard as stated in the ancient texts and that they could be associated with certain information-processing capabilities of the right hemisphere, this need not lead to his conclusion that they represent nothing beyond the split psychological functioning of early man. Rather, his evidence can be used in support of the ancient textual claims of divine auditory experience, later to become the prophetic experience, seeing the very right hemispheric capacities to which he refers not simply as processors of information originating in the individual but as a receiving mechanism for transpersonal information.

But as Jaynes has also demonstrated, where such voices are experienced, there is no possibility for the exercise of free will:

Sound is a very special modality. We cannot handle it. We cannot push it away. . . . To hear is actually a kind of obedience. Indeed, both words come from the same root and therefore were probably the same word originally. This is true in Greek, Latin, Hebrew, French, German, Russian, as well as in English, where "obey" comes from the Latin *obedire*, which is a composite of *ob* + *audire*, to hear facing someone. . . . [I]n bicameral men, this *was* volition.

> Another way to say it is that volition came as a voice that was in
> the nature of a neurological command, in which the command
> and the action were not separated, in which to hear was to obey.[16]

Where Schwaller de Lubicz's unfallen man acts upon unspoken impulses derived "by merging with the creative Unity,"[17] which is the unitive response of the lower brain, with Jaynes's bicameral man the higher cortical functions of the double brain, most significantly its linguistic capacity, have emerged into history but in a dualistic form in which internally heard divine voices are recognized as other than the self and command obedience.

Though the Adamic and bicameral forms of man seem closer to the divine than is the fallen man of modern subjective consciousness, the paradox of the Fall is that it is just this fortunate growth of self-consciousness that liberated the human will, and that it is only through such freedom of the will that man can truly become the image of God. For it is not by modeling himself upon a past condition of divine unity but only upon the model of the future that man can fulfill his divine destiny. In Lurianic cosmology, the repair or Tikkun of the shattered divine vessels is to accomplish a transformation of the original single form of divinity, that of Adam Kadmon, into the Partzufim, the multiple divine personalities, and this way of the future is to be a product of man's own spiritual development. It is only by way of the Fall, the Shevirah, that man can accomplish, both below and above, this divine transformation, by modeling himself upon the future perfection of divine personality. It is not, then, through a past modeling, with its implied angelic takeover of the human will, that man can make his necessary contribution to the cosmic design, nor through such modern occult forms as trance mediumship that aim at a similar return to the cosmic past. Rather, it is through such future modeling as can only arise from a fully self-aware ego that man can both model and remodel the divine image.

Humans, then, have a choice between submitting to an angelic compulsion that harkens back to the past or the freedom of the soul urging them ever onward into the future. Although the Nefesh soul was earlier shown to be following a steadily "downward" course in its progress through the third and fourth worlds, it can also be understood to have been following the forward path to the future. This is even true of the final fallen form it may reach in the fourth world, that double-brained creature with a silent right hemisphere who wanders forlornly through a strange landscape seeking for a clue to the cause and cure of its alienation. The cause lies in this very impulse to actualize the future, which can lead to a premature acquisition of higher cognitive powers before the soul had developed sufficient mastery to be able to utilize them properly, at the animal Nefesh rather than the truly human Ruach level of the soul. We shall see that what the fallen animal soul contributes to human consciousness is a sense of the self together with higher powers of thought and feeling and the impulse to use these higher powers in a future-oriented development of the self. But its will, though subject to influence by the evil inclination, is still free and capable of a higher rather than lower enhancement of the ego.

The creation story tells us that it is the responsibility of man to establish "dominion" (Gen. 1:28) over all the animals, and this can be taken to include the animal propensities within himself. To fulfill the divine image in which he was created, man is told to follow the way of the plants, to "be fruitful, and multiply" (Gen. 1:28), and also to dominate the animal nature. The difference between the right way of the plants and wrong way of the animals is largely a matter of timing, the plants exhibiting a measured ripening process and the animals a restless impatience. If humans are to follow the original divine commandments, they must learn the patience of the plants and to control their lower animal nature, its anxiety, impulsiveness, and belligerence.

Entering the path of the Tikkun requires a process of spiritual discipline that can rectify the Nefesh soul. This involves a twofold effort. The first step, just considered, involves the control of the animal nature by submitting to a higher moral law and to the mindful monitoring of the impulses coming from the lower animal ego. The second step may be likened to the return to an unfallen, expansive state of the Nefesh Tzelem that may be achieved through the practice of meditative prayer. Such a twofold approach is, in fact, that taken by the world's religions to control the evil inclinations of fallen man and, at the same time, to lift him into a condition of higher consciousness. For the free will with which man is endowed was intended to function in just such a condition of expanded consciousness and a constrained animal nature. Stabilized in this state, man would have become the proper vessel for the Ruach consciousness of the fifth world, which in an ideal scenario can be understood to be the true source of the higher capacities of thought and feeling made prematurely available to fallen Nefesh man, and at the rate appropriate for such development. But given the Fall, these capacities cannot be annihilated. Rather they must be uplifted through spiritual development. To understand something of the perils and promise awaiting the Nefesh soul in its fourth-world embodiment in man, we should now attempt to further define the Nefesh soul in both its unfallen and fallen forms.

THE STRUCTURE OF THE NEFESH SOUL

As already partly suggested, the Nefesh soul is characterized by an essential polarity between a more collective center of consciousness and an individualized center. As with the brain, so the soul would seem to be bicameral. Where the brain is divided into right and left sides, so may the soul be thought to begin with a central essence and a lateral surrounding shell and to maintain this distinction between what I shall be calling "central" and "lateral" modes of consciousness throughout its later evolution. In the cosmic model developed in chapter 1, we saw that this major distinction between soul essence and soul vessel could be further distinguished into two such opposing soul essences and soul vessels, bringing the number of soul elements to four, the two of the first half of the world identified, as before, with the central mode and the two of the second half identified with the lateral.

The lateral individualized center may be further identified with conscious awareness and the central collective center with the unconscious, the former also associated with waking Nefesh consciousness and the latter with the Nefesh consciousness during sleep. The collective central center would seem, in fact, to be a perfect model for Jung's concept of the "collective unconscious," and the dream state in which this form of consciousness is most structured does use an archetypal visual language consistent with Jung's concept of the collective nature of such consciousness. But the dream reality of such central consciousness, though characterized by psychic powers not normally available to the waking state, lacks the coherence and continuity of the waking state that largely obscures its existence. Since the normal state of Nefesh consciousness contains traces of unconscious activity, the waking state will, however, have some intimation of another order of reality. In the dream state, on the contrary, there is only central consciousness with no suspicion of a lateral realm of greater fixity and contraction.

The model of Nefesh consciousness being developed may also be said to define a daily progress through its four levels, one going first through its lower two levels from deep sleep to the dream state and then through its upper two levels to the awakening and fully awake state of consciousness. From the perspective of the mediating consciousness at the midpoint of the soul, these sleeping and awake states may also be viewed as defining a circuit, really the figure 8 that has in its horizontal form become the symbol of infinity. This progress may be viewed as going through a centrifugal phase, moving away from the original stability of collective consciousness to the new stability of individual consciousness, that going through the third and fourth quarters, followed by a complementary centripetal phase, one that moves back from such stabilized individuality, first to the midpoint and then to its original state of collective consciousness, by following the path from the second quarter to the first, after which it would return to the midpoint to repeat its round. These dual movements are representative of the daily functioning of the vital soul, the outgoing contraction of consciousness

representing the awakening and fully awake Nefesh soul and the ingo-
ing expansion its sleeping state, going from the dream state to that of
deep sleep. Both movements of consciousness are clearly necessary for
the healthy functioning of the Nefesh soul, daily recharging it both
with vitalizing energy and the inner assurance of its ultimate wholeness.
In this balanced circuit of lateral and central elements we may also read
the biological round of anabolic and catabolic functions as well as the
further dynamics of the biophysical world, in which life forces build up
higher forms of informational order to counter the physical effects of
entropy. In the central and lateral centers we can see the basic polarities
of this world, that between collective and individual consciousness,
darkness and light. The forces propelling these centrifugal and centripetal phases bind this functional polarity of central and lateral consciousness into a regenerating whole whose oscillation creates the
rhythmic processes that inform all things. This combination of centers
and binding forces represents the minimum needed to maintain the
vital functioning of the body at the lower level of consciousness that
may be equated with the animal state, the state of the Nefesh Chayah,
or living soul, which characterized the animals brought before Adam
for naming.

The centrifugal and centripetal forces just defined may be further
understood to represent faculties in the service of the two main centers
of Nefesh consciousness. If we can identify the centers of consciousness
with the soul essences of the two halves of the soul, those that may be
located in the "interior" first and third quarters of the divided "space"
of the fourth cosmic world, then the faculties that provide the data
these conscious centers are to interpret may be associated with the
more "exterior" aspects of these soul halves, those that may similarly be
located in the second and fourth quarters of this world.

Considering now what two psychic faculties might be correlated
with the level of the vital soul, they would seem to be those of instinct
and intuition, and it seems appropriate to identify instinct with the lateral center and intuition with the central center. Instinct may be said to

have a lateral character insofar as it defines a pattern of behaviors that is rational to the extent that it has proven survival value for the individual or species. Intuition, which serves as an emergency adjunct to such normal instinctual functioning, has a central character, however, since it arrives at its knowledge through irrational paths. But there would also seem to be some cross-connecting of these centers and faculties since instinct defines a collective mode of behavior suitable for the general case, while intuition allows for the unexpected through which the general can be individually adapted to fit the unusual case.

This simple model may be said to define the functioning of the animals, of man at his most primitive level of tribal development, and of the animal level of man at a higher level of his spiritual development. It may also be identified with the unfallen state of the Nefesh soul. To understand how the cosmic model developed in chapter 1 may further illuminate the process of the Nefesh Fall, we should now begin to consider it more directly. In the next section, this model will be more precisely detailed than is necessary for the present discussion, but the most important point to be reviewed here involves the surrounding cosmic environment into which the soul must extend to form its Tzelem. As will be remembered, this was understood to be the Reshimu, the residual light remaining in the cosmic space after the Tzimtzum, into which the fragments of shells broken in the Shevirah intermingled in a chaotic fashion. It was then suggested that the most forward element of the soul, that which can now be identified with the fourth quarter defining the lateral shell, would need to extend into this chaotic substance of the not yet realized future world in order to shape its soul vessel, and that, in so doing, it would risk the danger of becoming stuck in this chaos. Let us now apply this model to the just completed definition of the unfallen Nefesh soul.

In that analysis, we have seen that the lateral faculty identified with the outer shell of lateral consciousness is that of instinct. And earlier in this chapter we saw that the freedom of the Nefesh soul in its earliest stages is more of an instinctual process to proceed toward the ever denser and more efficient embodiment that could be associated with the future direction from Yetzirah to Asiyah. Now again, in the formative stage of Asiyah, we may project the same propensity of the Nefesh instincts to move precipitously to acquire future powers of the soul from the still chaotic soul surroundings into which it is moving, a movement to capture higher faculties that may be identified with an Asiyic Fall.

In the more complex psyche of such a fallen Nefesh soul, involving a development both of the emotions and the intellect, greater sophistication will have been achieved without the spiritual development necessary for its proper use. Since these heart and mind faculties of the now fallen Nefesh soul were acquired by and serve its lateral center of personalized consciousness, they may also be considered lateral. These faculties would now be added to that of instinct in the enclosure of the lateral center of consciousness, and they complete the natural endowment of fallen man. But these additions also interrupt the simple balance of the unfallen model by extensions that can now only be rebalanced by the Ruach consciousness of the fifth world and so should not be utilized without the further spiritual development that can direct their activities toward such higher ends. Rather than serving the social purposes of Messianic society through the Ruach centers that they would have ideally served had the dimension of the fifth world been added to that of an unfallen form of the fourth world, they have now become adjunct faculties of a lower lateral center of consciousness still essentially at the reptilian level of the inner brain. Their greater sophistication is now serving an animal level of consciousness at its initial point of ego development, of its assertion of territorial rights and willingness to fight for their protection and extension. The faculties of feeling and thought have thus become dominated, indeed contaminated, by the impulses deriving from the primary lateral faculty of the Nefesh soul, that of the instincts, primarily those of self-preservation and sex. In serving the lowest center of lateral consciousness, the faculties of emotion and intellect have become molded into conformity with the mode designed to serve this center, that of instinctual gratification, and now employ all their talents to enhancing both the quantity and quality of such lower gratification.

The problem with this fourth-world development of the emotions and reason is that they are directed backward to the lateral center of Nefesh consciousness rather than forward to the centers of Ruach consciousness that should be the level at which humankind is operating. The development of these faculties at the level of the fallen Nefesh soul has distorted the natural functioning of the unfallen vital soul so that it reflects a state of disease rather than of health, the misused and unintegrated higher faculties interfering with the proper functioning of the lower soul as well as losing all sense of their own proper sphere and direction. In the chapters to follow, we shall trace the upward path of the soul that will remedy the Fall through its development of the purified individuality that can give the highest fulfillment to the process of cosmic evolution, the process of Tikkun that will bring the soul far higher than its simple unfallen state. But first we should review the various alternative pathways whose false allure has tempted man to transgress the limits of his Garden state for a life of exile.

TEMPTATIONS OF A FALLEN CULTURE

Introduction: Tohu or Tikkun

At the edge of each completed cosmic world there is a shell that separates the order within from the chaos without, the chaos of a future world not yet formed, each successive world pushing the surrounding chaos further away and increasing the island of order within. To continue to apply the cosmic model proposed in the introductory chapter and just briefly reconsidered to our understanding of the Fall of the Nefesh soul, we should review some of its further details. In that introductory analysis, we saw that the Reshimu, the residual light left within the cosmic sphere produced in the process of Tzimtzum, has a dual character. On the one hand, it is inscribed with the laws involving each stage in the cosmic process; on the other, it is in the state of chaos produced by the failure of the original, noninteracting Sefirot to contain the divine light, which caused their vessels to shatter. A way in which this apparent conflict in Lurianic theory could be resolved was also suggested in the first chapter, the former inscription of the Reshimu, which represents the ideal plan for cosmic evolution, being associated with the first stage of the Tzimtzum, while the subsequent shattering of the vessels was seen to define the second cosmic stage of the Shevirah, a stage productive of a world of chaos (Tohu) in which the broken vessels intermingled with the previously law-inscribed residual light. It is this final definition of a double-aspected Reshimu that is especially pertinent here, its opposing potentialities for chaos or higher purpose providing the soul with the alternative pathways of Tohu or Tikkun. Following its inclination for the coevolution of the self and cosmos, it will proceed in a disciplined way to construct its Tzelem from the constructive elements in the surrounding Reshimu. Following its inclination only for self-aggrandizement or satisfaction, it will rush precipitously into what seems to promise such power or pleasure and become stuck in this chaos. The initial work of the evolving soul at each of its levels, then, is to distinguish the path of Tikkun from that of Tohu.

What distinguishes the paths of Tikkun and Tohu is that in the former the elements of higher consciousness are achieved by spiritual discipline, while in the latter the attempt to achieve higher powers is not only made without such discipline but with a further violation of the law of limitation. Though the growth necessary for the Tikkun always carries the danger of following a false path into Tohu, what primarily differentiates the path of Tikkun from that of Tohu is the observance of some form of Torah, the recognition that there is a border of law that distinguishes the permissible from the forbidden and that it is only in the former that the divine order is expressed. That this broader concept of Torah expresses the understanding of the Kabbalah has been attested to by Aryeh Kaplan: "When the Torah is discussed, it normally refers to the Five Books of Moses, or in a broader sense, to the entire theological structure based on these Books. In the Kabbalistic sense, however, the word 'Torah' refers to the entire spiritual blueprint of creation."[18] Before proceeding further with the application of this concept, we should briefly explore this meaning of Torah.

The best place to start would be with the epitome of Torah, the Ten Commandments. This essence of the covenant and of the spiritual life of Israel contains the guidelines for the creation of a holy community, one that has learned respect for that on which its continuing existence and that of its members depend. Although the concept of honoring only appears in the phrasing of the fifth commandment, "Honor thy father and thy mother," the remaining commandments can also be rephrased as expressions of honoring. Thus the first four commandments not only distinguish the one God from the surrounding polytheism as alone worthy of honor but also forbid the use of graven images and the name of God as, for instance, in magical practices aimed at controlling God in a manner that certainly does no honor to Him; and this honoring of God is reinforced through the memorial honoring of His Sabbath. As the first four commandments teach the individual to honor his God and the fifth commandment to honor his parents, so the last five commandments create a community in which the individual is taught to honor his neighbors. For such a community to exist, one should honor his neighbor by not killing him, betraying his marriage, or stealing from him; and one should not commit such sins either directly or indirectly through false witness or even in one's mind through coveting what is truly his. In other words, the last five commandments teach one how to honor one's neighbor by allowing his right to live and prosper regardless of one's own needs or grievances, by recognizing that one has no right to infringe upon the domain of another. And it is only such mutual honoring that can create a human community. The Ten Commandments attempt to create a holy nation composed of those who, through respect for the law, have been taught to honor their neighbors, their elders, and their God.

This most famous epitome of the Law represents God's second attempt to spell out His Torah to the children of Israel. The first is contained in the terms of the remarkable gift of manna: "Then said the Lord unto Moses, Behold, I will rain bread from heaven for you; and the people shall go out and gather a certain rate every day, that I may prove them, whether they will walk in my law, or no. And it shall come to pass, that on the sixth day they shall prepare that which they bring in; and it shall be twice as much as they gather daily" (Exod. 16:4–5). The most important point about God's initial announcement is that the path of Torah involves the capacity for just measure, gathering at a prescribed rate, this rate being doubled on the sixth day to provide for the needs of the Sabbath: "Six days ye shall gather it; but on the seventh day, which is the sabbath, in it there shall be none" (Exod. 16:26). A remarkable aspect of this "rate" is that man is commanded to gather exactly and only what he needs, the amount in each case measuring an omer: "Gather of it every man according to his eating, an omer for every man. . . . And when they did meet it with an omer, he that gathered much had nothing over, and he that gathered little had no lack; they gathered every man according to his eating. And Moses said, Let no man leave of it till the morning" (Exod. 16:16–19).

The way of the divine law is, then, the assured trust that God will provide one exactly what one needs and to be daily satisfied with this knowledge and gift of the divine. Such blessed trust is hard to sustain, and there were those who hoarded the manna overnight only to have it breed worms and stink, those who went out to gather it on the Sabbath only to find there was none and that on this day the extra portion from the previous day did not stink. The Torah of the manna teaches us, then, that we must see all that we get as a divine gift, one that is exactly what we require, and that the process of receiving this gift involves six days of gathering and one day of rest, for which the instruction is: "let no man go out of his place on the seventh day" (Exod. 16:29). This last expression is perhaps the most perfect definition of Sabbath consciousness, man's recognition of his proper "place" in the cosmic scheme and his willingness to abide there. But as the manna story also shows, the Torah is not only to be apprehended contemplatively as one retires within oneself and one's house on the day of Sabbath rest; it is also to be apprehended within the work one is required to do when this work is properly approached as the gathering in of that which is given.

Joseph Conrad's Marlow, the captain of a battered steamboat in *Heart of Darkness*, is most instructive regarding his attitude toward work: "No, I don't like work. I had rather laze about and think of all the fine things that can be done. I don't like work—no man does—but I like what is in the work,—the chance to find yourself. . . . I had to watch the steering, and circumvent those snags, and get the tin-pot along by hook or by crook. There was surface-truth enough in these things to save a wiser man."[19] When you "find yourself" through work, you find yourself in your proper place. By attending to the "surface-truth" of what can get an old tin-pot of a steamboat to *work,* one must displace oneself from the center of consciousness sufficiently to learn the laws by which something operates external to one's will. Thus Marlow feels he has "come upon something unmistakably real" when he finds an old book on seamanship in the jungle that shows "an honest concern for the right way of going to work, which made these humble pages, thought out so many years ago, luminous with another than a professional light." This earnest inquiry into "The breaking strain of ships' chains and tackle, and other such matters"[20] recognizes that there are laws external to one's will that one must learn in order to make anything work and that such learning involves a subordination of the ego that can lead to spiritual illumination.

Although this concept of work might seem to apply primarily to machinery, one not only has to figure out the nature of the machine that one hopes to operate but the nature of any form of work in which one hopes to succeed. In an office, there are certain modes of behavior that will work, get the job done, and others that will not and will get you fired. If you want to keep your job and even get promoted, you have to learn what the whole organization, of which you are now a part, requires that you do to make it operate more efficiently. If you are the leader of an industry or a country, you have to discover what potentials the market or the moment may hold that may enhance your position or cause. If you simply try to coerce the whole to obey your will, you will be defeated, as with Conrad's misguided Kurtz: "You should have heard him say . . . 'my ivory, my station, my river, my'— everything belonged to him. It made me hold my breath in expectation of hearing the wilderness burst into a prodigious peal of laughter that would shake the fixed stars in their places. . . . They only showed that Mr. Kurtz lacked restraint in the gratification of his various lusts, that there was something wanting in him . . . because he was hollow at the core."[21]

True charisma involves an intuition into what, under the special set of circumstances with which a leader is confronted, will work. It does not labor against the grain of history but apprehends its deeper direction and goes with it. In all such cases, what works is what observes the laws that govern the whole, and these laws can work for the individual only when he learns that he truly is a part of this larger whole. While the contemplative Sabbath mode may appear to bring one closer to God, there is always the danger in turning inward that the god one discovers is only a reflection of one's own ego needs. Such a danger is impossible in the outward direction required for work since this ensures that one learns to subordinate the ego to the true source of power beyond, to find and abide in one's proper place. What the Torah of work teaches is a proper respect for limitation, both one's own limits and the limits of that arena in which one is operating. With such an understanding of the meaning of Torah, we can now return to a consideration of that departure from the proper place of the Nefesh soul that may be considered to constitute his "Fall" into the state of chaos lying just outside the realm of his optimal functioning and the alternative temptations it offers.

In interpreting the alternative paths of temptation we shall now be discussing, it will be most helpful to use the particularly relevant terminology appearing in the second sentence of Genesis: "And the earth was without form [Tohu] and void [Bohu]." For these Hebrew terms for formlessness and emptiness are most appropriate to this discussion. Using this biblical terminology, a Bohu would define a formal entity devoid of content, while a Tohu would define a state of formless content, paths that lead nowhere and experiences without consistent form. Although the initial analyses to follow will relate to temptations of the unfallen Nefesh soul, in the final discussions, we shall be able to chart a yet deeper form of the Fall, one that has moved from the defining quality of Bohu, meaninglessness, to that of Tohu, total psychic disintegration.

Beyond the Place of the Unfallen Nefesh Soul: Particular Dangers to the Nefesh Lateral Personality

The proper place in which the Nefesh individuality should abide is within its lateral center of consciousness. It is only within this structure that the individualized Nefesh consciousness can achieve the stability necessary for it to play its proper role in the Tikkun, the role of a part conscious of its participation in a larger enveloping and supporting whole and so at peace with its position in the cosmic scheme. On the Nefesh level of soul development, such peace is only possible for that stabilized lateral consciousness that feels at home in a world of physical solids it recognizes as divine and with whose limitations its individuality is in harmony.

If such individualized consciousness has not learned to abide within the world sanctified by observance of the divine laws of limitation, it can follow one of two unhallowed paths. The more accessible of these paths is that which represents such narcissistic inflation of the ego as recognizes no operative restraints to the pursuit of its own self-aggrandizement. Having lost the sacramental sense of life, it can only worship the false idols of secular society, power and pleasure.

On the more benign level of general mankind, this may mean no more than the pursuit of a prestigious position in society, one embracing the right job, spouse, and possessions by which society measures success and that are advertised to bring happiness. But when the goal of a lifetime's striving has been achieved, when one arrives at the place of social success, it will be found empty of all true contentment. It is normally only at such moments of consummation that the hollowness of a life directed primarily to personal success is revealed. Though such individuals may be model citizens and even formally committed to their religion, their real belief is only in themselves and in taking whatever they may safely get away with. But the self whose never-satisfied needs they serve is as hollow as the success they may finally win. The utopia to which the materialism of the modern world beckons the self-enfranchised individual turns out to be the "no place" that Thomas More signified by his neologism "Utopia," "no place" for a Nefesh soul to abide. Its utopia turns out to be a chaotic Bohu in which the soul can find no meaning that can integrate its elements and restore it to its proper place of peaceful stability.

On the more malignant level of unrestrained individuality, this same path to "no place" is that taken by the great villains of history and literature. This is particularly the path of the Shakespearean villain, of Iago, who says, "Virtue! a fig! 'tis in ourselves that we are thus or thus" (1.3.322), and of Macbeth, who similarly says, "For mine own good, / All causes shall give way" (3.4.35–36). But neither villain is as much the master of causality as he believes and both are left empty and defeated by the fulfillment of their destructive pursuit of ego satisfaction, Iago concluding "From this time forth I never will speak word" (5.2.304) and Macbeth expressing a similar emptiness: "I 'gin to be aweary of the sun, / And wish th' estate o' th' world were now undone" (5.5.49–50). The ultimate punishment for all those who have followed the path that leads individualized consciousness away from the sacred space in which it experiences its harmony with the whole is not the just defeat or death that may overtake it but the emptiness to which that individual must inevitably arrive who cuts himself off from all sense of connection with his neighbors, his parents, and his God.

Though originally motivated by a spiritually undeveloped egocentricity, there was yet about this course a certain buoyant self-confidence that promised the soul much good through fulfillment of its worldly aims. Marlowe's Tamburlaine shows such innocent enthusiasm when he asks: "Is it not passing brave to be a king, / And ride in triumph through Persepolis?" (2.5.53–54). And it is "our souls," he argues, which bid us "never rest / Until we reach the ripest fruit of all, / That perfect bliss and sole felicity, / The sweet fruition of an earthly crown" (2.7.21, 26–29). The soul pursued this course in the mistaken though happy belief that the unbridled fulfillment of its individual will must be attended with "perfect bliss." It is only when the soul experiences the failure of this expectation in the finally empty consummation of its wishes that it may then experience the inverse side of its disconnected individuality, the anguished perception of its alienation and the meaninglessness of existence. Thus Macbeth, in a dramatic world filled with signs of supernatural power and purpose, can only find life to be "a tale / Told by an idiot, full of sound and fury, / Signifying nothing" (5.5.26–28).

If this first path represents the unrestrained individuality that mistakenly seeks its bliss in ego enhancement, the second would seem to represent the alienated individuality whose consciousness of being imprisoned in a disconnected psyche is filled with existential despair. It defines the logical last step in the lateral path of an individuality that, by knowing no bounds, is brought to emptiness and final alienation. The dream of worldly success, which cut it off from its deeper roots, turns into a nightmare of bitterness with the frustration of its expectations and loss of faith in the false gods it had substituted for the true. Having cut itself off from all limiting connections with a bold impunity, it now finds itself in an alienated state of self-created isolation from which there is "no exit," this disconnected state proving a fit illustration for Sartre's hell.

But this final hellish state of alienated individuality is not only approached through such successive steps; it seems directly available to some few spirits that have apprehended only the isolating effects of their individuality with no appreciation of the bonds to community and cosmos without which it could have no being. Such a consciousness is expressed by Matthew Arnold in "To Marguerite—Continued": "Yes! in the sea of life enisled, / With echoing straits between us thrown, / Dotting the shoreless watery wild, / We mortal millions live *alone*" (lines 1–4). The archetypal form of such consciousness is that of Melville's Bartleby, the gentle scrivener whose negative assertion of individuality—"I would prefer not to"—leaves him "alone, absolutely alone in the universe. A bit of wreck in the mid-Atlantic."[22]

These two paths, not to be safely approached with Nefesh consciousness, would also seem to represent forms of the drug experience by which some undeveloped souls have attempted to precipitate a state of higher consciousness. In these terms the first seems representative of a "good trip" and the second of a "bad trip." But the "good trip" at best leads only to an experience without meaningful content, and at worst it can lead to the permanent "bad trip" of addiction, leaving one alienated from normal society and the prey to one's inner demons, as in Malcolm Lawry's *Under the Volcano,* a consummate portrayal of alcoholism. It is in this total vulnerability to such inner demons and the frightening sense of isolation from any possible source of rescue that the bad drug trip consists. But whether induced by drugs or the false idols and philosophies promulgated by secular materialism, these are the negative states to which the lateral elements within the Nefesh soul are prey when not abiding in the Sabbath consciousness of their proper cosmic place.

Particular Dangers to the Unfallen Nefesh Central Personality

The proper functioning of the Nefesh soul is not only endangered by the lateral attempt to enhance its individuality through a disconnecting breach of its limitations. It can also leave the stability of its lateral individuality by entering too fully into the unitive consciousness of the central system or by never having sufficiently emerged from this consciousness into the stable lateral acceptance of physical limitation and multiplicity. For the Nefesh level of soul development is structured to give a necessary dominance to its lateral elements, without which dominance it cannot function in the physical world. We have also seen such lateral dominance to be encoded in the diatonic scale of the soul, whose fourth whole tone gives dominance to its second half of Sol. On the level of the unfallen Nefesh soul, the central system can achieve no stable fulfillment in the physical world and should remain recessive.

There are, however, many individuals and even societies and historical periods in which the recessive central elements in consciousness have achieved a premature Nefesh development. One such literary portrayal is that of the Reverend Arthur Dimmesdale in Hawthorne's *The Scarlet Letter*: "Notwithstanding his high native gifts and scholar-like attainments, there was an air about this young minister,—an apprehensive, a startled, a half-frightened look,—as of a being who felt himself quite astray and at a loss in the pathway of human existence, and could only be at ease in some seclusion of his own. . . . Coming forth, when occasion was, with a freshness, and fragrance and dewy purity of thought, which, as many people said, affected them like the speech of an angel."[23] Dimmesdale is one who has not fully emerged from the central consciousness of unfallen Yetzirah, where the pre-incarnate Nefesh soul is hardly to be distinguished from the collective consciousness of the angels. "Quite astray and at a loss in the pathway of human existence," he cannot deal with the moral ambiguities inherent in the human condition, atoning so extremely for what he conceives to be his fall into sin that, like the proverbial good, he dies young.

Though monastic forms of religion and martyrdom provide one mode of escape for such angelic personalities from the complex demands of human existence, the primary cultural modes of commitment to the absolute have been romantic or "courtly" love and honor. Both demand a fidelity to absolute values that, in a world of often dishonorable contingencies, can lead, as with Romeo, to making "a dateless bargain to engrossing death" (5.3.115). To prefer death before dishonor in an imperfect world is to win a spiritual victory over mortal limitation by a paradoxical choosing of its ultimate form, which is death.

This choosing of death for honor is everywhere displayed in Homer's *Iliad,* but its best representative is probably Sarpedon, who stirs others to battle with the argument: "Ah, my friend, if after living through this war we could be sure of ageless immortality, I should neither take my place in the front line nor send you out to win honour in the field. But things are not like that. Death has a thousand pitfalls for our feet; and nobody can save himself and cheat him. So in we go, whether we yield the glory to some other man or win it for ourselves."[24] It is precisely because of the power and permanence of death that man's honor resides in such a pursuit of glory as will bring death the sooner upon himself. And in Sarpedon's own death "he breathed defiance, like some proud tawny bull who is brought down among the shambling cows by a lion that has attacked the herd, and bellows as the lion's jaws destroy him."[25] The hero's victory over death consists in just this defiant bellowing "as the lion's jaws destroy him." For the ultimate hero, Achilles, the choice is also clear. Recognizing that "you cannot steal or buy back a man's life, when once the breath has left his lips," he continues: "My divine Mother, Thetis of the Silver Feet, says that Destiny has left two courses open to me on my journey to the grave. If I stay here and play my part in the siege of Troy, there is no home-coming for me, though I shall win undying fame. But if I go home to my country, my good name will be lost, though I shall have long life, and shall be spared an early death."[26] Since the choice between long life and early death is placed in this context of shame or undying fame, Achilles' Hellenic destiny is determined. As his mother had earlier said, he is "doomed to an early death."[27]

This same structure of values informs the courtly love tragedy of *Romeo and Juliet,* "The fearful passage of their death-mark'd love" (pro. 9). Like Achilles, Romeo is faced with the choice: "I must be gone and live, or stay and die" (3.5.11). He had earlier said to the Friar: "Do thou but close our hands with holy words, / Then love-devouring death do what he dare" (2.6.7–8). Thinking her dead, his absolute fidelity demands he join her in a defiant love-death, triumphing over detestable death through bringing it upon himself:[28]

> *Thou detestable maw, thou womb of death,*
> *Gorg'd with the dearest morsel of the earth,*
> *Thus I enforce thy rotten jaws to open,*
> *And, in despite, I'll cram thee with more food!*
> *(5.3.45–48)*

Thus does the romantic idealist Romeo "shake the yoke of inauspicious stars / From this world-wearied flesh" (5.3.111–12).

None of these devotees to absolute love or honor chooses a death he believes will be a gateway to personal immortality but rather the reverse, a death that will annihilate his personality. They are "world-wearied" and want no more of individuality, with all its compromising limitations. The cry of their hearts is forever contained in the title of an old musical show by Anthony Newley: *Stop the World, I Want to Get Off.*

The reason that central consciousness on the Nefesh soul level develops what might be called, with Freud, a "death wish" is that there is only one direction in which the central personality at this level can move, and that is back to the source. But this source of individuated consciousness is, itself, still in a state of collective consciousness. Thus a premature return to this source, before the central consciousness has become stabilized at the Ruach soul level, can only mean the permanent loss of individual personality with its total reabsorption into collective consciousness. From the lateral perspective, whose consciousness is enjoying its incarnation in physical matter, such a death of individual consciousness appears to be a tragic waste. As Milton says in the words of the fallen angel Belial:

> *To be no more: sad cure for who would lose,*
> *Though full of pain, this intellectual being,*
> *Those thoughts that wander through eternity,*
> *To perish rather, swallowed up and lost*
> *In the wide womb of uncreated night,*
> *Devoid of sense and motion?*
> (Paradise Lost, *2.146–51*)

And however desirable the return to a state that is at best one of collective consciousness may appear to that minority of Nefesh souls in which the central system is more strongly marked than the lateral, it certainly does signify a short-circuiting of the process and, it would seem, purpose of cosmic manifestation. For these forms of individual consciousness are now forever lost, as is their contribution, to the perfecting process of cosmic evolution.

There has always been that spiritual minority, more cursed than blessed, in which the central system has achieved dominance before the soul has developed sufficiently to harmonize its higher sensitivities with the limitations that alone permit individuality. As Blake put it in "Auguries of Innocence": "Some are Born to sweet delight. / Some are Born to Endless Night" (123–24). And the two major forms of Nefesh religion develop from these two polarities of personality, as Blake further shows in the conclusion to this poem:

> *God Appears & God is Light*
> *To those poor Souls who dwell in Night,*
> *But does a Human Form Display*
> *To those who Dwell in Realms of day.*
> *(129–32)*

Though those "Born to Endless Night" may perceive a higher image of God than the happier inhabitants of the lateral day world, they are nonetheless "poor Souls," ill equipped to survive in a world of imperfect contingencies[29] whose demands soon make them world-weary and anxious for such annihilation of individual consciousness as that expressed by Keats, when transported by the nightingale's song:

> *Darkling I listen; and for many a time*
> *I have been half in love with easeful Death,*
>
> . . . .
>
> *Now more than ever seems it rich to die,*

To cease upon the midnight with no pain,

. . . .

Still wouldst thou sing, and I have ears in vain—
To thy high requiem become a sod.
(51–60)

The suffering artist is a cultural stereotype because so many artists, especially when young, have a markedly central character without the soul development necessary to give proper perspective to their visions. Though their heightened attunement to the source of being may endow them with enormous creative power, their vision of life is largely that of the young and, though he knew it not yet, shortly to die Keats, a vision "Where palsy shakes a few, sad, last gray hairs, / Where youth grows pale, and specter-thin, and dies; / Where but to think is to be full of sorrow" (25–27).

But though the beauty with which such tragic visions have been expressed has given the artist's agony a power to move and uplift that can redeem both the artist's suffering and that which it has aroused in a sympathetic heart, there is another kind of art that, though no greater, yet springs from a higher source of inspiration. From Bach to Wagner, from Michelangelo to Rodin, and from Milton to Tolstoy, there have been commanding artists who have reached a sublime level of art beyond tragedy, an epic art illuminated with a sense of cosmic purpose in which the enduring human will is allowed to play a meaningful role. Though chapter 3 will correlate all artistic creativity with the lowest level of Ruach power, we may now say that epic art is inspired by a higher level of the Ruach soul than that of even the greatest tragic art, whose Ruach inspiration springs from that initial level still expressive of the remaining power of Nefesh proclivities. For epic art, though ever aware of the sufferings of the human condition, yet places these sufferings in an affirmative cosmic perspective that finally transmutes them into joy. This is the highest art, for the creative utterances of Neshamah souls do not clothe themselves in imaginative fictions but become the prophetic foundations of civilizations and their religions.

It is epic endurance that is especially required of those marked for the central path. Though it makes possible an accelerated spiritual development for those who have committed themselves to such development, it is not until the Ruach soul level has been attained that central consciousness can rise above the pain of its mortality that drives it to suicidal modes of behavior, preferring to "become a sod" rather than longer to endure the pain of thought. To strengthen this capacity of the undeveloped central consciousness to endure, to resist the centripetal pull back to collective consciousness that spells the death of personality and to stay firmly on the path to a saving spiritual development, the safest course may well be that of strict, even monastic, forms of organized religion. Hawthorne shows us that his Dimmesdale required just such a restraining support. "Mr. Dimmesdale was a true priest, a true religionist, with the reverential sentiment largely developed, and an order of mind that impelled itself powerfully along the track of a creed, and wore its passage continually deeper with the lapse of time. . . . [I]t would always be essential to his peace to feel the pressure of a faith about him, supporting, while it confined him, within its iron framework."[30] For those Nefesh souls with central dominance who might otherwise kill themselves for love or honor, or just to annihilate thought through drugs, death-defying thrills, or suicide, the strict spiritual discipline provided by some organized religions can give a positive focus to their true spiritual cravings even as it lifts them to the higher stability of Ruach consciousness. For such, monasteries and Eastern cults have been truly life saving, as have the stricter forms of Judaism, especially those of the more spiritually informed hasidic sects. By teaching them to abide in their proper place, such religious communities provide a sacred space that increases the resonance of their own cosmic attunement.

This religious form of life—which sacramentalizes all permissible activities through spiritual devotions that, by bringing the divine dimension into everyday consciousness, educates the Nefesh soul as to its true spiritual direction—provides a well-tried way of conforming to that culminating commandment with which Moses concludes and contains the whole of the law: "See, I have set before thee this day life and good, and death and evil. . . . I call heaven and earth to record this day against you, that I have set before you life and death, blessing and cursing: therefore choose life, that both thou and thy seed may live: That thou mayest love the Lord thy God, and that thou mayest obey his voice, and that thou mayest cleave unto him: for he is thy life, and the length of thy days. . . " (Deut. 30:15, 19–20). Against Achilles' Hellenic choice of death, the Hebraic tradition commands one to "choose life." Not recognizing the validity of that pursuit of personal honor and glory for whose realization death may be chosen, it can only condemn such a choice of death as evil and a fit punishment for those who would arrogate to themselves the glory belonging only to God. But the life one is commanded to choose is to be one not so forgetful of its origins as to say, "My power and the might of mine hand hath gotten me this wealth" (Deut. 8:17). Rather, it is the choice of a life that recognizes its dependence upon a greater, divine whole and willingly abides within its limitations to realize its true nature: "For he is thy life, and the length of thy days."

Particular Dangers to
the Fallen Nefesh Central Personality

In this discussion of the dangers to the Nefesh soul, we have seen that they can provide an archetypal model of the main paths away from the sacred space bounded by some form of Torah that define the fallen behavior of the Nefesh soul. But before closing this subject, we should examine more extreme dangers to its further spiritual growth. Because we have just been considering the sad character of premature central dominance at the Nefesh level of development, it seems best to continue with the further plight to which such centrally dominant Nefesh souls are prone.

In analyzing the unfallen Nefesh soul, we saw that there was no place for a central consciousness individualized at the level of the fourth world to go except back to the central source of collective consciousness. In the previous section such a returning central movement was shown to be as necessary as the outgoing lateral movement for optimal functioning in the material world. The problem only arises when the Sabbath is so extended that no food is gathered, when the dream state is confused with consensus reality, when the breath is held too long. Then the forces meant for periodic regeneration of life prove its death. This is the suicidal malaise that we understood to afflict the prematurely developed central type of Nefesh soul in the prior discussion. But though such centrally dominated Nefesh souls may eventually commit suicide after a most melancholic life, they are yet more fortunate than those whom a completely unbalanced central development has blighted almost from the beginning of their physical incarnation. Those who have somehow been born to the fallen condition would seem almost immediately to stray past its limitations to inhabit a Tohu of fifth-world centrality, a psyche of such complete chaos as characterizes psychosis, primarily schizophrenia but also its most extreme form of infantile autism. For the difference between the central predicament in the unfallen and fallen stages of the fourth world is that the fallen stage does now provide a forward position to which central consciousness can progress. Rather than being drawn back to the central stability at the center, it can now be caught by a not yet stabilized form of the Ruach level of central consciousness. Such schizophrenics may well display some of the higher psychic powers that characterize the Ruach soul, particularly in its central aspect.

For there is a kind of quantum leap between the manifestations of the individualized central system in the fourth and fifth worlds. Its manifestation in the fourth world is as a subtle form of energy whose activities seem to contradict the normal perceptions of lateral consciousness and so are largely dismissed as coincidental, whereas its appearance in the fifth world is in the form of commanding visions. The central system appears here only in the form of discrete structures, of immediately embodied thought, a circumstance that may explain many features of what is called the astral plane. The indications of entry into the central system of Ruach consciousness would thus appear to be quite pronounced, almost like a light switch that dispels the darkness of disturbing paranormal hints on the Nefesh level with the certainty of meaningful visions, an astral realm as real as the physical but following different laws that must be learned for successful navigation. For as we will see in the next chapter, it is as important at the fifth world level as at the fourth for the central system to remain under the unremitting control of the lateral. Though the Ruach soul represents a higher level of consciousness than that of the Nefesh, it operates on a dimension that may be compared with the Shamanic concept of the Lower World, not a hell but a spiritual realm characterized by a fluid form of consciousness and a sense of descent. But the central system of Ruach as of Nefesh consciousness represents a danger to the soul's ultimate form of spiritual development because it is, in truth, going in a different direction from that of the lateral system that defines its abiding personality. It would lead man away from his development of the purified personality that can finally direct the highest of cosmic powers to their purposed end, leading him to the destruction rather than empowerment of personality.

From the foregoing, it should be apparent why a premature entry into the unstabilized form of the Ruach central system present beyond the limitations of the fourth world would be characterized by the cacophony of commanding visions definitive of schizophrenia. For the visions meant to enlighten Ruach consciousness as to the proper direction of its higher energies have here no such larger context of individual and social spiritual development. Lacking both the stability of vision and the control of this visionary center by a still inactive lateral center, it can only torment the psychotic consciousness with a confusion of visionary states masquerading as reality and commanding the individual to perform either impossible or destructive acts.

Particular Dangers to
the Fallen Nefesh Lateral Personality

Turning now to the fallen lateral system, what we find is that the power promised by the earlier lateral temptation will no longer be an empty Bohu but real. This is essentially the distinction between worldly and spiritual power. The previous discussion of transgression beyond the limitations of the unfallen Nefesh soul was concerned with just such worldly power, whether in its physical or social forms. For whether man has harnessed the power of the atom or of empire, such power has not fulfilled its promise of conferring meaning to his life, its very achievement revealing the spiritual emptiness of worldly power. At this less developed stage, the lure of Ruach power glimpsed by the Nefesh soul was only that outer form which it sensed it needed but only knew how to fill with the selfish, physical counters of its own Nefesh level of understanding. But at the more advanced stage of the fallen Nefesh soul, it has, indeed, forced its entry into a source of genuine spiritual power.

As we shall further see in the next chapter, the lateral center of the fifth world is, in fact, the powerhouse of the whole fully developed soul. Thus even a forced entry into this center will endow an individual with certain psychic powers, the powers of the black magician. In the next chapter this completed center will be fully analyzed in terms of the true powers available to such a white magician as can be called a Ruach Master. The difference between the holy and unholy uses of this power center is not simply in the greater power of the spiritual master but also in the self-defeating nature of all such occult power as has been perverted to lower ends. For a sorcerer, who through the use of black arts has gained access to sources of power beyond his Nefesh level of spiritual development, can only pervert such power to the Nefesh ends of ego aggrandizement and personal profit. Its effects will be as self defeating as was Jepthah's victory, purchased with divine power at what proved to be the price of his only child (Judges 11). Without a properly prepared spiritual vessel, the invocation of such supernatural powers can only produce a psychic overload leading to such a derangement as that just considered for the central personality. In a laterally dominated individual, however, it can be a formidable combination, its further access to central power leading to the derangement not of schizophrenia but megalomania. But perhaps the most serious though less drastic effect of such misbegotten and misdirected spiritual power is that its counterfeit of spiritual mastery is believed by the self and so prevents all further true spiritual development. What little psychic power has been falsely mimicked or truly acquired has been at the price of short-circuiting the further spiritual development that alone could yield the lasting satisfaction to the self that results from the perfect coherence of the individual will with benefit to the whole. But we must now close this psychological analysis of fourth-world consciousness with a final comment on what truly distinguishes the right- from the left-handed path to enlightenment.

As we have seen, what distinguishes the spiritual master from a false guru is that true observance of the law of cosmic limitation which enables one to find his or her proper "place" in the cosmic scheme, the place of a dependent part that, through grateful acknowledgment of this dependence, can grow in consciousness until it can become aware of its participation in the power of the whole. In every cosmic dimension or world there are conditions and limitations that must be discovered and obeyed if spiritual experience of such higher states is to be the path of Tikkun rather than of Tohu, if the increased power available to those who have found their way there is to be directed to the good, which includes that of the larger whole as well as of the individual concerned, or is to lead not only to the destruction of that individual's own goodness but, extending outward, to the potential destruction of many lives.

The means of progressing from one soul level to the next is that of appropriate spiritual discipline, of religious observance or a meditative practice. Because such traditional practices transmit a spiritual energy accumulated through the millennia of devotional observance, they can greatly enhance the power of individual devotions as well as guide the person along a safe path of spiritual evolution.[31] The left-handed path, time honored though it may be among some forms of Tantric Buddhism and other scattered groups primitive and modern, has always been more dangerous. For it seeks to violate the boundaries of normal consciousness through such aids as sex, hallucinatory drugs, and other mind-altering practices that can violently enlarge the consciousness before the individual has been spiritually prepared to navigate safely in those spaces and so can exercise some measure of control over the direction and purpose of these experiences. Though the very violence of such enlargement of consciousness may have some success in reaching that part of the self whose resistance to participation in the cosmic harmony can best be overcome through the proof of just such an experience of expanded consciousness, it is an unsure and ill-advised way. In each cosmic world there is an outer boundary whose Torah must be honored if understanding is not to go astray. And this study of the consequences of Nefesh transgressions should also reveal its true meaning, that Torah is that law of limitation whose observance can accomplish a crowning liberation from the negative constraints of the lower Nefesh ego because it can lift and integrate that ego into the rhythmic flow of the whole.

In this section we have viewed a premature entry into the higher faculties of heart and mind as constituting the Fall of Nefesh consciousness. But there is another way of understanding the position of the fourth world on the cusp of cosmic history, as providing a model of transformative consciousness, that consciously controlled transformation from a past to a future orientation that, in a fallen world, already marks the path of Tikkun. In the next section we shall develop a meditative model based on an understanding of the unique cosmic position of our world, a model of what can be called the "Transformative Moment."

THE TRANSFORMATIVE MOMENT:
A THERAPEUTIC FORM OF MEDITATION

Once the fourth world is understood as the turning point between the worlds of Emanation and those of Tikkun, its transformative nature can also be realized. The proposed model is one that can take an individual or an age from one world orientation to another through a life-altering moment of creative insight that can be called the Transformative Moment. In the following analysis, the focus will be on such an application of the fourth world to human consciousness.

In the cosmic model developed in chapter 1, we saw that the cosmic worlds could be divided into four parts: the innermost quarter attached to and modeling itself on the vessel of the prior world; the second quarter reaching to the balancing midpoint of the world, which is less molded by the past; the third quarter, which is beginning to feel the influence of its outer, future vessel; and the fourth quarter, which is attached to and directly molded by this outer vessel. This scheme may be paralleled in the thought of the sixth Lubavitcher Rebbe, Rabbi Joseph Isaac Schnerson, concerning the two types of divine light, apparent and hidden, each of which has its own vessel: "There are two modes [of light] which reveal the will of the Most High flowing from the very Being of the Infinite One . . . the mode of the apparent and the mode of the hidden. Even in the mode of the apparent, there exist both the apparent and the hidden. And in the mode of the hidden, there exist both the apparent and the hidden."[32]

Using this terminology, we can consider the innermost quarter of a world to represent the hiddenness of the hidden, its purest collective essence; the second to represent the apparent aspect of the hidden, which enclothes this essence; the third the hidden aspect of the apparent, its individualizing essence; and the fourth the most apparent form of the apparent, that whose definition of individuality makes the whole fully manifest. To complete this model, we must now add the forms of the inner and outer vessels and the balancing consciousness at the midpoint.

The four stages into which the fourth world of material reality may be divided can be identified in various ways. The most inclusive would be the standard understanding of these stages as divided into the categories of the minerals, plants, animals, and man. Viewed in the terms of Rabbi Schnerson, of two successively contrasting "hidden" essences with their two "apparent" vessels, these four categories can be further divided into the two larger stages of earthly life defined in the biblical account of creation, those of the third and the sixth "days." The creation account of Genesis 1 was treated in chapter 1, but we are now to see further meanings in its account of the special days of creation earlier associated with the harmonics of the Sol tone, the third and the sixth. On the third day, the dry land is first created and then "the earth brought forth grass, and herb yielding seed after his kind, and the tree yielding fruit" (Gen. 1:12). In the biblical understanding, the potential for plant life is already present in the minerals, and together they form the first larger stage of the earth as the bearer of life. This same potential of the material earth also appears in the manifestation of animal life: "And God said, Let the earth bring forth the living creature after his kind, cattle, and creeping things" (Gen. 1:24). But where in the third day plant life was seen as the covering of the earth, in the sixth day it is the unique creation of man in the divine image that becomes the most perfect garment for the animal nature. In both cases, the covering of the "apparent" is represented as being the highest form of its "hidden" essence, that of the third day being judged "good" (Gen. 1:10, 12), and that of the sixth "very good" (Gen. 1:31). The problem of how to transform the potential of the first larger stage into the realization of the second, the unconscious vegetative life on the earth into the animal forms of increasingly self-aware consciousness, is not addressed, however, in the biblical account. But if we can consider the need for this midcourse correction or redirection to be taking place in the divine mind, and man to be created in its image, then a further study of such an operation of human consciousness may provide a clue to the transformative process informing all the major changes of cosmic evolution.

The fourth world will thus be divided now into the four successive stages identified with the periods within a human life span of the biblical seventy years. In this revised model, the first stage could be equated with the first seventeen and one-half years of such a life, years that, in the normal American educational scheme, would take students almost up to their high school diploma. During these formative years, students can develop most productively by absorbing the knowledge of the past and becoming skilled in the adaptations of the collective traditional forms that can best sharpen their talents. This would provide the most vital foundation for further growth, one that has deep roots of continuity with the past. Should the youths have such special intuitive powers that they can already perceive the dim outlines of the future and the inappropriateness of adapting themselves to past models, the explosive force of their revolutionary rebellion against accepted traditions will generally prove more destructive than vital. This is the effect of a premature movement to future patterning before a firm foundation of traditional knowledge and skills has been acquired. Explosive, indelicate, and lacking in true creativity, this alternate pattern can equally model the course of adolescent rebellion in the case of individual youths and of such artistic movements as Dadaism. At the first quarter and well into the second quarter stages in the development of an individual, an artistic or scientific tradition, or an age, the most vital and creative efforts will be those that expand upon the resources of the past rather than rebelling too early against its limitations.

By the midpoint of development, however, it should become clear that the vitality is seeping out of the traditional patterns that formerly worked so well. At age thirty-five it is possible to get an insight into the inappropriateness of past patterns of behavior for future growth, to see that the techniques that were successful in coping with the circumstances of the past have ceased to work positively for such individuals and, if continued, will make them increasingly rigid, a shell lacking in true vitality and so unable to adapt to changing circumstances. What is needed at this point is a mediating consciousness able to make the shift from a past to a future orientation that can keep the course of creative vitality flowing through the second half of a life or era. From this center of transformative consciousness we can chart the elements of what can be called the Transformative Moment from its perspective, the moment at which an insight into the inappropriateness of persisting patterns of behavior can produce real change.

Though this moment can occur many times during a lifetime and with more highly developed individuals can become a habit of mind, for many individuals it occurs just once, at that midlife crisis for which the fourth world can provide the model. In this model, consciousness is alerted at this midpoint to some behavior or situation causing acute pain that is suddenly recognized to be part of a whole pattern of inappropriate behavior or involvements, a pattern that, if persisted in, will result in greater rigidity. Recognizing this negative patterning, the next step is to trace it back to its cause. This second step is necessary since one cannot be released from the grip of the past until one has learned to understand and accept its former influence, to recognize that such modeling on the past, in our model of the first quarter on the form of the inner vessel, was the only way in which the forms of appropriate behavior could have been originally developed but that it is no longer appropriate for further creativity.

The transformative process cannot end, however, with such analysis of past causation. Without a new image of the self that seems attainable, the individual will cling to the old self, whose failings and foibles have been so lovingly understood and forgiven in the process of analysis. Two further steps are necessary for true transformation to take place. First a new ideal image of the self must be projected, that image derived from the fourth quarter's attachment to the mold of the future. But this is not enough, for its very perfection is so far from the recognized imperfection of the self as not only to be daunting but undesirable, undesirable because it seems to offer no continuity to the present personality that could make its attainment appear to be other than the death of the self.

What is necessary is a creative specification of the ideal model to the peculiarities that give one's essential self its identity, the individual-izing essence of the third quarter or stage, a specification that can enable the self to identify with the new image derived from the final stage because it can see the continuity of its personality in this new and improved form. If the first stage, modeled on the past, can be taken to represent the birth of the individual self, so this third stage, modeled on the future, would seem to signify the recreation or rebirth of the self.

If it is this progression that can ensure continuing vitality, then it would seem that life and all forms of development are programmed to require such a midcourse correction as, in personal terms, can be con-sidered a spiritual rebirth. He or she who before had been an appren-tice can now display the mark of the master, the ability to redefine the tradition with a creative power that not only expresses the original spirit of its creator but of its age. Only such a progression can provide the continuity of a living tradition, that which was received being trans-formed through a creative refashioning that can leave its own legacy for the future because it is in harmony with that future. It is only with the projection of a new ideal model and the creative adaptation of this ideal to fit the personality that the individual can be released from its past patterning.

The Transformative Moment occurs, then, when both the pattern derived from the past is seen to produce a form no longer coherent with the emerging design of the present, and the future form needed to replace it can be envisioned in terms with which the self can iden-tify. It is only with such a creative revisioning of the self that the old self can be sacrificed. Indeed, this creative revisioning effects just such a sac-rifice, producing that transformation in which all distinguishing traces of past determinism have been immolated and the essence freed to ascend upward. In this final form, the four stages just distinguished in the median sphere of the fourth world can be seen to define a trans-formative process in which past patterning must be sacrificed to permit further creative evolution in accordance with a projected model of future perfection. This modeling of the Transformative Moment will be expanded in chapter 3 into the meditative model of Nefesh/Ruach functioning, and in chapter 4 it will be seen to represent the essential nature of Neshamah consciousness. Finally, in appendix A it will be incorporated into a guided meditation.

As was just seen in the analysis of the median fourth world as a model of transformative change, the purpose of this fourth world of material manifestation would seem to be none other than to transform the cosmic process from one that expanded upon past models in a series of emanations consistent with the four cosmic worlds of the classical Kabbalah to one that nests within the virtual dimensions of future, more perfected worlds reaching to the final circle of the Tzimtzum, that finite circumference whose enclosure of the cosmic octave is most fully coherent with the future orientation of the Lurianic Tikkun. And it provides as well a model of the process by which one world can be transformed into another, moving from past patterning to find its own identity that, in turn, can provide a foundation for the evolution of further worlds or the higher dimensions of consciousness they can also be understood to represent. For though the fourth world contains the previous three worlds and its own prior stages still accessible within it, it also contains implicit within it the potentiality for further spiritual development, one that can retain the complex individuality acquired by the soul during its cosmic development while purifying it of the gross materiality that impedes the full utilization of its powers. Man is not, then, fixed in his fallen condition but has the possibility of reorienting himself in the very direction of his future perfection. The necessity of such soul development will become clearer in the following consideration of this future perfecting process.

THE FUTURE DEVELOPMENT OF THE SOUL

In its most basic meaning, the Nefesh soul is the vital spirit or intelligence of the sense body as it exists on a purely animal level of instinctual and intuitive response. On the human level, however, it is considered to contain the full mental and emotional endowment of the natural man, what may be considered to define its "fall" insofar as these higher faculties are dominated by the appetites of the animal senses. In moving from the Nefesh to the Ruach soul levels, we are also moving from the given spiritual endowment of the fallen fourth world to the potential for redemptive spiritual development, a potential that, though present in the fourth world, can only be fully actualized in the higher dimension of the fifth world. It is generally agreed among Kabbalists that the Nefesh soul is born with every man. The Ruach soul, however, is a personal acquirement that enlarges the heart beyond the selfish and sensual imperatives of personal satisfaction. Normally associated with the emotions, it lifts these to an ethical level, opening out the self-centered appetites of the Nefesh soul to the joys of the winged heart and sharing its energies with larger and larger wholes. But where man's Nefesh Tzelem is given him at birth, he must build his Ruach Tzelem through his personal efforts of soul growth.

This is more true as it is more rare of the Neshamah Tzelem, which opens the soul still wider to embrace a divine level of intellectual illumination and mystical experience. In the *Midrash ha-Ne'elam* section of the *Zohar*, it is alone this level of soul that is thought to achieve immortality.[33] This belief can be paralleled in the system of Gurdjieff and in that informing the ancient Chinese text *The Secret of the Golden Flower*.[34] Both esoteric systems claim that immortality is not universal but that man must, through his own efforts of spiritual discipline, build an immortal spiritual body. The immortal golden flower of the Chinese text, unfolded through a strenuous discipline of meditation, is certainly suggestive of the thousand-petalled lotus of the Hindu crown chakra as that can be correlated with the highest Sefirah of the Tree of Life Diagram, that of Keter, meaning "crown." And if man is thought capable of climbing this Sefirotic Tree, then he does have access to this higher immortalizing soul and is, in fact, incomplete without it.

It is just such an esoteric belief in the personal achievement of immortality that Milton expresses when, in *Comus,* he speaks of the relationship possible between a saintly soul and the angelic guides who

> *. . . in clear dream and solemn vision*
> *Tell her of things that no gross ear can hear,*
> *Till oft converse with heav'nly habitants*
> *Begin to cast a beam on th'outward shape,*
> *The unpolluted temple of the mind,*
> *And turns it by degrees to the soul's essence,*
> *Till all be made immortal: but when lust*
>
> . . . .
>
> *Lets in defilement to the inward parts,*
> *The soul grows clotted by contagion,*
> *Imbodies and imbrutes, till she quite lose*
> *The divine property of her first being.*
> *Such are those thick and gloomy shadows damp*
> *Oft seen in Charnel vaults and Sepulchers. . . .*
> *(457–71)*

Milton, a student of the Kabbalah, seems to be distinguishing an immortalizing level of the soul from its polar opposite, the animal soul as it is kabbalistically defined, it being generally considered that the Nefesh soul confers no permanent immortality but maintains only a brief, ghostlike existence around the grave before dissipating and returning to the earth.

The question of immortality is, of course, a much debated subject and neither the Kabbalah nor other parallel esoteric systems offer any definitive answers. If, however, we are to entertain the Zoharic suggestion as to the immortality exclusively associated with the Neshamah soul, what then is the destiny of the personally acquired lower spiritual body of the Ruach soul? Here another kabbalistic doctrine may be of help, the doctrine of *gilgul*, or reincarnation. As already suggested in the first chapter, it may be that it is the Ruach soul which undergoes reincarnation and that what is meant by the immortality of the Neshamah soul is that it is only the full development of the Neshamah soul body that can maintain its permanent identity and overcome the cycle of *gilgulim.*

Thus the higher levels of the soul are not given to man as his birthright but are there to be developed. Whereas his Nefesh soul is fully manifested in the fourth world, his Ruach soul is given in only a chaotic, unfinished form that he must personally perfect, and, at the unfinished state of his Ruach soul, his Neshamah soul cannot even be hinted at. But insofar as humans can reach this highest attainment of soul development, they can become one with the very source of cosmic love, knowledge, and power, enclothing the divine in their own perfected personality.

Alexander Pope, in *An Essay on Man*, has defined man as

> *Placed on this isthmus of a middle state,*
> *A being darkly wise, and rudely great:*
>
> . . . .
>
> *Sole judge of truth, in endless error hurled:*
> *The glory, jest, and riddle of the world;*
> *(2.3–4, 17–18)*

Caught between the two pulls of carnal contraction and spiritual expansion, man still has his cosmically unique power of free will. Siding with the pleasures of the Nefesh soul, it can leave the Ruach potential unfulfilled and become imbruted in the more contracted form of the animal soul appropriate to a lower level of evolution, as Milton has shown. Siding with the attraction of the Ruach soul, it can develop the discipline to rectify the Nefesh soul body and build a Ruach Tzelem, one incorporating the purified Nefesh Tzelem into its own higher path of spiritual mastery, itself the prelude to the still higher power and purpose of the Neshamah Tzelem and the souls of even higher dimensions.

But in being attracted to its own spiritual development, the human will is being affected not by past but future causes. Aristotle had a word for it. He called it the *telos*, the final cause, which contains "the purpose and the good"[35] for which the three prior causes of form, matter, and the transformative power called the "entelechy" are intended. This concept has had more modern proponents. For Shelley, the future can inspire the most highly attuned spirits to new modes of being that become models of the new age. "Poets are the hierophants of an unapprehended inspiration; the mirrors of the gigantic shadows which futurity casts upon the present; the words which express what they understand not; the trumpets which sing to battle and feel not what they inspire; the influence which is moved not, but moves. Poets are the unacknowledged legislators of the world."[36] And central to the more recent thought of Teilhard de Chardin is the evolutionary force exerted by such a future "Omega point": "this kind of attraction . . . must be linked at its root with the radiations of some ultimate Centre (at once transcendent and immanent) of psychic congregation: the same Centre as that whose existence . . . seems indispensable (the supreme condition of the future!), for the preservation of the *will* to advance, in defiance of the shadow of death, upon an evolutionary path become reflective, conscious of the future. . . ."[37]

There is, then, a long tradition stemming from Aristotle that regards the future as exercising an influence over the present, and our cosmic model can offer graphic corroboration of this in the influence of the form of each containing sphere upon its contents. Although I have previously focused upon its temporal aspect—the order in which the various spheres may be said to have emerged from a cosmic center—as significant of cosmic history, its final spatial aspect is equally important. The metaphor changes from before and after to beneath and above, within and without. We can now picture ourselves as looking down into a cone of concentric rings, the larger of these rings progressively containing everything both within and beneath them. This cone of continuous creation would appear to contain not a temporal sequence but a layering of different levels of spiritual worlds or of consciousness all perceived as simultaneously present, though the surface level conceals as much as it reveals of the deeper levels beneath it. The question of the Fall becomes, then, an illusion, as Eden, with the Tree of Life in its midst, is seen to be perpetually present, an illusion and a choice as to which level should be the focus of attention. The paradox of the future altering the past is also seen to be an illusion when both are recognized to be simultaneously present. For an understanding of the fourth world as itself bounded by the sphere of the fifth world dissolves the paradox of the future exerting an influence upon man's choice of spiritual direction. And when in the following chapters we contemplate these future worlds, we shall see that these worlds, with their higher soul bodies completed, are already present and just as interpenetrating with the fourth world, which our near-focus lens tells us is the only world present, as are the prior worlds of cosmic emanation.

But though this final spatial perspective seems to render time an illusion, it still retains a temporal aspect, and not simply as a metaphor to aid our analytic powers of discrimination. For both aspects of our model are true. It is imperative, then, that neither aspect of the model be discarded in favor of the other. Similarly, neither the concept of linear time nor that of eternity should so dominate our consciousness of reality as to make the other seem an illusion. Rather, they should both be contained and synthesized in a fuller concept of time.

Such a concept has been defined by Robert Lawlor as the "gnomonic principle" of time, to understand which we must first comprehend the meaning of the gnomon. As defined by the Greek mathematician, Hero of Alexandria, "A Gnomon is any figure which, when added to an original figure, leaves the resultant figure similar to the original."[38] From this definition, our cosmic model exhibits the gnomonic principle of growth, each enclosing sphere being a gnomon that, when added to an earlier sphere, leaves a resultant figure larger than but similar to the original. Showing how the gnomonic principle works within the organic process of growth by accretion, as in the growth of bony tissues and most remarkably in the shell of the nautilus, Lawlor finally arrives at his culminating definition of gnomonic time:

To these two characteristics of Time—Passing Time, or the perception of a fleeting directional movement from a dissolving past through an imperceptible present to an imaginary future, and Static Time, which is an all-containing eternal fullness—the Gnomonic Principle adds a further description. This is Time as Growth . . . revealing a continuous evolution and having, at every given moment, a past with its fundamental results still in evidence, a present in which the results are still in the process of becoming, and a future in which yet unevolved powers and forms of being are implied and must appear for there to be a full and perfect manifestation.[39]

Viewed in this way, the fourth world, which represents that central moment in the cosmic scale constituting our present, not only contains all of the past present in the form of gnomonic accretion but all of the laws from which the future will evolve. It tells us what we are given and what we must contribute to the enduring cosmic process. And in the gnomonic growth of the encircling cosmic spheres it encodes the great mystery of human destiny, that the only way to preserve the identity given man with his Nefesh soul is to expand it.

3

THE FIFTH WORLD OF MESSIANIC AND RUACH CONSCIOUSNESS

INTRODUCTION

The fifth world of our modified Lurianic cosmos marks a crucial movement beyond the four cosmic worlds of the classical Kabbalah, most immediately to a world or dimension corresponding not only to Ruach consciousness but to the chronologically future Messianic Age. Such movement to the future "worlds" of the Tikkun was a major subject of chapter 1, and it took us into such areas as the biblical creation account and the concept of the Shemitot derived from it, both necessary to lay the theoretical foundation for what is probably the major innovation of this study, the projection of a seven-dimensional cosmos in terms compatible with the Jewish mystical tradition. In this chapter we shall move directly into the dual aspects of this fifth dimension of consciousness, its correlation with the Messianic Age and with the Ruach level of the soul.

In the following section of this chapter summarizing traditional Messianic chronology, we shall see that this traditional chronology provides new illumination as to the nature of this future ideal. The next section on Ruach consciousness will then apply this chronology to a study of the stages of Messianic or Ruach consciousness, its approach emphasizing the development of such consciousness both individually and in relationship to community, and it will show this relationship to be both characteristic of the Ruach soul corresponding to the fifth world and the means of its final perfection. Also characteristic of the Ruach soul is a level of consciousness that may be related to the meditative experience. The section that then follows will provide a study of two kabbalistic texts on meditation as a background for the next two sections on the structure of the Ruach soul, showing how it builds upon the structure of the Nefesh soul, developed in chapter 2, to define a model of meditative power. Finally, the remaining four sections will show how this model functions on the four levels of Ruach spiritual mastery, whose powers will be the crowning subject of this chapter.

Ruach consciousness has thus far been identified with the consciousness of the Messianic Age and so with the future. But a caveat must be offered before proceeding further with what will be an essentially future-oriented analysis. For as the final sections will show, the fifth world's dimension of consciousness can best be seen as corresponding to the symbolizing faculty that has been considered definitive of man, that which is a function of true personality and can be considered to occupy a systems level between the *impersonal* realm below and the *transpersonal*, symbolic realm above. Thus in its fifth emanation our cosmic model is defining the dimension of consciousness that should be normal to man as he passes beyond the state of individual or racial childhood and enters into the full powers of his maturity. Had the passage from the childlike nature of the animal or unfallen Nefesh soul to the higher functioning of the Ruach soul followed the path ideally programmed for the human soul, all the higher spiritual powers that will be unfolded in the last four sections would have been the common property of all normal human beings.

But, alas, humanity seems rather to have followed the path of precipitant development represented by the improperly motivated future modeling of Nefesh behavior, which produced what can be considered the fallen form of this soul, with the result that some measure of Ruach power became available to man while he was still locked into the more limited perspective of Nefesh consciousness. Using such usurped power only to facilitate his acquisition of worldly power and pleasure had the further effect, moreover, of blocking the natural development of this power to its full Ruach potential. Thus the mental level available to all people became the property only of the extraordinary few, those who through special grace or spiritual discipline were able so to perfect their souls that they could overcome the Fall and reascend to the purposed level of earthly human functioning.

It is important to remember, nonetheless, that the powers of the Ruach Master we shall be exploring do not truly belong to an abnormal spiritual state, rather to the state to which humankind is naturally heir, and that the way now trodden only by the spiritually gifted is the path meant for all. The Ruach dimension can be assigned to the Messianic future only because we still allow ourselves to be victims of the mistakes of our forebears, such mistakes as have been transmitted through the alienating institutions and habits of our society and the neuroses of our equally victimized parents. But though such influences rob each of us of our native Paradise, we have it in our power to regain a greater Paradise, the optimal condition of physical and psychological well-being that represents the full realization of the human potential *on earth*. In the concluding sections of chapters 4 and 5 we shall be considering the full development of soul levels that *are* properly associated with the World(s) to Come and whose appearance in human form *is* abnormal. But the Ruach level represents a spiritual dimension that should be readily available to earthly man and in some measure is present in all symbolic activity. Incorporating and redeeming the Nefesh soul in its fuller cognitive and emotive scope, it is the Ruach rather than the Nefesh soul that is designed for the most effective and, at the same time, harmonious activity in the bodily state, and its powers are ours to reclaim, making the future evolution of the race a present reality for ever increasing numbers. Though such powers must remain only a future hope to fallen man, they are already present, then, to those who have perfected their Ruach souls and redeemed their fallen condition, this, indeed, the work we are set on earth to do. The section on stages of Ruach consciousness should help to chart the steps of the soul work necessary to reclaim this lost heritage of spiritual power, and it can be read from dual perspectives, in its ideal form as a present reality or only as a future possibility, if humanity be deemed to be trapped in the persistent reality of the fallen fourth world.

In chapter 1 the seven worlds of our cosmic model were also related to the seven dimensions of the *Sefer Yetzirah* (1:5), that of the fifth dimension—"a depth of good, a depth of evil"—being identified with a moral dimension woven into the fabric of space-time that can be further identified with the processes of Providence. Such processes may finally be related to the "curious principle" Jung has termed "synchronicity":

> synchronicity takes the coincidence of events in space and time as meaning something more than mere chance, namely, a peculiar interdependence of objective events among themselves as well as with the subjective (psychic) states of the observer or observers. . . . [C]ausality describes the sequence of events. . . . The synchronistic view on the other hand tries to produce an equally meaningful picture of coincidence . . . [showing that synchronous events] all are the exponents of one and the same momentary situation.[1]

As we proceed further in the analysis of the fifth world, we shall see how it is possible for a Providential order of causality to express itself through the synchronicity of events that may be said to define the fifth dimension. But first we should investigate the traditional chronology of the Messianic Age to see what clues it can offer to the developmental stages of Ruach consciousness.

TRADITIONAL MESSIANIC CHRONOLOGY

Needless to say, there is no such thing as a hard-and-fast Messianic chronology in the Hebraic tradition, or of any other hard-and-fast dogmas, for that matter. Nonetheless, in the long history of the Messianic idea, from the biblical prophets through the apocalyptic literature to the Talmud and beyond, certain prophesied events did crystallize as essential elements of a generally accepted tradition. Of these, two were clearly of overriding importance, the appearance of a Messianic personality and the subsequent inauguration of the Messianic millennium. Because of their supreme importance and chronological order, their identifications seem obvious, and we can categorically assign them to the two most significant stages in this or any other cosmic world, those defined by the semitones of the solfeggio scale. These assignments would be of the Messiah to the midpoint of the fifth sphere, corresponding to the chromatic Si tone, and the Messianic millennium to its completion, corresponding to the diatonic La tone. As the culminating tone of the fourth world, Sol, can finally be correlated with fallen man, so the Si tone may be said to signify the perfected man who constitutes the Tikkun or reconstitution of man in his originally conceived but never so fully actualized perfection.

In applying our cosmic model to the fourth world, we saw that the midpoint could be considered the "Transformative Moment" mediating the transfer of consciousness from patterns of causality influenced by the past to those influenced by an intuited perception of the future. In the Messianic Age this midpoint becomes identified with *a transformative personality*, that Messianic personality who may also be identified with the full realization of the Ruach soul. In this process of Ruach soul development we may further say that its first half shows the continuing rectified presence of the Nefesh soul as it becomes ever more identified with the functioning of higher Ruach consciousness, and that in its second half the Ruach soul becomes increasingly informed with a growing Neshamah presence.

Where the Messiah may be identified with the Si stage of perfected individuality, the identification of the La stage with the millennium gives it a communal character. Though history should properly balance the records of individual achievement and mass movements, it is the latter that seem most reflective of a Zeitgeist, the defining spirit of an age; the changing epochs of history incorporate it and the individuals whose achievements are to be epical, non-tragic in their outstanding success, must bring themselves into harmony with the age. If we now follow our earlier practice in defining the fourth world, again subdividing each of the two halves of this cosmic world into two further halves, the best place to look for definitions of these four quarters of the fifth cosmic sphere would be in traditional Messianic chronology.

In his definitive history of the subject, *The Messianic Idea in Israel,* Joseph Klausner concludes his survey of the middle period in the development of the Messianic idea, that of the Apocrypha and Pseudepigrapha, with the following Messianic chronology:

> And thus was forged that complete Messianic chain whose separate links are: the signs of the Messiah, the birth pangs of Messiah, the coming of Elijah, the trumpet of Messiah, the ingathering of the exiles, the reception of proselytes, the war with Gog and Magog, the Days of the Messiah, the renovation of the world, the Day of Judgment, the resurrection of the dead, the World to Come. Not all the links of this chain are found in every book of the Apocrypha and Pseudepigrapha, or in this order; but in general you find it with these links and in the order mentioned. These links are also found in the Talmudic-Midrashic literature, to which the Apocryphal and Pseudepigraphical books serve as a transition from the Bible.[2]

In his following section on the talmudic literature, however, Klausner excludes at least the last three items in this list as belonging to the period after the Messianic Age, that of the World to Come, and so properly to Jewish eschatology, the study of "last things:" "Those passages in which we find this expression [what is destined to come] must be treated exactly as those containing the expression 'the World to Come': we must exclude everything referring to the life after death, the resurrection of the dead, the last judgment, and the New World. What is left belongs to the Messianic idea; and only this can we fairly include in work on the Jewish Messianic idea. The rest belongs to Jewish eschatology. . . ."[3] Excluding items that properly belong to the sixth world, the World to Come, we are left with an extended list of events, some of which can be combined with others.

Of Klausner's list there seems good reason to unite two items as the elements that define entry into the fifth world of the Messianic Age. These are "the coming of Elijah" and "the trumpet of Messiah." Elijah was generally considered to be the forerunner of the Messiah, and he was charged with various specific functions, as shown by Klausner:

> as early as the time of Ben-Sira, it was the function of Elijah "to make ready the tribes of Israel. . . . [In the Mishnah passage at the end of Eduyyoth, Elijah] is in the Messianic age transformed into an angel of peace for the whole nation, or even a "refining fire" coming to burn out of the world all unrighteousness and all doubt.
>
> But Elijah has still other functions. He will, in the Messianic age, restore three things to Israel: "The flask of manna, the flask of water for purification, and the flask of oil for anointing. . . ."
>
> "The flask of oil for anointing" is of a very special kind. . . . Elijah, who will restore this marvelous flask to Israel, will of course himself anoint the Messiah with its oil.
>
> . . . Elijah must come one day before the Son of David. Apparently, he will announce the Messiah's coming from the top of Mount Carmel. . . . Elijah will also appear in the days of Gog and Magog. . . .[4]

The functions of Elijah associated with the three flasks would seem to

place him in both of the stages that will shortly be defined as preceding the coming of the Messiah as well as at that midpoint of the age, in
which the Messiah actually appears to be anointed by Elijah's flask of
oil. We shall later see that his role as purifier of the nation, associated
with the flask of water, can place him in the previous second stage as
well. Can the flask of manna that Elijah also brings be similarly associated with the first stage of the fifth world, which we are now to define?

As the stage marking the new vibratory level that distinguishes the
fifth world, it is fitting that it should be identified with the "trumpet of
Messiah." In Klausner's explanation, this "is not a trumpet blown by the
Messiah, but the trumpet of the Messianic age,"[5] a concept derived
from the biblical prophets: "the prophets speak also of the blowing of a
horn (Isa. 27:13; Zech. 9:14) something that gives place afterward to the
idea of 'the trumpet of Messiah.'"[6]

As I have shown elsewhere,[7] the great shofar that heralds the
Messianic Age is to be blown by God Himself or His surrogate and as
such is a means of bringing the divine spirit, the Ruach ha-Kodesh,
into communion with man. Further, this communion brings man into
the higher level of attunement that empowers him to participate in the
new dimension of Ruach consciousness. The "trumpet of Messiah" is,
then, the necessary first stage and thus herald of the Messianic Age, the
means of effecting a radical reattunement of consciousness. Finally, it is
this new attunement that constitutes the new covenant, the law written in the heart. Whether this means an abrogation of the old Torah of
Gevurah or, conversely, a new capacity to observe the law in the
stricter construction of Shammai (the looser construction of Hillel, in
the great talmudic controversies, being normally preferred in the present condition of the world) is not important. For in either case the
heart will now be attuned to apprehend the operation of the law in all
elements of creation and will naturally conform itself to the Way of
God thus manifested.

It is in this last point that we may see a connection between the
Messianic shofar and the "flask of manna" Elijah is to restore to Israel in

the Messianic Age. For if, as both symbol and demonstration of the power of God working through history, the shofar represents the Way of God, so too is it with the manna. As explained more fully in the previous chapter, God tells Moses that the manna is given "that I may prove them, whether they will walk in my law, or no" (Exod. 16:4). The Torah of the manna is another expression of the divine Way, a path that here commands one to gather exactly and only what he or she needs and that develops an assured trust in divine Providence, the knowledge that God will provide exactly what one requires. Since it was recently suggested that the fifth dimension may be considered the dimension of Providential causality, it is particularly urgent that the "flask of manna," the law originally given in the Exodus, be restored to Israel in this Messianic new world. The manna is, then, as much a direct revelation of the Way of God as is the shofar that conveys the empowering breath of God.

As Elijah is associated with the "flask of manna," so can his function be related to that of the shofar. Klausner was earlier quoted to the effect that Elijah "will announce the Messiah's coming," and he had shown that such prophets as "Nahum and Deutero-Isaiah also speak of a *herald* (or 'messenger of good news to Zion'), who in later times was confused with *Elijah*."[8] So Elijah becomes the talmudic herald of the Messiah in concert with the shofar, whether or not he is supposed to be the spirit that actually is to sound this horn. But since the Messiah is to be heralded by a shofar and Elijah is the appointed herald, it seems appropriate that it should be he who blows the horn as God's surrogate. Although Elijah may be said to animate all stages up to the midpoint of the fifth world, it is possible to associate his name more closely with this first stage in which he appears, as we shall see the name of the Messiah ben Joseph can be associated with the second and that of the Messiah ben David with the transformative consciousness defining the turning point of this age.

Turning now to the second quarter, the Messianic event in Klausner's list that seems most identifiable with the stage just preceding the advent of the Messiah is the war of Gog and Magog, first prophesied by Ezekiel. As developed in chapters 38 and 39 of Ezekiel, "Gog, the land of Magog" (38:2), shall attempt to conquer Israel only to be defeated by God and left as "a great sacrifice upon the mountains of Israel" (39:17). In its later talmudic development, this great war of the Messianic Age becomes connected with the concept of a second Messiah, not the Messiah ben David who will reign in the Messianic kingdom but the Messiah ben Joseph from the Ten Lost Tribes of Israel who will command the armies of the Lord and fall in battle:

> So *Messiah ben Joseph* became a *Messiah who dies:* he is fated to fall in the war with Gog and Magog, as Bar-Cochbah had fallen in his war against Rome. . . . the Messianic age itself comes after "the wars of the dragons" and after the war with Gog and Magog. The military commander in these great battles can be none other than Messiah ben Joseph. . . . Messiah ben Joseph, the first in time but the second in rank of the two Messiahs, is already present at the time of this war. But the Messianic age reaches its *culmination* only *after* the war with Gog and Magog, when Messiah ben David appears in all his glory.[9]

The great collective event that occurs before the coming of the Messiah ben David and that epitomizes the national woes referred to under the general title of "the birth pangs of Messiah" is, then, the apocalyptic war of Israel with ultimate evil that goes under the name of Gog and Magog. As further developed in the Talmud and still later in the Kabbalah, this collective event is also seen as synchronous with the personal tragedy of the Messiah ben Joseph, who leads the army of Israel but dies a sacrifice to its victory. It is in this stage that Elijah may also play a role, bringing the flask of water that will purify the spiritual warriors for their coming struggle. In alliance with the Messiah ben Joseph, he has a part to play in preparing the tribes of Israel for the warfare that will "burn out of the world all unrighteousness and all doubt."

Having determined that the war with Gog and Magog best defines the great communal action preceding the advent of the Messiah, we have now to determine what should be considered the major action of masses of people to follow the Messiah's appearance. Returning to Klausner's list, this would seem to be the twofold "ingathering of the exiles" and "reception of proselytes." Although the former particularly is featured in many early prophecies as a sign of the Messiah's approaching appearance, the tradition also conceives it as an ongoing process that would vastly accelerate with the coming of the Messiah and the establishment of his kingdom. Klausner shows that "according to the Psalms of Solomon (17:26–28) and the Targum Psuedo-Jonathan (on Deut. 30:4 and Jer. 33:13) the Messiah will bring back the dispersed nation to its own land."[10] And he shows a similar treatment of the subject of proselytes:

> The Messiah will be cordial and gracious to all the peoples. . . .
> Closely connected with this conception of the Messianic age
> expressed by R. Jose is the following saying of his contemporary,
> R. Simeon ben Gamaliel II: "In Jerusalem all nations and all king-
> doms are destined to be gathered together, as it is written (Jer.
> 3:17), 'And all the nations shall be gathered unto it, to the name of
> the LORD.'" . . . The Gentiles will become proselytes of their own
> accord, without exhortation on the part of the Jews: for they will
> be irresistibly attracted by the model kingdom where all are priests
> and all combine to make a holy nation.[11]

The stage in which all Jews and all other nations are gathered together seems the most significant communal response to the presence of the Messiah and the one that should be associated with the third quarter of the fifth world.

The two larger communal expressions of the Messianic Age, those that precede and follow the coming of the Messiah and are correlated with the second and third quarters of this age, form an interesting contrast. The former represents a process of exclusion and the latter of inclusion, both of which may tell us something about the Messiah and the development of the consciousness he exemplifies. It would seem that the necessary preliminary to such an advent is a period of sacrificial purification but that, once the vessel has been thus prepared for the influx of a higher level of spirit, this higher spiritual nature will be all-accepting, able to harmonize itself with what had formerly to be excluded in virtue of its own purified vision into the underlying goodness of all. The Messiah will, then, only appear to a people that has defeated the evil in and around itself, and the appearance of such a holy nation will subsequently lead to the conversion of the surrounding nations, formerly a snare to Israel but now attracted by its example.

Before turning to the fourth quarter of the Messianic Age, that of the millennium, we should briefly review our progress to this point. The Messianic Age will begin, then, with the process of reattunement that will lead to a more formal practice of the spiritual discipline necessary for one who is to fight in the Messianic battle. And this spiritual war will prepare the way for the coming of the Messiah, whose presence is to effect the central transformation of this age. For the Messiah's presence will lead to the final ingathering of Jewish exiles and Gentile proselytes, an inclusiveness in marked contrast to the exclusiveness of the apocalyptic warriors, that will set the stage for the culmination of the Messianic Age, the millennium or "Days of the Messiah," exemplifying the "signs of the Messiah," that changed earth of effortless fertility and animal harmony referred to in the Messianic writings, which may be identified with the "renovation of the world" listed by Klausner. The three listings just given can all be ascribed to the final La stage of the fifth world, the extended millennium in which man achieves a harmony not only with his fellows and former enemies but with all of nature.

In the millennium there will be that transformation of animal nature recalled by Isaiah's words: "The wolf also shall dwell with the lamb, and the leopard shall lie down with the kid; and the calf and the young lion and the fatling together; and a little child shall lead them" (Isa. 11:6). Whether the new attunement, to which the animals will apparently be the most responsive, will immediately lift them above the predator instinct or this final transcendence will be reserved for the last stage of the millennium, there will certainly be an evolution of animal consciousness and a movement of man to overcome his lower instincts.

Such an evolution of animal consciousness is already beginning to take place in the animals that humanity has domesticated, whether for work, study, or companionship. All have learned to respond to verbal signals, some chimps even having been taught to communicate with sophisticated forms of sign language. And can we doubt that, as humankind cultivates more and more of the earth and segregates the remaining "wild" animals to carefully patrolled parks and zoos aimed at preserving them from extinction, animals largely fed by humans will gradually lose the instinct to kill for food. However the change be defined, in the final millennial stage animal nature will be so transformed that only its outer shape will be retained, and man will begin to undergo a similar change.

The nature of vegetation will also be so transformed that it would seem to approximate such Messianic prophecies as those of Ezekiel, much elaborated upon in the later tradition: "And I will raise up for them a plant of renown, and they shall be no more consumed with hunger in the land. . . . And I will multiply the fruit of the tree, and the increase of the field" (Ezek. 34:29; 36:30). Needless to say, such an increase in agricultural productivity, with the accompanying hope that famine will finally disappear from the earth, is already well under way. Even before the millennium arrives, then, plant, animal, and human nature will have been completely transformed. And yet these individual forms of life will still be recognizable as such.

Finally, in the millennium, time itself will seem to lengthen.[12] But time becomes elastic in other ways as well, furthering the properly directed will of the Messiah, as of the Ruach Masters he will inspire, and bringing all their aims to fruition. For in this final stage, the Messianic Masters will go beyond their former embrace of community to recognize their interconnectedness with all aspects of nature and all the levels of causality determining the shape of natural behavior to perform the wonders that complete their Ruach development.

STAGES OF RUACH CONSCIOUSNESS

In the previous section, the four main stages of the fifth world were identified with traditional stages of Messianic chronology. The Jewish tradition, both in itself and in the legacy it has bequeathed to the Western world, maintains that the Messianic Age will become a historical reality in the world of the future, and we have seen that its essential phases have a logic that can be correlated with the next cosmic world. But in addition to its correlation with kabbalistic cosmology, we shall now see how this chronology can also function as a model of personal and cosmic consciousness, for all these cosmic "worlds" should be understood to delineate the successive dimensions of such consciousness. Having defined the stages of the fifth world in traditional terms, we are now in a position to reframe the preceding discussion into an analysis of the stages by which the Ruach dimension of the soul becomes actualized. This mystic internalizing of the Messianic process and personality represents, in fact, the major approach of the Kabbalah to the prophecies of a Messianic Age, as scholars have recently shown.[13]

The first stage to higher consciousness corresponds to the traditional blowing of the great shofar. It is the deliberate process of attunement to higher spiritual vibrations that forms the heart of all spiritual disciplines. In most cases this involves some form of meditative prayer accompanied by silent or audible chanting of divine names or other frequently repeated liturgical passages. As the repeated phrases fall into remembered cadences, the chatter of the rational mind becomes stilled and its silence permits the normally recessive aspects of consciousness to expand beyond the constrictions imposed by the particularizing lens of consciousness. This expanded state is such a blissful experience that it inspires a greater commitment to the process of spiritual development and the stricter disciplines by which it can be accelerated.

This first stage of Ruach consciousness differs sharply from the first Nefesh stage. Where that was understood to be particularly shaped by the form of the past, the first Ruach stage marks such a redirection of the spirit as was only reached in the third stage of Nefesh development. Indeed, as we shall see the midpoint of the fifth world to mark the beginning of a growing Neshamah presence, so may the midpoint of the fourth world mark a similar beginning of the Ruach dimension's functioning in the rectification of the Nefesh soul, each dimension being given the taste of a higher dimension that can strengthen and direct its own expansion of consciousness.

The movement from the Nefesh to the Ruach level of soul is also one from an orientation dominated by the instinct for personal survival to one dominated by a sense of communal belonging. By the second stage, it involves an empathic embrace of the Other with an accompanying concern for social justice. At this stage we become involved in the evil that good men do in their obsessive desire to improve society, such a desire always implying some measure of Ruach development. But it is at this stage of Ruach development that such souls can also go astray.

There are three separate forms that can be taken by the overall second stage corresponding to "the birth pangs of the Messiah." Whatever its form, however, this is the one stage in the development of Ruach consciousness that promises to be painful. Taking it in its individualized form, this can reflect the pain caused by the internal war between old attachments and new aspirations as one attempts for the first time the service that will hopefully aid the development of a new heart. Taking it in its collective form, this can reflect the destructive limitation of the self, with or without the desired elimination of the enemy, experienced by most who become totally involved in mass political action.

In its individualized form it may take some form of withdrawal from general society and attachment to a group that will support adherence to a strict discipline penetrating all of the day's activities. If less individuality is sacrificed, less purification will be accomplished. But the purification process must be constantly monitored to ensure that the vitality of the spirit will not become impaired rather than transformed. The collective form of this stage may or may not be a product of deliberate spiritual practice. The individual may simply be seized by the Zeitgeist summoning him or her to an enthusiastic embrace of some social cause that promises to rid the world of evil in one or all of its guises. Or a specific spiritual awakening may render the individual more sensitive to the social urgencies of the moment and lead his path away from reclusive discipline to communal activism. In any case, the individual who embarks on the path of social activism without sufficient spiritual development may find that his efforts have, indeed, served to purify some aspect of society but at the sacrifice of his own spiritual health.

In addition to those primarily concerned to change the self and those primarily concerned to change the world, the synchronicity of these two modes of change suggests that there may be a third path that synthesizes their polar opposition. On such a path those concerned with personal transformation would also take part in the process of political change, while political activists would also devote themselves to spiritual development, the two becoming part of a larger movement of positive transformation that would help protect the spirit from the potential deadening threatened by either polarity in isolation.[14] This fuller mode of the second stage incorporates the two defining characteristics of Ruach consciousness, its purification of the egocentric aspects of spirit and its redirection into social channels. But at this stage of consciousness, such development can only be achieved through some exclusionary mode of behavior that pits the emerging righteousness of the self and of the elitist movement of which it is so proudly a part against an evil to be vanquished. It is no wonder, then, that even this third path will be filled with much frustration, prior to victory, over the recalcitrance of entrenched forces to change. But since such frustration is itself a sign that this recalcitrance is as much internal as it is external, it behooves the aspirant to spiritual mastery to continue his or her efforts at spiritual growth despite all the pain attendant upon this stage.

This pain reflects the last vestiges of the Nefesh soul as an independent center within the enlarged consciousness of the emerging Ruach soul. The tragic sense is a product of Nefesh consciousness and it extends up to and through this stage of Ruach development. It is brought about essentially by the central aspect of the Nefesh soul, which experiences the loss of an earlier expansiveness of being most profoundly in its present physical incarnation and yet has learned to cherish its new humanizing sensitivity to pain. Shakespeare expresses this tension in his depiction of a character "Who, by the art of known and feeling sorrows, / Am pregnant to good pity."[15] The pain of physical embodiment, nowadays referred to as the "birth trauma," proves to be precisely the quality that makes the community of mankind possible. A similar understanding is expressed by Wordsworth when he says: "A power is gone which nothing can restore; / A deep distress hath humanized my Soul."[16] The humaneness that crowns humanity, though born, as Shakespeare notes, of "feeling sorrows," is its own reward, and it contains a promise. As Wordsworth concludes his poem: "Not without hope we suffer and we mourn."

It is a humanity purged of its sorrows that is promised for the later stages of Messianic or Ruach consciousness, and this makes it possible for the aspiring soul to endure the sufferings of this second stage. Such purgation will come when the soul begins to experience the new empowerment attendant upon its individuality once it has been purified of its limiting egocentricity. But before the beginnings of empowerment that will attend the third stage lies the pain of the second stage, and its pain is a symptom of the subtle efficacy of the purifying process as it attacks the egotism to which the Nefesh soul still clings. As the shell must crack to permit the seed to sprout, so all religious traditions agree that there is no spiritual growth without pain. If the sacrifice has been faithfully performed, flesh will be transformed into spirit, and a new form of consciousness will be born, that of the master.

The spiritual mastery that emerges at the midpoint of Ruach development has been the result of the previous stages of attunement and training, and its power will be further enhanced in the following stage. Though such mastery cannot be assured even by the most punctilious observance of a course prescribed to that end, it will only come through the diligent practice of such a discipline. Taking it first in a purely vocational sense, a master is one who has served an apprenticeship, a course of discipline, in a profession or craft for which he ideally has a vocation, a calling, and can now both guide others to a similar proficiency and use his training creatively. There is another sense, however, in which the mastery is not over some skill but over some person or persons who can be considered enslaved or conquered. The two come together in a chess master, who defeats his opponents through original applications of his skill. These two definitions of mastery can be related to the distinction between the two modes of the second stage leading to this status, the attempt to discipline the evil within and the attempt to conquer the evil without, and they are clearly connected through the one quality that both forms of mastery share, control. The master is the one who gains control, and what he must ultimately control, if his dominion is not to be subject to revolt, is himself.[17] It is to such self-mastery that the skills of spiritual discipline are aimed. But the power to exercise such control comes not from the discipline itself; it comes, rather, from what this discipline releases, the will.

What the transformative midpoint of Ruach development releases is the true controlling will. Perhaps the best definition of such will is given in the system attributed to Gurdjieff: "Instead of the mechanical process of thinking there is *consciousness*. And there is *will,* that is, a power, not merely composed of various often contradictory desires belonging to different 'I's, but issuing from consciousness and governed by individuality or a single and permanent I. Only such a will can be called free, for it is independent of accident and cannot be altered or directed from without."[18] The will of the master can be self-directed rather than directed by external influences, be a cause rather than a result, because it is one with the true individuality of the self that can only become manifest at the Ruach level of development. The Nefesh soul, in its primary desire for personal success and security, had submitted to the social conditioning that promised to satisfy these desires as well as secondary needs such conditioning had instigated. The result is that the soul developed a mechanical, mass-produced personality that could no longer distinguish its true nature and affinities. In kabbalistic terms, it has lost contact with the root of its soul and can no longer distinguish the other souls derived from this root, those with which it has a special affinity. It is only by purifying the soul of its egocentricity that it can escape such mechanical conditioning and discover its true individuality, that unique vibration stamped on the fingerprints and the scent that can unerringly select those companions with which it is in vibratory resonance. It is only on the Ruach level that the most intimate of such associations, marriage, can be a true soul mating. The will that can make such a correct choice of partners is one that has a proper sense of its affinities, and it is this quality that the master must most especially cultivate since it is the necessary foundation of all work with the energies.

Once the individual will has developed, it is able to harmonize all aspects of the body, heart, and mind, and this harmonious being will develop a special attunement to deeper cosmic currents that will transform it into a medium of divine revelation. It is only when the individual Ruach will and the cosmic Neshamah will have become thus harmonized that the master can proceed to the third stage of true empowerment. The master who has not become one with the community of mankind and thinks to use this power to gain control over the world would, if he could gain such premature access, surely blow himself up in the process, such Providential justice being built into this fifth dimension, but he could also accomplish much evil in the meantime. In the third stage, then, he undergoes a second apprenticeship, working with the higher *lateral* energies that empower him to be a charismatic leader and teacher able to change the hearts of men and the course of history. It is, in fact, the momentum of his charisma, as it attracts more and more followers, that connects him with the human community and draws him into this third stage of his development.

This third stage of the fifth world reflects a decisive change in its spirit. Whereas the first half of Ruach development was concerned with purifying the vestiges of Nefesh consciousness within and without the self, its second half is concerned with giving greater and greater expression to the inspirations and power of its Neshamah connection. Its spiritual communities, therefore, have a different character from those of the earlier phase. No longer needing to raise consciousness through rigid practices and beliefs aimed primarily at exclusion, these communities are so filled with spirit that all their activities are marked by creativity. Both serve necessary functions, but the more rigid communities are normally those with long-established traditions, whereas those filled with creative spirit are normally possessed of a living master or are within only a few generations of that infusion.

Perhaps the best recent example of such a creative spiritual community is that known as the Shakers. The creative imprint of this tiny community upon nineteenth- and early-twentieth-century America is remarkable and extends to every area it touched. It developed the famous styles of furniture and knitting that bear its name as well as being innovative in the architecture of its communal buildings and barns. It was the first to package seeds and herbs for sale, to develop new hospital beds, new teaching methods, and a list of inventions ranging from the flat straw broom, the steel pen-point, and the circular saw to the first washing machines. In the arts, it practiced new forms of spiritual dancing and painting, and it has left us its beautiful hymn, "'Tis a Gift to be Simple." Founded by Mother Ann Lee in 1776, this celibate "Millennial Church" was also advanced in its social ideals, practicing communism, pacifism, and complete sexual equality. The broad and varied list of its accomplishments indicates that here was a community that gave its members the freedom to think creatively about everything they did and provided the spiritual and financial support to build the experimental models necessary to test the ideas of its inventors.

Though the creativity of such a community has been largely geared to the practical, history also gives us examples of unusual flowerings of genius in small civic communities. In the Athens of the fifth century B.C.E. and in fourteenth-century Florence, towns no larger than my own sleepy hamlet, we may see a similar ability to rethink all aspects of the cultural heritage that suddenly and only briefly manifests itself. Whether it gives us the Aristotle of Athens or the iron nail of the Shakers, what is significant is the numbers of the talented that can suddenly appear in a small community.

This fact indicates two things, first that the capacity for genius lies dormant in most of us, and second that the likelihood of such genius flowering is greatly increased by a community environment that encourages such creativity. Indeed, as the resonance of group meditation can increase the depth of one's own experience, and artists working within close proximity of each other can be mutually stimulated to a heightened expression of their own individualities, so any factor that fosters the unfettering of spirit in a community will lead to a dramatic increase in creative thought.

The factor that can be most readily ascertained in most cases is the appearance of a charismatic master. A further meaning of "master" is an original from which copies can be made. Whatever their subject, masters are those who make original contributions to their field, who absorb and go beyond received traditions, and their very presence provides a model of creative expression. Both by example and by direct infusions of their spirit, the communities founded by such masters retain the efficacy of their living spirit. But as the living example of such a master fades, the conservators of the rituals that embody that spirit lose the elasticity of their founder. All traditions, therefore, require periodic infusions from new charismatic masters capable of transforming the rituals that embody the living spirit of their lineage and of infusing these new forms with their own spirit. One such line would take us from the Temple service established by Moses and developed to include liturgical prayer by the Zadokite priesthood,[19] to that redeveloped by Ezra, its new emphasis on Torah observance being further infused by the mystical intentions, Kavanot, established by Isaac Luria, and the later spiritual additions in the sects founded by the various hasidic masters. At each stage, the presence or recent memory of a living master can produce a charismatic community filled with creative spirit.

But as the community needs such a master to release its spiritual potential, so does the master need the vessel of a community to extend the power of his personal revelation. A master whose primary concern is his own spiritual development will never reach his full potential. It is paradoxically only by moving beyond himself to share his heightened power of understanding that he can receive the reciprocal infusion of energy that can complete the higher circuit of individual with collective consciousness, a unification that is the source of all true magical power.

Stage performers or political orators can sense the psychic state of their audience, how far they can heighten and extend it without breaking the mood they inspire, and their own performance is heightened and its intentions clarified by the clues they pick up in this communal response. Between master and community, as between performer and audience, a magical entity is created, larger than either in isolation and informing both with its own intelligence. It is only when the master has learned to work with communal human energies that the *central* cosmic energies may open up to him and empower him to perform miracles.

But what is true of the relationship of master to community is also true of the relationship of each member of the community to the whole. All must learn to adjust their own energies to those of the community in a manner that not only retains but enhances their creative sensitivity. A community of such members will be alive with joy and its characteristic expression will be laughter. Henri Bergson's analysis of the societal source of laughter is most illuminating in this regard:

> Another thing it [society] must fear is that the members of whom it is made up, instead of aiming after an increasingly delicate adjustment of wills which will fit more and more perfectly into one another, will confine themselves to respecting simply the fundamental conditions of this adjustment: a cut-and-dried agreement

among the persons will not satisfy it, it insists on a constant
striving after reciprocal adaptation. Society will therefore be sus-
picious of all inelasticity of character, of mind and even of body,
because it is the possible sign of a slumbering activity as well as of
an activity with separatist tendencies. . . . It is confronted with
something that makes it uneasy, but only as a symptom—scarcely
a threat, at the very most a gesture. A gesture, therefore, will be its
reply. Laughter must be something of this kind, a sort of social
gesture. . . . Laughter, then, does not belong to the province of
esthetics alone, since unconsciously . . . it pursues a utilitarian aim
of general improvement.[20]

In the impulse to laughter, Bergson sees the highest cultivation of the
communal spirit, the elasticity that strives for an ever more delicate
reciprocal adjustment. Communal laughter, and it does have a curiously
healing infectiousness, is directed, then, at whatever just misses that
mark of higher development, and it serves as a gentle corrective.

A good example of this occurs at the beginning of the *Iliad* when
the clumsy attempt of the lame god Hephaestus to reconcile his quar-
reling parents, Zeus and Hera, permits the dinner to proceed in a new
atmosphere of healing: "a fit of helpless laughter seized the happy gods
as they watched him bustling up and down the hall."[21] This "laughter of
the gods" can also be found ever ready to erupt in any true spiritual
community and is the tone that marks its most perfect communion
with the master, the tone that lifts all to the same level of mastery.

The Knesset Yisrael that is ideally realized in this third stage is,
indeed, a holy community in which all can serve as priests, in which
each member is both master and communicant. For the great masters
of history, there is no other path of development but that which leads
to community. For those whose mastery is less distinguished, though
genuine, the path is still the same. It will take them from an initial stage
of attunement, followed by austere personal and social activities aimed
at general spiritual improvement, to the first signs of mastery, and this

will cause them to reach out to humanity in a new spirit of acceptance and joy. There they may meet others who followed a less arduous path but who are ready to be uplifted through the joint endeavor of communal growth in which each can make a unique contribution.

As already suggested, there are two paths to reach this point, the simpler process followed by the commonality and the more arduous process taken by those blessed or cursed by more powerful individuality. At both the second- and third-quarter stages, the individual has a chance to rejoin the collective, temporarily or permanently, and if such reunion at the second stage is advisable, it becomes an absolute necessity at the next opportunity if one's mastery is not to remain at half its potential power. Thus at the three-quarter point the individual path becomes indistinguishable from that of the collective, and the master's future development will grow out of this larger harmony. It is only when masters recognize their membership in this interconnected social whole that they can proceed to the final stage of Ruach consciousness.

But just as the Ruach dimension has two paths, so does it indicate the necessity for both. As all stages of kabbalistic cosmology are marked by the necessary balancing of force and form, of influx and vessel, so is it only by maintaining and balancing the influences of the broader and narrower paths that humanity can truly progress. The path of the individual Ruach Master is necessary to ensure the highest development of the Ruach community that we shall meet in the fourth stage, a stage whose creative energy will either propel the Tikkun further into the next world or render it a sterile revelation of no lasting significance. But it is the community that must be ready to receive the Messianic energy and transmute it into ever new creative forms, since without the prepared vessel of the holy nation even the true Messiah will have come in vain.

It is this extension of individual revelation into collective experience that is the final prerequisite before the arrival of the millennium. And this culminating stage will contain all the accumulated transformations of animal, plant, and human nature that have marked the development of the fifth world but that are only a prelude to the final transformation to be here accomplished of time itself, that through which "the earth shall be full of the knowledge [Da'at] of the Lord, as the waters cover the sea" (Isa. 11:9). One aspect of this knowledge will be a new penetration into the meaning of what formerly appeared to be evil. No longer will the necessity of spiritual purification require its exclusion as a source of evil and pollution. The purified consciousness can now forget the former battles and severity of its second Ruach stage and can reembrace this subdued power as a necessary aspect of its enlarged consciousness, one without which the treasured pearl of individuality could never have been formed. In this final stage, the largely Neshamah-informed Ruach consciousness can now become a codeterminer of a new dimension, the fifth dimension of Providence. It is this new dimension that is the essential characteristic of the millennium. And it marks the final development of Ruach consciousness as it moves from individual awakening to the embrace of collective humanity and from there to a still higher union with the cosmic flow.

In this section we have seen how the traditional Messianic chronology can model the stages of Ruach consciousness, a level of consciousness that we shall see in the following sections is perhaps best understood through the experience of meditation. But before we arrive at our analysis of the structure of the Ruach soul as a model of meditative consciousness, we should turn to a preliminary consideration. This is the study of two classic kabbalistic texts on meditation whose definition of the specifically kabbalistic approach to meditation will be shown to have special affinities to the meditative model to be developed and serve as the best introduction to its meaning.

KABBALISTIC TEXTS ON MEDITATION

In *Renewing the Covenant* I devoted a chapter to kabbalistic meditation, including an attunement process derived from the *Sefer Yetzirah*,[22] and that work provides an important base for the present discussion, just as the model of kabbalistic meditation shortly to be offered can expand that earlier treatment by providing a new understanding of the psychic mechanism of guided meditation. Also included in that earlier treatment is a fuller survey of classic kabbalistic texts on meditation than can here be offered. The following discussion will focus on the two classic texts that can especially illuminate our present meditative model.

The first of these texts is the *Chayah ha-Olam ha-Bah* (Life of the World to Come) of Abraham Abulafia, the thirteenth century Kabbalist of the Aristotelean philosophic school. Beginning with the process of attunement through letter permutations, the major kabbalistic technique for altering the consciousness and one that is shown to affect the emotional system centered in the heart, Abulafia then takes us to the higher spiritual work that may be accomplished after the Shefa, the spiritual influx, is experienced:

Meditate *(hitboded)* alone. . . . [B]egin to permute a number of letters . . . until your heart is warmed as a result of these permutations. . . . The influx will then come, bestowed to you. . . .

Then prepare your inner thoughts to depict God and His highest angels. Depict them in your heart as if they were human beings, sitting or standing around you. You are in their midst, like a messenger whom the King and His servants wish to send on a mission. You are ready to hear the words of the message. . . .

After you have depicted all this, prepare your mind and heart so that your thoughts should understand the many things that come to you through the letters that your heart imagines. Understand each concept and its reasons, both as a whole and in its parts. Ponder them, like a person who has a parable or example revealed in a dream. . . .

Take each concept that you hear, and interpret it with the best and closest interpretation that you can. Judge yourself according to what you understand from it. And what you are told can also relate to others.[23]

It is interesting that Abulafia identifies the imagination as an activity of the heart although clearly distinguishing its operations from the purely emotional response of the heart to the letter permutations. In so doing, he would seem to be recognizing the distinction between the Nefesh and Ruach faculties of the heart. Another point of contact between Abulafia's conceptions and those being here advanced is his view that the meditative experience of higher consciousness does not take the soul back to the prior cosmic worlds of Atzilut, Beriah, and Yetzirah, whether chronologically or logically so understood, but forward to the World to Come, the Olam ha-Bah. In this passage we can see Abulafia guiding the meditative process toward a precise imaginative projection of an astral scene containing God and his angels that is meant to facil-itate the reception of a divine message. In this state of prepared readi-ness for higher knowledge, the message will be transmitted through what the "heart imagines." This may come as letters, concepts, or sym-bolic images as in a dream.[24] But the imaginative reception of the sym-bolic message is only half of the process. What is next required is that the image be interpreted, and this is a function of the analytic mind, our old friend the alienated intellect now connected to the Ruach soul in the meditative experience and functioning with new harmony and purpose.

Thus Abulafia, after instructing us to "interpret it with the best and closest interpretation that you can," concludes: "Judge yourself according to what you understand from it." If one can rightly judge what one's condition and prospects may be from the way one interprets such imag-inatively projected material, the implication is that this mental process can impress itself on reality with the force of truth, that it can determine one's own reality and also that of others to whom it is applied: "And what you are told can also relate to others." Abulafia's method can be taken as a model for psychic healing, both of oneself and others, and I shall shortly expand upon this topic in conjunction with a full treatment of the Ruach model of higher consciousness. But there is another kab-balistic text whose concepts will aid in the final treatment of this model.

This is a work contemporaneous with that of Abulafia, the *Sha'ar ha-Kavanah le-Metubalim ha-Rishonim* (The Gate of Kavanah of the Early Kabbalists), attributed to Rabbi Azriel of Gerona, a disciple of the Provençal kabbalistic master Isaac the Blind. In the following, I shall not enter into the details of the light meditation it gives, the varieties and positions of the lights to be visualized, but focus rather on the essential methodology of this short work: "When a person sets his mind on something, its essence returns to him. . . . According to the strength of his concentration, he will then transmit power through his desire. . . . When there is no other thought or desire intermingled with [his concentration] it can become so strong, that it can transmit an influence from the Infinite *(Ain Sof)*."[25] The text tells us that a focusing of the will powerful enough to elevate an object of desire to the Infinite becomes a channel by which a reciprocal influence from the Infinite can be transmitted that has the power to effectuate the fulfillment of this desire.

The next and most vital step in this spiritual process truly distinguishes the practice of the master:

An individual thus ascends with the power of his concentration from one thing to the next, until he reaches the Infinite *(Ain Sof)*.

He must then direct his concentration in a proper manner so as to perfect it, so that the Highest Will should be clothed in his will, and not only that his will should be clothed in the Highest Will. . . .

The Highest Will and the lower will are then unified. The individual identifies himself with his attachment to the Unity. The divine influx can then be transmitted in order to perfect him.

The lower will is not perfected when the individual approaches for his own needs. Rather, one must approach while clothed in the will and desire to reveal the identification that is hidden in the concealed Mystery.

When one approaches in this manner, the Highest Will then brings itself close to him. It increases his power and motivates his will until he can accomplish anything. This will even include things that he himself desires, in which the Highest Will does not have any portion.[26]

Whereas most spiritual teachings are directed only to the attainment of that sense of divine union in which the individual will becomes clothed in the Highest Will, the practice being here taught retains and so directs the master's will "that the Highest Will should be clothed in his will." Rather than dissolving his will in the bliss of the Infinite, the aspirant to spiritual mastery is taught to perfect his will by attaching itself to this unification with his higher will, not as final consummation but "to reveal the identification that is hidden in the concealed Mystery." As the work later concludes: "This is one of the ways of prophecy. One who accustoms himself to it will be worthy of attaining the prophetic level."[27] The master is one whose words and deeds "reveal the identification" of such an individual with the divine power, and his purpose is to perfect himself into an instrument of divine revelation. Such an instrument "can accomplish anything" but only so long as he does not use his power of concentration "for his own needs." Yet if his will is properly directed toward revealing the Highest Will as working through all his words and deeds, his purified personal desires will also be fulfilled and all his needs met. The master is one who can perform miracles through the power of his concentration. Abulafia also speaks of "the mystery of the true discipline, through which you can alter the laws of nature."[28]

For both Abulafia and the author of the *Sha'ar ha-Kavanah,* the mystery of this true discipline involves three things: a process of attunement that can initiate the divine influx, followed by a process employing both visual symbols and words—influx, symbols, and words. The concluding discussion of the *Sha'ar ha-Kavanah* defines these three elements of master meditation and relates them to the talmudic description of the spiritual practices of the early Hasidim in *Mishnah, Berakhot* 5, 1:

The individual must be clothed in spirit *(Ruach),* expressing his concentration with words, and making a symbolic act. According to how he does this, the influx will be transmitted from potential to potential, from cause to cause, until the result is completed according to his will.

It was in this manner that the early [saints] would linger an hour before praying. During this period, they would dispel all other thoughts, fixing the paths of their concentration and the power of its direction.

They would then spend an hour in prayer, verbally expressing this concentration with words. Finally, they would spend an hour after their prayers, contemplating how the power of their verbally expressed concentration would have a visible effect.[29]

The sentence with which this quotation begins defines the three essential elements of transformative meditation. To change the course of events or "alter the laws of nature," the master must feel enveloped by spirit and focus this spirit with words while "making a symbolic act." The meaning of this last phrase would seem to be that suggested by the last sentence, the use of the imagination to symbolize the desired result visually.

According to how powerfully he is able to focus his spirit through words and visible symbols "the influx will be transmitted from potential to potential, from cause to cause, until the result is completed according to his will." From this it seems clear that the Ruach Master can alter the workings of causality by effectuating certain potentialities that might otherwise have remained dormant but are still available within the realm of possibility. His power involves a mastery of the fifth dimension of Providence, a dimension that influences the apparent randomness of events to bring about a desired result that is consistent with justice and that may operate through the improbable possibilities at the further limits of the bell-shaped curve of probability.[30]

In the first quoted paragraph, the three elements appear to be simultaneous. With a properly attuned spirit, the master visualizes a desired result and decrees its manifestation with such words as "Let there be. . . ."[31] But the reference to the three-hour meditative practice of the early Hasidim, alluding in part to the Talmud, in correlating these three elements with a three-stage process, appears to add a step. Here the visualization does not accompany the verbal affirmation but appears in response to a verbal prayer, as a symbolic answer to a question and guide to future action. As the *Sha'ar ha-Kavanah* opens with instructions for the visualizing of light, it is clear, however, that it also understands the first stage of the process, by which the Hasidim spent an hour "fixing the paths of their concentration and the power of its direction," as involving a visual focusing of the imagination toward a specific purpose. It would seem, then, that there are two separate visualizations, a first visualization of a problem, whether internal or external, that impedes spiritual perfection, a verbal carrying of this visualized problem to the Infinite, and a revisualization of the transmitted solution that must then, as Abulafia had earlier told us, be verbally interpreted to give it potency. Abulafia had also presented his initial visualization of God and the angels as an aid to reception of a divine message, which would come through what the "heart imagines," that is, as a second visualization.

The masters of kabbalistic meditation whose works we have examined convey the same essential understanding of meditation as a discipline not aimed solely at spiritual purification for the purpose of eternal union with God but at such purification for the purpose of channeling the divine energy back into the human realm as a means of perfecting that realm. It is aimed not at the dissolution of personality but at the achievement of the transformed personality of the spiritual master who, in the words of the *Sha'ar ha-Kavanah*, "can accomplish anything."

In the advanced classic texts of kabbalistic meditation we have been examining, the soul of the meditator is always depicted as rising at some stage in the process to the level of the Infinite. Although Abulafia does not distinguish between Ruach and Neshamah meditation and includes all meditative levels within the single Olam ha-Bah, it is still true that some experiences and powers described by him and others go beyond the fifth-world level of the Olam ha-Tikkun to that of the true Olam ha-Bah.

We shall later more fully understand that the final Ruach power can only be utilized by a Neshamah Master, and it may well be that the full powers of the entire Ruach system can only be activated by such a Neshamah Master. It would appear, nonetheless, that the miraculous effects of such a master are performed through the mechanism of the fifth world rather than that of the sixth. As the Messiah must join with a ready community to release his highest power, so must the Neshamah Master who would influence the historical process come down again, clothing the Highest Will in his own will and revisualizing the desired effect with the Ruach imagination. But the mechanism of Ruach consciousness does not demand this higher spiritual development and is sufficient to effect at least the lower manifestations of the will of a Ruach Master.

With the understanding gained from this study of the kabbalistic meditative tradition, we can now turn to a closer examination of the proposed model of Ruach consciousness and more clearly see how its masters can perform their miracles. In what follows we shall see that this model defines four levels of Ruach spiritual power, and we now turn to the preliminary definition of the structure of the Ruach soul that will help us understand the mechanism at work in all its levels of power.

THE STRUCTURE OF THE RUACH SOUL

The Ruach Master was previously discussed in the context of the Messianic community, but now we must finally turn to the analysis of the structure of the Ruach soul that can enable it to reach such Messianic heights. And we shall see that it also provides a new model for the transformative state of meditation. In the second chapter I discussed another such therapeutic model based on a particular characteristic of the fourth world, the fact that, in a seven-dimensional cosmos, the fourth world is situated on the cusp between past and future. This circumstance permitted an understanding of the fourth world that could enable it to model a "Transformative Moment" of insight into the failure of past patterning that can permit the projection of a new possibility of future behavior, a moment that chapter 4 will show to be the defining characteristic of Neshamah consciousness. But in this chapter we shall develop a model of Ruach consciousness that also defines the dynamics of the meditative state, a model centered on a similar moment of transformative insight.

Before defining the fifth-world elements of consciousness, it would be helpful to review the elements of the fourth-world model. This modeling of the Nefesh soul was understood to be composed of a "central" collective center of consciousness and a "lateral" individualized center, the former having the further power of intuition and the latter of instinct. The central center was also taken to represent the collective form of consciousness that normally functions only when the rest of the system is "unconscious," whereas the lateral center was taken to represent self-consciousness and was associated with the ego. The fallen form of the Nefesh soul was further understood to have developed higher powers of emotion and reason, both of these higher powers being considered to have been brought prematurely into the service of a will still arrested at the reptilian stage of development corresponding to the inner bulb of the brain, a possible reason for associating the Fall of this level of consciousness with a snake! In the fifth world, however, these disassociated aspects of Nefesh consciousness will all become hooked up to a larger system in which they evidently have important roles to play. But to understand how all the elements of the fifth world operate, we shall first have to determine the functions of the major centers of Ruach consciousness, the Ruach soul continuing to distinguish between the same central and lateral systems of the Nefesh soul.

Turning first to the lateral center of Ruach consciousness, this can be identified with the essential lateral quality that can be associated with the Ruach Master, the truly free and individual will, whose earlier given definition by Gurdjieff bears a somewhat enlarged repetition:

Instead of the discordant and often contradictory activity of different desires, there is *one single* I, whole, indivisible, and permanent;
there is *individuality,* dominating the physical body and its desires
and able to overcome both its reluctance and its resistance. Instead
of the mechanical process of thinking there is *consciousness.* And
there is *will,* that is, a power, not merely composed of various often
contradictory desires belonging to different "I"s, but issuing from
consciousness and governed by individuality or a single and permanent I. Only such a will can be called "free," for it is independent of accident and cannot be altered or directed from without."[32]

Unlike the Nefesh soul, whose mechanical personality is the result of
social conditioning, the will of the master is self-directed, a cause rather
than the result of external influences, and can thus express the true individuality of the self. It is in the Ruach lateral center that the higher "I"
of Ruach consciousness resides, and when the whole psychic entity
moves either permanently or temporarily from a Nefesh to a Ruach
state of consciousness, the transfer of identity from the lower to the
higher ego that then takes place is from the earlier lateral center of
Nefesh self-awareness to this new lateral center. The difference between
these two levels of self-awareness can be largely attributed to the quality of the wills they express, the lower will being overly determined by
external forces while the higher will expresses a genuine individuality
in tune with its highest self-realization, an individuality whose expression is marked by just such creativity as will later be identified as the
Ruach faculty serving this lateral center of Ruach consciousness. In
contrast, the still primitive level of Nefesh individuation may well be
influenced subconsciously, and the term is used advisedly, to rejoin a
state of collective central consciousness.

For the most part, the detribalized man of the last five thousand
years is not truly civilized, insofar as truly valuing his independent
voice, and seeks in mass conformity a return to a sense of tribal belonging. Thus Nefesh consciousness is perhaps best described as tribal, the

mechanization of the will that Gurdjieff described being the result of the unsatisfactory way in which human beings, thrust prematurely into a higher civilization for which they are spiritually unprepared, attempt to recreate the lost tribe of their dreams. Few are the truly civilized who, valuing their hard won capacity for individual creative thought, can answer the invitation of tribal howling as does Conrad's Marlow in *Heart of Darkness:* "An appeal to me in this fiendish row is there? Very well; I hear; I admit, but I have a voice, too, and for good or evil mine is the speech that cannot be silenced."[33]

If the voice of the truly individual will can be associated with the lateral center, the central center can be associated with a power just as essential to Ruach consciousness, that of the imagination. The best definition of the imagination is still that given by Coleridge in his discussion of the ideal poet:

> He diffuses a tone and spirit of unity, that blends, and (as it were) *fuses,* each into each, by that synthetic and magical power, to which we have exclusively appropriated the name of imagination. This power, first put in action by the will and understanding, and retained under their irremissive, though gentle and unnoticed, control (*laxis effertur habenis*) reveals itself in the balance or reconciliation of opposite or discordant qualities: of sameness, with difference; of the general, with the concrete; the idea with the image; the individual, with the representative; the sense of novelty and freshness, with old and familiar objects; a more than usual state of emotion, with more than usual order ...[34]

The higher imagination of which Coleridge speaks is a "synthetic and magical power." It is in truth the aspect of consciousness most necessary for producing those effects that shall be here unabashedly referred to as magic. And this aspect is closely dependent upon the power for which it was named, the power of imaging, of visualization. But it is also a "synthetic" power, and that which it synthesizes first and foremost is "the idea with the image." It provides an individual and concrete form for a general truth or idea, thus lifting its images to the level of symbols. Such symbolic forms express in the language of imagery the truths perceived by that inner vision known as insight, and the source of its insights is a heightened state of emotional sensitivity, of empathy, of seeing into the heart of the Other. Such empathic emotion, in fact, is the operational mode of the further central faculty that serves the Ruach central center of consciousness, as it will later be more fully defined. Beyond all this, the Ruach imagination is a power that seeks to balance, reconcile, or fuse all "opposite or discordant qualities," that "diffuses a tone and spirit of unity."

Many of the above qualities will sound like the familiar, popular descriptions of the "right side of the brain." For the current theory based on split-brain research divides all mental processes into those of the analytic left brain and the synthetic right brain, and one goal of popular psychology has been to develop the power of the normally recessive right brain in the belief that a more "holistic" person will thereby emerge. But what is being asked of the poor, mute, image-processing faculty of the right brain is impossible without further spiritual development, and is, indeed, a description of higher consciousness. The right hemisphere of the neocortex corresponds to what Coleridge calls the "primary imagination," the "prime Agent of all human Perception."[35] It processes the perceptions of the physical eye for interpretation by other portions of the brain. The "secondary imagination," earlier discussed, is a higher faculty of the inner eye that "dissolves, diffuses, dissipates, in order to re-create."[36]

If the distinction between the functions ascribed to the right and left sides of the brain has any validity, it is on the higher level of Ruach consciousness and may be associated with the central and lateral centers currently under discussion. But the relationship of these two centers of higher consciousness must still be as Coleridge defined them, for the imagination should be activated and ever under the control of the will. We have seen that the central pursuit of the ideal on the Nefesh level can lead to various forms of suicidal behavior and to psychosis. And even more than at the Nefesh level, the Ruach imagination, if allowed unfettered expression of its visionary power, can lead to psychosis. Its power of astral projection can threaten the body as well as the mind. And even in milder forms it can unleash a power of the irrational that can make a virtue of vice. In the excessive enthusiasm of its emotive faculty, it can champion the holiness of sin. But the real danger of its emotional excesses is in so identifying with the needs of the Other that it does not adequately provide for the needs of the self.

All of these aspects of the imagination are brought together at the conclusion of Coleridge's great poem on the irrational, *Kubla Khan*. Composed in a drug-induced state, the symbolic images of the poem first describe the "stately pleasure-dome" that Kubla Khan had built beside underground caverns, and then the imagery switches to a vision of a damsel singing, concluding:

> *Could I revive within me*
> *Her symphony and song,*
> *To such a deep delight 'twould win me,*
> *That with music loud and long,*
> *I would build that dome in air,*
> *That sunny dome! those caves of ice!*
> *And all who heard should see them there,*
> *And all should cry, Beware! Beware!*
> *His flashing eyes, his floating hair!*
> *Weave a circle round him thrice,*
> *And close your eyes with holy dread,*
> *For he on honey-dew hath fed,*
> *And drunk the milk of Paradise. (42–54)*

The truly creative imagination depends on a special state of attunement, of higher harmony, but such a magical power of creation, though fed by Paradise, is threatening to the normal consciousness of auditors and seer alike. For magical effects that inspire rather than threaten, Coleridge insists that the imagination must be under the "irremissive" control of the will.

A similar distinction between correct and improper uses of the imagination was earlier voiced by the master of kabbalistic meditation, Abraham Abulafia. Warning against its improper use, he writes, "You [*sic*] mind will be confused, your thoughts confounded, and you will not find any way to escape the reveries of your mind. The power of your imagination will overwhelm you, making you imagine many utterly useless fantasies. Your imaginative faculty will grow stronger, weakening your intellect, until your reveries cast you into a great sea. You will not have the wisdom ever to escape from it, and will therefore drown."[37] Elsewhere he shows us what can be accomplished through the proper control of the imagination by the will: "if his mind can control its fantasies, then he can ride [his mind] like a horse. He can control it as he desires, spurring it on to go forward, or reining it to stop where he pleases. At all times, his imagination remains subject to his will, not straying from its authority, even by a hairbreadth."[38]

Our primary definitions of the Ruach centers of consciousness were determined by the larger consideration of this chapter, the development of a model for the functioning of higher consciousness, particularly in the meditative state. But there is a more general way of defining them that can be integrated with the identifications already made. As earlier suggested, the way the distinction between right- and left-brain functioning is often put could be better applied to the two aspects of Ruach consciousness, those associated with what I am calling the central and lateral systems, respectively. We can go further and identify the Ruach central system with the Ruach heart and its lateral system with the Ruach mind, understanding the imagination and the will to be lodged in the Ruach heart and mind thus defined. Such an association of the imagination with the heart is reflected in the biblical phrase "the imagination of man's heart" (Gen. 8:12).

As earlier indicated, we can further assign to the Ruach heart the higher central emotional faculty whose characteristic quality of empathy distinguishes its emotions from those of the Nefesh soul. For as the Nefesh emotional faculty serves its egocentric lateral center, it can be considered to be selfish. Its Ruach counterpart, on the other hand, in serving the higher central center of consciousness, should be considered selfless. Its identification with the needs of the Other represents the highest quality of the Ruach soul and is the very quality that can make possible the coming of the Messianic Kingdom. But as its very selflessness can constitute a danger to personal survival at the Ruach level and so short-circuit the higher development of the soul to the Neshamah level, the imaginative Ruach heart must remain ever subject to the will of the Ruach mind, "not straying from its authority," in Abulafia's words, "even by a hairbreadth."

The reason that the Ruach mind can exert such authority is that it is, in fact, the power center of the whole multidimensional soul, and the four levels of its power will be developed in the last four sections of this chapter. It is the very beginnings of such empowerment that drives the individual at this level of soul development to become a spiritual master. But it is only the exercise of Ruach power in a manner consistent with the desires of the Ruach heart for communal sharing that is ultimately rewarding, perversions of this power to private ends proving to be equally self-defeating because of that built-in fifth dimension of Providential justice operating precisely through this spiritual power.

It is only when we come to the Ruach level that the mind and heart functions can express their true natures rather than being dominated by the shaping influence of the animal instincts upon the Nefesh soul. This is in accord with the earlier depiction of the Ruach soul as the level proper for optimal human functioning on earth. What we can thus far understand of this ideal condition is that it is one in which the mind, with its extraordinary level of will power, operates in concert with the heart, whose equally extraordinary quality is its capacity for imaginative projection into the state of another recognized to be one with the self, to lift that self and all else on the planet to a level of heightened empowerment and harmony that can only be called Messianic. But it is because this Promised Land remains only our potential heritage that it must here be treated not as our normal condition but rather as a mode of higher consciousness, one that can be both apprehended and achieved through such spiritual practices as meditation. Central to the meditative experience are the two centers of consciousness just defined. But functioning importantly with them are those elements of feeling and thought earlier identified with the fallen Nefesh soul. What contribution they have to make at the expanded level of Ruach consciousness we are now to consider.

In *Kubla Khan* Coleridge had shown, through its absence, that the first step to the properly controlled exercise of the imagination must be one of attunement to higher harmony, that the magic of creativity could only arise from the "deep delight" experienced in such attunement. Abulafia describes a similar state resulting from use of his meditative techniques: "You will then feel as if an additional spirit is within you, arousing you and strengthening you, passing through your entire body and giving you pleasure. It will seem as if you have been anointed with perfumed oil, from head to foot."[39] The power of such attunement as can lift normal consciousness into the expanded dimension of the Ruach soul, that earlier also identified with the first stage of the Messianic Age, would seem to be lodged in the emotional-limbic system, most probably in the hippocampal circuit of this system that is noted for its emissions of the theta frequencies,[40] the brain-wave pattern associated with the meditative state. The power of attunement by which the identity can be enlarged from the Nefesh to the Ruach soul is lodged in the emotional system; and it would seem to effect an ascent of its lower lateral faculty into the union with its higher central faculty that can represent a new understanding of the concept of the "double heart."[41] The lower lateral faculty of feeling is where the process of attunement begins, and it would seem to be activated either by the Nefesh will to higher consciousness or by some spontaneous experience of central harmony, as sunset over still waters or the satisfied silence of a congenial group. This state of meditative attunement is the highest experience of fallen Nefesh consciousness. But it can go beyond this, achieving the goal of spiritual discipline in the activation of higher spiritual powers.

In chapter 2 we observed some of the dangers to which the fallen Nefesh emotional system is prone. Now we can see that its highest extension and probably its truest purpose lies in hooking up to and activating the Ruach level of the emotions, that it functions like an electrical circuit that, when switched on (or, in the more evocative vernacular, "turned on"), passes an energy current through it that powers the whole mechanism of Ruach consciousness. The same may be said for the lateral power earlier identified with the analytic functioning of the fallen Nefesh mind. Where in the fourth world its condition was one of intellectual alienation, in the fifth world we discover the higher purposes of this analytic function. Hooked up to the mechanism of the Ruach lateral center, it becomes an essential factor in all its higher spiritual work. In the meditative process with which the remainder of this chapter will be largely concerned, it is this analytic power that would supply the initial instructions given by the will to the imagination and that would then first interpret the images summoned by the imagination in obedience to the will. If the higher function of the first emotional faculty is its power to begin the attunement of the soul to the higher vibrational level of the Ruach dimension, that of the first intellectual faculty is its capacity to define the focus of concentration and to diagnose its initial condition, an activity that distinguishes the meditative practice of the true master from that which is no more than a mode of relaxation. We have thus far reviewed the meditative functions of the lower emotional and rational faculties or powers. The specifically meditative functions of the remaining four elements of the Nefesh soul should now be defined as well as one additional Ruach element.

Simplest is the first lateral power, associated with the reptilian bulb of the inner brain and the Nefesh animal instincts, whose function it is to maintain and monitor the bodily functions during the exalted states of meditation and particularly during any out-of-body experience. Should any internal or external danger to the body arise, this instinctual lateral power would activate the dormant lateral center so that it can bring the soul down and safely ground it. But this lateral Nefesh center can sometimes improperly interfere with Ruach functioning, responding with fear to unfamiliar Ruach experiences and calling the soul back prematurely. When such an identity shift suddenly occurs during high Ruach states, it is due to the arousal of Nefesh self-consciousness suddenly made aware that its identity is truly imperiled and, like Augustine, saying "God make me chaste—but not yet." It is because Nefesh self-consciousness can provide such an impediment to higher spiritual work that all the practices of spiritual discipline are necessary; for these are geared to purifying the Nefesh soul prior to engaging in such high meditative states so that it will not be resistant to the soul's higher development and play its correct role of preserving the body as the vessel of the soul.

There are two remaining central elements of the Nefesh soul that have not yet been mentioned, its collective center and the intuitive power that most directly connects it to the Ruach central center. The function of these two elements in this model would seem to be that suggested by such a connection. That is, when the Ruach imagination is asked to supply an image of a condition, to "show what it looks like," it may be thought to send such a message through the circuitry of the central system, the connecting link of the central intuitive faculty to the central center of consciousness representing the "collective unconscious," to use Jung's terminology. This collective unconscious contains the knowledge of all that is presently existent, on both the gross and subtle levels, together with the chain of causality linking past to present to probable future, and it files this information under various archetypal symbols. When so called upon, it would select the appropriate image that is storing the precise information requested and send it back through the central faculty of intuition to the Ruach central center, where it would finally appear on the screen of the imagination for interpretation by the lower lateral intellect, which, when so connected to Ruach consciousness, also serves as the analytic faculty of the Ruach mind. The last element necessary for normal Ruach functioning in this model is a Ruach lateral mental faculty that, as earlier suggested, provides the Ruach mind with its capacity for creative thought.

As the Ruach heart has upper and lower faculties of feeling, so does the Ruach mind have two major faculties of thought, a lower analytic and a higher creative faculty, and it is the joining of the two that results in Ruach sagacity. As the lower analytic faculty connects the Ruach and Nefesh levels of consciousness, so would it seem that the higher creative faculty joins the Ruach level of consciousness to that of the Neshamah. Though not itself of the sixth world, as the highest of fifth-world elements, and the one wholly uninfluenced by fourth-world legacies, it is in the best position to receive and transmit the purity of the highest messages, and its authentic voice, when not joined to that of the lower analytic function, may be considered prophetic. But however inspired, creative, and synthetic this faculty may be, it cannot be associated with the right brain since its principle tool of thought is language. As earlier insisted upon, it represents, rather, the distinctive characteristics of the higher Ruach mind.

We earlier saw that the four quarters of the fifth-world model could define the four stages of the Messianic Age corresponding to the fifth-world sphere; but we should now see how they can also model the centers and faculties of Ruach consciousness. In psychological terms, the fifth-world sphere, like that of the fourth world, is divided into its two halves, each further divided into a center of consciousness and the outer instrument through which it functions, the central half also contained within the lateral half. It will be remembered that there were two forms of the Nefesh soul. In its unfallen form, the first central half was identified both with a collective center and with the instrument of intuition housed in its shell, its second lateral half likewise identified with an individuated center and a shell housing its instrument of instinct. But the healthy round of its functions was seen to be unbalanced in its fallen form by its lateral acquisition of emotional and intellectual powers ideally belonging to the Ruach dimension of the fifth world.

Going further back to the initial cosmic model developed in the first chapter, it was there suggested that the soul at each of its levels would have to build the vessel of its Tzelem from the residual light of the Reshimu within the cosmic limits defined in the process of the Tzimtzum, and that this Reshimu was in a chaotic stage following the cosmic Shevirah, the Lurianic version of the Fall. This circumstance was then imagined to provide an opportunity for certain precipitant elements in the soul to capture higher powers from the still chaotic contents of this cosmic environment before its more deliberate elements could construct from such contents its defining boundary. In the second chapter, this circumstance was taken to explain the Fall of the Nefesh soul, the most advanced lateral aspect being thought to acquire the Ruach faculties of thought and feeling from the surrounding chaos before it had defined the boundary that would have made such capture not only impossible but also impermissible. And these captured faculties were thought to have unbalanced the Nefesh soul and defined the character of its Fall. When the Ruach soul is added to the Nefesh, however, this joint soul becomes rebalanced, as these extra Nefesh faculties reattach themselves to the higher Ruach faculties of thought and feeling and henceforth function in concert with them as their intended and now rectified lower halves. But since these lower halves have also become a permanent feature of independent Nefesh functioning on the human level, the forms of their attachment to their upper mates are different.

The lower lateral emotions can be unified with the upper central heart because they are adjacent to each other, these emotions being located on the outer lateral shell of the Nefesh soul just within the Ruach central heart. As this center of the Ruach central system surrounds the Nefesh lateral shell and is, in turn, surrounded by its own shell, each containing a faculty of the Ruach heart, it may be supposed that these upper and lower faculties could be unified by the heart that connects them. But in the case of the upper and lower mental faculties, there can be no such functional joining since the creative mental faculty of the Ruach mind occupies the highest position in its world, that of the lateral shell, while the Nefesh analytic faculty on its lateral shell is separated from the Ruach mind by the Ruach heart. These two mental faculties remain separate, therefore, and make independent contributions to the understanding of the Ruach mind, though this separation also allows for the possibility that the analytic faculty may at times relapse to its alienated Nefesh state. These details of the model reinforce the more general understanding of the heart as an organ of fusion and the mind of distinctions, though the intermediate position of the heart may here allow the upper and lower mental faculties to work more harmoniously together. But as the functioning of the Ruach soul involves all elements of the Nefesh soul and may be considered to effect its rectification, we should understand the captured or fallen faculties of the Nefesh soul, those of thought and feeling, as now functioning only as the lower halves of these Ruach faculties and so to be counted with them in a rebalanced whole.

A final difference between the modeling of the four temporal stages of development and of the four spatially defined aspects of the fully evolved psyche involves the function of the midpoint. For the temporal modeling of the cosmic worlds, it involves the power of transformation, that which can bring its world consciousness from a past to a future orientation. But for the spatially defined modeling of the fully evolved soul, it involves the power of balance, a balancing of lateral dominance with central input that gives full allowance to the importance of central understanding. Having defined all the elements of the joint Nefesh–Ruach soul, we should now look more closely at how it may function as a model for transformative meditation.

THE RUACH SOUL MODEL
OF TRANSFORMATIVE MEDITATION

How the model of the conjoined Nefesh–Ruach soul can in general define the meditative process we are now to see, beginning with an attempt to use this model to demonstrate the nature of psychic healing, perhaps the simplest and most accessible of all "magical" processes. This is not to say that all such healing, and other transformative processes with which it can be allied, follow the same step-by-step procedure that shall be outlined here. For many adepts, or those of natural talent, the process may be both spontaneous and instantaneous. Nonetheless, it is possible to analyze even such a natural process into the steps now to be given, and they can certainly be consciously practiced with increasing effectiveness.

We begin, then, with the process of attunement that was earlier identified as lifting the lower emotional faculty of the Nefesh lateral system to the more expansive realm of the upper emotional faculty of the central Ruach heart. Such an attunement process was also identified with the first temporal stage of the corresponding Messianic Age. For some this meditative process need be no more than a conscious focusing on the subject at hand and a dissociation from mundane matters and tensions, a redirection of the consciousness to a higher level of concentration. For most, however, this redirection can be facilitated by one or more of the meditative techniques taught in the kabbalistic or other traditions. Most effective is the silent repetition of a divine name, known in the Yoga tradition as a mantra, accompanied by a conscious regulation of the breath. Various such techniques of classical Kabbalah are given in Aryeh Kaplan's book *Meditation and Kabbalah,* and the modern student is well advised to study and practice them. In addition, I would also suggest use of the "mantra" I have decoded in the *Sefer Yetzirah,* this being the name of the first Sefirah in this text, Ruach Elohim Chayyim (Breath of the Living God), breathing in to "Ruach," holding the breath for the divine name "Elohim," and exhaling to "Chayyim." This mantra is best used in the attunement phase of the fuller process of kabbalistic meditation, a guided form of such "master meditation" being offered in appendix A.

By this stage in the meditative process, an experience of higher spirituality can be felt, in the words of Abulafia, "passing through your entire body and giving you pleasure." For many, this experience is sufficient. It relaxes the stress of the mind and the body, which in itself can promote both healing and happiness. But its spiritual effects can be still greater; for it can open a channel through which the highest spiritual forces can work on an unconscious level, developing and perfecting the soul even to its attainment of Ruach ha-Kodesh, that Holy Spirit informing the highest state of spiritual enlightenment. Because the effects of meditation consistently practiced can be so great, many traditions are content simply to teach the various simple techniques by which it can be stimulated. But as we have seen, the primary thrust of the kabbalistic tradition of meditation has been on those conscious and directed processes by which the powers of a spiritual master can be both developed and manifested. It is to the techniques of such master meditation that we now turn, with particular emphasis on healing.

When the properly activated and attuned higher will wishes to heal the self or another, it will direct the visual center to provide an image of the body either of the healer or of another, absent or present, that will reveal any condition, physical or spiritual, requiring treatment. The image that the "heart imagines" will now be presented to the lower analytic function of the mind for diagnosis. To translate the process thus far to the Ruach model, we can say that the lateral center of the Ruach will, working through its mind, directs the center of the central imaginative heart to provide a symbolic image of a condition, which the latter accomplishes by going to the depths of the central system, the Nefesh collective center contacted through the Nefesh central faculty of intuition. The image that can be thought to appear on the screen of the Ruach central imagination is now subject to interpretation by the lower analytic faculty at the direction of the Ruach lateral center. This lower lateral faculty of the mind, the highest power of the fallen Nefesh soul, has the capacity, when enlisted in such higher Ruach processes, of interpreting psychological and spiritual causes and probable effects as well as purely physical causes and effects, but its capacity is limited to deterministic analysis. It can diagnose, often brilliantly, the causes and course of a condition and even prescribe any known treatments for this condition. But it cannot discover or implement any new solution or cure.

This is a function of the higher creative faculty of the mind at its first level of true Ruach power. When the conscious will has received the diagnosis of the analytic faculty, it then calls upon its creative power to prescribe a cure. The source of this remedy will not be from the accumulated record of the past, represented by the collective unconscious of the center of the Nefesh central system, but from the still unmanifest future, the World to Come or Olam ha-Bah, for which this Ruach creative faculty serves as a channel. This may be considered to transmit the breath of the living God, Ruach Elohim Chayyim, lifting the person so inspired through the power of the holy spirit to higher levels of prophetic revelation.

It is in this state of higher consciousness initiated by silent repetition of the divine name Ruach Elohim Chayyim that the breath of God can communicate to the highest faculty of man, inspiring his understanding with a new vision of possibility. This new cognitive vision is then transmitted through the higher will to the imagination for translation into visual form. This is the most important step in the process. The imagination, which had before projected an image of a diseased condition, is now asked to revisualize the same subject in terms not only of its cure but of the highest perfection that can be imagined as still coherent with one's sense of personal identity. With this image before the central visual center of the Ruach heart, the lateral verbal center of the Ruach mind should now express its will with an affirmation of its purpose that this image be translated into manifest reality.

This is the technique but the extent of its effectiveness will depend on the development of the consciousness. Before turning to these levels of spiritual mastery, we should note the clear parallels between the processes related to the functioning of the cumulative Ruach soul and the stages of the "Transformative Moment" defined near the end of chapter 2. In the latter model, the transformative consciousness first focused on the perception of a self-defeating pattern that revealed the clue to its origin in the past, and this first focus on the enduring influence of the past can be seen to parallel the first visualization of a recognized unhealthy condition traced by the analytic function to its past causes. Similarly, the second process of both is virtually identical. Where the transformative consciousness first looks to the future for an ideal solution and then—the most important step—modifies it to fit the individual case, so does the creative mind in its direction and interpretation of the second visualization, to which it then adds the verbal expression of its will that this transformation be manifested. What the present analysis has added to the previous model has been a filling in of the mechanism of soul psychology operative at each of the stages of what can now be called Transformative Meditation. It may be possible, however, to use the four-fold temporal model in still another way, not to define the stages of an era but the levels of the individual who has arrived at Ruach mastery. In what follows we shall survey the four levels of Ruach spiritual power, utilizing the psychological model earlier defined and just expanded into a model for the practice of Transformative Meditation.

THE FIRST LEVEL OF RUACH POWER: CREATIVE THOUGHT

We have thus far examined only the mechanisms of Ruach consciousness and are now to consider it more precisely when only its lowest level has become empowered, whether through spiritual practices or some spontaneous spiritual development. In terms of healing, this minimal model of Ruach consciousness, which contains all of the rebalanced Nefesh and Ruach elements, is most effective for self-healing and problem solving. If one understands the causes and nature of one's illnesses or problems and, rather than resting indulgently with such knowledge, then projects a positive image to the self of its health and prospects, it is clear that this positive mental outlook will go far, in and of itself, to cure the disease that has attacked the body and spirit as well as marred the self's social and professional relationships. But this positive attitude is most effective when it does not rely wholly on the will, though even this can ensure significant results, but is also informed by new insight into the causes of a negative condition and a creative approach to remedying it. For such insights can encourage the normal rational consciousness to believe that change is possible and then to decide to take such steps as will bring this change about.

Though all of this may sound quite normal and even sensible, it nonetheless contains unexplained or magical elements, but elements so usual in our experience that we do not generally stop to wonder at them. The influence of spirit on matter by which negative attitudes can produce disease and positive attitudes cures is so accepted in medical practice today that the spiritual implications of such psychosomatic effects are not even remarked upon. And all our normal functioning is so dependent upon our capacity for insight and creative solutions that we rarely question how it is possible to arrive at such insight.

But it is not only in healing that these features of Ruach consciousness are present. They are present in all modes of creative thought and expression and their effects are just as magical. The process of composing a new work of music can be analyzed as easily in terms of this model as the act of healing. Thus composers must first have a deep knowledge of their art, what its various forms can express and how these forms have traditionally been used. When moved to begin a new work, they will imaginatively file through the traditional forms until they focus on the form that best seems to fit their mood, intention, or vision. Examining this form with their mind's eye, they will be able to see what its capabilities are. If their analytic vision clicks with the feeling they wish to express, their creativity will be inspired to flow into this form in such a manner as to reshape it into the expressive medium of their own identity. If none of the traditional forms seems capable, upon analytic examination, of expressing the power of their vision, they will feel called upon to create a new form to express this vision. But whether new or transformed, each new work of true originality will result from a revisualization of the possibilities of form as traditionally understood. Finally, between such a revisualization of form as can express new meaning and the completion of the work, there must come an act of will, an act of such positive motivation as shall not falter until the work is completed in a form as close as possible to that originally envisioned and held ever before the mind's eye in the process of composition. When one listens to Beethoven's ninth symphony or one of his late quartets, who does not find such creations miraculous, even were Beethoven not deaf at the time of composition? So too with Einstein's revisioning of all of modern physics in the single equation $E = mc^2$. For such commanding acts of creative thought as can transform the nature of an art or science, there is no adequate explanation provided through physiology and the laws of cause and effect. The imagination of such a creative being is, as Coleridge said, a "magical power," and its mode of operation is that of all magic: "it dissolves, diffuses, dissipates, in order to re-create."

The lowest level of Ruach magical power is, then, a very high level, indeed. It accounts for all the creative thought and expression that informs the various arts, sciences, and social movements. But though such creativity always springs from inspired moments of insight, moments that must be prepared for but that cannot be determined, it is accepted as a normal mode of human functioning. In fact, it is the normal mode of Ruach functioning and already implies a development of consciousness beyond the requirements for animal satisfaction and survival. Whether employed to write a symphony, solve the problem of pollution, or heal an ulcer, its results will always be considered natural and within the higher limits of normalcy. But in the process of arriving at these results, a certain restructuring of the consciousness will ordinarily occur that will facilitate the development of the next level of Ruach power.

THE SECOND LEVEL OF RUACH POWER:
THE MASTER OF SYNCHRONICITY

The process of creative revisioning, which we have seen to define the normal functioning of Ruach consciousness, depends on the adoption of a positive approach to the possibility of change. Rather than remaining a prisoner to the treadmill of mechanical responses, a condition that when recognized without an accompanying hope of correction can lead to an ever increasing negativity of spirit, those people who can creatively refashion their lives through a positive belief in its possibility will find such positiveness reinforced in theory and strengthened in power by the very success of this endeavor to be freed from a life of unproductive limitation. And as their spirit becomes increasingly positive, increasingly relaxed and joyous, so will the circumstances of their lives become increasingly easy. Their health will improve, as will their social relationships, and all their projects will prosper. Doors will suddenly open and opportunities arise just when they are ready to make use of them. Indeed, as expressed in a completely different context in Webster's *The White Devil:* "So perfect shall be thy happiness that, as men at sea think land and trees and ships go that way they go, so both heaven and earth shall seem to go your voyage."[42]

Of course, all such effects will be put down by the disbeliever as the product of chance and coincidence, at best as the natural result of the person's increased charm and charisma. But note those words, the former associated with magic as the latter is with miraculous spiritual power. The very language has enshrined the belief that a certain kind of personality can influence events in its favor. The subject is normally dismissed by considering such a person as lucky. But rather than closing the subject, the existence of people who are consistently lucky poses a mystery. Let me recount a personal anecdote on the unsettling effects of meeting such a person, on realizing that there was more in heaven and earth than had been dreamt of in my philosophy.

His name was Jose Lopez, and he appeared many years ago in a third-class railway carriage on a train between Seville and Granada. It was the day after the Seville spring fair, and the train was very crowded with all seats taken. A fat well-to-do man entered and a young soldier got up to give him his seat. The soldier then stood for much of the trip by an open window singing his Moorish songs like a bird. A beggar came through the train singing dreadfully and everybody gave him something because, as one person told me, he sang so badly. The soldier gave him his week's meat rations. Then a peddler came on the train and went through all the cars raffling off a bag of candy. Everybody again took a raffle, costing one peseta. Presently the peddler returned with the winning ticket. It was the soldier who won and he immediately passed out all the candy. On this trip between Seville and Granada, three separate peddlers boarded the train at various stops to raffle off similar bags of candy. And each time, in a train of some ten cars, the soldier Jose won—and gave away all the candy. I began speaking to him through an interpreter. "Do you always win," I asked. "Oh, yes," he answered. "Then you must win a lot of money gambling," I continued. "Oh, no," he quickly responded; "I never gamble. I'm religious." It turned out in further conversation, when we later took him out to dinner in Grenada, that Jose was nineteen and just completing his two years of military service. A trained bullfighter, he already had a contract for his first professional bullfights that coming summer in Mexico. Whether he became a famous matador or died in the bullring I do not know, for I never heard of him again after that remarkable incident so many years ago. He was a very pure soul who gave everything away only to have it all returned to him more abundantly, who was no longer surprised but still frightened by his lifelong ability to win against the odds.

Jose's mysterious power to win against the odds of mechanically determined chance is one experienced intermittently in all successful gambling and the secret of its appeal. Gamblers strive for that state of altered consciousness in which they feel "hot," in which they know the dice or the cards will turn up in accordance with their wishes—clearly a feeling of godlike power. The concept of sacred lots, cast by the early

Hebrew priests as well as the priests in other religious traditions, implies that the outcome of such lots will not be determined by chance but by a divine force, that spiritual power can manipulate the instruments of mechanical chance to influence the outcome. Beneath the more modern concept of luck as chance lies the older belief in Fortune or destiny as an overriding force determining the shape of one's life. To be fortunate was to be in the grace of God or the gods. The biblical belief that the reward of goodness is prosperity and long life also reflects this understanding that to the person living in the Way of God all riches and health will flow.

It is this power to influence the complex strands of causality so that two such lines meet just when one, a person moving "in the spirit," has need of what the other has to offer that I am identifying with the second level of Ruach power. It operates through what Jung has called synchronicity, and always assumes the appearance of chance. Most who are favored by this power have no idea what they are doing to cause such desirable effects. A book will come to their attention or be published just when they have need of that information and they may even open it to exactly the right page. They will start to meet the people needed for their personal or professional development, according to the old saying: "When the student is ready, the teacher appears." They will start remarking that they always seem to find parking spaces just when they arrive. At most, such people will recognize that at such times and at more and more of the time they are feeling "in the flow," that they are feeling a flow of heightened, exhilarating energy through their beings and also that they are moving in harmony with a larger, surrounding flow of events, with a cosmic energy.

Since the feeling is so fulfilling, they will start to do all they consciously can to enhance it, monitoring themselves with a kind of natural biofeedback that tells them when the "vibes" are good or bad and so increasing those experiences and associations that produce the former while eliminating those with negative results. And as their vibrational level becomes higher and purer, so will its influence on external events seem to increase. The breaks will all fall their way and, as the doors of opportunity open, so will they gain increasing command of their faculties, always knowing exactly what to say and do. This is a characteristic Mark Twain attributed to Huck Finn, as when he says, "I went right along, not fixing up any particular plan, but just trusting to Providence to put the right words in my mouth when the time come; for I'd noticed that Providence always did put the right words in my mouth, if I left it alone."[43] Such characters will have enormous charm and seem to live a charmed life, for this is the level on which what is normally called "magic" does operate. Such fortunate people are natural magicians, working with the higher energies without conscious awareness of what they are doing.

Some, and there are more and more of them in this New Age when all self-realizing techniques are being everywhere taught, will go beyond such natural magic to apply the techniques of Transformative Meditation for practical results. They will visualize the more desirable job or apartment to be found with verbal affirmations of their success, even to the point of visualizing and affirming the finding of parking spaces. It will work to some extent, for these techniques do have magical power, but their full power can only be released by a highly developed spirit who will use them for purposes higher than the satisfaction of its own needs.

It is only such a person who will be consciously able to command the power manifested in synchronicity. Such a person will be able to heal others as well as himself, though the former will be put down to coincidence as the latter is to nature. But as the *Sha'ar ha-Kavanah* points out, when one approaches spiritual work with the desire to fulfill the Highest Will: "he can accomplish anything. This will even include things that he himself desires, in which the Highest Will does not have any portion." The Ruach Master can, of course, use his power to meet human needs that must be satisfied for him to continue his higher work, but he will ordinarily prefer that these needs be met by natural means and not pervert higher powers to lower purposes. The apprentice who uses these techniques only for personal gain may become surprised that the indices of personal success seem less favorable than when he was just starting spiritual training and that others without such training seem to be far luckier than him. If the techniques work and he gets what he asked for, he will discover that he did not understand what to ask for and is being punished by getting what he ignorantly wanted. But more often he will find that all his spiritual techniques and—if he goes further into standard magical practices—charms will fail, that the abuse of spiritual techniques will close off their power and prove them sterile, even causing his natural power to fail. Nonetheless, if a person is in the flow, is motivated by the Ruach desires to help others and fulfill the Highest Will, then he can increase the natural magic that will strew his path with good fortune by conscious techniques of visualization and affirmation.

But the true master of synchronicity will do more than this. He will have perfected his willpower so that it can be applied precisely as required to accomplish its purpose. Such perfecting of the will, which is the task and test of the master, is achieved through a process similar to that of natural biofeedback and is, in fact, the same process on a higher and more conscious level. It involves an attunement of the master's will to the vibrational level of the event to be influenced and then a transmission of directed energy on that wavelength such that all on its frequency will resonate to that influence and be pulled into the orbit of its purpose. The technique will be similar to that earlier defined for the minimal Ruach system, except that the visualizations will not be on the object but on its vibrational level and will be concerned not with static images but processes. It is as though the focus of attention is not on the aspect of reality as particle but as wave, and the wave pattern is not so much visualized as felt imaginatively.

Spiritual masters will project themselves imaginatively into a given situation and feel the quality of its vibration. From this they will be able to understand analytically the factors that are at play in it. They will then arrive at a creative understanding of how that situation should be altered to bring it into conformity with their intention and then translate their revisualization of this situation into a retuning of the original vibration within the limits of its affinities. Finally, they will transmit this retuned vibration through the power of their will to the situation at issue with such directed force that it will be pulled into resonance with their will. This developing situation will then begin so to evolve that it will be ready to embrace their purpose when the time comes for them to enter it. What seems coincidental when it occurs will have been carefully prepared for on the subtler planes of reality. Even when the process is not this conscious, a high and pure will attracts to its purposes all those latent possibilities within circumstances that have an affinity for them and empowers these latencies to become actualized. The master's will and the potentialities within historical process are mutually reinforcing, and their mutual powers arrive at a future convergence.

We have thus far spoken of such manifestations under the term *synchronicity*, for this is how such events may appear in the present culture, but an older and truer name for it is Providence. I have often stated that the fifth dimension is the dimension of Providence,[44] and the true Ruach Master is the one for whom this dimension is as palpable as time and space, who apprehends its operations in all the mundane events of human experience. While its general direction is set and monitored by the spiritual hierarchy of the sixth world, the Ruach Master can fine tune its processes in the particular space-time frame in which he is located. It is true that all great events occur through the meeting of the person with the moment, neither being sufficient without the other. So can it be said that the force of Providence requires the vessel of a living master to achieve its larger historical purposes. But their alliance is operative even in smaller matters. Just as Einstein tells us that matter bends space, so the power of a master bends the Providential dimension of reality to support and effect his will, and he does this not alone through techniques of conscious focusing but simply through being. He is both a master and agent of Providence.[45]

THE THIRD LEVEL OF RUACH POWER: THE MASTER OF TRANSFORMATION

As the master develops his or her power to influence the operations of Providence, so will still higher powers be developed that can no longer be explained away as coincidence but must be considered miraculous. Such is the power of the third level of the Ruach soul, the highest power attainable exclusively through the fifth world, though most often exercised by masters whose souls have already developed to the Neshamah level of the sixth world. It would seem, indeed, that the masters who have learned to operate through the Providential dimension begin to move into the sixth world while still perfecting the Ruach powers through which they can directly influence and communicate with the world of ordinary humanity. Once they begin to operate successfully with the higher energies, their development will accelerate and become multifaceted. At this next level, the master of Providence also becomes the master of transformation.

While it is true that all Ruach spirituality is transformative, that the same technique of creative revisualization with verbal affirmation can be employed on all its levels, the scope of this transformative power expands with each level of development. Where the Ruach will is only able to function on the lowest level of its power, its effects will be largely subjective. It will be able to transform the health of the body housing it and function more creatively and positively in all areas of that person's life, even to the point of producing creative works of art and thought and of organizing or reorganizing groups of people for special creative projects. But all its operations, however truly miraculous in transformative power, will be considered normal and natural in effect. When the Ruach will has developed its second level of power, it begins to be able to affect the external world through purely spiritual means. Working primarily through the higher fifth dimension that can be called Providential, its influence over events would have to be considered magical if such events were not dismissed as coincidental. But the point about this level, and one secret of its effectiveness, is that all its effects can be dismissed by the uninitiated as the products of chance while still operating effectively on behalf of those who know how to channel this power.

When we arrive at the third level of Ruach power, however, the secret is out. The master must become public, for there is no other explanation for his powers than that they are miraculous. No longer confined to the temporal processes of history, he can now directly affect and transform material substance. The blind can suddenly see, and by his will, according to Dov Baer, the Maggid of Mezrich, lead can be transformed into gold: "This is how a miracle comes about, changing the laws of nature. . . . When a person gazes at an object, he elevates it into his thought. If his thought is then attached to the supernal Thought, he can elevate it to the supernal Thought. From there it can be elevated to the level of Nothingness, where the object itself becomes absolute nothingness. This person can then lower it once again to the level of Thought, which is somethingness. At the end of all levels, he can transform it into gold."[46]

He who can transform external matter through spirit can truly be called a charismatic master. Although the Mezricher Maggid had said that such material transformations were dependent upon the ability to lift the original visualization up to the highest world of Nothingness, Ayin, before revisualizing it, we should also remember that Coleridge had defined the creative imagination as a power that "dissolves . . . in order to re-create." If it is possible to identify Coleridge's concept of the "secondary imagination" with what is here being defined as the Ruach imagination, then the power of transformative revisualization would seem to be fully within the mechanism of fifth-world consciousness.

What changes as one after another of the fifth world's levels of power become activated is the depth of such visualizations. At the lowest degree of Ruach power, the imagination can visualize and revisualize only images of objects in space. At the next degree of power, the imagination can visualize such spatial entities as particular vibrations, as events in time as well as space. But the vibrational attunement is still to particulars, to the macrostructural distinctions of molecular chemistry and biology, which are apprehended not simply in class terms but in their absolute individuality, as this person, that group event. At the third degree of power to which we have now come, the Ruach imagination has achieved a degree of magnification by which it can focus on the microstructure of objects, people, or events, a level at which all individual distinctions disappear and the ground of all performs its quantum dance. The difference between those who have seen such quanta in bubble-chamber tracks and in the higher imagination is that the latter tend to speak of such patterns of energy as manifestations of a divine or conscious force.

Swami Muktananda, known as Baba, in his remarkable spiritual autobiography, speaks in this manner of the light patterns he began to see when first initiated by his guru and that he continued to see throughout his life:

> For a short while, I experienced the One in many, abandoning the tendency that differentiates the inner from the outer and shows many in One. . . . I could perceive infinitesimal dots shimmering and rushing throughout my body with astonishing velocity. I was overwhelmed with joy and wonder. I opened my eyes and looked outside. Lo! There too legions of the minutest blue particles were scintillating in rows upon rows. . . . Even today I can vividly recollect that experience of oneness. I am still seeing those minute blue dots . . . the extremely subtle, tranquil, all-pervasive, conscious blue light. . . . Whenever I look at anyone, I first see the blue light and then him. When I look at an object, I first see the honeyed, subtle, conscious rays and then the object. Regardless of where my mind is directed, I perceive the universe within the lustrous mass of light. [47]

If we read these statements in the light of the present discussion, it would seem that Baba Muktananda's normal perception was focused on the microstructure, the quantum or divine level of energy, and that he had constantly to refocus his attention to the macrostructure of individualized persons and objects. In doing this, however, he did not lose sight of the "all-pervasive, conscious blue light" within and without the particular object of his attention. He perceived an interfacing of the microstructure with the macrostructure, the "all-pervasive, conscious blue light" of the microstructure being delineated into the individualized forms of the macrostructure within his field of vision.

Once such a level of consciousness is defined, it is fairly easy to see how it can be employed in transformative magic, a practice Baba Muktananda, himself, ever eschewed: "The seers who attain this state become omniscient. Our great sages of ancient India had risen to this height through the yoga of meditation. They could also tap this omniscient centre at will during their waking hours. . . . Some yogis acquire extraordinary powers at this stage. It does not take long to obtain these through meditation. But a true seeker longs only for perfection, being a true child of his Guru. He does not attach any importance to supernatural powers, nor would he reveal them to others."[48] Of the Yogis noted for such extraordinary powers, perhaps the most celebrated in recent memory is Satya Sai Baba. It is alleged that Satya Sai Baba could pass his hand through sand and transform it into a ruby. Indeed, motion pictures have been made that purport to demonstrate this miraculous power of transformation.

If we are to accept this or other accounts of magical transformation, the mechanism would seem to be explicable through the process of master meditation being defined. A master must visualize the all-pervasive microstructure in and around the object on which his concentration is focused, sand or lead as the case may be, while also attuning himself to the vibrational frequency of its particular molecular structure. He must then reattune himself to the vibration of the imaginatively transformed object, ruby or gold, while directing his will to the quanta within the original physical object. Such influence will be more easily accepted if we can also accept Baba Muktananda's belief that the infinitesimal particles of light he perceived are "conscious." In such a case, the particularized consciousness of the master would communicate its will to the all-pervasive consciousness within and identified with the quanta of the original object, telling them to change their arrangement from that of their present molecular structure to that of the molecular structure desired by the master. If his will is of such a pure energy that it can be accepted by the quanta as their own, they will begin to resonate to it and will then respond by mimicking any morphic changes communicated within the field of vibratory sympathy they share with the master. Thus the quanta within a piece of lead, accepting the master's vibration as their own, will rearrange themselves to define the characteristics of gold when the master transmits both the new vibrational frequency of gold and the influence of his more powerful will. The power of this new frequency can be said to produce a rhythm entrainment of the weaker or slower frequency of the quanta, forcing it to operate at the new frequency of gold rather than the old vibratory pattern of lead. Whether the influence of mind over matter be explained by the consciousness of matter or the physics of rhythm entrainment, that subtle process by which one frequency can force others that are close to oscillate in phase with it,[49] there is evidence to suggest that the proper direction of mental frequencies can develop a power capable of affecting the structure of matter.

More subtle and yet more significant than such alchemical magic is the most celebrated instance of magical transformation in Western history, Jesus' transubstantiation of the bread and wine of his last Passover feast into his body and blood without any visible sign of such a change. It is more significant because the Christian sacrament of the Eucharist, which Jesus thus instituted with a verbal declaration, continues to exert its power to communicate the spirit of this master to the devout communicant to this day. Here we see the true power of ritual, which is to conserve and convey the living spirit of its founding master and, through this, the divine spirit and source of all. All religions are structures designed to conserve and perpetuate the divine fire manifested through a master spirit and transferred by him into specific rituals. Such communion is facilitated by an ordained priesthood, initiated in a ceremony directly transferring a portion of the master's spirit in an unbroken lineage, for these priests become empowered to perform the ritual transubstantiation by which matter becomes a vehicle for spiritual experience.

The sacrament of the Eucharist holds a central place in Roman Catholic ritual observance, and its greater significance in Catholic than in Protestant worship may derive from the fact of the unbroken lineage of its priesthood. If the laying on of hands, which is a feature of ordination ceremonies in most religious heritages, does confer a power to reinvest a ritual act with its original spirit, then we may see in the continuing power of Catholic Communion an explanation for the difference in the character of Catholic and Protestant countries. There seems no reason to doubt the testimony of countless Catholics in all countries and ages, as well as this main focus of Catholic theology, that something miraculous does happen to them when, in a state absolved of sin, they taste the Communion wafer. The very structure of the Mass recognizes this by providing a period of meditation for the congregation after it has taken Communion, for most congregants seem to enter into a state of what we would today call spontaneous meditation. The sense of a compelling spiritual Presence seems to be widespread during the portion of the service called the Communion Meditation, experienced both as within the individual communicant and as containing the whole congregation.

The existence of such evidential weekly experience of a higher spiritual realm on such a large scale in Catholic countries may account for the lack of driving motivation for worldly success in such countries and their toleration for conditions of widespread poverty and disease. Conversely, the great Protestant countries of the West—England, Germany, and twentieth-century America—may have released the springs of worldly progress and success precisely through having broken the priestly lineage through which the sacramental power of the Eucharist had been passed down. This is not to say that Protestantism is lacking in spiritual power, rather that the sources of this power are of a different character, deriving largely from inspired preaching and the direct experience of grace, both powerful but rather chancy and subject to lapses. The final development of Reformation Protestantism may perhaps be seen in Southern Baptism and forms of Pentecostalism that, whether black or white, in tents or tabernacles, manage to develop a group religious fervor that for many is evidential of the true workings of the Holy Spirit. Nonetheless, the dependence of such congregations on individual preachers rather than a structure of priestly ritual leads to an emphasis on individualism and personal expressiveness that has historically been compatible with the progress of science and the rise of capitalism.[50]

A phenomenon similar to that of Catholic countries can be found in India, where more extreme forms of poverty go hand in hand with the most highly developed techniques of spiritual mastery yet manifested in human history. And here too the power of transformative magic is widespread. As Jesus is credited with having transformed the nature of bread and wine so that, under certain specified conditions, they could contain and transmit his spirit, so does the Yoga tradition claim a similar mode of spirit transmission. This is the power of mantra, a power we will see to be similar to that which Jewish mysticism has ever attributed to the dinvine names. As Baba Muktananda explains this power:

Truly speaking, the divine name is the mantra obtained from the Guru. Repetition of the name activates the inner Shakti with full vigour. . . . Never stop repeating and identifying yourself with the mantra, which bears a conscious force. It is a boon of the Siddha Guru. It embodies your Guru. A mantra charged with the potency of Parashiva, the highest Guru, is not merely an inert pattern of sounds. The supremely glorious, universal, divine power is hidden within it. In such a mantra, Parashiva and the Guru are united. Therefore, it is endowed with consciousness. . . . [51]

Baba Muktananda tells us that the reason a particular pattern of sounds has the power to transform an individual has nothing to do with natural human physiology, endorphins and the like, but is the result of a spiritual process by which an "inert pattern of sounds" has, itself, become transformed into a carrier of Shakti, that of the guru who gives it and of the deity by which he gives it. When a meditator takes such a divinely charged mantra into his consciousness, what is working within him is the real spirit of his guru, his guru's lineage, and the deity whose name appears in the mantra, Shiva in the case of Baba Muktananda's mantra "Om Namah Shivaya."

Most religious traditions treat certain phrases with a special reverence. For Muslims it is the *zikr*, which translated means "There is no God but God." For Jews the most highly charged phrases are the Mosaic Sh'ma, normally translated "Hear, oh Israel, the Lord your God, the Lord is one"[52] (Deut. 6:4) and the Kedushah of Isaiah: "Holy, Holy, Holy is the Lord of Hosts: the whole earth is filled with His Glory" (6:3). Greater than these and felt to be so highly charged that it could not be pronounced by any but the high priest and only on Yom Kippur is the Tetragrammaton, the most holy four letter name of God.[53] The transubstantiation of matter through the power of blessing is also a feature of Jewish ritual, of the Sabbath wine, challah and, perhaps most powerfully, in the lighting of the Sabbath candles.[54]

Of course, the effects on Catholic communicants of taking the wafer, on Yogic meditators of repeating the mantra, and on Jewish women of lighting the Sabbath candles can and have been explained in terms of natural, if abnormal, psychology and physiology. What I am doing here is looking seriously at the claims of Catholic, Hindu, and Jewish theologians and practitioners that miraculous transformations of ordinary foods, words, and candles do occur that make them the transmitters of higher spiritual energies. But though masters in all spiritual traditions are capable both of initiating such rituals of transformative magic and of empowering their successors to reenact them with undiminished potency for as long as their traditions persist, the true concern of spiritual masters is not with material transformations but with the transformation of persons. When we speak of a charismatic master, it is not simply in a figurative sense that such charisma or spirit should be understood. For the power to attract and influence large groups of people *is* a spiritual power. In the Yoga tradition it is precisely defined as *shaktipat*, the direct transmission of spiritual energy, normally by touch. As Baba Muktananda defines it: "The true Guru is one who awakens the disciple's inner Shakti through Shaktipat and makes the divine energy active within him. . . . Whatever work he imparts constitutes a mantra, endowed with conscious force. The sublime Guru in whom Chiti is manifested, enters his disciple by his mantra, thought, touch or look."[55] Through his speech, thought, and look, as well as touch, the charismatic master enters and transforms his disciples. It is this power, far more than the miraculous healings performed by such figures as the prophet Elisha, Jesus, Baba Nityananda (Baba Muktananda's guru), and the legions of contemporary psychic healers, or even the miracles of material transformations, that constitutes the highest expression of the third degree of Ruach power.

THE FOURTH LEVEL OF RUACH POWER: THE MASTER OF CREATION

If the third degree of Ruach power can only be activated by Ruach Masters who have already largely evolved to the Neshamah soul level, the final degree of Ruach power is one that is available only to Neshamah Masters and normally not utilized even by them, who prefer to interact with humanity through the second and third degrees of Ruach power. As the defining characteristic of the third degree of this power is transformative, so that of this fourth degree can be considered truly creative, not simply the creation of art from thought as with the first degree of Ruach power, but of something from nothing. It is here, not with alchemical magic, that we meet the Mezricher Maggid's concept of the Ayin. And the reason for this is that at this level of power the Ruach imagination is no longer operative. To be able to perceive the source of that which materializes out of "nothing," the master would have to place his consciousness in the Neshamah imagination of the sixth world. But if he does this, he will not be able to function in the fifth dimension, the bridge between the highest consciousness and the consciousness of ordinary humanity defined by space-time.

The ability to materialize something out of nothing is the most spectacular of magical effects, whether true or contrived, and the very fact that stage magicians regularly feature such magic tricks as the high point of their shows merely underscores the preeminent position stories of such powers hold in the annals of all spiritual traditions of holy men. One such story I personally heard Baba Muktananda tell of another Yoga master. I believe it probably was of Hari Giri Baba,[56] though I am not absolutely sure and the story, to my knowledge, has not been published. The event took place when Baba Muktananda was young and traveling with the older renunciate. They were on a train and, when the conductor approached to ask them for their tickets, it appeared that Hari Giri Baba had neglected to purchase them since such men as he were normally honored with the charity of free travel. When this conductor insisted that they could not ride without tickets, despite Baba Muktananda's avowals of the greatness of his companion, Hari Giri Baba simply proceeded to materialize the exact tickets required out of his hand, to the general confusion and apologies of the conductor and the astonishment of all the passengers. The story continues that Hari Giri Baba then offered to teach the young swami how to do such feats of magic since he recognized that his spiritual development was sufficient to learn the techniques of materialization. But Baba Muktananda refused the offer on the grounds that he could not learn magic and do his *sadhana*, his spiritual discipline, at the same time. Upon hearing this, Hari Giri Baba exclaimed, "You will be a great prince and live in a palace," a statement Baba Muktananda seemed to apply with a glance to his exalted position on a throne-like chair in a palace-like Ashram. Whether or not Hari Giri Baba actually had those correctly printed tickets up his sleeve and imposed on the credulity of the young swami, the fact remains that the incident left an indelible impression on him and was consistent with the powers he believed such yogis to possess.

Since the production of something out of nothing is a feat that directly corresponds to the traditional understanding of the divine creation of the universe, it would be possible only through the participation of elements from the sixth world, the lowest realm of the divine. For the fourth Ruach level to be empowered, then, it would seem that the Neshamah elements would have to be already in place, the divine working through the level of perfected Ruach consciousness. In the Jewish tradition, the most remarkable legends involving this highest level of power are centered on the divine ability to imbue a clay figure with life, an ability attributed by the *Sefer Yetzirah* to the patriarch Abraham, by the Talmud to various sages, and in the later legends of the Golem primarily to Rabbi Loew of Prague.[57] The *Sefer Yetzirah* reference and the many medieval commentaries upon it all derive from the biblical verse "And Abram took Sarai his wife . . . and the souls that they had gotten in Haran" (Gen. 12:5). Thus to Abraham, above all other figures in Jewish history and legend, was attributed the divine ability to create souls. Less spectacular but more largely reported was the legendary ability of the prophet Elisha who, like Jesus, was able to restore the dead to life (2 Kings 4:32–6). Nonetheless, it is said of Moses and only of him: "And there arose not a prophet since in Israel like unto Moses, whom the Lord knew face to face, In all the signs and the wonders . . . which Moses showed in the sight of all Israel" (Deut. 34:10–12).

The mighty power of Moses derives from the face-to-face knowledge of Himself that God granted only to Moses. In this mystical union of Da'at, some portion of the divine spirit was imparted to him that could be seen and that endowed him with a special holiness:

> And it came to pass, when Moses came down from mount Sinai
> with the two tables of testimony . . . that Moses wist not that the

skin of his face shone. . . . And when Aaron and all the children of
Israel saw Moses . . . they were afraid to come nigh him. And Moses
called unto them; and Aaron and all the rulers of the congregation
returned unto him: and Moses talked with them. And afterward all
the children of Israel came nigh: and he gave them in commandment all that the Lord had spoken with him in mount Sinai.
(Exod. 34:29–32)

The holy dread that Moses inspires results in part from, and is attached
as well to, the laws of the covenant that God imparted to Israel through
Moses; for it is the special power of this covenant to transmit holiness
to all who obey it: "Now therefore, if ye will obey my voice indeed, and
keep my covenant, then ye shall be a peculiar treasure unto me above
all peoples: for all the earth is mine: And ye shall be unto me a kingdom of priests and a holy nation" (Exod.19:5–6). The distinction
between "Aaron and all the rulers of the congregation," with whom
Moses talked directly, and the "children of Israel," to whom he gave the
Lord's commandments, attaches also to the quality of the holiness transmitted by and through Moses. When Moses is overburdened by his
responsibilities, God provides for a transfer of a portion of Moses' spiritual power to the elders: "And the Lord came down in a cloud, and
spake unto him, and took of the spirit that was upon him, and gave it
unto the seventy elders: and it came to pass, that, when the spirit rested
upon them, they prophesied, and did not cease" (Num. 11:25). But it is
not only to those who have directly received the Mosaic spirit, and presumably their descendants, that the capacity for true prophecy resides.
When Moses is informed that two men remaining in the camp also
began to prophesy, he says: "Enviest thou for my sake? would God that
all the Lord's people were prophets, and that the Lord would put his
spirit upon them!" (Num. 11:29).

There are, then, two ways in which Moses was able to transmit the
spirit of God that rested on him, through the direct communication of
the prophetic spirit and through the commandments, and the presence

of one does not obviate the need for the other. As the highest development of the children of Israel would be if all were to become prophets, so the special laws of priestly purity attest to the fact that the prophetic power imparted to the leaders of the congregation does not excuse them from obedience to the laws but rather is designed to increase observance. It is through both the Mosaic spirit of prophecy and the Mosaic covenant that all of Israel is to become "a kingdom of priests and a holy nation." If "there arose not a prophet since in Israel like unto Moses," it was not because of "all the signs and the wonders . . . which Moses showed in the sight of all Israel" but because he established the basis for creating a holy nation. It is in such creation that the higher souls can truly be begotten that testify to the supreme manifestation of the Ruach spirit on earth, the Ruach ha-Kodesh. And it is only through the descent of this Holy Spirit that one can experience a reality that seems to "come down" (Num. 11:17) from nothing, Ayin. Moses' great teaching is of the sacramental nature of the divine commandments, that when properly empowered the ritual commandments can become the transmitters of holiness both to the individual and the whole community of the faithful. For observance of the commandments brings the presence of God into the life of the observer: "If ye walk in my statutes, and keep my commandments, and do them; Then . . . I will walk among you, and will be your God, and ye shall be my people" (Lev. 26: 3, 12).

Of all the commandments, that which is considered by the rabbinical tradition to be so holy that its performance alone can be regarded as fulfilling the entire covenant is the Sabbath. It is the only ritual observance to be included in the Ten Commandments and the only one of these commandments to be designated as holy: "Remember the sabbath day, to keep it holy. Six days shalt thou labour, and do all thy work: But the seventh day is the sabbath of the Lord thy God: in it thou shalt not do any work, thou, nor thy son, nor thy daughter, thy manservant, nor thy maidservant, nor thy cattle, nor the stranger that is within thy gates: For in six days the Lord made heaven and earth, the sea, and all that in them is, and rested the seventh day: wherefore the

Lord blessed the sabbath day, and hallowed it" (Exod. 20: 8–11). In the last phrase of the Fourth Commandment, we are told that the Lord blessed and hallowed the Sabbath, that it is a vessel containing that divine Presence which constitutes holiness. Moreover, the act of remembering to keep the Sabbath holy is the means of communicating this holiness to the observer: "Verily my sabbaths ye shall keep: for it is a sign between me and you throughout your generations; that ye may know that I am the Lord that doth sanctify you" (Exod. 31:13). The Sabbath becomes the sign of God's covenant to sanctify Israel through its observance of the holiness of the seventh day.

The concept of hallowing time implies that time is not empty but contains a spiritual power and purpose, one to which the Ruach Master can so attune himself that he can enhance in his own being and empower for others the special spirituality conveyed through observance of its rhythms. It is the ritual empowerment of the apparent nothingness of time so that its divinely invested spirituality can be apprehended that constitutes the highest development of the Jewish revelation and the source of its strength. It is the holy jewel of the Mosaic legacy. There are many Jews today, as in the past, who observe the Sabbath because of the trait that God so often bemoaned, a stiff-necked refusal to let secular time reduce the Jewish people to oblivion, a stiff-necked commitment simply to endure, to triumph over the millennia that have consumed so many empires. But the true triumph over the nothingness of time that the Sabbath can provide is the holiness its ritual observance can instill in all those who participate in its spirit. Nor is this holiness to be understood as a metaphor for a purely subjective affect. The Torah meaning can best be appreciated by taking it seriously, that is, literally, by understanding that it is a real spiritual entity that comes from beyond the individual to rest on him, to infuse and engulf him, in the performance of certain prescribed rituals. As Abraham J. Heschel has shown:

> The legitimate question concerning the forms of Jewish observance is, therefore, the question: Are they spiritually meaningful? . . .

Religion is not within but beyond the limits of mere reason. . . .
Its meaning must be understood in terms compatible with the sense
of the ineffable. . . . Ceremonies are created for the purpose of signifying: mitzvoth [commandments] were given for the purpose of
sanctifying. This is their function: to refine, to ennoble, to sanctify
man. They confer holiness upon us, whether or not we know
exactly what they signify.[58]

In his uniquely meaningful book on the Sabbath, Heschel further explores the manner in which this crowning mitzvah serves to sanctify time:

Judaism is a religion of time aiming at the sanctification of time. . . .
The Sabbaths are our great cathedrals. . . . When we celebrate the
Sabbath we adore precisely something we do not see. To name it
queen, to call it bride is merely to allude to the fact that its spirit
is a reality we meet rather than an empty span of time which we
choose to set aside for comfort or recuperation. . . . The Sabbath is
the presence of God in the world, open to the soul of man. . . .
What is the Sabbath? Spirit in the form of time. . . . Something
happens to a man on the Sabbath Day. On the eve of the Sabbath
the Lord gives man *neshamah yeterah* [additional soul]. . . . [A]n
actual spiritual entity, a second soul, becomes embodied in man on
the seventh day. . . . This is the task of men: to conquer space and
sanctify time.[59]

In the Sabbath, then, Moses transmitted to Israel and the world the
highest degree of spiritual holiness, "the presence of God in the world,
open to the soul of man." And the wonder of this highest degree of
Ruach power, the Ruach ha-Kodesh, is that it is available to every man,
woman, and child who takes the time to receive it, who has learned to
sanctify the Sabbath.

With this brief tribute to the Sabbath, we bring to a close the
analysis of the fifth-world model for both the Messianic Age and the

complementary four degrees of Ruach spirituality. And it seems not coincidental that the holiness of the Sabbath should emerge as the highest expression of the degrees of its power. In chapter 5 we shall see that the seventh world of our cosmic model provides an explanation for that unification of the finite with the infinite in which the holiness of the Sabbath may be said to consist. The periodicity of the seventh seems to carry a special spiritual quality or meaning in all sorts of circumstances but most particularly in that other domain with such significant correspondences to our cosmic model, music.

It is remarkable that the seventh harmonic should also prove to be the interval of the seventh, the slightly flat minor seventh, to be precise. In the first chapter I reviewed what I have elsewhere demonstrated, that the biblical creation account was based on the twin keys of geometry and music, specifically on the hexagram and the harmonic series,[60] and with respect to the latter that the seventh day could be associated with the seventh harmonic. It is the modulating quality of its minor seventh interval—that which to modern ears demands resolution by the chord of the subdominant key, as in the modulation from the key of C to the key of F—which in that earlier discussion of creation was associated with the essence of the Sabbath, its transformative effect upon the consciousness.

Such a musical power to modulate and lift the consciousness is coherent with the understanding of this interval shown by one of the twentieth century's most gifted seers, Rudolf Steiner. Claiming that this was the interval that dominated the music of Atlantis, he states:

> This musical experience, which was based on an experience of the seventh through the full range of octaves, always consisted of man feeling completely transported [*entruckt*]. He felt free of this earth-bound existence and transported into another world in his experience of the seventh. . . . When they made music they were transported completely beyond themselves; they were within the great, all-pervading spirituality of the universe in an absolute motion. . . . Their musical experience converged with a direct reli-

gious experience. . . . . [T]hey sensed how the gods, who pervaded
and wove through the world, revealed themselves in sevenths.[61]

Steiner's testimony to the transporting power of the musical seventh
upon a less fallen sensibility can illuminate the corresponding power of
the Sabbath, as recognized by Heschel, to reveal "the presence of God
in the world," an experience of the seventh that can bring rectification
to the fallen soul.

Synthesizing the biblical concept of the days of creation with the
kabbalistic concept of cosmic worlds has led to an understanding of the
multidimensional structure of the cosmos as containing seven cosmic
worlds. A further correlation was made between the full structure of
this cosmic model and music, that each of the seven spheres contained
in this model has its own tonality corresponding to the tones of the diatonic scale, a possibility rich in Pythagorean associations. With the fifth
world, which is the proper concern of this chapter, we have reached the
tonal equivalent of La, that which defines the interval of the musical
sixth. And of this interval, Steiner has said "The form of the soul's composition during the experience of the sixth is that of inspiration with
clairvoyance."[62] Inspiration, the inhaling of spirit, and clairvoyance, the
power of imaginative projection, are what the dimension of the Ruach
soul is all about. We have already considered Steiner's understanding of
the musical power of the seventh, which is the interval corresponding
to the tonality of the sixth world, and when we finally arrive at the seventh world, which contains the musical octave, we shall be fully able to
appreciate his observation that "the feeling for the octave brings us to
find our own self on a higher level."[63] Thus as we explore the higher
dimensions of our cosmic model, we may be said to partake in some
measure of that highest spiritual state experienced by the father of
Western geometry and music, Pythagoras, the soul's ascending experience of the music of the spheres.

4

THE SIXTH WORLD
OF TRANSFORMATIVE
NESHAMAH
CONSCIOUSNESS:
THE PATRIARCHS AND
THE PARTZUFIM

THE TRANSFORMATIVE MOMENT
OF NESHAMAH CONSCIOUSNESS

It is fitting that we follow the discussion of Ruach or Messianic consciousness in chapter 3 with a fuller consideration of Neshamah consciousness, the highest level of consciousness that, though normally associated with the psychic condition of the World to Come, can still be manifested on earth. There is one prior analysis that will prove most suggestive in attempting to grasp the very timelessness that must surely be a central characteristic of the World to Come. This is the model of the Transformative Moment, first developed in chapter 2, which will here be reinterpreted to serve as a window into our study of the nature of that sixth dimension of consciousness shared by the Neshamah soul and the Partzufim, the divine personalities. In fact, we shall see that what was earlier defined as the Transformative Moment is precisely a moment of Neshamah consciousness, its focus on transformative insight being reflective of the essentially mental nature that has traditionally been attributed to the Neshamah soul. While it is the capacity to sustain such moments that defines both the Neshamah Masters and the Partzufim, the following far-ranging exploration, proceeding from the Patriarchs to the cosmic consciousness of Ze'ir Anpin, the Partzuf of the son, will show that these moments are available to any of us and provide an inspiring sample of the World to Come.

It may seem paradoxical to approach an understanding of qualitative timelessness through study of something like its chronology, but even the timeless has a structure and one that would seem to contain two major phases, phases whose archetypal meaning may be defined in forward progression as sacrifice and creation. In addition, it is the nature of Neshamah consciousness to act as a mediating force, one that is truly transformative in bringing opposing forces into harmony. It serves especially to mediate between the powers of sacrifice and of creation, powers that can be associated as well with death and life. As such, its primary role would be to mediate between the forces of entropic death and intelligent life, transforming the death of the patterning derived from past causes into the potential for creative redirection in conformity to a vision of final purpose. It is this process that defines the Transformative Moment, which is the essence of the sixth dimension identified with the World to Come and Neshamah consciousness.

Not only does the seat of Neshamah consciousness mediate between the more centered stages of sacrifice and creation but also between the more extreme stages modeled on the final patterning of the fifth and sixth worlds, and in these five phases we may identify the various aspects of the moment in which one worldview becomes sacrificially transformed into another. Although not exactly parallel, these aspects bear some resemblance to Cordovero's concept of the Behinot, the aspects of the Sefirot that define the inner dynamics enabling one Sefirah to be connected to that preceding it and to emanate the next.[1] Even closer, at least with respect to the nature of past causality, is the Greek concept of the Fates: Clotho, who spun the web or thread of life; Lachesis, who measured, wove, or gave it specific form; and Atropos, who cut it. This final cutting of the web of life has been identified with death, but Atropos, like the parallel Hindu god Shiva, can also be viewed as the agent of transformation in which the sacrifice of an old pattern makes possible the genesis of higher forms.

The Transformative Moment may be said to arise with the perception of a fatal pattern to past causality. It is not simply that the source of the present can be traced to past causes, to Clotho, but that these causes are suddenly recognized to constitute a pattern, to betray the shaping hand of Lachesis. For transformation to occur, however, for Atropos to be able to cut the thread of Fate so that the death of the old can become the sacrificial agent of change, something more is required, something more than the Greek concept of Fate can yield. As many long-term Freudian analysands can avow, it is not enough to be able to recognize the sources and patterns of self-defeating behavior. To break the negative patterns that have hitherto defined one's personality, one must also have a vision of a new and better life and see how its vision can be fitted to conform to some surviving sense of one's own identity. Without such a believable envisioning of one's past identity in a new pattern, the sacrifice of past patterning will seem to be the true death of personality, and one will cling to the old patterns as to life, however negative they are now recognized to be and however beautiful the vision of future alternatives. In the transformative vision, the moment must become transparent to the near and far influences from both the past and future. As past causes are seen to constitute a past pattern, so the future pattern, the Aristotelian telos, or final cause, must be creatively specified into the new pattern of the future before past and future can meet in the mediating consciousness of that moment in which the past pattern can be sacrificed and the new pattern initiated, the Transformative Moment.

It is because no true transformation can occur without sacrifice that sacrifice has ever been recognized to be the essential gateway to the highest consciousness, and this consciousness has been identified with fire. Sacrifice and enlightenment are both associated in their essence with fire, the former consumed by it and the latter radiating it. It is fire, itself, that is the prime agent and symbol of transformation, as has long been recognized in the alchemical tradition, and its inverse relationship to sacrifice and enlightenment, engrossing the first and informing the second, suggests how enlightenment can be fueled by the power of sacrifice.

In alchemy, the transformative agent of fire is symbolized by the ascending triangle of the hexagram while its opposite, water, is symbolized by the descending triangle, a difference in which we may be able to read the distinction between Neshamah and Ruach consciousness.[2] In the first chapter we saw that the biblical "days" of creation provided both the overall bases for projecting a seven-dimensional cosmos and the specific symbolic bases for interpreting it. If the fifth day of creation may be associated with the Ruach soul of our fifth world, then this soul level would be identified with what characterizes that day, the fish, birds, and especially the flowing elements of water and air they inhabit. The Ruach dimension can thus be understood to represent the divine flow, the Way of God, or Derekh ha-Shem. Similarly, the sixth day of creation brought forth the crowning work of man: "And God said, Let us make man in our image, after our likeness and let them have dominion over the fish of the sea, and over the fowl of the air, and over the cattle, and over all the earth. . . ." (Gen. 1:26). As the association of the Ruach soul with the flowing element of water relates it to the descending triangle of the alchemical hexagram, that signifying the downward vortex of water, so the association of the Neshamah soul with the higher divine image can relate it to the ascending triangle of this alchemical symbol, that signifying the upward vortex of fire. Considered the divine soul in man, the Neshamah expresses its divine resemblance through its primary characteristic of "dominion . . . over all the earth." Thus the Neshamah dimension is that which transcends and also directs the flow of the lower Ruach dimension.

Where the Ruach soul, as a flowing mode of consciousness, is still involved with linear chronology, Neshamah consciousness involves an instantaneous apperception of interrelationships that endows their formerly disparate members with a unifying meaning, a moment of recognition momentous, indeed, for it releases the power of creation. And where Ruach consciousness is primarily concerned with attuning the self to the divine force flowing through time and nature and with joining in its direction, Neshamah consciousness differs in being self-determining, in liberating itself from the course of external determinism so that it may, in becoming its own cause, also become a determining force for the whole. In defining the four levels of Ruach power in chapter 3, it was suggested that the purely Ruach Master operates primarily through the lower two levels of creative thought and synchronicity, whereas the two more magical upper levels of transformation and creation from nothing are properly the domain of the Neshamah Master working in this world through that Ruach level of his soul still native to it. In this higher Transformative Moment of Neshamah consciousness all the prior forces of causality are severed, those transmitted through parents or the stars or the environment at birth and all the karma since built up. All their power is broken, burned up in the sacrificial fire of Neshamah consciousness. Indeed, that which must be sacrificed to its transformative power is precisely the chains of causality forged by the Nefesh soul and still influencing the intermediate Ruach level, particularly those that link cause to effect through linear time.

That this causal linkage through linear time is a function of ordinary perception may perhaps be gleaned from a study of senility. Anyone who has had contact with the senile knows that the first mental power they appear to lose is the ability to keep the experiences of a lifetime strung out on the evenly measured nodes of linear time. A phone call from a mother long dead will be thought to have occurred that morning; future appointments can no longer be kept *straight*; all the past and future become crowded into the increasingly disordered present. For whatever reason the brain's energy decreases, it would seem that the maintenance of minimal functioning requires that the sense of linear time be sacrificed. It thus appears that an enormous amount of brain power must be devoted to maintaining this sense, to forcing the curvature of space-time, as Einsteinian physics now defines it, into an unnatural straightness. One can imagine that it is with a profound sense of relief, even of glee, that the senile give up the weary task of keeping temporal events straight. But the disorientation they experience in so doing attests to their lack of operational knowledge of the sphere into which they have been thus prematurely thrust. As the Fool tells King Lear: "Thou shouldst not have been old till thou hadst been wise" (1.5.41).

What distinguishes Neshamah consciousness from senile dementia is that its liberation from linear time is accompanied by increased order rather than disorder, by a build-up of the information first defined by the linear space-time grid that can be released from this grid because of the higher perception of its patterning. In such patterning, events from near and far in both space and time are seen to overlap in meaningful configurations. In senile perception, however, the same overlapping does not yield its meaning to the containing consciousness. Such meaningfulness knocks at the doors of perception, events overlap in consciousness because of some affinity, but the affinity and its implications cannot be grasped, and the only experience is one of terror, terror at the entropy, the increasing disorder, of the only informational grid with which this shrinking consciousness is familiar, a grid stuffed with discrete entities without markers of their subtle relationships.

But Neshamah consciousness does not rest in the perception of meaningful patterning. It is ever occupied in perfecting that patterning, in tuning it into greater harmony. It does not rest in forgiving all that it can understand but, when recognizing a source of dissonance or disease, retunes and heals it. It takes in the full pattern given it in the moment and transforms any dissonant factors into new sources for the increased harmony of the whole. Where Ruach consciousness attunes itself to the larger flow, Neshamah consciousness is the tuner of the divine symphony, the higher source of the Providence whose flow constitutes the fifth dimension. It *is* the Way.

THE PATRIARCHS

Most individuals have no more than one experience in a lifetime of Neshamah consciousness, of a Transformative Moment. The Bible gives us two archetypal examples of such insightful moments of change, those of Jacob and Joseph. Together with Abraham, they form a pattern of the major personality types as given in Genesis, types whose early pattern of behavior may be chronologically defined in moral terms as: righteousness, unrighteousness, and self-righteousness. In the first instance no Transformative Moment seems to have occurred. Though God changes Abram's name to Abraham, His command—"walk before me, and be thou perfect" (Gen. 17:1)—does not require a radical reorientation of Abraham's direction since Abraham had ever been willing to follow the perfecting Way of God, a willingness only confirmed by the final testing and refining of his righteousness in the virtual sacrifice of Isaac. The cases of Jacob and Joseph are far different. In both instances we may see the hand of Providence shaping the direction of events so that imperfect behavior will be brought to a crucial moment of insight. Such an understanding of Providence is given by John Milton in *The Christian Doctrine* and it underlies his portrait of Satan in *Paradise Lost*:

> Nor does God make that will evil which was before good, but the will being already in a state of perversion, he influences it in such a manner, that out of its own wickedness it either operates good for others or, punishment for itself. . . . By this means he proves the inmost intentions of men, that is, he makes man to have a thorough insight into the latent wickedness of his own heart, that he

may either be induced thereby to forsake his sins, or if not, that he may become notorious and inexcusable. . . .[3]

Jacob's pattern was early established when, rather than being his brother's keeper, he took his birthright for the bowl of pottage that Esau thought would save his life. When he followed this by then stealing Esau's blessing, despite his hesitance about appearing a "deceiver" (Gen. 27:12), he is forced to "flee" (Gen. 27:43) from the murderous anger he has aroused in Esau's heart. During his journey to Laban, he awakes from the dream of an angelic ladder connecting earth and heaven with the startled recognition: "Surely the Lord is in this place; and I knew it not" (Gen. 28:16). But he calms his fear by vowing to return to God a tenth of all He had promised to give him in his dream.

His subsequent behavior with Laban shows, however, that he was insufficiently changed by the divine vision he had experienced despite the empowerment it had imparted to him. Though Laban is just as deceptive as Jacob, changing brides and wages on him without excuse, the fact remains that through magical use of the rods Jacob has so enriched himself at the expense of Laban that Laban's sons are moved to say, "Jacob hath taken away all that was our father's; and of that which was our father's hath he gotten all this glory" (Gen. 31:1). His response to the outrage of Laban's family is the same as it had earlier been to that of Esau, for "Jacob stole away unawares to Laban the Syrian, in that he told him not that he fled" (Gen. 31:20).

Negotiating a truce with the pursuing Laban that bars Jacob's return to Laban without "harm" (Gen. 31:52), he is suddenly confronted with the approaching army of Esau. His past behavior catching up with him as he finds himself unable to go either forward or back, he suddenly gains a transformative insight into the unworthiness of his character, and he prays to God for deliverance not only from his enemies but from his own past self: "I am not worthy of the least of all the mercies, and of all the truth, which thou hast showed unto thy servant. . . . Deliver me, I pray thee" (Gen. 32:10–11). Where before he had felt himself entitled to whatever he could get and by whatever means, whether from Esau, from Laban, or from God, his insight into the fundamental dependence of all his power upon a source beyond himself initiates a purgative process that finally proves redemptive. He must now wrestle the night with the personification of the liabilities his behavior has incurred, and he can prevail over this angel of Providential judgment because of his prior vision of his true cosmic position. His name transformed to Israel as his nature is to righteousness, he can now make peace with his brother and see God in his former enemy's face: "I have seen thy face, as though I had seen the face of God" (Gen. 33:10).

Where Jacob had taken advantage of others to enrich himself and thus gained their enmity, Joseph is always careful to align himself with the source of immediate power within his sphere, with his father Jacob, his master Potiphar, and finally with Pharaoh. The status and riches he thus gains are, however, always at the expense of others whose fury he arouses. The pattern of Joseph's behavior seems to have been set by the early choice he made between his father's favoritism and his brothers' acceptance. Rather than placating their jealousy, "Joseph brought unto his father their evil report" (Gen. 37:2). Still worse, he had a dream which he interpreted to mean that they will bow down to him, and he "told it his brethren: and they hated him yet the more" (Gen. 37:5). When Jacob now reinforces this pattern by sending him to spy on his brothers, they respond to his superior gifts and airs by conspiring to kill "this dreamer" (Gen. 37:19). As he had coped with their enmity by dreaming of his eventual triumph over them, so does the presumption of this proclaimed dream become a new source of their escalating anger. They strip Joseph of the hated, multicolored coat, symbol of their father's favoritism, and then, rather than slaying him, sell him into slavery for their own profit and his greater degradation.

At the slavemaster's house, he follows his previous pattern of supporting power with both fidelity and skill until Potiphar makes him "overseer over his house" (Gen. 39:4). When he is again confronted with a choice between power and an even greater personal intimacy than that of fraternity, he resists the desires of Potiphar's wife on the double basis of his fidelity to her husband and to the image of his own righteousness: "how can I do this great wickedness, and sin against God?" (Gen. 39:9). His self-righteousness so enrages her that she condemns him to her husband for precisely what he had refused to do and has him cast into prison.

But he still does not recognize the pattern of his own behavior that arouses such retributive anger: "For indeed I was stolen away out of the land of the Hebrews: and here also have I done nothing that they should put me into the dungeon" (Gen. 40:15). Yet even in the dungeon he is sufficiently forward in using his talent for dream interpretation and asking that it be brought to Pharaoh's attention that he is finally rewarded. Once before Pharaoh, he is quick not only to interpret his dreams but to suggest that "Pharaoh look out a man discreet and wise, and set him over the land of Egypt" (Gen. 41:33). Again he builds his position on the greater prosperity of his power source, using the grain reserves in his keeping to reduce the famished Egyptians to little more than serfs to Pharaoh upon what was formerly their own land and enormously increasing and consolidating Pharaoh's power.

It is only when Joseph's own famine-stricken brethren are bowed down before him that he begins to suffer from any self-conflict: "And Joseph remembered the dreams which he dreamed of them, and said unto them, Ye are spies. . . . And he turned himself about from them, and wept; and returned to them again, and communed with them, and took from them Simeon, and bound him before their eyes" (Gen. 42:9, 24). The fulfillment of his dream fills him first with vindictiveness and then with sorrow at what he cannot refrain from doing, his private weeping unable to keep him from still acting vindictively toward his brothers. Even when his mother's son Benjamin is finally before him, "Joseph made haste; for his bowels did yearn upon his brother: and he sought where to weep; and he entered into his chamber, and wept there. And he washed his face, and went out, and refrained himself" (Gen. 43:30–31). After continuing his self-punishing vindictiveness against his brothers through yet other maneuvers, he is finally brought to a trans-formative insight into his self-defeating course by Judah's prayer that he spare Jacob any further grief.[4] He now recognizes that his superior gifts were given him not that others should bow down to him but that he might deliver those less gifted than himself: "Now therefore be not grieved, nor angry with yourselves, that ye sold me hither: for God did send me before you to preserve life . . . to preserve you a posterity in the earth, and to save your lives by a great deliverance" (Gen. 45:5, 7). With healing words, he sacrifices his past vindictiveness to a new vision of brotherhood under the guiding patrimony of God.

For both Jacob and Joseph the Transformative Moment to which their whole lives had been leading was one that not only recognized the part they played in relation to the whole but the way in which they were linked by this whole to other parts, that those from whom they had formerly felt alienated were in truth connected to themselves. They return from the Transformative Moment to the sense of human brotherhood under God that is the essence of the Messianic Age and of Ruach consciousness. Jacob and Joseph were both great Ruach Masters who rose to an even greater moment of transformative Ne-shamah consciousness.

From the least to the most spiritually developed, human beings do not normally have more than one such moment in a lifetime. In most cases it is called the "midlife crisis," and it operates in a manner remark-ably similar to what we have just been examining in the Genesis accounts. An individual has to come to the fulfillment of the contours of success defined by his early conditioning before he can recognize any misalignment between the goals programmed for him by his home and social environment and the true needs of his soul. The success that was supposed to guarantee happiness must, itself, turn into the source of inescapable psychological pain. Thus Jacob, programmed by Rebekah to seek power through deception, discovers that wealth cannot save him from the fearful effects of his alienation from all ties of blood; and Joseph, programmed by Jacob to seek position through a self-serving alignment with the power structure, discovers himself unable to love his brothers when he yearns for their embrace.

But as Milton has shown, it is the nature of Providence to bring man to such a moment of confrontation with the pattern of his past as will make him have "a thorough insight into the latent wickedness of his own heart, that he may either be induced thereby to forsake his sins, or if not, that he may become notorious," in the words of *Paradise Lost*, "hard be hard'n'd, blind be blinded more" (3.200). If one resists the transformative process demanded by such insight, the unrewarding patterns to which one would still cling become ever more involuted and rigid, a protective armor that prevents all freedom and grace of movement. In so doing, Milton's Satan discovers that now, and only now, "all Good to me is lost" (4.109). Because it nonetheless proves easier for most to cling to familiar patterns, however self-defeating, Jacob and Joseph can be accounted heroes of the spiritual Way for allowing such insight to work a transformative change on their souls. If their stories become less "interesting" from this point on, it may well be because the last seventy or so years of their lives were spent on the higher dimension of Neshamah consciousness.

To have one's consciousness ever focused on the Transformative Moment is beyond the capacity of almost all living masters. The immediate problems of ministering to their flocks are ever pulling them down to the level of Ruach consciousness at which such earthly problems must be handled. And this is even truer for those of more modest spiritual development. Most function on a sustaining level of Ruach consciousness whose Way is illuminated only by intermittent moments of transformative insight. For those operating more continuously on the Neshamah dimension of mastery, the term that is most appropriate in the Jewish tradition is *tzaddik*.

This term is applied most significantly to Abraham: "And he believed in the Lord; and he counted it to him for righteousness [*tzedakah*]" (Gen. 15:6). God further defines the nature of such a Tzaddik when He says of Abraham: "he is a prophet, and he shall pray for thee, and thou shalt live" (Gen. 20:7). Only the Tzaddik is a true prophet, empowered to *determine* the course of Providence. That the Tzaddik's nature is essentially tuned to the Neshamah dimension is shown by Abraham's eagerness to drop everything for moments of divine contact. When God appeared to Abraham in the form of three men, "he ran to meet them. . . . hastened into the tent unto Sarah, and said, Make ready quickly three measures of fine meal . . . ran unto the herd, and fetched a calf tender and good, and . . . hasted to dress it" (Gen. 18: 2–7).

But it is the courage to believe that is tested most crucially in the story of Abraham. At the age of seventy-five, the childless Abraham is told by the Lord: "Get thee out of thy country, and from thy kindred, and from thy father's house, unto a land that I will show thee: And I will make of thee a great nation. . . . [A]nd in thee shall all families of the earth be blessed" (Gen. 12:1–3). And Abraham leaves his house, following the Lord's voice for many years without question. It is only on the fourth reiteration of the promise that Abraham voices his perplexity: "the word of the Lord came unto Abram in a vision, saying, Fear not, Abram: I am thy shield, and thy exceeding great reward. And Abram said, Lord God, what wilt thou give me, seeing I go childless" (Gen. 15:1–2). If he "laughed" (Gen. 17:17) at the prospect of fathering a child at one hundred years of age, he still waits patiently, as he has for twenty-five years, for the promised birth.

A more severe test is posed when God admits him to His counsel concerning the fate of Sodom and Gomorrah. In the conflict this arouses between his compassion and faith, it is with the desire to resolve his doubt concerning God's justice that Abraham questions the Lord: "Wilt thou also destroy the righteous with the wicked. . . . [T]hat be far from thee: Shall not the Judge of all the earth do right" (Gen. 18: 23, 25). Abraham questions God's purposes not to undermine but to support his faith on a yet higher level of understanding. Though Abraham is only left with the assurance that the ten righteous for which he had bargained would save those cities, God's true though harsh justice is never biblically in doubt since there proves to be only one righteous man, Lot, in the cities of the plain and God has made provision to deliver him and his family.

The final and most severe test comes some years after the miraculous birth when God commands him to make a burnt offering of the child of promise, "thine only son Isaac, whom thou lovest" (Gen. 22:2). Obedience to this demand not only touches his deepest affections but would destroy the seed of the covenant and God's promise to man. Caught in this tragic conflict of command and promise, both of which demand his faith, Abraham rises above the temptation to doubt God's purposes. We may today fault Abraham for not being as good a father as he is a true believer, for not pleading with God for his son's life, that with wordless alacrity, "he rose up early in the morning" (22:3), obedient to the direct command of God and with abiding faith that God will somehow reveal His truth, however it be that He "provide himself a lamb for a burnt offering" (Gen. 22:8). For though he may question divine decrees until satisfied with their justice, as with Sodom and Gomorrah, he unquestioningly obeys all direct divine commands,[5] at whatever cost to his human relationships and filial feelings, from the first direction to leave his father's house to the final test that converts sacrifice into blessing: "because thou hast . . . not withheld thy son. . . . in thy seed shall all the nations of the earth be blessed" (Gen. 22:16, 18). If man fell through Adam's disobedience, it is through Abraham's patient yet ever eager obedience, supported by his pious questioning of his doubts, that the promise of God's blessing is restored to all mankind. In this new covenant of grace, Abraham becomes the true father of mankind in its quest for the redemptive life.

In contrast to the heroic form of the Tzaddik personified by Abraham, it is in the more humble form of his son Isaac that we may find an even truer paradigm of the Tzaddik and of Neshamah consciousness. For Isaac's whole life is devoted to transforming the dread of sacrifice that afflicted his youth into the power of blessing that informs his old age. This task seems to have been aided by two factors, the first of which is his primary association with female consciousness. It is his mother who seems to have healed him from the sacrificial devotions of his father, and it seems to have been impossible for Isaac to fill her place until after her death: "And Isaac brought her into his mother Sarah's tent, and took Rebekah, and she became his wife; and he loved her: and Isaac was comforted after his mother's death" (Gen. 24:67). The second and most important factor is that Isaac, alone of all the figures in the Bible, is mentioned as a practitioner of meditation: "And Isaac went out to meditate [*suach*] in the field at the eventide" (Gen. 24:63). Isaac comes into his own only after the death of his father, and it is significant that it is not Abraham but God who blesses him: "And it came to pass after the death of Abraham, that God blessed his son Isaac; and Isaac dwelt by the well Lahairoi" (Gen. 25:11).

It is also from the well Lahairoi, or Beer Lachai Roi, that Isaac was coming at the time mention was made of his meditative practice, the time also when he first saw Rebekah (Gen. 24:62–63). Aryeh Kaplan's analysis of *suach* meditation shows it to represent "a mental state that is very 'smooth,' ultimately calm and tranquil."[6] Kaplan's reference to a nineteenth-century interpretation of the aforementioned well is particularly interesting in this context:

> One of the later commentaries, Rabbi Meir Lebush Malbim (1809–1879), clearly states that Isaac was engaged in a classical form of meditation. Beer Lachai Roi was the place where the angel had appeared to Hagar after she and Ishmael had been driven away by Sarah, and since an angel had appeared there, this place had become a shrine. Malbim writes, "This was a holy place at the time because an angel had been seen there, and Isaac went there each afternoon to meditate (hitboded)." It is significant to note that Malbim uses the term *hitboded*, which, as we have seen, refers to the "inner isolation" of meditation.[7]

In the note on Beer Lachai Roi in his translation of the Torah, Kaplan gives the following further references: "Some say that he [Isaac] prayed there because this was where an angel had been seen (Rambam). Others maintain that he had gone to visit Hagar (*Bereshith Rabbah* 60: Rashi)."[8] Whether Isaac was drawn to the well where he was later to reside because he was being spiritually instructed by Hagar or the angel who had appeared to her, he had much to learn from the harsh experience of Hagar, sent out to die by Abraham with their son Ishmael as a sacrifice to appease his wife Sarah after the birth of Isaac and in accordance with divine command (Gen. 21:10–14). For Hagar's despair was transformed to hope by the voice of the angel telling her to "fear not" (Gen. 21:17), to strengthen her son with her hand, and to know that God would be with him (Gen. 21:18). With such knowledge, her eyes were now opened to the well of saving water in the wilderness (Gen. 21:19–20). So, too, God twice appears to Isaac with the primary message: "I will be with thee, and will bless thee" (Gen. 26:3); "fear not, for I am with thee, and will bless thee" (Gen. 26:24). And Isaac's main activity seems to be the digging of wells in the wilderness.

Even more significant is his nonbelligerence. When the first two wells he discovers are challenged, he withdraws from the possibility of conflict and only settles near the third, unchallenged well, thus peaceably finding his proper place on the divine ground of being: "For now the Lord hath made room for us, and we will be fruitful in the land" (Gen. 26:22). Where Abraham had fought a war to rescue Lot, Isaac lives at peace with all and earns the enmity of none. He is thus not only divinely blessed but becomes a force for the direction of divine blessedness, a power he reveals most forcibly in the blessing of his sons. That such sublime simplicity of being may make him vulnerable to the power machinations of his wife and son Jacob is but one of the classic signs of the Tzaddik. He is the fool of God, the man whose spirit cannot descend to the power games of the world and who continues to bless and live in amity even with those he knows to have deceived him.

It was to accomplish such a spiritual development that Isaac's soul, if not his body, had early been put through the sacrificial fire that burnt away all the dross and left him only with his saving fear of God, that reverential awe by which Jacob was later to swear as tribute to the highest consciousness he had known: "And Jacob sware by the fear of his father Isaac" (Gen. 31:53). It is to accomplish a similar development of the whole nation of Israel that it was given both hardships and law in the desert:

> And thou shalt remember all the way which the Lord thy God led thee forty years in the wilderness, to humble thee, and to prove thee, to know what was in thine heart, whether thou wouldest keep his commandments, or no. And he humbled thee, and suffered thee to hunger, and fed thee with manna, which thou knewest not, neither did thy fathers know; that he might make thee know that man doth not live by bread only, but by every word that proceedeth out of the mouth of the Lord doth man live . . . to do thee good at thy latter end. (Deut. 8:2–3, 16)

If the great biblical epic is a divine comedy, Isaac is the personification of its joy. His very name signifies laughter, the incredulous laughter of his aged parents at the divine announcement of his coming birth and the final laughter of a life twice divinely given whose sufferings were all transformed into blessing, "Gaiety transfiguring all that dread," in the words of Yeats.[9] Isaac lived another eighty years after the mixed-up blessing that would determine the fate of nations and that, after a momentary fit of trembling, he accepted and reiterated. His dim eyes must have sparkled with laughter over the absurd fitness of it all; and we can further imagine that in their silent years, Isaac, Jacob, and Joseph all meet on a high plateau like that to which Yeats's Chinese characters climb, that, like them,

> *Their eyes mid many wrinkles, their eyes*
> *Their ancient, glittering eyes, are gay.*[10]

Though Jacob and Joseph are the primal figures representing the two often divergent but sometimes converging main streams of Jewish understanding, its esoteric and exoteric traditions,[11] Abraham and Isaac represent the dual forms of the Tzaddik among the Patriarchs, the heroic and the humble, and of the two it may well be Isaac whose lack of ego marks him as its most perfected form. The most telling sign of this would be that he appears to be the least significant. For unlike the spiritual master, the Tzaddik is rarely a public figure. In other traditions, he is to be found living in caves, seeming to live on air, rarely talking or focusing on those who may come to give him food or just to sit at his feet. Though still in the flesh, he is thought to be part of the spiritual hierarchy governing the world, his consciousness wholly absorbed in this transcendental work.

THE TZADDIKIM

The *Zohar* makes reference to celestial academies into which those still alive may sometimes be admitted, as in Rabbi Hiya's vision of the deceased Rabbi Simeon in the heavenly academy:

> there appeared a host of huge winged celestial beings upon whose wings R. Simeon and his son R. Eleazar were borne aloft into the heavenly Academy. . . . R. Simeon then opened his mouth and said, "Let R. Hiya enter and behold what the Holy One, blessed be He, has prepared for the rejoicing of the righteous in the world to come. Happy is he who enters here without misgiving, and happy is he who is established as a strong pillar in the world to come.". . . A voice thereupon went forth, saying . . . "O, ye unseen celestials, ye open-eyed who sweep to and fro throughout the world, behold and see! O, ye terrestrial beings who are sunk deep in slumber, awake! Who among you laboured to turn darkness into light and bitter into sweet before you entered here?". . . Meanwhile he beheld a number of his colleagues gather round, even all the

mighty pillars of wisdom, and he saw them ascend to the heavenly
Academy, while others in turn descended. At the head of them all
he saw the chief of the winged angels, who approached him and
solemnly declared that he had heard "from behind the curtain" that
the King visits each day and remembers his gazelle which is trodden in the dust, and that at the moment He does so He strikes the
three hundred and ninety heavens so they all quake and tremble
before Him. . . . The Messiah then entered.[12]

In this rich passage, we may see the essential nature of the sixth world,
the Olam ha-Ba or World to Come. Though this world is thought to
be primarily inhabited by the righteous souls of the departed, those still
in the flesh, such as Rabbi Hiya and his human colleagues, are seen to
be freely able to ascend to and descend from the heavenly Academy.
What distinguishes these righteous souls and empowers them to make
such flights to the World to Come is that before their admittance they
have "laboured to turn darkness into light and bitter into sweet." Their
consciousness has been devoted to transforming the spiritual energies
of the earth in accordance with a heavenly model of sweetness and
light. In so doing, they become "established as a strong pillar in the
world to come" while still in the flesh and contribute to its work of
cosmic transformation.

The Olam ha-Ba has two levels, however, a disclosed form and one
hidden "behind the curtain," the Pargod. The hidden portion of this
world is the abode of the Holy One, blessed be He, and of ultimate
knowledge, the disclosed portion contains the discrete entities of the
righteous souls and is visited by the presiding authority of the Messianic
King, who "puts his seal on all the expositions that issue from the
mouths of the teachers."[13] Thus the work of the Academy is to expound
the implications of the ultimate truth at a lower order of particularity,
and these sealed explications become the force of Providence as it functions in the material world. These are not, however, linear explications
but follow the model of consciousness provided by the celestial

Messiah, a moment that sets the heavens trembling. The striking of the heavens by the force of consciousness enables that consciousness to hear its pitch and harmony or disharmony and to retune it to resonate at its own frequency. As we shall soon see, this is probably the most satisfactory model for the functioning of cosmic consciousness.

This Zoharic passage has given us models both of the highest cosmic consciousness and of the individuals, living and dead, who participate in it. Of its living members the Jewish tradition has a legend, that of the thirty-six just men who must be alive at any one time to ensure the survival of the world. Although some may appear in the world, usually in the form of victims and fools, more are to be found in various hermitages: caves, monasteries, ashrams, and yeshivas. These centers of spiritual energy may not appear to be contributing anything to the solution of the world's problems, but it may well be the subtle energies they are transmitting that have thus far saved the world from the catastrophic build-up of negative forces being transmitted by the agents of worldly power. Whether the monks and other spiritual recluses of the world will be sufficient to combat the escalating danger such forces of mechanistic power pose for our own time is another question. To combat the build-up of man-made nuclear and electromagnetic power, it may be necessary for the world to experience a massive generation of spiritual power such as has never been known before, a general transmission of the traditions of the masters to an inspired populace that will transform it into a spiritual army fit to successfully wage the apocalyptic war of Gog and Magog, the wholly spiritual warfare between the sons of light and darkness that will usher in the Messianic Age. Then will the divine covenant with Isaac be fulfilled: "in thy seed shall all the nations of the earth be blessed" (Gen. 26:4). Then will the way of the meek prosper, the sound of laughter be heard on high, and the world become the mirror of transformative consciousness.

To move from the way of Jacob and Joseph to that of Isaac, from the Transformative Moment that forces itself Providentially upon the consciousness to that which is the product of one's conscious direction and discipline, it is best to follow Isaac's model of meditative practice. To engage in *suach* meditation, to bring one's soul into a state of cosmic harmony, can enable the soul to recognize its true vibration. With this knowledge, it can then make any moment of stress transformative. Focusing on the source of the stress and then on its affinities, those other instances that resonate with it to form a pattern, one can then compare the tenor of this information with the pure tone of one's soul and retune the affective content of the moment into harmony with it through the creative projection of a new pattern to replace the old. Where such moments may at first be prolonged, with sufficient training and conscious alertness they can become instantaneous and continuously transformative of the quality of one's own life.

As consciousness becomes thus transformed, so does it become extended, the stress upon it no longer arising from the private life but from the disharmony of the world, and its primary activity becomes one of retuning the spiritual energies of this world, of focusing on the source of this disharmony and sending out a spiritual beam to transform its negativity and bring it into harmony with the whole. As it comes to function more and more on this cosmic dimension, so does it begin to encounter the energies of other souls engaged in the same work of cosmic transformation, sometimes on the physical plane but more often on completely spiritual planes, and to join with them in what has been called "the spiritual hierarchy of the world." And as it becomes more and more engaged in this work, in response both to the cosmic appeal it receives for its particular contribution and the still greater appeal of the ecstasy it experiences in bringing its extended consciousness into harmony, it starts to spend more and more of its earth time so engaged and needs to disengage itself progressively from the worldly demands upon its time, a process of progressive simplification of lifestyle that may well end with withdrawal to a Himalayan cave. At this point there is little to distinguish the consciousness of a Neshamah Master from the cosmic consciousness of which it is a part, and we can now turn from the human to the divine polarity of the sixth world.

THE PARTZUFIM

The Kabbalah distinguishes three main levels of the divine associated with the Sefirot of Keter, Tiferet, and Malkhut on the Tree of Life Diagram. Associated with Keter is the transcendent form known as Ein Sof, the Unlimited One, who is wholly beyond the cosmos. Associated with Malkhut is the form of divine immanence variously termed the Shekhinah or the Partzuf of the Nukvah and identified with the divine femininity. Finally, there is the association of Tiferet with an intermediate form of divine transcendence operating within the cosmos, which is variously termed the Holy One, Blessed be He, and the Partzuf of Ze'ir Anpin, and which is identified with the divine masculinity. The Kabbalah defines five such Partzufim: the uppermost is Arikh Anpin (the Long Face), viewed either as the equivalent of Ein Sof or just below it but like it wholly transcendent and identified with Keter; the parental Partzufim of Abba (Father) and Imma (Mother) derived from Arikh Anpin and identified with the Sefirot of Chokhmah and Binah, respectively; Ze'ir Anpin (the Short Face), who represents the divine personality of the son, is identified with the six Sefirot from Chesed to Yesod; and the Nukvah (Female), the sister and bride of Ze'ir Anpin, is identified with the Sefirot of Malkhut. The lower female Partzuf, also identified with the indwelling spirit of God known as the Shekhinah, may be understood to be present in the human soul and to be particularly realized within the consciousness of the Neshamah Masters who form the supernal Knesset Yisrael. But it is with the form of cosmic transcendence signified by the terms the Holy One, Blessed be He,[14] or Ze'ir Anpin that we shall be primarily concerned in the following attempt to understand the nature of cosmic consciousness.

The following discussion will focus on the consciousness of the prime divine personality, that of Ze'ir Anpin, and this for a few reasons. As was shown in the final section of chapter 1, it is to him that the Lurianic concepts of the Shevirah (Breaking of the Vessels) and Tikkun (Reconfiguration) most apply, since it was his vessels alone that were broken and he alone who is twice-born;[15] thus it is possible to see in this divine history of Fall and Reconfiguration a model for man's own spiritual perfection. It is also he in whose consciousness the power of Providence is primarily lodged. Finally, it is he who can be most closely associated with that celestial Messiah of the *Zohar* whose consciousness resonates the heavens and who is actively engaged with the world of dust, a portrayal that may serve as a model for the way in which Providence functions. To understand the workings of Providence, this most characteristic operation of Neshamah consciousness on both the divine and human planes, we shall have to pay particular attention, therefore, to the Partzuf who most resembles man, Ze'ir Anpin; and the remainder of this chapter will explore the nature of his consciousness.

We should first conceive of the consciousness governing the cosmic environment of our earth as one in which the myriad forces affecting it are perceived in their essential resonant form. The more harmonious their combined vibrational pattern may be, the more ecstatic is the rejoicing of the perceiving consciousness, and the more dissonant its sound, the more is its ecstasy impaired. For the sixth dimension is essentially one of sound, a world of information and joy communicated to the perceiving consciousness through the higher sense of hearing. It was to reach this highest development of spirit that Israel has been called, in the Sh'ma, to "hear."

In the tradition of Yoga, the entrance to this dimension is known as *nadaloka*. This "domain of celestial melodies" is described at length by Baba Muktananda in the autobiography of his spiritual awakening:

> these rapturous sounds do not originate in the ear but in the *akasha* or *sahasrar*. . . . The *nada* is indeed the Absolute Reality. It forms a kind of sound-body of Sri Guru Nityananda. It is the vibrating current, set in motion by Kundalini. About the *nada,* the scriptures say: God originally manifested Himself as sound. I perceived God with these sounds. They represented the last phase of my dynamic Kundalini awakening. Thus while hearing *nada,* my mind would converge on its source. I witnessed the center which, activated by

nada, emits divine sparks. All my senses were drawn towards it. Even my tongue rushed in that very direction. . . . I felt as if a gentle fire were burning in my body. Sometimes a tiny drop of nectar dripped from the upper *akasha*. While enjoying these unearthly melodies and knowing that they are *Shabda-Brahman*, I directly experienced It in them. My dynamic Kundalini felt delighted on meeting Her husband in the form of *nada*. The currents of Her joy flowed through my entire body. . . . As the waves of *nada* played within me, my mind also became sharp and agile. . . . I began to comprehend mysterious matters. . . . I would obtain clairvoyant vision. . . . Finally, I heard the ultimate *nada*, namely the rolling thunder, which is the most significant and powerful. When it emerges, the upper *akasha* trembles with its impact. . . . This is the *nada* which leads to *samadhi*, the goal of yoga.[16]

Baba Muktananda paints a double portrait of *nada* as both a product of his own awakening Kundalini and of her husband, who would also seem to be identified with the sound-body of his guru, Nityananda, and the divine source of creation. These sounds are also perceived as coming from "the *akasha* of *sahasrar*," the space of the crown chakra. If these *akashic* sounds can be associated with Shabda-Brahman, God in the form of sound, then it may be that the crown center of the living master functions like a radio receiver to transform vibrational information picked up from space into sound, including the linguistic communication of "mysterious matters." If this can be said for the highest subtle center of man, then a similar center may be postulated for Shabda-Brahman. Indeed, his whole body of sound can be conceived as the consciousness of such an organ of perception, that it is the medium, quite apart from molecular air, which transforms vibrations into psychic sound.

If we can now relate this Hindu conceptualization with kabbalistic cosmology, we can conceive of Ze'ir Anpin as composed of such a sound-body, the perceived sum of cosmic vibrations transformed by its sensing organ into sound. Experiencing the cosmos as his own sense body, his primary activity would be that by which Neshamah consciousness was earlier defined, the transformation of dissonance into harmony to reduce stress and multiply joy. Projecting what was earlier discussed in human terms onto a cosmic scale, one can speculate that when Ze'ir Anpin becomes conscious of a dissonant tone, he will focus in on it to determine its source and then send a signal back on the same beam that will carry the harmonious tone to this source.

If this source of dissonance is human, the signal would probably be retranslated into information, incontrovertible proof of some truth that confounds all of such a person's preconceptions. He has now been brought to a Transformative Moment in which he must either bring his life into harmony with this new truth or find his life becoming increasingly dissonant because of the persistence of the supernal tone at odds with his own. This, in brief, is a model of how Providence may be said to work upon an individual. If the human transforms his consciousness and begins to be a source of harmony, this will increase the harmony of the whole and contribute to its consciousness of joy. If he does not, Ze'ir Anpin would need to increase the power of his own corrective tone both to increase the pressure on its recipient and also to drown out its influence on his sound-body, a process that may end with the destruction of the inharmonious source, be it an individual or a whole society.

When the societies on earth are in harmony both with their mother planet and with the cosmic source of their own transcendence, then earth and heaven experience a cosmic Yichud, the coupling of Ze'ir Anpin and the Nukvah. Baba Muktananda described such a joyous union within his own body of the divine Kundalini within with "her husband" beyond, and it seems clear that such a coupling of the earthly and heavenly can take place in and through the consciousness of the righteous at their most exalted moments, particularly during prayer.

The Partzuf of the Nukvah is identified with the Sefirah Malkhut and represents both the earthly terminus of the process of cosmic emanation and the ground of the subliming process of the Tikkun. Like the

Greek goddess Gaia, she is the Partzuf who may be said to ensoul the earth and give it the capacity for balancing its energies. And she has two husbands, man and the heavenly Partzuf of Ze'ir Anpin. It is only man's good husbanding of her natural resources that can place her in a state of harmonious receptivity to cosmic influence; chemical, electromagnetic, and nuclear pollutants block her responsiveness, the raising of her "female waters." Ze'ir Anpin, the soul of the surrounding cosmic environment, must for his part also be brought into a state of harmony before he can engage in Yichud with his mate, the soul of the earth. As the earth is affected by the physical pollutants resulting from man's sudden industrial and post-industrial evolution, so are the more subtle surrounding realms affected by the mental energies man puts forth, the misdirected individualism whose physical manifestation has been in such environmental pollution. Human evolution so out of harmony with its own world can only add a source of increasing dissonance to the natural cosmic harmony and divorce the earth and its fate from the larger sphere in which it revolves. But when human societies were in harmony with the welfare of the earth and responsive to higher cosmic influence, then heaven and earth met in an embrace that released a tremendous burst of creative power, a sublime knowledge that could rear pyramids, cathedrals, and a holy nation in the desert.

While the embrace of earth and heaven can be taken metaphorically, it is also valuable to respect the pervasive understanding of all spiritual traditions that such metaphors are pointing to deeper truths about reality, that there are, indeed, fields of conscious energies, variously called gods and goddesses or Partzufim, that meet in ecstatic embrace when they come into a state of harmony with themselves and each other. And if such interpenetration and sharing of energies becomes both possible and pleasurable, then in such Yichud we may see the essential motivation and reward for the constant preoccupation of such overlapping fields of cosmic consciousness with the transformation of discord into harmony. As above, so below. For the highest evolution of the soul involves just such a Yichud of its finite and infinite aspects as has traditionally been conveyed through the Throne vision, that source of the Jewish mystical tradition with which chapter 5 will both begin and end its comprehensive revisioning of the multileveled soul. The present chapter has explored the sixth dimension of Neshamah consciousness in both its human and divine aspects, and its culminating image of an embracing heaven and earth is one to which we will return at the end of the final chapter, an embrace that will finally include the fully realized soul.

5

THE SIX PATHS
TO DIVINE KNOWLEDGE

THE SIX PATHS TO ENLIGHTENMENT
AS GRADES OF THE SOUL

We come now to a kabbalistic model for transpersonal psychology reaching finally to the highest levels of the soul. And we shall see how this model can be correlated both with what I have elsewhere called "the secret doctrine of the son," the doctrine I have shown to be at the heart of the Jewish mystical tradition,[1] and also with six paths to divine knowledge, analyses that should shed new light on each of the paths forming an ascending ladder of spiritual development: the paths of sex, love, power, knowledge, holiness, and unification. The whole should provide an overview of the entire process of spiritual evolution, one detailing the birthing of that androgynous "son" who can unite in its own divine personality the finite and the infinite.

Let us begin by looking again at an abbreviated form of the primary definition of the soul given in the *Zohar*, a definition that distinguishes a lower and an upper triad of soul levels. "Three names has the soul of man: *nefesh, ruah, neshamah.* They are all comprised one within the other . . . for all three are one, forming one whole, united in a mystical bond, according to the prototype above, in which *nefesh, ruah,* and

229

neshamah constitute together one totality."[2] In this Zoharic model, the first three levels relate to the human forms of the Nefesh, Ruach, and Neshamah soul levels and the last three to their supernal forms, all six finally constituting "one totality." With these initial identifications, we can further place the five soul levels of the later Kabbalah on our model. Thus to the first three levels of the *Zohar*—the first level identified with the Nefesh soul, the second level with the Ruach soul, and the third level with the Neshamah soul—the fourth level could now be further identified with the Chayah soul, a level not previously treated, which would leave the fifth and sixth Zoharic levels for identification with the Yechidah soul, a double identification that will later be clarified.

To begin to understand how these six spiritual levels can also provide paths to mystical knowledge, we should now return to the source of the entire Jewish mystical tradition, Ezekiel's Throne vision:

> Now it came to pass . . . that the heavens were opened, and I saw visions of God. . . . And I looked and, behold, a whirlwind came out of the north, a great cloud, and a fire infolding itself, and a brightness was about it. . . . [O]ut of the midst thereof came the likeness of four living creatures. And this was their appearance; they had the likeness of a man. And every one had four faces. . . . As for the likeness of their faces, they four had the face of a man, and the face of a lion, on the right side and they four had the face of an ox on the left side; they four also had the face of an eagle. . . . Now as I beheld the living creatures, behold one wheel upon the earth by the living creatures, with his four faces. . . . And when the living creatures went, the wheels went by them. . . . [F]or the spirit of the living creature was in the wheels. . . . And above the firmament that was over their heads was the likeness of a throne, as the appearance of a sapphire stone: and upon the likeness of the throne was the likeness as the appearance of a man above upon it. . . . This was the appearance of the likeness of the glory of the Lord. And when I

saw it, I fell upon my face, and I heard a voice of one that spake. And he said unto me, Son of man, stand upon thy feet, and I will speak unto thee. And the spirit entered into me when he spake unto me, and set me upon my feet. . . . . (Ezekiel 1:1, 4, 5, 10, 15, 21, 22, 26, 28; 5:1, 2)[3]

As shown in chapter 1, the chariot (Merkabah) envisioned by Ezekiel has four levels, later correlated with the four worlds of the Kabbalah, those of the wheels, the living creatures (Chayot), the firmament, and the divine glory (Kavod) in "the likeness as the appearance of a man above upon" a "throne." We shall return to the seer, called "son of man" (Ben Adam) many times in his book, and his vision of glorified man on the Throne. But first we should study the faces of the Chayot, which we have not previously considered.

The four Chayot each have four faces: the face of an ox, of a lion, of an eagle, and of man. These four faces form the basis of the ancient esoteric science of morphology, more commonly known as physiognomy, the practice of interpreting human character from facial features, which has undergone something of a renaissance in French medical circles as well as in Israel and has also come to the United States.[4] This science or art associates the four facial types of Ezekiel's Chayot with the four "humors" (bodily fluids) or temperaments of ancient medicine. The ox, whose category is expanded to include the uncastrated form of the adult bovine male, the bull, is associated primarily with the lymphatic system and the phlegmatic temperament; the lion is associated with the blood and the sanguine (optimistic) temperament; the eagle, which had been associated with the black bile and melancholic temperament, is now associated with the electrical system and nervous temperament, and the humanoid face is associated with the yellow bile and choleric (angry) temperament.

What is most interesting about these identifications is that the animal faces so arranged seem to represent a succession of psychic conditions similar to those of the lower three soul levels. That is, the ox-faced signifier of lymphatic dominance in the phlegmatic type would seem to be related to the Nefesh soul level insofar as it defines the animal level of instinctive functioning, the lymphatic system being associated in part with the autonomic functions of digestion and elimination, with a phlegmatic chewing of the cud, as it were. In its further association with the bull it would also signify the instinctual responses of sexuality and the whole range of sensual experience. The leonine face may similarly be associated with the predominantly heart level of the Ruach soul since its humor is that of the blood, a correspondence that has entered the folk consciousness in the concept of the lionhearted. Finally, the eagle face, identified with the electrical-nervous system associated with cerebral functioning, would seem to correspond to the Neshamah soul, the highest, predominantly mental body that, like the eagle, soars upward.

A final point about the Chayot faces is that the humanoid face is identified with the bilious or choleric personality, that characterized by a quick or short temper. This is interesting because such short temper may also be considered the defining characteristic of Ze'ir Anpin, the divine personality (Partzuf) of the son. For the name Ze'ir Anpin literally means "short face," and it has traditionally been taken to suggest short temper. The Fall of man is also kabbalistically explained by human impatience, by a premature eating of the fruit on the sixth rather than the seventh day. Thus the lowest level of the three upper states of spiritual development—that represented by the human face of the Chayot—is that of choleric man, associated both with the Fall of Supernal Adam and his partial reconstitution as Ze'ir Anpin.

The particular animals appearing in Ezekiel's Chayot are remarkably appropriate to the lower three soul levels with which they have just been correlated, and the evolution through these soul levels can be further illuminated by observing additional aspects of these animals, particularly as related to the tradition of the Hebrew Temple. We may even regard the first three faces as representatives of the guiding intelligence informing both these animal species and soul levels. The first Chayah may thus be viewed as embodying the Nefesh capacities for survival and reproduction on the instinctual level epitomized by the ox or bull, the animal class of cattle that, in sacrificial form, provides the lowest level of communion with the divine. The second Chayah would similarly embody the Ruach capacities for courage, liveliness, and dominance, heart qualities showing an evolution of the emotions well epitomized by the lion, that king of the wild animals whose reflection of the divine freedom and grace has led to its becoming the emblem of Judah and so of the surviving Community of Israel. The third Chayah would finally embody the Neshamah capacity for divine transcendence or salvation in the functional definition of flight epitomized by the eagle. As the bull-ox is associated with the sacrifices Israel is to offer to God and the lion is identified with the collective soul of Israel, so can the eagle be identified with the God of Israel: "Ye have seen what I did unto the Egyptians, and how I bare you on eagles' wings, and brought you unto myself" (Exod. 19:4). By proceeding through these three functional levels, the soul may thus be said to evolve from the level of sacrifice, to that of sacrificer—embodying the ritual power of "a kingdom of priests, and an holy nation" (Exod. 19:6)—finally to emerge as the very image of the divine. So transformed into the divine image, the soul can now begin its higher evolution, represented by its human face, as it evolves into the ever more etherealized faces we are now to identify.

If we are to use the Zoharic model of six soul levels in relation to Ezekiel's Throne vision of ultimate knowledge, then we should be able to identify two further faces in this spiritual encounter to complete our proposed correlation of six Zoharic soul levels with six paths to divine knowledge. Once this problem is so posed, the solution becomes apparent. The first face must be that of the prophet, given the name "son of man" that implies God's adoption of the human Ezekiel as His son, a name that has a most significant history in relation to the prophet Daniel, the legendary Enoch, and finally Jesus. The remaining face that may be identified in Ezekiel's vision would have to be that of glorified man on the Throne. But as we saw in the first chapter, the deepest meaning of this vision of deified man by a divine son is of their identity, that Ezekiel is recognizing the man on the divine Throne to be his own higher self, that there is an identity between the seer and the seen. Thus the term *son of man* seems to signify the achievement of that enlightened state in which the mystic can recognize the divine nature of his higher self.

In the earlier treatment of Ezekiel's vision in chapter 1, a kabbalistic tradition, exemplified by Abraham Abulafia, was further noted that holds that at the highest level of mystical ascent the face one sees on the Throne will be one's own. As we also then saw, this understanding of Ezekiel's vision was already clear in the derivative visions of the prophet Daniel and the legendary figure of Enoch appearing in the fairly contemporaneous nonbiblical Book of Enoch, both of whose Throne visions include a supernal figure called the son of man, a term later angelically applied to themselves. In Enoch's vision, particularly, the son of man sitting on the Throne of Glory with the Head of Days is recognized to be his own final transfiguration in the World to Come, as it is of all the righteous who have followed his path to divine sonship.

The further development in the post-biblical period of what I have called the secret doctrine of the son occurs in such Merkabah-Hekhalot texts as 3 Enoch and the *Shi'ur Komah*, dated between the second and seventh centuries C.E., the main difference of these works from Daniel and 1 Enoch being the substitute name of Metatron given to the supernal figure earlier called the son of man. The work now known as 3 Enoch clarifies the deepest implications of Merkabah mysticism and of its kabbalistic legacy. Because of its importance for the following analysis, this text, in which Rabbi Ishmael converses mystically with Metatron, will be largely requoted:

> [IV] (1) I asked Metatron and said to him: "Why art thou called by the name of thy Creator, by seventy names? Thou art greater than all the princes, higher than all the angels . . . why do they call thee 'Youth' in the high heavens?"

(2) He answered and said to me: "Because I am Enoch, the son of Jared. . . .

(10) And because I am small and a youth among them in days, months and years, therefore they call me "Youth" (*Na'ar*).

[IX] (2) And I was raised and enlarged to the size of the length and width of the world. . . .

[X] (1) All these things the Holy One, blessed be He, made for me: He made me a Throne, similar to the Throne of Glory. . . .

[XII] (5) And He called me THE LESSER YHVH in the presence of all His heavenly household; as it is written (Ex. XXIII. 21): "For my name is in him."

[XV] (1) As soon as the Holy One, blessed be He, took me in (His) service . . . forthwith my flesh was changed into flames. . . .[5]

Though serving the Holy One, blessed be He, and seated upon a throne only "similar to the Throne of Glory," Metatron's size equals the whole of creation, he is called "THE LESSER YHVH," and he rules over all the heavenly hosts. But what makes Metatron of singular significance is the fact that he is not simply a supernatural being but the transfigured form of the biblical human figure Enoch. The former humanity of this fiery being on a heavenly "throne" is designated by the term of Youth applied to him, a covert suggestion of his sonship to that king he serves as prince, since the son of a king is a prince.

Metatron is also called Youth in the *Shi'ur Komah*. Though he is not here associated with a human son figure, his own divine sonship is suggested, as in 3 Enoch, by use of the term *na'ar*, Youth. But the *Shi'ur Komah* introduces another form of the secret doctrine of the son I have defined, that adept who has secret knowledge of the "measure of the (divine) body": "It is said that he who knows this mystery, is assured of his portion in the world to come (is assured to be a son of the world to come). . . . I [Rabbi Yishmael] and Rabbi Aquiba vouch for this, that whoever knows this measure of our Creator, and the praise of the Holy One, blessed be He, he will surely be a son of the world to come."[6] Thus the further mystery conveyed through the secret doctrine of the son is that the mystical understanding of one's higher divine self also carries with it the assurance of one's own immortality.

Scholem summarizes the dual forms of Metatron as follows:

> It is already observed in *Shi'ur Komah* that the name Metatron has two forms, "written with six letters and with seven letters." . . . The kabbalists regarded the different forms as signifying two prototypes for Metatron. They reintroduced the distinction between the various components that had been combined in the Hebrew *Book of Enoch* in their possession. They identified the seven-lettered Metatron with the Supreme emanation from the *Shekhinah*, dwelling since then in the heavenly world, while the six-lettered Metatron was Enoch, who ascended later to heaven and possesses only some of the splendor and power of the primordial Metatron.[7]

Metatron, then, can be understood both as the formerly human Enoch and his apotheosis, and both of these forms will be utilized in the following analyses.

As the Merkabah texts go back to Ezekiel's Throne vision, so does this tradition continue into the later Kabbalah, especially in the importance and special history given to the Partzuf of the son, Ze'ir Anpin. The centrality of this son figure is shown when the five Partzufim are placed on the Tree of Life Diagram, Ze'ir Anpin occupying six of the ten Sefirot on the reconfigured Tree, those from Chesed to Yesod. As it is only his six Sefirot that shatter, so does his reconstruction involve a curious second birth,[8] two factors that particularly make him a paradigm for man. Finally, his mating with the Nukvah, which is facilitated by the prayers of the righteous, may be said to generate the higher souls of these twice-born humans, a connection again being established between such human and supernal sons. But as the relationship of the human and divine sons of man is most clearly defined in the figures of Enoch and Metatron, it is these names, enshrining the Hebraic secret doctrine of the son, that will be adopted to define the fifth and sixth paths to mystical truth.

Returning to the earlier discussion of Metatron, it is clear that he has the two forms associated with the six-lettered and seven-lettered spelling of his name, the former identified with Enoch and the latter with Metatron proper. Thus the ascending Enoch may be viewed as the lower portion of Metatron associated with the cosmos, and Metatron proper as occupying a still higher place just above his Enochian self and associated primarily with the infinite light surrounding the circle of the Tzimtzum that, in Lurianic cosmology, provides the space for a finite cosmos. Together they form the seventh world of our cosmic model, whose cosmic key of the diatonic scale is particularly illuminating for its seventh world. For the correspondence of the first half of this world with the upper octave was the reason given in the first chapter to assign the outer sphere of the Tzimtzum to the border between the first and second halves of the seventh world. On the basis of this distinction, we can now identify the lower, cosmic portion of the Yechidah soul with the Enochian or six-lettered Metatron and its higher, extracosmic half with the ultimate seven-lettered form of Metatron. We earlier saw that the fourth soul level and path could be identified both with the Zoharic upper Nefesh soul and the Lurianic Chayah soul. Some overlapping should be noted, however, between the Chayah soul, as the culmination of the cosmic octave, and Enoch, as the lower half of the complete seventh world, that which both contains and transcends the cosmic sphere.

The six levels of spiritual development can thus be defined as the four Chayot and the two forms of Metatron, the first Chayah displaying its bull-ox face, the second Chayah its lion face, the third Chayah its eagle face, the fourth Chayah its human face, the fifth level, which is the lower portion of Metatron, the face of Enoch, and the sixth level the human face of the final exalted form of Metatron proper. But though such a sequence of faces can be projected, we should recognize that on the Yechidah level they may finally all be equated. On the other hand, though each of these six faces signifies a spiritual dimension that is no less perfect or cosmically required than another and must follow its own path to cosmic contribution, the six displayed faces can be more richly appreciated by viewing them as also representing one grand progression of the soul through all its dimensions, from that of the animal soul to the most exalted state of the divine Presence.

Not only does each of the Chayot have all four faces and Metatron have two forms but the Chayot and Metatron may also be taken to represent two different perspectives concerning that human personalizing of the divine in which the divine and the human are united, the Chayot representing the divine descent into the cosmos and Metatron the human ascent into the Infinite. As such they may be represented by the central Jewish symbol of such divine descent balanced with human ascent, the six-pointed Star of David. Adding this hexagram to our spherical cosmic model can further illuminate both this model and the following analyses. If we now refer back to figure 1.4, we can better imagine this hexagram as forming a horizontal cross section at the equator of the total cosmic sphere, placing ourselves before its lowest point and viewing the diagram horizontally. We can then identify its forward point with the bull-faced Chayah, the point at the lower left side with the lion-faced Chayah, the point at the upper left side with the eagle-faced Chayah, the point at the furthest position away from us with the human-faced Chayah, the point at the upper right side with the Enochian face of Metatron, and the point at the lower right side with the face of Metatron proper.

Use of this hexagram cross section can further demonstrate the relationship of the lower and upper soul triads since they are now arranged around the three axes of the hexagram. Those of the lower and upper Nefesh are connected on the vertical axis, of the lower and upper Ruach on the axis going from the lower left to the upper right, and of the lower and upper Neshamah on the axis going from the upper left to the lower right. We should also understand the human Chayot face of the upper Nefesh position to correspond to the Chayah soul as the faces of Enoch and Metatron, representing the two levels of the Yechidah soul, correspond to the axis positions of the upper Ruach and upper Neshamah levels, all these levels being finally understood to be retained in the all-encompassing perfection of the Yechidah soul.

Viewing each of these soul levels as representative of a separate but equal path to ultimate gnosis can invest their individual faces with new symbolic import. The first, which will hereafter be identified with the bull rather than the ox, would define the path of the senses to carnal "knowledge," a path epitomized by sexual ecstasy. The lion face can similarly be identified with the path of the heart, a path culminating in the beatitude of love. And the eagle face can be identified with the spiritual path of power, the path of mastery by which the spirit can prevail. Of the three remaining human faces, the identification of the human face of the Chayot with the fourth path of cognitive knowledge, with the ecstasy of insight, is especially appropriate to its position at the upper point of the vertical axis, whose lower point was seen to define carnal knowledge. Similarly, the fifth path of holiness, that which can now be identified with the human face of Enoch, may be considered the higher resonance of the second path on its axis, ultimately that of holy love, both characterized by a selflessness that may be considered archetypally feminine. And the sixth and final path of unification, now identified with the human face of Metatron, shares with the lower third path of power on its axis the dominating power of the purified self, a quality archetypally masculine.

But since the fourth path is also being identified with the Lurianic Chayah soul, its association with the concept of life may also relate it to the archetypal associations of the other two axes just given, as the life resulting from their symbolically "sexual" interaction. In the Lurianic form of the Tree of Life Diagram, its one large equilateral triangle connects the Sefirot of Chokhmah, symbolizing the Partzuf of Abba (Father), Binah, symbolizing the Partzuf of Imma (Mother), and Tiferet, symbolizing the Partzuf of their son, Ze'ir Anpin. In the same way, one can view the higher levels of the present three axes, in descending order, as symbolizing the same father, mother, and son.

These six faces have now been associated both with six human paths to divine knowledge and with soul levels, and both associations will continue to inform the following analyses. The previous distinction between three animal and three human faces could thus be reinterpreted as the distinction between three human soul levels and the witnessing consciousness of the three divine levels linked to them, a further implication being that the lower triad of soul levels is that at which the human soul is still connected with the prior level of animal evolution while the upper triad represents the human potential for ultimate connection with the divine.

Finally, this model of the soul can be defined as comprising two divisions. The first would consist both of the lower animal faces and human soul levels, which may be arranged on the forward and left half of the cosmic circumference, with the upper human faces and divine soul levels arranged on its back and right side, each of these faces appropriately placed in this model on the six points of an inscribed Jewish star. As this hexagram model can first be divided into these primarily left and right sides, so can it be divided a second way into the three hierarchical levels defined by its axes. The six faces of this soul model may thus be associated with the two main distinctions in modern theories of consciousness and the brain, that which distinguishes faculties into a right and left side of the brain and that which distinguishes three ascending levels of brain evolution, those of the reptilian brain bulb, of the mammalian limbic brain, and of the human neocortex. Our six faces, so arranged and understood, would seem to offer, then, a complete model of transpersonal human consciousness, one that may also be said to contain six separate but related pathways to knowledge that it is the task of Yechidah consciousness both to allow and to orchestrate.

Though the five Lurianic soul levels, synthesized in this model with the six Zoharic levels, are hierarchically ranked, what distinguishes the

Yechidah soul from all of the soul's lower levels is the virtual equality among its various levels and sides of consciousness. Thus it is only at the highest level of the Yechidah soul that the full human potential can be both articulated and modeled. But it is not until we arrive at the final section of this chapter that we shall consider the Yechidah soul as such an independent entity. In the five intervening sections, we shall be following the ever higher pathways to knowledge of the divine taken by the soul in the course of its evolution. It is nonetheless true to say that each of these paths does arrive at the same divine knowledge, however different the garments in which it is clothed by the different organs through which it is perceived, garments through which God may be perceived as generative, loving, all-powerful, all-knowing, holy, and One. What we shall be exploring, then, are but different encodings of the same knowledge as apprehended by the senses, the emotions, and the mind at both their lower and higher levels of development. In fact, as we shall next see, the whole of this knowledge is not only contained in the first of these paths but can best be modeled by it.

THE SEXUAL PATH OF THE BULL

Concerning the first, sexual path to divine knowledge, the Kabbalah has much to say. Nor should what it says be viewed as only symbolic. From the Song of Songs, through Luria, to the Baal Shem Tov, the mystical tradition of Judaism has taught the way in which sexual union can be lifted into a path of ultimate salvation and knowledge. This involves the drawing of higher spiritual energies into the sexual act both through its ideal placement within the sanctifying context of the Sabbath and through a proper understanding of the preliminary mystery of the kiss, the point at which we shall also begin this analysis.

The Song of Songs begins: "Let him kiss me with the kisses of his mouth" (1:2). This mystery is explained at length in chapter 2 of the "Sha'ar ha-Kelalim," the introductory section to the *Eitz Chayyim*, which is the chief work of Lurianic cosmology compiled by Chayyim

Vital, with respect to the first mental conception of Ze'ir Anpin as a Partzuf composed of six Sefirot:

> When Abba and Imma cohabit there is also the concept of the Kiss. First Abba kisses Imma. After that Imma kisses Abba. During the kiss, Abba sucks vapor from Imma, as is known and can be observed with the faculty of sight, and likewise when Imma kisses Abba she sucks some vapor from Abba. . . . Each kiss is divided into two parts and likewise each vapor is divided into two parts in accordance with what was given and what was taken. . . . Since the kisses and vapors are doubled one Neshamah can come into another Neshamah as this comes from the kiss. Likewise one Ruach can go into another Ruach for they come from the vapors. . . . Thus we have explained the concept of the six Sefirot of Ze'ir Anpin, the origin of their roots and how they came into being.[9]

Most important is the reference to the vapor sucked from each during the act of kissing, a vapor that the author claims "is known and can be observed with the faculty of sight." A similar claim to perceiving such a soul vapor is made by Marlowe's Doctor Faustus in his famous speech to Helen of Troy:

> *Sweet Helen, make me immortal with a kiss.—*
> *Her lips sucks forth my soul; see where it flies!—*
> *Come, Helen, come, give me my soul again.*
> *Here will I dwell, for Heaven be in these lips,*
> *And all is dross that is not Helena. (5.1.96–100)*

The need for two kisses, one coming from each partner, is similarly explained by both Vital and Marlowe as necessary to complete that higher circuit of the lovers' souls through heaven. As further shown in the *Eitz Chayyim,* it is through the kisses that the Neshamah soul of each can enter that of the other and through the vapors that their

Ruach souls can do the same. Finally, it is through such kisses that the soul body of a magical child is produced, a psychic entity that embodies this spiritual union during the course of its passion and would seem to have an immortalizing power. Through such soul sensitizing and communicating kisses, the soul can enter the sensual path of the Tikkun, as the Baal Shem Tov declares: "It was revealed to me from above that the reason for the delay in the coming of the Messiah is that people do not enter the mystery of the kiss before the great loving."[10]

It is not that the whole path can be traversed through kissing alone, but that the lips are the organs through which the Neshamah energies of the crown and the Ruach energies of the heart can be aroused to participate in a sexual union and lift it above the Nefesh level into a spiritual passion. By kissing and embracing, the heads and the hearts are allowed to interpenetrate on a spiritual level before physical penetration transpires, and this permits the sexual act to take place within the larger soul bodies of the couple's conjoined souls, on a dimension in which pleasure becomes a teacher of that ultimate knowledge revealed through the path of the bull.

If the bull-faced Chayah can be so interpreted, and can be considered a necessary faculty of the completed Yechidah soul, this implies that its Tzelem, its soul body, will retain a capacity for sensual experience, earned both through its inhabiting of a physical body and spiritual purification of the Nefesh Tzelem associated with that mortal body, which can fit it for incorporation into the immortalizing Ruach and Neshamah soul bodies. And if the preceding analysis of sanctified sexuality can be admitted, then the highest form of sexual ecstasy, even when experienced in a physical body, can only be explained as a function of the higher soul bodies in whose consciousness this union is truly taking place. It follows that such a capacity for ecstatic sensual pleasure is one that the disembodied soul not only would not want to lose but is perfectly able to retain. One explanation of how spiritual bodies may so function is given by Milton, in the angel Raphael's answer to Adam on this question in *Paradise Lost*:

Let it suffice thee that thou know'st
Us happy, and without Love no happiness.
Whatever pure thou in the body enjoy'st
(And pure thou wert created) we enjoy
In eminence, and obstacle find none
Of membrane, joint, or limb, exclusive bars:
Easier than Air with Air, if Spirits embrace,
Total they mix, Union of Pure with Pure
Desiring; nor restrain'd conveyance need
As Flesh to mix with Flesh, or Soul with Soul. (8.620–29)

It is not, then, simply as metaphor that the Song of Songs was included in the biblical canon, that its "garden . . . of pomegranates" (4:12–13) was chosen as the title of Cordovero's great work of kabbalistic cosmology, that its lily introduces the *Zohar,* and that its description of the beloved King's body (5:11–16) provides the basis of the *Shi'ur Komah.* All these sources, and preeminently the Zoharic and Lurianic preoccupation with cosmic coupling and its facilitation, reveal an understanding of cosmic functioning as not exclusively but yet intrinsically sexual. It is no wonder that this Foundation (Yesod) of our Knowledge (Da'at) of the ultimate truth should be given such centrality in the esoteric traditions of most religions, for it provides the model as well as the base of all the other paths. To understand the sexual model for the division and reuniting of those cosmic energies termed masculine and feminine that would seem to be the driving force of creation, how in his deepest understanding of the Kabbalah A. E. Waite could say "the Supreme Wisdom is a Mystery of Sex,"[11] we should further explore this archetypal sexual model.

The classical form of this model is summed up by Spenser in *The Faerie Queene*:

It hath bene through all ages ever seene,
That with the praise of armes and chevalrie
The prize of beautie still hath joyned beene;

> *And that for reasons speciall privitie:*
> *For either doth on other much relie.*
> *For he me seemes most fit the faire to serve.*
> *That can her best defend from villenie;*
> *And she most fit his service doth deserve,*
> *That fairest is and from her faith will never swerve.*[12]

This model is further epitomized in Dryden's definitive words: "Happy, happy, happy pair! . . . / None but the brave deserves the fair."[13] The mutual reliance of power and beauty upon each other and of sexual generation upon their successful union is understandable once one appreciates the nature and function of each. To know why "none but the brave deserves the fair" we must first understand the meaning of *bravery,* a word best defined through the Latin derivations of its synonyms, courage and confidence, the first related to the heart and the second to the quality of being "with faith."

The Hebraic tradition of holy war is, in fact, based on this awareness that bravery in battle must spring from a heartfelt assurance of the availability of the requisite power to meet a warrior's need. Though the source of this power differs between the Hebraic and Hellenic traditions of warfare, being divine in the former case and personal in the latter, the Greek warrior must have just as much faith in his own power not to flinch in the face of danger as the Hebrew warrior does that God's power will not fail him.[14] True courage involves making just such a leap of faith that the source of one's power is reliable, that one's horse, lance, and heart will be stout enough to be victorious over the enemies without and within, the champions without that might reinforce the doubt within. Such a brave warrior will be powerful in battle and his air of self-confidence can give assurance as well of his sexual potency, the two forms of power arising from the same necessary self-assurance. If the "prize of beautie" is justly to be awarded to the brave, it is because only this quality can assure the potency that the male partner must contribute to a "happy pair."

But if the male must be archetypally strong to be sexually successful, the question remains as to why the necessary female contribution
to such successful union should archetypally be beauty, and particularly
facial beauty. When we consider the nature of such beauty, however, it
would seem to arise not only from the harmonious proportion of the
features but still more from the refinement of those features, a refinement that seems expressive of sensitivity. Indeed, a sensitive expression
can give a cast of beauty to any features, rendering them beautiful in
the eyes of the beholder. If the reward of a man's prowess is beauty, this
is largely because it promises him such a sensitive receptacle for his sexual desire as his potency deserves.

Another aspect of beauty is equally important, the power of beauty
to arouse desire. Another word for *beauty* is *attractiveness*, and this conveys beauty's mysterious power of attraction. As Pope puts it, "beauty
draws us with a single hair."[15] And Marlowe attests to the mystery of its
power when he says:

> *If all the pens that ever poets held*
>
> .   .   .   .
>
> *. . . combin'd in beauty's worthiness,*
> *Yet should there hover in their restless heads*
> *One thought, one grace, one wonder, at the least,*
> *Which into words no virtue can digest.*[16]

Beauty arouses the response of wonder that can lift physical desire into
a spiritual passion, a response we shall later see to be the basis of Plato's
theory of love. Marlowe's character Tamburlaine also sees "in beauty's
just applause" some quality "With whose instinct the soul of man is
touch'd" and that "every warrior that is rapt with love / Of fame, of
valor, and of victory, / Must needs have beauty beat on his conceits
[thoughts]."[17] It would seem, then, that beauty, particularly the possibility of its possession, has the power to inspire the very valor that will
merit its just applause and acceptance.

More generally, beauty would seem to have a mysterious power to touch a soul with the desire for its possession. All the possessions for which we labor are marked by its special quality, their superior beauty in our eyes being the final determinant that singled them out from their competitors for our purchase. We strive, by adorning and surrounding ourselves with beauty, to gain something of its power of attraction.

We should now be able to understand why "none but the brave deserve the fair" and reciprocally why "she most fit his service doth deserve, / That fairest is." For the female's beauty can both inspire male desire and promise it a sensitive reception, while the male's self-confidence can promise the power to carry such desire to its highest consummation, to draw out the full capacities of the feminine instrument and play his soul's melody upon it. In such an ideal sexual union we may see that union of vitalizing power and sensitive vessel that informs all of creation and is everywhere revealed by it.

But that this is often more ideal than real is indicated by the humor that an arrogantly self-confident male will inspire, a humor classically expressed in the dramatic figure of the Miles Gloriosus, the braggart soldier, and it suggests that there is a missing ingredient in the above account that renders it less than ideal. This is love and it proves to be both the source and result of a sense of empowerment. The genesis of such love in a sexual relationship may perhaps be seen more clearly in the reverse model of the beautiful but weak male and the strong woman, though it is true in all relationships that generate love. Venus had two significant lovers, the powerful Mars and the beautiful Adonis, and what she gave to Adonis was just what she received from Mars, a sense of empowerment. The weak male is attracted to the strong woman not only because she can protect his sensitive nature from the rude shocks of gross reality but because he can draw from her the strength and confidence he needs to perform effectively. For the strength he derives from her, he will repay her with love and a sense of sweetness, the special gift of the weak. As Spenser says of Venus and Adonis: "But she her self, when ever that she will, / Possesseth him, and of his sweetness takes her fill."[18] This sweetness inspires her tenderest love in return, for it serves both to validate the relationship and her own sense of desirability, her own power.

Similarly with those relationships that more nearly conform to the sexual stereotypes, at least outwardly. A woman's love for a man is a sign of her faith in his power, and it can give him such faith in himself where his own self-confidence is uncertain. This is, indeed, part of the ideal model defined by Spenser in its fullest form: "she most fit his service doth deserve, / That fairest is and from her faith will never swerve." So it is not enough for the woman simply to be fair; she must also give the man her unswerving faith in him. But just as much male self-confidence seems to depend on the love of a woman, so does female self-confidence largely derive from the love of a man, from the proof of her power to attract.

Thus the receipt of love would seem to be empowering, to validate the sense of our own worth, and our own love for the other would similarly seem to be inspired by the sense of such empowerment and directed to whatever we recognize to be its source. On the deepest of levels, it is only when one recognizes that God "is thy life and the length of thy days" (Deut. 30:20), the ultimate source of one's power, that one can "love the Lord thy God with all thine heart" (Deut. 6:5). Love is the gratitude with which we repay the gift of power, the gift, ultimately, of life. For power is attractive precisely because it is vitalizing, because it conveys the energy by which we live. Love and power are normally seen as opposites, and spiritual teachers will often urge the forgoing of power in favor of love. But if ego empowerment may sometimes be at the expense of love, at a deeper level they are reciprocals, neither possible without the other and both necessary for the act of creation whose model is sexual union.

Though we began by the functional definition of the male in terms of self-confident power and of the female in terms of beauty, the true ideal would seem to be that both partners should be both attractive and powerful, each able to arouse the desire of the other and to meet it sensitively with the power of his or her own passion. But for such power to be mutually present and joined, the necessary ingredient would seem to be love, the gratified feeling of empowerment that stimulates and sustains the very desire whose consummation serves to recharge the feelings with yet stronger love. True sexual union can always be defined as "making love," for this is, in fact, what it does produce in an ever increasing cycle of empowerment and fulfillment.

It is, then, the union of love and power that marks the path of the bull, the sexual path to divine knowledge; and what it teaches is precisely the reciprocal relationship of these two spiritual spheres whose separate development marks the successive paths of the lion and the eagle. If the path of the bull is the foundation for these next levels of spiritual development, it is just because it both contains them and can explain their relationship. And it is the foundation as well because it provides the first evidential experience of the operations and laws of spirit, the dependency of power upon something as immaterial as feeling and the behavioral training it provides in working with such spiritual energies, rewarding a proper adjustment of force to vessel with ecstasy and punishing an improper adjustment of the individual to the conjoined passion with a loss of power and frustration of pleasure.

More than this, it provides the first evidence of a realm of experience so powerful that it can only be called divine, the realm accessed by spirit through the sensual. In *Death in Venice*, Thomas Mann has expressed such an understanding of the sensual path to knowledge of the divine in the Platonic ruminations of his passion-obsessed aging artist, Aschenbach:

> with an outburst of rapture he told himself that what he saw was beauty's very essence; form as divine thought. . . . [T]he god, in order to make visible the spirit, avails himself of the forms and colours of human youth, gilding it with all imaginable beauty that it may serve memory as a tool, the very sight of which then sets us afire. . . . [B]eauty alone, is lovely and visible at once. For,

mark you, it is the sole aspect of the spiritual which we can perceive through our senses. . . . [B]eauty alone is both divine and
visible; and so it is the sense way, the artist's way . . . to the spirit.[19]

The desire that beauty sets afire is "the sense way" to reach the level of
"spirit" and, through this level, finally to gain the experiential knowledge of the divine.

There has been a long tradition in Judaism, as in other religious cultures, of regarding the inclinations of the body as a source of sin,
claimed by the diabolic Sitra Ochra, the Other Side,[20] but this is, in
large part, a testament to its power. Indeed, Mann's Aschenbach continues his previous thoughts on the sense way to the spirit by asking: "do
you believe that such a man can ever attain wisdom and true manly
worth, for whom the path to the spirit must lead through the senses?
Or do you rather think—for I leave the point to you—that it is a path
of perilous sweetness, a way of transgression, and must surely lead him
who walks in it astray?"[21] If the sensual path is one of "perilous sweetness," it is precisely because of its power to lift the body to a realm of
ecstasy not otherwise accessible to the undeveloped soul. But as Dov
Baer of Lubavitch has shown, "[There is a] separate ecstasy of the natural soul . . . which comes into the fleshly heart with a sensed ecstasy,
with sparks of the fire of longing. . . . For the divine soul this is the category of essential ecstasy in the fleshly heart, which results from actual
comprehension of the divine by the divine soul clothed in comprehension by the natural soul. As the verse says: 'My heart and my flesh
sing for joy unto the living God.'"[22] At the beginning of this section we
have also seen how the mystical tradition within Judaism has appreciated and sought to channel for higher uses this very sensual power. For
it is the foundational portal of the Nefesh soul to the higher realms of
spirit. In so teaching the soul of these higher dimensions of spirit and
particularly of the emotion of love experienced in the "fleshly heart,"
the path of the senses leads directly to the next path of the heart, the
path of the lion.

THE LOVE PATH OF THE LION

In the previous section we have seen how love can both arise from and perfect the ecstasy of sexual union, but it is still the sexual ecstasy of the Nefesh soul that was understood to provide the gateway to a more ultimate knowledge. Now we must consider love, in itself, as a path to such knowledge, first in its romantic and then in its religious aspects. That romantic love between two individuals could be a path to knowledge of the ultimate has been recognized since the time of Plato. But before turning to this foundation of Western love theorizing, we should consider what characterizes love as a passion in its own right.

Perhaps the first characteristic that should be noted is the time differential between these passions. Where the experience of sexual passion, however much preliminary desire it may arouse, is limited to the actual time of sexual intercourse, that of love is a more or less continuous current of feeling in the heart. Though it can be interrupted by the business of daily life, it is always there, ready, at the least opportunity of relaxation, to flood back into the heart and assert its sovereignty once more over the whole of consciousness. It is the power of this flood of feelings that most characterizes the passion of love and allows it to become a path to spiritual knowledge. For this power seems disproportionate to the actual qualities of the beloved and raises the profound wonder as to its actual source that most enchants the lover's soul.

This enchanting magnification is at the center of the most significant modern work on the subject, Stendhal's *On Love*. For Stendhal, the "passion-love" with which he is primarily concerned requires a process he calls "crystallization," using the analogy of a stripped bough dropped into a Salzburg salt mine for a few months that comes forth covered with a vast number of sparkling crystals. The romantic process of such crystallization has for him seven stages: "1. Admiration; / 2. One says to one's self 'What pleasure,' etc; / 3. Hope; / 4. Love is born; / 5. The first crystallization; / 6. Doubt is born; / 7. Second crystallization."[23] Love begins with genuine admiration for another, which inspires both the desire for a relationship with this superior being and the hope for reciprocation, the hope that defines love as "the most noble of the passions of the human heart, the one which, in order to be truly happy, must inspire the same degree of passion that it feels."[24]

The first crystallization of love is virtually simultaneous with the generation of hope, and its intense happiness leads lovers to endow their beloveds with the "thousand perfections" commensurate with the sense of what "has just fallen to us from Heaven in some way we do not understand."[25] It is the very wonder of the lover's experience that leads to the doubt so necessary for the second crystallization that can ensure the duration of this love. This doubt, it seems to me, is not so much of the beloved's faithfulness, as of the very contingency of the lover's happiness, the realization that he or she is not in control of the situation, which can produce that loss of ego necessary for true love, for that felt need of a salvific merger with a superior being that has such mystic resonances.

Stendhal does find such a resonance in the German approach to love, an appraisal of which he quotes: "'The emotion of love is regarded by the Germans as a virtue, as a divine emanation, as something mystic. . . . it is profound and has something of illuminism about it.'"[26] He further indicates his agreement when he says: "Love of the Werther kind . . . changes the face of everything. Passion-love spreads before a man's eyes the whole of nature in its sublime aspects. . . . Everything is new, everything is alive, everything breathes the most passionate interest."[27]

Ortega y Gasset, in his similarly titled work *On Love*, rejects Stendhal's whole concept of crystallization: "Note that, in sum, this theory defines love as an essential fiction. It is not that love sometimes makes mistakes, but that it is, essentially, a mistake. We fall in love when our imagination projects non-existent perfections onto another person. . . . For Stendhal it is less than blind: it is imaginary."[28] He must nonetheless agree: "There is an undeniable and evident germ of truth in the theory of 'crystallization.'"[29] Though he reduces this to the fact that lovers are often mistaken, this germ of truth might better have been related to a more general criticism Ortega has about modern theories of love: "The ideology of recent times has lost cosmological inspiration and has become almost exclusively psychological. Refinements in the psychology of love, by multiplying subtle casuistry, have drawn away our attention from this cosmic dimension, which is elemental to love."[30] Ortega does make this connection in support of his far poorer theory "that 'falling in love' is a phenomenon of attention, but of an abnormal state of attention which occurs in a normal man."[31] But his correlations of love and mysticism do not speak too well of either:

> the highest moment in the course of mysticism will be that moment in which the mystic feels saturated with God, like a sponge of divinity. . . . now actually working as an automaton of God . . . This extreme situation finds its equal in the development of "falling in love.". . . [T]he beloved is no longer an object to be thought about, for the simple reason that you have him within you. . . . In the "state of grace," whether mystical or sexual, life loses all weight and bitterness. . . . This surprising parallel between [religious] ecstasy and "love" takes on, however, a more complex aspect when we compare both with another abnormal state of being: hypnotism.[32]

But though neither Stendhal nor Ortega are cosmologically inspired, the phenomenon they describe can only be adequately explained by taking its cosmological implications seriously. Thus the overplus of response to the perceived graces of the beloved need not be taken as a mistaken fiction but as a true perception by one's higher Neshamah soul of the possibility of a soul mating with the Neshamah soul of the beloved. As the Neshamah soul level is the divine element in the human soul and as such endows any activity in which it participates with meaningfulness, its participation in one's admiration for a particular person can only cast a

sheen of divinity over that other and cause the realization that a love relationship with this divine mortal would bring the utmost meaningfulness
to one's life.

Now although it was earlier said that the love path of the lion-faced
Chayah could be identified with the Ruach soul, there is clearly some
unification also taking place in the passion of romantic love between
the Ruach and Neshamah souls of each of the lovers as between these
soul levels of the individual lovers. I have elsewhere suggested that an
important stage in the course of spiritual development involves the unification of the double heart, taking this traditional term not to signify
the conflict of the good and evil inclinations but rather the unification
of the Ruach and Neshamah hearts,[33] both good but heading in different directions, the Ruach toward fulfillment on earth and the
Neshamah toward the participation of a heavenly element. Where the
Ruach level yearns to be one with the other, the Neshamah level
endows such heart union with the special sense of meaningfulness that
defines this passion. The warm, satisfying feeling of heart expansion that
floods the senses conveys such a sense of the fulfilling presence of the
other as to banish all personal and existential loneliness in a present
radiance that answers all questions, whether through the embrace of a
heavenly here-and-now or of its intimation of a far vaster and enduring spiritual realm that is making itself manifest through the very power
of this passion.

For the wonder of this passion is not only its power but that it
seems to be directed by some will beyond personal consciousness. As
William James has said:

> there is no rationally deducible connection between any outer fact
> and the sentiments it may happen to provoke. These have their
> source in another sphere of existence altogether, in the animal and
> spiritual region of the subject's being. . . . The passion of love is the
> most familiar and extreme example of this fact. If it comes, it
> comes; if it does not come no process of reasoning can force it. Yet

it transforms the value of the creature loved as utterly as the sunrise transforms Mont Blanc from a corpse-like gray to a rosy enchantment; and it sets the whole world to a new tune for the lover and gives a new issue to his life. . . . [J]ust so are the passions themselves *gifts*—gifts to us, from sources sometimes low and sometimes high; but almost always non-logical and beyond our control.[34]

This experience of grace, as Ortega has called it, which is experienced so powerfully by lovers as to seem evidential of the most sublime truth, may perhaps be explained by the kabbalistic understanding of the Neshamah soul as both one's personal higher self and divine, as belonging to a supernal realm that is directing the cosmic process toward an ideal end, one that in this case appears to have chosen these two lovers' souls to meet in a union whose fruit will somehow contribute to this process.

The kabbalistic understanding of ideal love as a mating of the higher souls of the lovers has a long history and has never been more delightfully expressed than in the myth Plato has put in the mouth of the comic dramatist Aristophanes in *The Symposium*. In this myth the original humans were divided in half:

And when one of them finds his other half . . . the pair are lost in an amazement of love and friendship and intimacy . . . and yet they could not explain what they desire of one another. For the intense yearning which each of them has towards the other does not appear to be the desire of intercourse, but of something else which the soul desires and can not tell, and of which she has only a dark and doubtful presentiment. . . . [T]here is not a man among them . . . who would not acknowledge that this meeting and melting in one another's arms, this becoming one instead of two, was the very expression of his ancient need. And the reason is that human nature was originally one and we were a whole, and the desire and pursuit of the whole is called love. . . . Therefore we shall do well to praise the god Love, who is the author of this gift, and who is also our greatest benefactor, leading us in this life back to our own nature, and giving us high hopes for the future, that if we are pious, he will restore us to our original state, and heal us and make us happy and blessed.[35]

This myth of division and reunification is true to the psychological facts of love as a desire for a merger that goes beyond the physical to express the soul's desire for some ultimate healing and blessing greater than human love can provide but of whose possibility this love has given us a presentiment.

But there are evident problems in such an identification of human with divine love, the problems attendant upon the waning of the very idealizing of the beloved that had given this love its power, a waning due to the greater familiarity that can only reveal her or his very human failings. This may lead to the search for a new love who can inspire the same ascension of passion-love, with all the problems of the ever decreasing returns from the cycles of what may well become a promiscuous and jaded love addiction. The opposite problem may result from the attempt to domesticate such passion, which may lead to feelings much more useful for a shared life but such affections as, however deep, cannot fly. As Chaucer has observed:

> *Love wol not be constrained by maistrye:*
> *When maistrye comth, the God of Love anoon*
> *Beteth his winges and farewel, he is goon!*
> *Love is a thing as any spirit free; . . .*[36]

Although I have elsewhere written much in praise of the different love fulfilled in such familiar relationships as characterize marriage,[37] the question before us now is not how we should best live our lives here but of love as a spiritual path, and we have begun our search with what Stendhal calls passion-love precisely because it is the power of this love that some-how conveys such a presentiment of the true spiritual object of the soul's yearning as can convert romance into a genuine spiritual quest.

This, Plato recognizes, can only occur if one first becomes con-scious of being on such a love path. As Diotima has instructed Socrates:

> And the true order of going or being led by another to the things
> of love, is to use the beauties of earth as steps along which he
> mounts upwards for the sake of that other beauty, going from one
> to two, and from two to all fair forms, and from fair forms to fair
> actions, and from fair actions to fair notions, until from fair notions
> he arrives at the notion of absolute beauty . . . the divine beauty, I
> mean, pure and clear and unalloyed, not clogged with the pollu-
> tions of mortality, and all the colors and vanities of human life. . . .
> Do you not see that in that communion only, beholding beauty
> with the eye of the mind, we will . . . become a friend of God and
> be immortal, if mortal man may.[38]

The idea that has distressed the Western tradition with the true nature of Platonic love is, of course, the notion that we should "use" our lovers and the feelings they inspire "for the sake of that other beauty," the "divine beauty." But this is only a stage on the ladder of love before one leaves the lovers of this world behind in a direct spiritual ascent. As Diotima instructs her pupil: "This my dear Socrates . . . is that life above all others which man should live, in the contemplation of beauty absolute; a beauty which if you once beheld, you would see not to be after the measure of gold, and garments, and fair boys and youths, which when you now behold you are in fond amazement."[39] For Plato, then, the presentiment of a divine reality that one gets from the passion of love in even greater degree than from sexual consummation is what can open the spirit both to the true existence of this spiritual realm and to the pursuit of the more direct encounter with it that can finally be termed that of mystical religion.

In Plato, as in Stendhal, the meaningful experience of this quasi-spiritual passion is wholly positive, if not slightly tinged with comedy. There is, however, another formulation of such love passion whose tragic nature is more attuned to melancholy souls, the "courtly love" that developed in twelfth-century Provence. That such polarities, deriving from personality type, can be found in traditions of romantic idealization can be supported by the major thesis of William James in *The Varieties of Religious Experience*. James distinguishes the religion of the "healthy-minded" from that of "sick souls" and asks: "Does it not appear as if one who lived more habitually on one side of the pain-threshold might need a different sort of religion from one who habitually lived on the other?"[40] His own kinship is with the broken-hearted melancholics:

> The method of averting one's attention from evil, and living simply in the light of good is splendid, as long as it will work.... [A]nd within the sphere of its successful operation there is nothing to be said against it as a religious solution. But it breaks down impotently as soon as melancholy comes . . . there is no doubt that healthy-mindedness is inadequate as a philosophical doctrine, because the evil facts which it refuses positively to account for are a genuine portion of reality; and they may after all be the best key to life's significance, and possibly the only openers of our eyes to the deepest levels of truth.[41]

If not even Socrates can be presented as an exemplar of the highest level of Platonic love, the love of divine beauty or perfection that is celibate precisely because it has left the beauties of this world behind, then the optimistic view of such love as an attainable spiritual path becomes seriously open to question.

To the troubadours of twelfth-century Provence, it was clear that love is rather a wounding passion, born in a condition of obstruction and able to be fulfilled only in death. In his important work on courtly love, *Love in the Western World*, Denis de Rougemont has traced this love to the Catharist heresy, that Church of Love whose tenets he sees exemplified in *Tristan and Iseult*: "But the fundamental mistake of this love is not only that the sin [drinking the love potion and its consequences] must be redeemed. The *askesis* of self-redemption must also, and above all, deliver a man from having been born into this world of darkness and lead him to the state of final and fortunate detachment in which he can undergo the deliberate death of the Perfect."[42] In the courtly model, love is defined in its very nature as a spiritual path: the divine qualities of the beloved are understood to be symbolically true, the obstructions surrounding her to represent all that prevents the manifestation of the ideal in an imperfect world, and the love-death the means of transcending the particular for a redemptive union with the Absolute. This can be seen in the love-death of Romeo at the tomb of Juliet as he first addresses the unfortunate Paris that he had just killed:

> *I'll bury thee in a triumphant grave.*
> *A grave? O, no, a lanthorn, slaught'red youth,*
> *For here lies Juliet, and her beauty makes*
> *This vault a feasting presence full of light.*
>
> . . . .
>
> *. . . O, here,*
> *Will I set up my everlasting rest*
> *And shake the yoke of inauspicious stars*
> *From this world-wearied flesh. Eyes, look your last!*
> *. . . And, lips . . .*
> *. . . seal with a righteous kiss*
> *A dateless bargain to engrossing death!* (5.3.83–86,
>   109–15)

Juliet's believed triumph over death through love illuminates for Romeo the path to transcendence of the inauspicious stars of his mortal existence, and his love enables him to embrace the horror of engrossing death, to which it has ever been leading, with a like sense of triumphant glory.

The symbolic depiction in the literature of courtly love of what is essentially a religious path to salvation achieves its greatest expression in the works of Dante, where a beloved child he had hardly known before her untimely death becomes the angelic guide to his Paradisal vision. The artistic expressions of such love as is incapable of realization in this world just because of its purity and whose sufferings lead inexorably to death have continued to affect the sensibilities of modern Western audiences, whether in ballets, operas, novels, or B movies. But what has most distinguished such expression has been its fictitious nature. As Rosalind, in Shakespeare's *As You Like It,* says of various literary examples of the love-death: "But these are all lies: men have died from time to time and worms have eaten them, but not for love" (4.1.106–8). So, like its happier counterpart, Platonic love, the path of suffering love has been no easier to follow in real life. Whether thought to be capable of fulfillment in this life or only beyond it, the raptures of love have been felt to intimate a more infinite love that could provide a path to an essentially religious salvation. But however unsuccessful the model of such romantic love has largely been as a complete path to ultimate knowledge, it has pointed the way to the true spiritual path of the heart, the path of love trodden by the saints.

It is this path of spiritual love that has been most inculcated by the world's religions, and this because it serves to develop the quality most needed to redeem humanity from the negative effects of the soul's necessary fall into individuality, the quality of unconditional love. The movement from the conditional love produced by the paths of the senses and of romantic love to such unconditional love is a measure of the distance between them, and yet the source of both the conditional and unconditional forms of love is the same. As was suggested earlier, the love "made" or consummated in the true sexual union of two complementary souls results from and is conditional upon two things, the sense of the other's special worth and the sense of vital empowerment each receives and gives as, ideally, a new life is conceived. Where the ideal new life of the sexual path is not only the conception of a child but of a conjoined physical passion, for romantic lovers it is a whole new sense of the meaningfulness of existence derived from the power of the love uplifting them to new heights of perception. The love of which we now speak also derives from a sense of empowerment, the individual feeling such a sense of plenitude that he or she can freely dispense it without fear of loss, but this feeling, as with the true religious passion of Platonic love, has now become freed from dependence on a specific source of such power; it has an unfailing and continuous connection with the ultimate source of its being, such love being the sign of the soul's own rebirth in the spirit.

The soul twice-born in unconditional love can give to all the world that quality most characterizing the feminine personality and its archetypal contribution to both sexual and romantic union, the ability to accept and validate the other. The path of the eagle will similarly emphasize the assertive use of power that characterizes the archetypal male contribution to sexual union and the source of masculine personality. But such concepts of the masculine and feminine derive, as we have seen, from the fundamental sexual model of cosmic functioning that is experientially realized only in the path of the bull. For the spiritual path of the lion, as that of the eagle, this model becomes symbolic, and its two complementary modes, finally freed from their dependence upon the physical organs of procreation, can now become asexual, both unrelated to sexual relations and also equally available and required of both males and females. Though it might be easier for most women to follow the heart path of unconditional love and most men the path of power, the fully developed soul will have need to perfect both of these complementary capacities.

The best order of presenting such development, and perhaps of achieving such soul growth, is the one we have been following, proceeding from the sensual path of the bull, through the romantic path of the lion, to the power path of the eagle, a progression that, on the

Yechidah level, retraces the soul's path from the Nefesh through the Ruach to the Neshamah soul levels, a course taking it as well through the elements of water, air, and fire. As the path of the senses is fluid and, particularly in its sexual manifestation, depends on the arousal and discharge of lubricants, so that of the heart is aerial—lofty and spacious. The path of power can similarly be associated with fire, as in the standard description of military might in terms of "firepower."

The spiritual path of the heart, is, then, that which primarily follows the Ruach definition of the heart, the expansive state of feeling that can intuit and identify with the Other. It is because the Ruach heart can truly identify itself with the needs of the Other that it is not afflicted with personal ego and can give its love unconditionally. The path of such love involves the learning of the consequences of such a general gift of love. The external effects of such giving have already been learned by those on the sensual path, but for those on the heart path who are devoted to celibacy, it is important that it be repeated. This is the fact that love is powerful and, as is true of all forms of power, can communicate something of its nature to the powerless. Thus the universal love of a selfless soul is empowering to all those with whom it comes in contact, communicating to them something of its unflagging energy and vision. It strengthens the weak by causing them to regain faith in their own capacities and in the fecundity of opportunity, and it does this both through the experience it gives them of being unconditionally loved and also through the power of example. For what unconditional love teaches the heart capable of it is that selfless giving is, in fact, self-empowering, that in giving up the claims of the ego, a space is cleared that immediately becomes filled with the powerful beatitude of unconditional love. Such individuals become radiant, their eyes shining with the spiritual power that fills and lifts them to seemingly impossible accomplishments, to the miraculous.

It is this lesson that must be learned in both its essentials and particulars. Thus it is not enough to have a general understanding of the inverse relationship of selfless love to personal empowerment but such a soul must also learn to monitor itself, to trace any flagging of power to a surreptitious reemergence of ego, for only by this means can it really learn the negative effects of the personal ego, its ability to obstruct the influx of divine power that is the soul's true desire and fulfillment. Though it might seem that the paths of sensual or romantic love give more immediate feedback than that of unconditional love, this is only true for the external effects of love. It may take patience to watch the seed of love flower into effective living, but the internal truths taught by such loving can be just as immediately monitored as the rise and fall of passion. A selfless lover is really having a love affair with his or her source, and any flagging of such devotion will be immediately experienced as a loss of beatitude. But this source is not only within and subject to some measure of self-delusion; it is also without, defining the total complex of the circumstances in which the loving soul finds itself and demanding of that soul the humility to discover the limits of the possible and to work concretely within them. The spiritual path of the heart teaches the soul what love can accomplish both within and without. It teaches the soul the loving path to power, further aspects of this heart path being considered in relationship to the path of power we shall now enter.

THE POWER PATH OF THE EAGLE

Once the soul has learned the secret of empowerment, it cannot rest there. It must now learn the proper uses of such power. It must embark on the path of the eagle. Most spiritual devotees, and particularly those on the heart path, are averse to the direct pursuit or even the acceptance of power, believing it to be unspiritual and corrupting. But, in fact, the path of power represents the purest form of spiritual learning and one at which all spiritual aspirants must finally become adept. For it is only in the arena of power that one can learn the highest form of mastery, to be, in Hesse's terms, a Magister Ludi, a Master of the Game. Whether the game is business, politics, war, or chess, it can only be played and won according to the rules that define the nature of power, and it is these rules that the soul begins to learn as it enters the flight path of the eagle. What only the arena of power can reveal is the infrastructure by which the world is ruled and that all the surface counters, which seem to be determining factors, are only part of a massive charade to hide the truly operative dimension on which issues of power are decided. The master player is one from whose eyes the scales of accident have dropped, who can see the spiritual dimension on which the game of power is truly to be played.

We operate, at one and the same time, on what might be considered both a literal and an allegorical level, the latter so called because literary allegory provides the best available guide to its functioning— only the levels in allegory are the reverse of what they appear to be in reality. In Spenser's great allegory *The Faerie Queene,* a male knight representing holiness or a female knight representing chastity, among other such figures, battle dragons, sorcerers, Saracen knights, and other representatives of the evils without and the temptations within until they have achieved mastery of the virtue that is the object of their quest. The literal level of knights on horseback, traveling unerringly through an uncharted wilderness to just the encounter needed to test their readiness, expose their weaknesses, and further the progress of their training, is supposed to signify a deeper level of meaning; but it is precisely this literal level of allegory that best represents the subtle dimension of our own reality. Though politicians may have platforms, campaign for votes with eloquent rhetoric, and seem to depend on the tally of votes cast, there is a sense in which they are knights in shining armor, mounted on horseback, and tilting at each other directly with outstretched lances. And it is the way they conduct themselves on this pure level of power, their ability to wound or weaken their adversaries while protecting themselves or regaining their balance after similar wounding, that ultimately decides who will be the victor at the ballot box.

We do create power figures whether we know it or not, and if we do not know it they are more apt to betray us than if we do. These spiritual projections, which exactly mirror the degree and nature of our inner power, go out and do battle for us in accordance with the concentration of our will. And it is the spiritual power we are thus able to project and control that will determine our success in the objective world below. The master will triumph over the novice for two reasons, because he understands the workings of power, knows when and how much pressure to apply and when to refrain, but more importantly because he has mastered the prime quality that assures success in the arena of power, self-possession. The master of power is one who is master of himself, who possesses and can control all aspects of himself and especially the power image he projects. Where the power image of a novice betrays his every weakness, that of a master is opaque and conveys above all else his invincibility. If the path of love requires a warm heart, that of power requires a cool head. In whatever area of power he is operating, he will master all the details and skills necessary for success and then treat his appointed task as a game whose prime requisite for victory will be his unfailing self-possession under stress. Viewing his manipulations of power as a game does not trivialize it, for the game is as serious as life. It is life more truly observed. But it permits him to be detached from its earthly fruits, from any fruits beyond the perfecting of his own mastery.

The classic form of such mastery is exhibited in the martial arts, particularly in their Eastern forms, where they are recognized and still practiced as techniques of spiritual discipline. In the caste system of India, as in less cast-iron stratifications elsewhere, the warrior class is just below that of the priests and this because the true knight is recognized to be noble, a pure soul whose deadly trade enacts with mortal stakes the archetypal battles in which we are all less consciously engaged. Mounted upon the power of his horse, he directs the force for which he becomes a conduit out through his lance to meet its mark. The horse has long been symbolic of the power of the passions, as in the figure of the centaur, of the passion-dominated man. He who would learn to master and direct such power must learn to bridle it, not to diminish it but to make it subject to the higher will. As Milton recognized in *Areopagitica,* the "passions within us . . . rightly tempered are the very ingredients of virtue."[43] In the power figure of the knight on horseback, the knight represents the transformer of the power on which he rests, the horse, and his lance is but another manifestation of the magical rods used by such figures as Jacob and Moses to direct the force thus transformed from potential into manifestation.[44] The master who would have such power of manifestation in any field must direct his force with exactly the same concentration and self-possession as a knight on horseback, with the same skill and purity of purpose. Whatever the details of his expertise, he must be aware of the two levels on which he is operating and remember that all he must finally be concerned with in the game of life is to maintain his projected power figure at its requisite strength, that if he can project his possession of such power, then all will follow in accordance with his will on the material plane.

In the path of power, as in those of love and the senses, the final learning is of the dependence of the material upon a spiritual dimension and that it is the laws governing the operations of spirit that are the final determinants of optimum physical functioning. All similarly follow the sexual model, on the sensual level with actual lovers, on the highest heart level in the previously mentioned love affair between the selfless lover and his or her source, and on the power level in a similar love affair between player and game. Though master knights may battle each other for victory, the traditional prize of such victory is the winning of a mistress. In the game of power, the knight's mistress is the arena in which he plays, which he must woo and bend to his will. Whether it is an actual electorate or potential buyers, he must solicit them as a gravitational mass bends space, by a magnetism that draws all uncommitted energies into resonance with his frequency. Indeed, it is such a drawing of the spiritual energies within the circumambient air, such "spirits that tend on mortal thought"[45] as have been called "the light militia of the lower sky,"[46] that so increases his own resonant power that it can captivate all purposes into alignment with his own master will. It is his successful wooing of these forces that so enlarges his projected power that it can triumph over all adversaries.

But though the unconditional lover and the warrior may be playing the same game, are both involved with the conversion of love into power, it is with this difference: the lover's selfless concern to empower the powerless diffuses his or her power, while the self-possession of the spiritual knight concentrates it. It is this concentration that is needed to direct spiritual power into manifestation, a concentration that depends upon possessing rather than losing the self. Such possession is also different from the self-confidence of the ordinary hero, for where the power of the merely brave warrior relies on his faith, that of the master warrior is recognized as a product of his own consciousness. He is not dependent on but is the maker of his moods. In possessing himself, he has brought all the levels of his being into the light and control of his conscious will. Such power is certainly formidable and, if placed in the service of a diseased will, can become most dangerous.

In a fight between those whose use of power is good or evil, the good master will always win because the right it adds to power will make it the more attractive. Such a master will be more relaxed and graceful in his manner, will exude an air of freedom exhilarating to all, offering the double attraction of power and beauty in one fully realized being. Where the evil or false master is coercive, whipping his followers into an obsessional frenzy, the good and true master is liberating, lifting his followers into creative joy. Offered a choice between two such masters, few would choose to serve the egomaniacal. But the choice is more often between those modes of power and love represented by the diseased master and the Ruach path of the heart, and in such a contest it is the warped master of evil that will win. He will win because he offers a more direct source of power than that of love, one already mature rather than the seedling offered by unconditional love. As any form of power is vitalizing, even coercive and destructive power will draw adherents in a power vacuum, such warped vitality being preferable to none insofar as it can organize otherwise dissipated energies into the production of some form of nourishment.

It is not love that can fight such evil power but only a form of equally masterful power ranged on the side of holiness. And this is not only true of a fallen world but of the whole structure of cosmic consciousness. To win the spiritual battle against entropy there must be warriors ready to fight the apocalyptic battle on the side of right. The devotees of spiritual love must be ready to accept power so that they may perfect the world as they perfect themselves on the Neshamah path of power. This is particularly important for the work of the Tikkun that, like power, is future oriented. The master in the arena of power is always figuring a few moves ahead and working with future probabilities. And his or her ultimate concern is for some form of divine communion without loss of self. The concept of the Tikkun has been primarily associated with the forward thrust of spiritual evolution, that reconstitution by which the cosmos, like man, can become twice-born, and it requires the spiritual mastery of the uses of power with which we have here been concerned.

But the development of such power should not necessitate the forgoing of personal love, these being as complementary for man as they are for the cosmos. On both the cosmic and human planes, we may distinguish between the personal and the impersonal. In the Lurianic system this is expressed as the distinction between the internal and the surrounding lights of the divine, of which we are told: "and the surrounding light is outside the vessel, and it is known that the surrounding light is greater than the internal light because the internal light is constricted within the vessel, which is not true of the surrounding light."[47] The surrounding light is more powerful than the internal light and can, indeed, be regarded not only under its infinite aspect but also under the aspect of power. But if the area surrounding the vessel of internal light can be associated primarily with the domain of power, so can the enclosed sphere be associated with the domain of love, the former with the impersonal and public and the latter with the personal and private. Both domains are as necessary to the individual person as they are to the cosmos, and they require the development of complementary capacities, power a self-assertiveness and love a receptivity to the Other. Both are also reciprocals, being the products of one another properly used. A natural example of the spiritual conversion of love into power, of the sweet feeling of fulfillment that results in the sense of empowerment, can be found in the nature of fruit and all sugars, that which is most sweet to the taste being most directly convertible into energy. As love properly receptive of the Other should lead to mutual empowerment, so power properly managed should lead to a reciprocal love of the governed.

If government can be considered a primary model for the domain of power, it can be seen that it requires a cooperation between the governor and the governed. When power is wrongfully used not to provide for the peace and nourishment of the governed but only their exploitation and repression, it is not the giving of love but only its withholding that can undermine it. Those who attempt to overcome evil power through love may temporarily disarm it but will probably end up being crucified. The power of evil government can, however, be broken through such passive resistance as Thoreau advocated, which is a true form of power held by the governed. For government to function, the few must be able to manage the many, and if the many refuse to work and obey, to support and cooperate with the agents of government, these agents will prove too weak to exert effective control.

Love and power are directed toward different ends and should remain within their own domains. Love is always directed toward persons, to the good of individuals, and while it may do much good to those individuals to whom it is devoted, it is not equipped to administer a whole society. It is only power that has the capacity to organize the whole, and it is ever directed to dominating larger and larger such wholes. Not only can love not organize a society, but it requires a power-devoted society to support its good works. This does not mean that such a society is wrong, rather that this is the only basis on which a larger whole can become self-sustaining. If love is properly directed to the good of individuals, power is properly directed to the good of the whole. Both are clearly necessary but should not be commingled. This is as true for individuals as it is for nations. An individual should have both a private and a public life but should try never to confuse them. There should be no power games in personal relationships and no personal considerations, whether respecting the self or individual solicitors, in the exercise of power.

When people go into the impersonal world to earn their daily bread and contribute to its value, they should learn to operate by the principles of power, to make things work; and if, as their power grows, they learn to administer it with ever greater wisdom, goodness, and elegance, both they and others will come to love such work. But in the impersonal world even love must be impersonal. It neither can nor should be allowed to warm the heart or it will distort the purity and success of the work. It is just because it is necessarily so lonely at the top that the individual, whether male or female, should ideally alternate between the public and private spheres, turning to the private realm for that heart's ease necessary both for private well-being and the human balance it can allow such people to bring back into the working world. Should they demand the rewards of love from power, they will either become ineffective or disappointed, and the latter can cause them to become cold monsters. Conversely should they demand the rewards of power from love, they will be met, just as surely as an unjust government, with passive resistance and the loss of the love that formerly was theirs. Though the natural sphere of love is the home, that enclosed garden of the personal devoted to the acceptance of our being, there is a place for what are called the caring professionals in the larger world, in those agencies and avenues that tend the sick and needy, those who cannot work; for power only interests itself in the productive elements of society. But since a society cannot be nourished by those who spend themselves on the unproductive, however worthy and needy their contribution may be, it is the proper uses of power that must finally be accepted and learned for the good both of society and for the spiritual evolution of the individual.

The paths of the bull, the lion, and the eagle can all be pursued simultaneously, each in its proper domain, or successively. As paths to divine knowledge, each has its own lessons to teach; and what the path of the eagle teaches its masters are the laws of manifestation. But as with the learning on the prior paths, this learning is primarily experiential, taught through the successful manipulation of spiritual energies, through a subtle form of self-monitoring. Where sensual lovers will check their level of arousal and spiritual lovers their feelings, the masters in the realm of power will check their level of spiritual power directly and, should it require some further charging, will retire briefly from the fray to center themselves, to repossess that self constituting their center in some form of disciplined or spontaneous meditative practice. Only when thus recharged with force will they reenter the field to learn what power has chiefly to teach, what will work, for only then can all the carefully prepared counters be properly marshaled to attack a problem with peak efficiency, to find that future-hidden solution whose receptivity to their power can transform will into manifestation. Whether in the purer forms of athletics, physical combat, and mental games or in the more worldly forms of politics and business, the master of the power game is being trained for the highest work, the spiritual government of the world and cosmos. For it is only the soul that has retained a sense of self while purifying that self of ego that can properly collaborate in the cosmic process, can properly focus the divine will into the specific works of Providence whose biofeedback-like rewards and punishments can propel the course of spiritual evolution to its fulfillment of the purpose of creation. Such a master soul has not only learned how to translate will into manifestation but that this translation involves a moral ingredient, that fifth dimension of good and evil, referred to in the *Sefer Yetzirah*,[48] whose Providential justice affects alike both the translation and the translator, in the latter case ensuring that the personal use of this power will prove self-defeating. It has learned experientially both the how-tos and the how-nots of manifestation, both what might be called the mechanical laws of manifestation and their Torah. What remains is only their cognitive comprehension and codification, the path of knowledge represented by the fourth face of the Chayot, the path of the human face, of man or Adam.

THE COGNITIVE PATH OF MAN

The path of cognitive knowledge, what in the Hindu system is known as Jñana Yoga, is the path that has most characterized the history of Jewish spirituality during the past two thousand years, first in the codification of the Talmud and then in the supreme value it has attributed to study of the Torah. The ecstasy to which such study can lead through the insights it can afford into the wisdom, goodness, and beauty of the cosmic Law is everywhere apparent in the *Zohar*, whose sages are ever filled with exaltation at yet a newer and more profound interpretation of Scriptures.

Such a saving ecstasy was also the desired culmination of the Aristotelian contemplative ideal of Maimonides and the later Jewish Aristotelian mystics, most notably Abulafia. Moshe Idel has shown that just as "the intellectual, contemplative ideal was . . . perceived by Maimonides to be the ultimate target of redemption,"[49] so for Abulafia "the salvific nature of the Agent Intellect is also implied,"[50] Abulafia emphasizing "the present intellectual attainment as the major religious experience."[51] Louis Jacobs has further shown that contemplative ecstasy was the religious ideal of Habad Hasidism: "The mind was to become engaged in the worship of God. It was to dwell in profound meditation on such matters as His Nature, His omnipresence and His relationship to the world, and ecstasy of the heart would follow automatically."[52] For knowledge can provide its own ecstasy, without recourse to the tools of sex, love, or power, and it can do so on the purest level because it adds to the self-possession of the master of power the highest value that the acquisition of selfhood can yield to consciousness, self-awareness, the soul's awareness not only of what it knows but that it knows.

In considering the path of pure cognitive knowledge, special attention should be paid to the three modes of such knowledge that have ever been the study of sacred science, those of sound, number, and geometry. For these modes are not only descriptive of other forms of functioning but able to provide direct knowledge of ultimate truth through study of their intrinsic properties.[53] Thus the distinction between the sound of consonants and vowels, between odd and even numbers, and between lines and circles, all reflect the same distinction between the masculine and feminine appearing in the basic sexual model and the two derivative models of power and love. But the modes of cognitive knowledge can go beyond those of experiential knowledge by providing information of the necessary coexistence of the finite with the infinite. Thus sound has a series of harmonics in which all the odd harmonics are individual and all the even harmonics multiply those individual tones to infinity, number also revealing this same distinction between odd and even. So too can space combine within a square the finitude of sides with the infinity of its diagonals, as within a circle the finitude of the radius with the infinity of the circumference. The gnosis of sacred science, then, is of that necessary coexistence of the finite and infinite in all aspects of the cosmos that it is also the task of the soul to realize and recognize in its own nature.

In addition, the mind can conceive of those imaginal realms where the fictive and impossible are as real as they can be imagined. As the scientist explores these modes of thought for the laws of nature and consciousness that can be symbolized by means of them, so the artist explores them through the realms of the imagination and with equal fidelity to truth. Whether it is the composer using harmonic proportions, the visual artist redefining the geometry of space, or the poet's use of the still greater cognitive resources of language, the artist who can move us is touched with a spirit that sees deeply into the nature of things and can teach us of its truths. The artist is near allied to the prophet, and as Shelley has said: "Poets are the unacknowledged legis-lators of the world."[54] The poet's power to intuit the leading direction of vital energy and give it symbolic form provides the channel of understanding through which less conscious energies can be enlisted to join in its flow.

All forms of arts and sciences follow the pattern of language, the primary mode through which the mind can talk to itself, in providing symbolic forms for the activity of perception, garments for conscious thought. It is this capacity for image making that is finally the most essential to the work and very existence of the soul. For what is the liv-ing soul with which God endowed Adam but just such a Tzelem, a divine image of itself? The soul of man is the imaginal body in which the divine consciousness can clothe itself, can give the form to its knowledge and power necessary for self-perception. And the task of the human soul is to build itself by stages into a vessel strong and vast enough to contain the full force of the divine influx.

In the Lurianic myth, the initial vessels emanating directly from the divine essence were inadequate to hold this influx and broke, a break-age that somehow led to the materialization of those husks of divine substance, the Kelipot, unable or too weighty to immediately rebound upward to rejoin the uncreated light. But it was from this material earth, Adamah, that the proper vessel of man, Adam, could be formed capable of holding the divine breath, its living soul, Nefesh Chayah, composed of both this dirt and breath. The task of the soul, which is the process of Tikkun, is to take the divine spark of its birthright and to amplify it into ever larger spiritual bodies, Tzelemim, each higher body containing the purified essence of its predecessors, until, at the Yechidah level, it can become an embodiment of the Limitless Light, the Or Ein Sof. It is just because the Nefesh, Ruach, Neshamah, and Chayah soul bodies are still contained within the all-encompassing body of the Yechidah soul that it is still necessary for it to maintain the separate paths to knowledge they can provide, the paths of the bull, the lion, the eagle, and man.

The association of the path of cognitive knowledge with both the fourth face of the Chayot and with the Chayah soul is most illuminating. As we saw in the analysis of the Chayah soul in the final section of chapter 1, the primary task of the Chayah soul is the necessity of integrating complementary opposites in a whole whose balance is also generative. To further understand this task, we ventured into new areas of the Jewish esoteric tradition, most importantly into an unprejudiced consideration of Sabbatian theory, particularly the concept of redemption through the Other Side. As the cosmology of the Sabbatian theorist Nathan of Gaza is summarized by Scholem:

> When the light substance of *En-Sof* entered the *tehiru* in a straight line, the divine forms crystallized, and . . . found their appropriate, positive place in the emergent structures. However, not the whole *tehiru* was affected by the irruption of the ray of light from En-Sof. The "straight line" penetrated only the upper half of the primordial space (which should be pictured as a sphere), and there built the world of its "thought"; it did not reach the lower half, described by Nathan as "the deep of the great abyss." The great work of cosmic *tiqqun*, which Israel has to accomplish through the strength of the Law and the divine commandments, relates to the upper part of the *tehiru* only. The lower part persists in its unformed and chaotic condition *(golem),* dominated by the *qelippah* until the advent of the messiah, who alone can perfect it. As a matter of fact, the thought-less lights too built worlds unto themselves, to wit the demonic worlds of the *qelippah*. . . . In the context of this doctrine, the Zoharic designation of the sphere of evil as the "other side" takes on a startlingly novel meaning. It refers to the "other side" of *En-Sof* itself, that is, that half of it which resists the process of differentiation and organization.[55]

Applying Nathan of Gaza's thought to our cosmic model, we can divide the space (Tehiru) of the multileveled cosmic sphere produced in the Tzimtzum into an upper hemisphere and a lower hemisphere, a division that may be thought to be marked by the hexagram cross section that it was suggested both in chapter 1 and the opening section of the present chapter should be inscribed at this equator to define the six paths we are currently traversing. In this revised understanding of figure 1.4, the upper hemisphere would contain the enduring structures produced by the thought-some light and the lower hemisphere the chaotic structures produced by the thought-less light. The task Nathan assigned to the Messiah for the Tikkun of the world is also that which, in our model, the Chayah soul must finally undertake for the redemption of the hitherto suppressed half of its own consciousness.

Nathan's concept of the thought-less light can clearly be related to the concept of the unconscious and also to the Jungian category of the shadow, and his understanding of the need for its final redemption also has an affinity with Jung's recognition of the need for the shadow to be integrated with the conscious self. Jung defines this concept in his discussion of the psychic opposition between archetype and instinct:

> But, just as between all opposites there obtains so close a bond that no position can be established or even thought of without its corresponding negation, so in this case also "les extremes se touchent." They belong together as correspondences. . . . True opposites are never incommensurables; if they were they could never unite. . . . These counter-positions . . . form the twin poles of that psychic one-sidedness which is typical of the normal man of today. . . . [B]ut the one-sidedness . . . can be removed by what I have called the "realization of the shadow". . . the growing awareness of the inferior part of the personality, which should not be twisted into an intellectual activity, for it has far more the meaning of a suffering and a passion that implicate the whole man. The essence of that which has to be realized and assimilated has been expressed so trenchantly and so plastically in poetic language by the word "shadow" that it would be almost presumptuous not to avail oneself of this linguistic heritage. . . . The "man without a

shadow" is statistically the commonest human type, one who imagines he actually *is* only what he cares to know about himself.[56]

Some such confrontation and working through this repressed material is desirable at various stages in the process of maturation, but it is the imperative step that must be taken upon entrance into the seventh world if its second half of communion with the Infinite is to be consummated without harm.

The movement to the Other Side, here of the hexagram-inscribed spherical equator that divides the upper hemisphere from the lower hemisphere of our revised cosmic model, is necessary to perfect the Chayah soul through the further spiritual work of self-redemption, through what Jung has called "the realization of the shadow," realization, one may suppose, in its double senses of growing awareness and emerging reality. For as the soul grows in its awareness of its own implication in the Other Side, its shadow life begins to be exchanged for the true vitality that characterizes the Chayah soul, the full vitality only possible to the whole self. In making the journey through the lower hemisphere of the unconscious, the Chayah soul also redeems it from Tohu and brings it into the light of its consciousness as a necessary part of its whole self. And as it becomes consciously aware that its upward spiritual journey has been accompanied at every point by a complementary downward journey, it can shift its attention to this previously unobserved journey. There the repressed desires of the personality are finally exposed to the light of Chayah consciousness and their lingering hold on the soul released. Beginning with the most recent and retracing its path to its earliest contributions to the shadow side, the Chayah soul relives all the conscious and unconscious distress it suffered in its earlier conformity to the difficult Abrahamic path demanded of the Tzaddik by God: "walk before me, and be thou perfect" (Gen. 17:1). But it does it now not with the ignorance of the outward journey, rather with the wisdom born of seeing the completed pattern.

If we can associate the positive/rational hemisphere with what can be considered the upward "solar" path, and the negative hemisphere, its intu-itive/irrational side, with the downward "lunar" path, then these dual hemispheres can also be associated with the figures of Jacob and Esau, respectively, biblical archetypes of polar opposition for which the talmu-dic sages foresaw an ultimate reconciliation. Though the brothers were reconciled in the Bible, the failure of Jacob to fulfill his promise to Esau that he would "come unto my lord unto Seir" (Gen. 33:14) became a source of Messianic allegory in the later tradition. As J. H. Hertz notes: "There is no record that Jacob went to Seir to see his brother. But, add the Rabbis, Jacob will yet visit Esau in the day of the Messiah when the reconciliation between Israel and Edom will be complete."[57]

For the followers of Jacob Frank, that time had come: "For the time has come that Jacob [was referring to when he promised] 'I will come unto my Lord unto Seir' [Gen. 33:14], for we know that until now he has not yet gone thither; and he [who will fulfill the verse] is our Holy Lord Jacob, 'the most perfect of all' [*Zohar,* 2.23a] and the most excellent of the patriarchs, for he grasps both sides [*Zohar,* 1.147a], binding one extreme to the other until the last extreme of all."[58] Though for Frank, himself, to "'come to Esau' . . . is . . . the passage through the 'abyss' with its unmiti-gated destruction and negation,"[59] such "destruction and negation" need not be nihilistic, the subversion of all law and goodness, but can rather involve the negation of negativity and contradiction, "binding one extreme to the other" in a whole productive only of good.

It was just suggested that the upper hemisphere be considered solar and the lower lunar, and that Jacob be associated with the solar side as Esau should be with the lunar. Such associations receive interesting sup-port from the biblical description of Esau: "and the first came out red, all over like an hairy garment. . . . And the boys grew: and Esau was a cunning hunter" (Gen. 25: 25, 27). What is interesting about this description is that it seems to have a medical basis in a

genetic disorder called erythropoietic porphyria, which has been blamed for the medieval legends that gave us the werewolf. The illness stems from an inborn lack of an enzyme. This lack leads to an accumulation of substances called porphyrins in body tissues, making them painfully sensitive to light. Victims of the disease tend to be excessively hairy. Their teeth have a reddish hue when exposed to light because of the accumulation of porphyrins. Sunlight brings out the most painful symptoms of the disease, prompting its sufferers to stay undercover until nightfall.[60]

Esau's occupation as a hunter would require him to spend most of his time in the forest, out of the sunlight that could only aggravate the genetic disease for which he would appear to have all the symptoms. Thus Esau is born doomed to inhabit the shadow side of biblical narrative while the aggressive Jacob, who supplants this figure of darkness, carries the blessing of Isaac into the light of history. But if Jacob waxes in biblical time, the time of this world, Esau's true value will only become apparent at the time of future perfection projected by the sages. At that time, what formerly had to be rigidly rejected as dangerous to proper growth and so evil can be reembraced as a necessary part of the higher good.[61]

As the Chayah soul completes its lower journey, it can view all its formerly repressed desires and resentments in the light of that hard-won wisdom whose present state of ease and fulfillment can make all such past bitterness seem foolishly trivial and so lose its force. It has not only achieved the liberation of those soul sparks of its own root that had been trapped in a purgatory of blasted delusions but of those parts of its own identity also held hostage there until they could be exposed to the light, and it experiences a greater and greater sense of its liberation in this process of expanding awareness. This process may be compared with the *tandra* state of which yogis speak, the state in which the unconscious, even in deep sleep, is opened to and experienced with full conscious awareness. In the Chayah soul, what was formerly lost in an unconscious Tohu, in what Nathan of Gaza calls the "thought-less light," insofar as thought is equated with consciousness, has been redeemed to conscious thought and redeemed through a process that heals its pain. Since whatever Jacob gained through his aggressive attachment to the upward thrust of his evolution was at the cost of his twin brother's suffering, his upward growth cannot proceed further until he can recognize his functional identity with his brother, that every wrong done another is also a wrong done oneself since it builds an immediate Providential or karmic liability that will eventually have to be discharged. Thus the suffering Esau is the true soul twin or shadow self of Jacob, and Jacob can only proceed higher by taking the downward path that can now release Esau, his shadow self, to take the upward reverse path through his own lower hemisphere.

From this perspective, then, there is nothing on the Other Side but the passion of passively suffering the sins of the world, and one moves to the Other Side not to *do* sin, since this can only increase this suffering, but to *undo* it, to undo its inhibiting effects on further soul growth. But in undoing the negative effects of sin, the soul also benefits from the suffering it caused, gaining heightened sensitivity and increased capacity to exist in the purely spiritual realm. For the shadow side of conscious awareness does exist on a plane free from all the limitations resulting from the space-time coordinates of material existence. It functions in the realm of pure, nonlinguistic imagination with perfect ease and considerable power, something the conscious self can do far less effectively. And this capacity is one it must acquire if it is to continue effective existence on the "other side" of material reality. But if Jacob needs Esau to teach him the pathways to spiritual power, Esau needs Jacob even more. For the nonmaterial night world he has hitherto inhabited provides no source of judgment or control. It functions on a "thought-less" instinctual level where all impulses are instantly manifested through some form of psychic action and all pain experienced with full intensity. The shadow side, while not losing its superior spiritual technology, needs to be raised to conscious self-control, to be enlightened.

The double hemispheres of cosmic consciousness can be read on two levels, on that of the higher soul dimensions of the World(s) to Come and on the dimension of ordinary human psychology. Clearly, there are implications for human psychology in what has just been developed, implications Jung and other psychoanalysts have already explored quite fully. But what the present analysis can contribute to an understanding of such therapeutic probing of the hidden side of consciousness is a note of caution. Bringing repressed materials up to an undeveloped consciousness is inviting exactly the same misapplication of such information as was historically expressed through the Sabbatians. This is the false belief that only harm can come from repression and that every desire or feeling must be given an overt outlet. While harm does come from all forms of repression, this harm may be outweighed by the good deriving from it, the space it gives for other more slowly developing fruits to be nurtured and for the social agents necessary for such husbandry. But when that fruit has ripened and the soul developed sufficient strength and wisdom, then the reconciliation with the negated self must be made and its silent suffering ended. So it is wise to delay the reconciliation with the shadow self until all aspects of the self have matured, to say with Jacob: "Let my lord, I pray thee, pass over before his servant: and I will lead on softly, according as the cattle that goeth before me and the children be able to endure, until I come unto my lord unto Seir" (Gen. 33:14). Jacob did not visit Esau at Seir in this world, when it seemed so close. He went "according as the cattle that goeth before me and the children be able to endure," at the slower pace of the upward journey that would allow for a more natural purification of the animal nature and outgrowing of the inner child.

Though there are some mature individuals who can profit from such an exploration and embrace of the Other Side in this life, for whom it can ease the various rites of passage, this process remains a necessity for the purely otherworldly work of the soul and is its primary rite of passage as it comes to that ultimate boundary between the cosmos and its further infinite journey, between the Chayah and the

Yechidah levels of the soul. Just as a partial "realization of the shadow" can take place in this life, unblocking the system for the further growth of self-realization, so it might be thought to take place between life-times at lower soul levels. But it is only at the Chayah level that the soul can complete its entire cosmic journey by venturing into the hitherto concealed lower half of its consciousness and integrating those dual aspects that complete its sphere of cosmic experience.

The Chayah soul, in comprehending both of its hemispheres, understands itself to be a whole made up of inverse but complementary halves. It understands that each action has an equal and opposite reaction and that both must be embraced as authentic aspects of any whole, especially of its own self. Thus after it has brought to light the desires and resentments it had previously repressed in its upward spiritual quest, and liberated the whole soul from the knots of guilt and pain that had silently afflicted it while impeding its further progress, the perfected Chayah soul is now able to recognize the just claims of the Other Side and give them some form of temperate expression. Milton is an example of one who, after having spent the first thirty-five years of his life in spiritually motivated austerity and celibacy, finally matures to the point that he can advise a similar young man:

> *For other things mild Heav'n a time ordains,*
> *And disapproves that care, though wise in show,*
> *That with superfluous burden loads the day,*
> *And when God sends a cheerful hour, refrains.*[62]

The Chayah soul recognizes that impulses from the Other Side are also God-sent, and that, since it is from the Other Side of God that they are ultimately derived, they cannot be evil. The Tikkun of the Other Side has accomplished its restoration to divine goodness.

Since the limited perspective of the lower soul levels could see only evil in such impulses and rightly so, as their very naturalness sought to chain the soul to the Nefesh level of the animal soul, it could only exaggerate the baneful effects of indulgence and by so doing pervert nature into sin. Once nature had been so perverted, the claims of the natural self could only be satisfied at much greater spiritual cost, warping the soul whether through indulgence or abstinence. But when the soul has finally reached the state where it can begin what Jung calls the "realization of the shadow," it can perceive nature as a divine garment, can feel "through all this fleshly dress / Bright *shoots* of everlastingness."[63] Animated by such a constant sense of divine influx, the Law becomes internalized and all its impulses can only be holy. This is not simply a semantic license to sin, as the Sabbatians would have had it, but involves a rectification of the impulses so that they will not desire what is injurious either to the self or to others. Such rectification is known in Christian theology by the term *right reason,* the ability to discern the difference between good and evil and to choose the good, a condition thought to have been lost in the Fall but one capable of redemption. But such rectification can only be accomplished through confronting the Other Side and redeeming it from a false dualism. By being able to discern between what is truly evil and what is actually good on that side, one can redeem the sparks of spirit that have become trapped in the Kelipot of a soulless materialism, dissolving this evil and leaving only good to the Other Side. Through such a Tikkun, the irrational can be transformed into the suprarational and inform the soul only with holiness. It is at this Chayah level, then, that the individual soul can embrace its own inner opposite and achieve its perfection.

To integrate this analysis with our earlier double focus on the human Chayot face as representing both the Chayah level of soul and the path of cognitive knowledge, we may say that this soul level is composed of the two complementary halves that unite the power of the sage and the prophet, lifting the analytic functions of thought to a new synthetic capacity, to a truly holistic mode of perception. For what the Chayah level of mentality is especially privileged to know is the truth of its own makeup, the necessary association of two complementary parts in any whole, its positive and negative aspects, the former identifiable with cognitive awareness, with such necessary awareness of self as may be termed masculine, and the latter with experiential awareness, with such receptivity to impressions as may be termed feminine. And as the union of these masculine and feminine partners results archetypally in the production of new life, so it seems no accident that the level of soul named for life, the Chayah soul, should be formed of complementary halves that may be associated with the masculine and feminine. What the Chayah soul is finally privileged to know, then, its gnosis, is no less than the secret of life, the secret of what gives enduring vitality to individual beings, the self-sustaining capacity for permanent psychic survival.

The triad of the masculine, the feminine, and the resultant new life has been stated in various forms. In terms of the major triangle on the Tree of Life Diagram, Chokhmah is identified with the male father figure of Abba, while Binah is the maternal Imma. When their union is understood sexually, its product may be regarded as Tiferet, the cosmic child known primarily by the name of Ze'ir Anpin, whose essential identification is with this Sefirah. Although this Sefirah, named Beauty, is normally associated with harmonious balance, its present identification with existent life suggests that vitality and new life are produced from such a harmonious balancing of the masculine and feminine, whether in a relationship between individuals or within the individual soul. Perhaps Norman Mailer put it best when, in lines that have been attributed to his knowledge of Kabbalah, he said: "Life comes from the meeting of opposites," more precisely that "life is gained every time opposites meet each other nicely."[64]

The Chayah soul, then, represents that beautiful meeting of cognition with experience, the subconscious lifted into consciousness and equally informing it to that "height of feeling intellect"[65] which would seem to define the source of spiritual life. As Descartes said of such thought: "I think, therefore I am." It is the image-making faculty of the soul upon which its continued existence depends, for it is only by its ability to make that image by which its essence becomes translated into the form of its spiritual body that the soul can become substantial, can become extended in time as in space, and not only in the limited four dimensions of our physical world but in the yet more extended dimensions beyond it. It should be no surprise, then, that the fourth face of the Chayot should be identified both with knowledge and life since both may be similarly traced to the same image-making faculty of the soul. It is only through images that we can name and know both our own experience and each other, including that carnal "knowledge" dependent upon bodies that, like creation itself, are ultimately the product of thought and language.

This identification of cognitive and carnal knowledge is supported by the Zoharic description of the six levels of the soul, in terms of which these two paths would represent the lower and the higher Nefesh. As paths to knowledge, the lower bull-faced Chayah may be identified with its carnal and the upper human-faced Chayah with its cognitive forms, the former leading to physical as the latter does to the highest spiritual life. The sexual model also serves to define the Chayah soul in another regard. As the production of new life is conjoined with the experience of physical ecstasy in the sexual model, so would that life produced by the activity of the Chayah soul seem to be conjoined with the height of spiritual ecstasy. This is an ecstasy, however, that preserves the distinctive individualities of each of its halves, and it would seem to be this preservation of differences that can make the Chayah soul a life-bearing receptacle for the vitalizing force of God.

As the Chayah soul learns to balance its own nature, so does it become more attuned to the life force on which it ultimately depends, and the moment its balance becomes perfect is the very moment it becomes the fit receptacle of the divine force of life. On the path of vitalizing knowledge, the Chayah soul is, then, engaged in a self-monitoring process similar to those on the other paths. It must ever be engaged in that delicate adjustment of its complementary parts, its conscious and subconscious halves whose perfect balance is rewarded by an ecstatic vision into the truth, one whose special property would seem to be its power to convey a sustaining vitality to that soul and, most probably, through that soul into the cosmos. In thus learning to become a fit receptacle and dispenser of the life force through its ability to balance its two opposing halves, the Chayah soul may be said to become self-sustaining and, itself, a source of cosmic sustenance.

We may finally say that the Chayah soul represents the culmination of the cosmic process, identified in our model with the octave portion of the seventh world, and that the primary task of its conscious awareness has been its confrontation and final unification with its subconscious self. The two hemispheres of our modified cosmic model were identified with the light of consciousness and the darkness of its shadow, using the terminology of its Jungian parallel. But in the original text of Nathan of Gaza, the upper hemisphere was identified with the World of Tikkun as was the lower with the World of Tohu. It is in these more traditional terms that Adin Steinsaltz has envisioned a similar integration that can prepare for the yet higher unification that is the focus of the remaining sections of this chapter.

> Man has to be a sturdy and well-built Vessel to receive the wild power of sanctity. . . . [W]hen the world of Tikun realizes its task and the Vessel is finished, it will be able to contain the power of the World of Tohu. Then a third situation will have been created, higher than either Tohu or Tikun, a world in which the infinite power of primordial Tohu will be within (controlled by) the perfection of the World of Tikun. This world is beyond the known and prescribed and substantial, a world in which men are no longer creatures of rigid and finite design but can begin to act as combinations of both the infinite and the finite in a single being.[66]

THE HOLY PATH OF ENOCH

When the octave portion of our cosmic model is seen as the culmination of the cosmic process, it may be identified with the Chayah soul.

But when it is seen as the lower half of an extracosmic seventh world, its transformed orientation creates a new path, the path that may be identified with Enoch. Our fourth and fifth paths, then, concern the same cosmic stage of the soul, a double aspecting that, when turned back to the cosmos, may be identified as a separate Chayah soul and, when turned forward to the Infinite, may be also identified as the lower half of the Yechidah soul. The fifth path, to which we now turn, is transitional, then, associated with the fourth in terms of their same cosmic position and with the sixth in terms of their final identity.

These final two paths, identified on the Zoharic model with the upper Ruach and upper Neshamah souls and on the Lurianic model with the highest Yechidah soul, represent most importantly the dual figures in the Throne vision, originally those of the prophet Ezekiel and of the glorified man he envisions on the Throne, figures that the Jewish mystical tradition will later identify with the human Enoch and his transfigured higher self as the heavenly Metatron. Enoch and Metatron may thus be said to represent the two significant phases of the Yechidah soul, as of the Throne vision, which are united in the highest ecstasy of Devekut (clinging). As Dov Baer of Lubavitch has said of this highest level of ecstasy, quoting the *Zohar*:

> Rabbi Simeon ben Yohai said: "I was bound to Him with one knot, to Him united.". . . This is the category of essential binding and attachment . . . of "surrounding and filling". . . the category of *yeḥidah* within him . . . of the binding of his "essence," known as "cleaving," where the soul cleaves and is drawn automatically as a result of the divine "essence" in the soul herself, just as the spark is drawn to the flame and so forth. It is this that is called actual divine ecstasy. . . . As Rabbi Simeon ben Yohai said: "With one knot," this is the "one knot" by which essence is attached to essence in the category of *yeḥidah*. . . .[67]

But though essentially united, a distinction can yet be drawn between the paths of Enoch and Metatron, that the latter concerns the part by which the whole is completed and formed into the unity of which it represents the governing identity, while the former remains a differentiated part of the whole. Since at the Yechidah level we are at that divine seventh world differentiated into cosmic and infinite halves, it would seem that the figure of Enoch may be associated with such a divine multiplicity as is represented by the Partzufim and the figure of Metatron may be associated with the divine unity.

In trying to determine what spiritual paths they might represent, we can begin by understanding each, on the Zoharic model, as the upper half of human-supernal poles. The Enochian pole would thus seem to symbolize the divine feminine and the Metatronic pole the divine masculine. These identifications follow from the definitions earlier given to the lower ends of these poles, that of Enoch being the "feminine" path of love and of Metatron the "masculine" path of power. With these preliminary identifications, let us now begin to explore the path of Enoch.

As suggested earlier, the path of Enoch may be said to serve a transitional function between the fourth and sixth paths and soul levels, bonding them together much as spirit (Ruach) is thought to bond soul (Neshamah) and vital body (Nefesh) together or, to take their counterparts in the three lower soul levels, love bonds the senses to power. The paths of love and Enoch are conjoined in that transitional pole signifying the dual feminine features of receptivity and concretization, the difference that allows for the Devekut or communion of the soul with the divine glory in the Throne vision. In the Devekut of the Yechidah soul, the human and the divine come into a union that preserves the distinctive individualities of each.

It is of such communion that the Bible speaks when it says, "And Enoch walked with God" (Gen. 5:22). But it goes on to say: "and he was not; for God took him" (Gen. 5:22). It is in this translated form that Enoch may be said to signify the uplifted human half of that which is taken out of itself in divine communion. This communion can be understood to involve the Enochian with the Metatronic forms of the Yechidah soul, the Enochian Yechidah soul rising up from the cosmos and the Metatronic Yechidah soul descending to meet it from the vastly larger expanse of the infinite surrounding light, Enoch facing forward and its Metatronic counterpart facing backward. We can now understand why a traditional interpretation of the Throne vision understands that vision as containing both an overwhelming sense of the "wholly other" and, at the same time, one's own face. For what these correlations suggest is that the only aspect of the ultimate that can be apprehended, can assume recognizable form, is that which is colored with one's own personality, and the throne vision brings the lower and higher selves together in a communion endowed with the special quality of the Sabbath, holiness.

It is of the communion that effects a sacrificial transformation of the human into the divine that the previously quoted description of Enoch speaks: "And Enoch walked with God: and he was not; for God took him." The association of sacrifice with the holy is central to the understanding of both, for both alike are related to the smoke resulting from fire. The sacrifice becomes holy in being transformed by fire into ascending smoke, and it is in the descent of "smoke" from the realm of heavenly fire that the divine holiness becomes apprehensible to man, as in Isaiah's Throne vision:

> I saw also the Lord sitting upon a throne, high and lifted up, and his train filled the temple. Above it stood the seraphims. . . . And one cried unto another, and said, Holy, holy, holy is the Lord of hosts: the whole earth is full of his glory. . . . [A]nd the house was filled with smoke. Then said I, Woe is me! . . . because I am a man of unclean lips. . . . Then flew one of the seraphims unto me, having a live coal in his hand, which he had taken with the tongs from off the altar: and he laid it upon my mouth, and said . . . thine iniquity is taken away, and thy sin purged. (Isa. 6:1–7)

We shall return later to other aspects of this Throne vision, but for the moment will only focus on its description of the holy. As apprehended by Isaiah, the holy is the quasi-substantial Presence that, in however indistinct a form, is capable of being apprehended and felt, as in the "smoke" filling the Temple. The referent of the term *holy,* Kadosh, is not to any conceivable notions of divine goodness, but precisely to the divine in the form of an experienced Presence, and this is what defines the Enochian realm of holiness. The path of Enoch is, then, the path of holiness, and in the human community it is trod by the priests and the Tzaddikim.

A true community is composed of all these paths or classes of occupation, though they should ideally not be hereditary. The path of the bull or the senses may be associated with the mercantile class, the producers of goods, the path of the lion or of love with the producers of services, the path of the eagle or of power with the military class, the path of man or of cognitive knowledge with the class of scholars, the path of Enoch or of holiness with the class of priests, and, as we shall finally see, the path of Metatron or of unification with that of the governor.

This identification of the priesthood with the holy is made clear in the consecration of Aaron, and is signified by the words "Holiness to the Lord" (Exod. 28:36) engraved on the forehead-plate of the High Priest's miter or turban, one of the priestly garments he is to wear "when he goeth in unto the holy place before the Lord, and when he cometh out, that he die not" (Exod. 28:35). Protected by the holy garments, he may commune with the divine Presence within the Holy of Holies and per-form the ritual sacrifices by which he makes atonement for the people. The prophet is also generally viewed as a holy man, particularly if he is a wonder-worker like Elijah, Elisha, and the more modern hasidic Tzaddikim. The holy man, whether priest or prophet, is one capable of performing miraculous transformations of the material either into the spiritual or by its means,[68] and this is a power he has gained through his consecration to God, through the passage of his own spirit through the purifying fires of sacrifice. Like Isaac, Jacob, and also Oedipus near their deaths, the suffering to which the holy man has submitted his being has exalted his spirit and endowed it with the divine power of blessing and cursing.

So does Oedipus at Colonus speak, beginning with an oracle of Apollo that foretold his life would end there:

> *That there I might round out my bitter life,*
> *Conferring benefit on those who received me,*
> *A curse on those who have driven me away.*
>
> .   .   .   .
>
> *For I come here as one endowed with grace*
> *By those who are over Nature; and I bring*
> *Advantage to this race, as you may learn*
>
> .   .   .   .
>
> *One soul, I think, often can make atonement*
> *For many others, if it be sincere. . . .*
> *The bloody deaths, the incest, the calamities*
> *You speak so glibly of: I suffered them,*
> *By fate, against my will! It was God's pleasure . . .*[69]

His presence, like that of the divine, can sanctify any place in which he abides, and this because he can finally accept both his sufferings and the holy power of blessing and cursing with which it has endowed him as derived from the same grace of God. Like Isaiah, his purgative sufferings have enabled him to perceive the immensity of the divine glory that both fills and rules over Nature.

But there is a difference between the divine glory and holiness; though the whole of creation attests to the glory of its source, the holy is always some thing or one specially chosen and consecrated to the divine service. The sacred is always set off from the profane. The chosenness of the sanctuary location, of particular prophets, and finally of a whole "holy nation," is the sign of its association with that aspect of the divine characterized by holiness, that is, by the distinguishable Presence that manifests the personality of God, the personal God. And that which characterizes all personality even to the level of the divine is the mystery of preference. On the divine level this is the mystery of grace, that which for its own unfathomable reasons prefers to exalt or heal one and not another.

The classical example of the operations of such grace and a model of the path of holiness is that involving the leper. This can only be understood in the context of the whole biblical approach to disease and healing, as it is first spelled out to the people of Israel by God: "If thou wilt diligently hearken to the voice of the Lord thy God, and wilt do that which is right in his sight, and wilt give ear to his commandments, and keep all his statutes, I will put none of these diseases upon thee, which I have brought upon the Egyptians: for I am the Lord that healeth thee" (Exod. 15:26). Disease results from an inability or refusal to live within the rule of Torah, to accept limitation, and to one so afflicted, healing can only come from a sense of the divine Presence, from the Lord. The most grievous form of such affliction in the Bible is that of leprosy since one so diseased is prevented from functioning normally in society, is exiled from community. None of the normal rituals of atonement can heal him, nor any priestly officer. All that the priests can do is to diagnose the presence of the disease and order his exile. The efficacious rituals of atonement and consecration all occur "*if* the plague of leprosy be healed in the leper" (Lev. 14:3), an "if" concerning which there can be no assurance and that can only result from the operations of grace, that which chooses to heal one leper and not another. The rituals of cleansing occur only after he is healed and are most interesting.

First there is a ceremony involving two birds, one of which is killed and the other dipped in its blood and allowed to fly free, a clear symbolic reenactment of the death of the old self and its rebirth in the spirit. The freeing of the live bird occurs at the moment the healed leper is, with another ritual, pronounced clean: "And he shall sprinkle upon him that is to be cleansed from the leprosy seven times, and shall pronounce him clean, and shall let go the living bird into the open field" (Lev. 14:7). The sprinkling of the leper seven times would seem to draw the Sabbatical holiness into the purification process, thus not only cleansing him but making him holy.

The following rituals support this understanding of the special holiness and consecration of the healed leper. First he must "shave off all his hair, and wash himself in water" (Lev. 14:8), a ceremony also required in the consecration of the Levites for service in the Sanctuary (Num. 8:7), and then he is taken through the further steps marking the consecration of the priests, the anointing of the right ear lobe, hand, and foot with sacrificial blood and of the head with oil (Lev. 14:14–18; Exod. 29: 7, 20). The implication is that one afflicted and healed by God has been brought through the fire of a special consecration that renders him more holy than either the Kohanim or Levites, combining their functions of atonement with humble service in a life henceforth totally devoted to the God of his salvation. It is of such a one that Isaiah's God speaks when He says: "Behold, I have refined thee, but not with silver; I have chosen thee in the furnace of affliction" (Isa. 48:10).

God is here speaking to "Israel," and Jacob, like the nation that bears his name, also went through such a refining fire before he was transformed into Israel. At each stage in its development the soul has been refined by tests of ever more painful fire; the purer the soul, the harsher the perfecting trial.[70] As Shakespeare's Isabella points out in *Measure for Measure:*

> *Merciful Heaven,*
> *Thou rather with thy sharp and sulphurous bolt*
> *Splits the unwedgeable and gnarled oak*
> *Than the soft myrtle. (2.3.114–17)*

But however progressively difficult the trials of the earlier stages may have been, the trial at this penultimate stage must be the harshest, for it must finally split "the unwedgeable and gnarled oak" of self-centeredness. It is this most difficult final passage that we have seen symbolized in the figure of the leper.

The transformation of the leper from one hopelessly afflicted to one exalted in holiness is particularly revealing in distinguishing the path of holiness from that of love on its middle axis. The leper, indeed, marks the limits of the path of spiritual love, being beyond its power of saving. He cannot be energized by love to a healing faith in his own capacities but persists in his alienated condition of dis-ease with creation. Of those most afflicted, particularly by some form of mental disease or addiction, the prognosis is always uncertain. It is a complete mystery why Alcoholics Anonymous will work with one alcoholic and not another, why therapy will save one rather than another from severe depression. But that alcoholic or depressive who is saved from a life of total incapacity and degradation will henceforth be totally devoted to spreading the good news of whatever it is that saved him, will become a disciple and servant of that saving truth. His eyes will not be radiant with happiness like those of one on the path of love but glow with a deeper fire that bespeaks a knowledge of unbearable suffering and inexplicable grace, most of all of the power of holiness to wound and to heal.

The suffering servant, the wounded savior, is one whose old self had to be shattered that a new and holy vessel could be recongealed by divine fire out of the shards of the old. Of such a broken and restructured heart, the hasidic Rabbi of Pshische has said: "There is nothing more whole and complete than a broken heart."[71] Why that fire selects one rather than another shattered vessel for repair is based primarily upon affinity, some liking for those particular materials. Part of the secret of this affinity may lie in the very nature of the Sabbath: "And God blessed the seventh day, and sanctified it: because that in it he had rested from all his work which God created and made" (Gen. 2:3). If it is rest as a cessation of work that provides the reason and vessel for holiness, then he who has permanently stopped working may provide extraordinary materials for such a vessel. The moral leper, he whose spiritual disease has made him incapable of functioning in society, is one who has stopped working because nothing prescribed by society does work for him. It is only through such a psychic breakdown of the old imperatives, whether of society or of ordinary religion, as with Job, that an opening can be made for an all-consuming higher truth.

When Job, the biblical model of the perfectly observant Jew, was afflicted by all manner of suffering, his patience, built on the conventional theology of a just God, finally gave out and he cursed his day, suffering now more from his religious despair in the apparent injustice of God than from his various afflictions. But it is the suffering born from his very refusal to accept such easy answers of his faith as those offered by Eliphaz that finally earns him a saving vision of God:

> Then answered the Lord unto Job out of the whirlwind and said, Gird up thy loins now like a man: I will demand of thee.... [W]ilt thou condemn me, that thou mayest be righteous? . . . Then Job answered the Lord and said. . . . I have heard of thee by the hearing of the ear: but now mine eye seeth thee. Wherefore I abhor myself, and repent in dust and ashes. . . . [T]he Lord said to Eliphaz . . . ye have not spoken of me the thing that is right, as my servant Job hath. Therefore . . . offer up for yourselves a burnt offering: and my servant Job shall pray for you: for him will I accept. . . . So the Lord blessed the latter end of Job more than his beginning . . . (Job 40:6, 8; 42:1, 5–6)

In condemning God for His injustice in punishing him despite his perfect performance of the commandments, Job had, indeed, demonstrated the failure of his faith and had proved the justice of God through this very recognition of his own failed righteousness. But through the profundity of his spiritual struggle, he gains a mystic vision of that *mysterium tremendum,*[72] upon which he and the whole of creation is dependent, the vision that reconstructs his righteousness on the higher reverential level of the true Tzaddik, one whose prayers for others will be answered, who has achieved the power to bless and to curse.

So also, when Jacob found himself immobilized by the destructive effects of his past behavior, did he finally stop running and turn to God for deliverance: "Deliver me, I pray thee, from the hand of my brother" (Gen. 32:11). And his prayer was answered by a vision of God that transformed his being into a vessel of divine power: "And he said, Thy name shall be called no more Jacob, but Israel: for as a prince hast thou power with God and with men, and hast prevailed" (Gen. 32:28). This deliverance finally gives him, as it had earlier his father, the power of blessing that determined the fate not only of their sons but of nations.

The power of holiness does not work with the kindness of love; it does not support but breaks down the malfunctioning psyche that a new spirit can be born out of the catastrophic destruction of the old. Such shock treatment is fortunately not required for the correction of most disorders and is not guaranteed to work, but it is the final mechanism by which those who otherwise would be hopelessly doomed may be redeemed, and redeemed, moreover, to the highest uses of the holy. Those who have passed through its fires become filled with the holy power both to bless and to curse, daunting the proud and healing the incurable as they themselves were daunted and healed. They become the model of that path of salvation all must eventually tread in the course of their spiritual evolution, that in which the human must finally be sacrificed for the divine. For some, such as Abraham and Elisha, the sacrificial transformation seems to have been easier. Others less graced must, like Isaiah, be purged by fire from the holy altar. Not only must all the chosen pass through the holy fire to be remade in its image, but the whole of the cosmos had likewise to suffer a Shevirah, a breakage, before it could begin to achieve the very reconstitution that would seem to have been the purpose of its creation, its reconstitution into the holiness of divine personality.

THE UNIFYING PATH OF METATRON

We have seen that each of the five paths we have thus far traversed makes a unique contribution to the composite of the Yechidah soul. That symbolized by the bull-faced Chayah contributes a capacity for sensual experience, that associated with the lion an emotional capacity, that with the eagle a capacity to enhance and control power, that with the human face a cognitive capacity for self-awareness, which seems to be the source of self-sustaining spiritual life, that with Enoch the capacity for the sanctification of all experience. And as we shall shortly see, the path symbolized by Metatron gives the capacity for unification both within and beyond the self. But the paths to divine knowledge taken by each of these facets of the Yechidah soul lead as well to different personifications of this knowledge, to different understandings of the personal God with which they may be associated. Thus those on the path of the senses will see their personal God in terms of the mystery of divine sexuality, the primary mystery of the Kabbalah. Those on the path of the heart will see their God as love, that aspect of the Hebrew tradition most emphasized by Christianity. Those on the path of power will see their God primarily in terms of greatness and size, the mystery of the *Shi'ur Komah*. Those on the path of cognitive knowledge and vitality will see their God both through the operations of the cosmic Law and as the Living God who is its great Lawgiver, the primary concern of talmudic and modern halakhic Judaism as well as of such scientists as Einstein. And those on the path of holiness will see their God as a holy Presence, the primary concern of biblical and hasidic Judaism. Finally, those on the path of unification, the path of philosophy and meditation, will see their God as the incomprehensible and infinite Unity beyond but influencing all of creation, the ultimate God of mystical contemplation. Thus, as earlier noted, the personal God can be defined from these various perspectives as generative, loving, all-powerful, all-knowing, holy and One.

Between the first five paths and the sixth there is, however, an important distinction, as would seem to be noted in the *Zohar:*

> there are six grades in the divine revelation to the prophets: "appearance" *(maḥzeh),* "vision" *(ḥazon),* "revelation" *(ḥezyon),* "aspect" *(ḥazuth),* "word," and "burden." The first five aspects are all like unto the vision of one who beholds a reflection of light from behind a wall. . . . But "burden" signifies that the light came with great difficulty, and was barely revealed . . . for which no words could be found . . . the reason being that the mystic object of Faith is contained in grades within grades, each more recondite than the other; shell within shell, brain within brain.[73]

Though one may speak of six grades of revealed knowledge, the final all-controlling brain is not properly an object of revelation. But the following analysis of the final Metatronic path will attempt to pierce the veil surrounding this highest level of the Yechidah soul and its divine cognates despite the "burden" of difficulty this poses. This final level, which may be distinguished from the previous five levels or paths as that which completes the whole and gives it the identity that makes it greater than the sum of its parts, is of so recondite a nature that it will, indeed, be difficult to treat it in terms of its more recognizable human parallels. Though an attempt will be made to continue the double focus of the preceding sections, treating it as a path of knowledge with both supernal and human correlatives, the main emphasis will fall upon the supernal nature of the Yechidah soul and of its association with the divine. But since this is the highest level of the human soul, the nature of its association with the divine is a matter of the utmost importance to humanity.

The two forms of the Yechidah soul that we have identified with the personalities of Enoch and Metatron derive ultimately from the meaning of its name. *Yechidah* has two primary meanings, "individual" and "unique," and, as earlier suggested, it seems possible to identify the former with the concept of an individualized personal God and the latter with the concept of the incomprehensible One. But where the path of Enoch, of divine individuality, teaches the lesson of transformative consciousness necessary for communion with the holy, that of Metatron, of the divine unity, teaches the even more essential lesson of psychic unification. Before further consideration of this process, however, we should review the ultimate composition of the soul as defined in the *Zohar*.

At the beginning of this chapter it was shown that this Zoharic definition involves two triads of souls, a lower triad of the Nefesh, Ruach, and Neshamah souls and the supernal forms of these same three soul levels. But the *Zohar* modifies the traditional understanding that the Nefesh is always destined to disintegrate with the decomposition of the body:

> A *nephesh* which is destined eventually to find rest, when in the course of its wanderings it meets with *Yuhudiam,* the chief angelic messenger . . . is taken by him through all the doors of the Garden of Eden . . . and then it invests itself in all serenity with its *ruah* . . . when that *ruah* ascends to be crowned with its *neshamah* which is above, the *nephesh* joins the *ruah* and clings thereto with all its strength, and receives illumination from it. . . . And that *ruah* then joins itself in the same wise to the *neshamah,* and the *neshamah* unites herself with the end of Thought, this being the mystery of the *Nephesh* which is above, and the *Nephesh* which is above unites itself with the *Ruah* which is above, and that *Ruah* again with its *Neshamah,* and that *Neshamah* with the Infinite *(En-Sof).* . . . This constitutes the attainment of the rest and quiet of the *nephesh* that is below . . . the lower *nephesh,* when it descends, similarly illumined from all sides—from the light of the *neshamah* and of the *ruah*—also illumines all the . . . limbs and bones of its body, and forms them into one complete body which emits light. . . . Blessed are the righteous who fear their Lord in this world, for they merit the threefold rest of saints in the world to come.[74]

In this remarkable statement, the Nefesh of the righteous is understood to be capable of forming a body of light that can be incorporated into a sixfold spiritual body comprised of both human and divine elements, those from below and from above, all of which can attain to the final rest of the Sabbatical World to Come. Thus the illuminated body of sense remains an integral part of the final sixfold Yechidah soul.

But it is with the sixth aspect of this soul, what the *Zohar* refers to as the upper Neshamah, that we are now primarily concerned. Like the lower Neshamah on its third pole, this highest aspect of the soul is informed by a dominating sense of self. Where the lower master of power had to be self-possessed, the upper soul master *is* the true self of the soul, what in Hinduism is termed the Atman, and it must dominate and govern its multiple dimensions. We all know from our most mundane experiences of the multiple personalities within us that compete for the limelight of consciousness. For the most part we slip seamlessly from one dimension to another, from experiences of the mind, heart, or senses, each with its own organs, urgencies, and understanding, without ever doubting that the same "I" with which we identify is present in all these experiences. But sometimes, most often when the heart and head are in conflict, an act of internal sabotage may occur that can cause us to wonder who is in charge. When the right hand does not know what the left hand is doing, when we discover that a part of us knew all the time what another part had forgotten, then we may glimpse the possibility that the senses, the emotions, and the reason really do have minds of their own, each having its own private memories, needs, and tactics. In some more seriously impaired individuals, these centers of consciousness may organize themselves into several different personalities, in each of which these centers assume different orders of dominance. But even so-called normal people don different roles for different occasions and may come to wonder, the better they play these roles, who they really are.

As we must work to integrate our lower self, so must such integration be achieved above. The Yechidah soul not only has five lower dimensions or bodies and a governing self but may also rearrange them into various personalities, the Partzufim. It is the task of this governing identity so to orchestrate the activities of its lower faculties that they all function smoothly as an integrated unit, each given its own play and providing necessary input for the whole. For each may be said to represent a separate body of consciousness that can take over the master soul when it is permitted to become intermittently dominant. What distinguishes the upper Yechidah soul is its ability to integrate its multiple personalities so that they do not conflict with and sabotage each other but are mutually illuminating and fulfilling. It recognizes that all these aspects are necessary to its best performance and fullest experiencing of its conscious individuality.

The Yechidah soul may be said both to fill and surround cosmic space. Thus the Yechidah soul body, at least in its lower Enochian form, may now be imagined to surround the cosmic Chayah soul body with an auralike radiance and that all of its lower levels are enclosed within the witnessing and governing intelligence of that unity definitive of the ultimate Yechidah soul. Containing all prior layers of the soul—the sensual body within the body of feelings, within the body of spiritual power, within the body of cognitive knowledge, within the body of holiness—it is able to "measure the body of its Creator" because it has become one with it in size, power, and knowledge. As the Chayah soul has been identified with life, we have seen that it seems possible to identify it further with that aspect of the divine known as the Living God. Beyond this are the two other aspects earlier identified with the lower and higher levels of the Yechidah soul. Of this threefold distinction the *Zohar* seems to speak in discussing a line from the Psalms: "In fact, there are three grades here: 'God,' 'My God,' 'Thou.' Yet, even though there are three designations, there is really only one grade, as all allude to the mystery of the Living God: 'God' is the supernal One, the Living One; 'My God' denotes His omnipotence 'from one end of the heaven to the other'; and 'Thou' expresses the personal grade of David's awareness of this Presence."[75] In our terms, the Chayah soul would be identified with the Living God, the lower Yechidah with the personal quality of the Presence, and the upper Yechidah with the omnipotence of the infinite ruling intelligence. In the Yechidah soul, a unification is made, then, between the lower three soul bodies or intelligences deriving from the human and the upper three deriving from and identifiable with the divine, and all are integrated by that controlling intelligence whose secret is taught on the sixth path of unification.

At the Yechidah level the soul becomes one with the divine, not losing its identity but expanding it so that its own perceptions become those of the whole and are experienced as such. It is the nature of the Yechidah soul, as of the Godhead, to move between the poles of personal condensation and infinite expansion, between its identification with Enoch and with Metatron. The cosmic rhythm reflected in the inhalation and exhalation of the breath, in the awake and sleep phases of the day, in the weekdays and the Sabbath, may be presumed to continue at the highest level of spiritual evolution and to be derived from that divine nature to which it ascends. In its Enochian phases it may be thought to condense its sense of individual personality into acts of communion and in its Metatronic phases to expand it until it may serve as a centering point of the Limitless Light. As Metatron, the Yechidah soul is encoded in the sixth portion that completes the whole and forms it into a larger unity. It is the governing portion of the whole and expresses its uniqueness.

Not only may the Yechidah soul be partially identified with divine personality but there seems good reason to identify it as well with the mystical understanding of the Knesset Yisrael, the supernal community of righteous souls that God proclaimed as his son when he said: "Israel is my son, even my first born" (Exod. 4:22). The six faces of the Yechidah soul may be associated with six such souls traditionally understood to have experienced a theophany—Enoch, Moses, Elijah, Isaiah, Ezekiel, and Rabbi Akiba—figures representative of the many more Tzaddikim who form the collective soul of this Community of Israel.

But whether the Yechidah soul is thought of as a collective of specific righteous souls, those of the mystical Community of Israel, or as a collective of those soul bodies or paths that were earlier identified with the bull, the lion, the eagle, Adam, Enoch, and Metatron, it is a collective entity, each of whose elements have individual natures but all of whom identify themselves with the whole. The Yechidah soul is able to alternate between its partial individualities and its uniqueness as a whole, each part able to be conscious both of its distinctive manner of functioning and also of its participation in the whole, to see itself alternately as a part or as the whole. But the integration of the parts that permits them all to see themselves uniquely as the whole is the work of the governing intelligence identified with Metatron and the final lesson the soul must learn in its sixth path of knowledge. For it is only through this ability to see itself uniquely as the whole that the Yechidah soul can achieve union with the One.

This union is achieved not directly with the Ein Sof, the Limitless One, but with its manifestation in the Limitless Light, the Or Ein Sof. Indeed, the Yechidah soul or souls may be regarded as finally composing this reconstructed Limitless Light. Its soul body is that to which the *Eitz Chayyim* refers in its phrase "the surrounding light," a light expanding infinitely around the finite sphere of creation within the Tzimtzum. Within this sphere are the spiritual bodies of sense, feelings, power, and knowledge that comprise the Chayah soul, and at the point at which the Chayah and Yechidah souls meet, at the boundary between the internal and surrounding light, the Yechidah light condenses into the cloud of the holy. It is the difference between the Nogah (glow) and the Arafel (cloud) of which Ezekiel speaks and which is central to the imagery of the Throne vision. If the Yechidah soul is viewed as a collective of souls, then it can be identified with the whole of the Limitless Light. But if it is viewed as the ultimate salvific form of an individual human personality, then it would be identified with a centering point of this Light, a particular knot in its network of light. All individuals who have reached this point could be thought of as individually filling and transcending cosmic space, each connected to all others while retaining its own personal definition. And in such interconnection, the soul can experience all the others with all the levels of its being, in its senses, heart, and mind, transmitting and receiving the holy power by which the self is regenerated in ecstasy.

It is the development of such Yechidah souls from the raw material of earth-formed man that is the purpose of creation, for only such a soul can provide the vessel through which the divine can know itself in all its infinite variety, becoming that cosmic child in which the human and the divine achieve a final unification. The Yechidah soul, the ultimate divine son, is that spiritual level, redemptive of the whole cosmos and attained in the dimension of the Sabbath, that originated with man on this earth.

As we complete our cosmic journey, it is fitting that we turn our thoughts one last time to this glory-filled earth and the question of its centrality in kabbalistic cosmology, a centrality based on the appearance here of intelligent life. Either this is the only cosmic abode of such intelligent life or it is not. If, as most astronomers seem to feel, there is a likelihood of such life on similar planets in many galaxies, then there is no reason that the earthly myths cannot be transposed to them, particularly the kabbalistic myth of the Partzufim. Thus the Nukvah or Shekhinah could always be understood to ensoul the habitation of intelligent life, and Ze'ir Anpin or the Holy One, blessed be He, its immediate cosmic environment, whether its solar system or its galaxy. As each outpost of intelligent life may sport its own brand of local governing consciousness, so may they unite in the common center of the cosmic whole. In any case, one must distinguish between Ze'ir Anpin and Arikh Anpin or the Ein Sof and recognize that the former is probably meant to refer to the local cosmic environment as is the latter to the cosmic and extra-cosmic whole.

But we must also consider the incredible possibility that the earth is the only point in cosmic space and time where the seed of intelligent life has been able to take root and flourish, that through countless possible expansions and contractions of cosmic mass, only once, in an out-of-the-way corner of an insignificant star system, could the divine image become manifest in physical form. Then *dayeinu,* "it would have been enough." For on this tiny bit of cosmic dust, billions of souls have been able to achieve embodiment and evolve, enough to populate and govern all heavenly mansions and any number of daughter cosmic systems. If the ultimate consciousness of Ein Sof has been dimly experimenting with all manner of cosmic combinations, then here, on this green earth, we arrive at infinity, that final cast in an infinite series of throws in which the incredible improbability is realized, the goal of divine self-expressiveness made manifest in the perfect combination of factors permitting the evolution of humanity. And if humankind is, indeed, the bearer of the divine seed and promise, then its cosmic position would attract to it and concentrate more diffuse fields of cosmic consciousness. The divine essence would embody herself in this home planet of humanity as an indwelling spirit, the Shekhinah, and this darling of space and time would attract to its increasing generation of information the most perceptive and solicitous of cosmic energies. Thus as the toil of humans enriched the earth and their thoughts the cosmos, so would the souls of earth and heaven meet in a joyous embrace that would radiate power back to humanity and generate those higher souls that can finally share in the ultimate unification, whose joint personalizing of the divine and divinizing of the fully realized soul can alone give meaning to the cosmos and fulfillment to its purpose.

We have now arrived at the culmination of our own voyage through the music of the spheres to witness that bridging of the finite and infinite worlds in which the multileveled soul achieves its highest realization. And at its octave apex, as we envisage the angelic chorus singing the Kedushah before the Throne of the Infinite, we may finally imagine that our heavenly hosts have changed their tune to that of "*dayeinu*" and its meaning to "it is enough."

Appendix A

THE PRACTICE OF
TRANSFORMATIVE
MEDITATION

INTRODUCTION

This appendix will provide a guided meditation that should increase the effectiveness of the more general techniques of meditation offered in chapters 2 through 4. This "Master Meditation" is adapted from chapter 2 of my *Renewing the Covenant: A Kabbalistic Guide to Jewish Spirituality*. But before beginning it, there are a few instructions contained in this meditation that require some explanation. To begin with, the guided stage of this meditation begins with an abbreviated form of the attunement process developed in far more detail in *Renewing the Covenant*. That extended attunement process concludes with twenty-six repetitions of the "mantra" I have decoded in the *Sefer Yetzirah,* the first extant text of the Kabbalah, dated as early as the third century, C.E. This is the Hebrew phrase, containing the divine name Elohim, that defines its first Sefirah: Ruach Elohim Chayyim (Breath of the Living God). The number twenty-six is the numerical equivalent of the holiest of divine names, the Tetragrammaton, in the kabbalistic science of Gematria, and this number of repetitions of Ruach Elohim Chayyim should also have brought one to a high state of resonant energy and ready to begin the process of creative revisualization that is the essence of Master Meditation.

Since the effectiveness of such meditation depends upon one's capacity for visualization, part of this meditative process should be devoted to training of the higher Ruach visual center, the "imagination of the heart." The major kabbalistic technique for such training has been the visualization of Hebrew letters and the unification of divine names containing them. In what follows, however, I will be recommending the visualization of the cube and octahedron as an effective means of improving one's power of visualization while at the same time contributing to the construction of the spiritual bodies that they will be representing throughout the meditation. In chapter 7 of *The Secret Doctrine of the Kabbalah: Recovering the Key to Hebraic Sacred Science,* I have shown that it is the interfacing of these two regular solids that solves the geometric enigma of the *Sefer Yetzirah;* and in chapter 8 of that book I have shown how the relationship of these same solids not only contains the secret doctrine of the Kabbalah but is encoded in the geometric source underlying the central kabbalistic Tree of Life Diagram. As these geometric solids would thus seem to be at the heart of Hebraic sacred science, their visualization adds to the power of the mantra that continues to be repeated during their imaginative construction, which will here be offered in a version more simplified than that appearing in *Renewing the Covenant.* So it is good before beginning the meditation to have a clear idea of the form of the three-dimensional octahedron and of its spatial relationship to the cube as well as the shapes of the Hebrew letters that will also be visualized in the imaginative process of visualizing these regular solids.

The octahedron is best pictured as two pyramids joined together at their square bases; it is composed of eight equilateral triangles, four above and four below, meeting at a square. Figure A.1 will help to make its visualization easier.

The octahedron and the cube are said to be dualing solids because

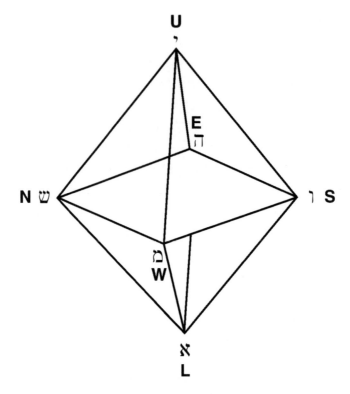

Figure A.1. The Octahedron

each can exactly contain the other. When the octahedron is positioned diagonally to the cube, the six points of the octahedron touch the centers of the six faces of the cube, and the eight points or corners of the cube touch the centers of the eight faces of the octahedron. In addition to these geometric forms, one should also be familiar with the form of the three letters in the Tetragrammaton, Yod, Hey, and Vuv, and the three Mother Letters of the *Sefer Yetzirah,* Aleph, Mem, and Shin, since the infinite cube to be visualized will be sealed by these letters, as specified in the *Sefer Yetzirah,* which has been an important source and inspiration for the meditation shortly to be given. To aid this visualization, the relevant Hebrew letters are reproduced in both figure A.1 and here: ׳ (Yod), ה (Hey), ו (Vuv), א (Aleph), מ (Mem), ש (Shin). After these visualizations of geometric forms and Hebrew letters, the meditation will move into its major phase with forms of visualizations and affirmations that continue the techniques of meditation specified in the classic kabbalistic texts discussed in chapter 3 of this book and more fully in chapter 2 of *Renewing the Covenant.* Each of the affirmations will conclude with the Hebrew word *vehayah,* normally translated as "and it shall come to pass," which is the reversed form of the Tetragrammaton, not Yod-Hey-Vuv-Hey but Vuv-Hey-Yod-Hey. In the appendix to *Renewing the Covenant,* I demonstrated that its consistent biblical use is as a power word, and its use in this meditation can strengthen and channel the manifesting power of these affirmations, as it can also be added to every good wish and carry every prayer into the manifesting work of time.

As earlier indicated, the guided portion of this meditation is most effectively performed after the initial process of attunement outlined above, which should ensure the *shefa,* the divine influx of energy, necessary to lift the meditator into the meditative state. It is from this point that the meditator will be guided forward to his re-creation as a divine personality. The spiritual progress through this meditation may be said to have four stages. In the twenty-six-breaths of the attunement process, one is still functioning from the Nefesh soul, the primary function of this attunement being to lift the Nefesh soul up to the Ruach level. In the subsequent work of geometric soul body construction and healing visualizations, the Ruach soul becomes activated, but it still is functioning in conjunction with a continuing Nefesh presence as long as its focus is on the individual. Finally, the consciousness moves fully into the Ruach soul body with the shift to relational vision, and one begins to experience as well the emerging presence of the Neshamah soul in the increase of information being filtered down, a presence that will continue to grow until it becomes dominant in the last phase of the meditation, a phase filled with the element of its light. With this brief introduction to some of the powerful tools and concepts, drawn from the Kabbalah, that will be used in the following guided meditation, we can proceed directly to it, using the second person grammatical form throughout to facilitate its use as a meditative aid.

THE MASTER MEDITATION

You should begin by seating yourself comfortably, closing your eyes and regulating your breath with the mantra Ruach Elohim Chayyim. In your silent pronunciation of this mantra, you should breathe in to the word for breath, Ruach, hold the breath for the divine name Elohim, and exhale the breath to Chayyim, the word for the living process made possible through the Ruach Elohim Chayyim, the Breath of the Living God. You should repeat this mantra twenty-six times, the numerical equivalent of the holiest four-letter Name of God, counting each repetition with your fingers, a process that should bring you into a state of higher attunement.

As you feel yourself filled by the divine breath, you should begin to build the permanent spiritual body, or Tzelem, of your Nefesh soul, visualizing it in the form of a cube of light. You should first imagine its square upper plane above your head, then its lower plane below your feet or cushion, then the planes in front of you, behind you, to your right, and to your left. As you experience yourself expanded into this resonant, crystalline body of light, you should imagine the cube to lift you a few feet into the air.

You should now imagine the octahedron, the visualized form of your Ruach spiritual body, and see it positioned diagonally to enclose the cube in which you are seated, the upper pyramid, with its forward point in front of you, coming down to join with the inverted pyramid rising to meet it, whose lower point may be imagined as just touching the floor. You should visualize all the triangles of the octahedron and be careful that all eight corners of your cube are exactly touching the centers of the triangles composing the octahedron before finally clamping the two pyramids together to form your Ruach soul body. As you begin to feel the concentrated force of this pyramid power, you should let it lift you out of your earthly space, guiding your octahedron chariot forward through the nearest window and swiftly up to the center of the galaxy.

In this starlit darkness of outer space, you should now construct the divine spiritual body of your Neshamah soul. From the Or Ein Sof, the Limitless Light, you should draw down the upper plane of your infinite cubic body, seeing it as composed of the same light as that which extends beyond it to infinity and sealing it to the upper octahedron point of your Ruach soul body with the letter Yod. You should draw this light down while inhaling your breath to the word *Ruach,* seal it with the Yod while holding the breath to the word *Elohim,* and then direct this light down through the Yod point of your octahedron Ruach body into your Nefesh and physical bodies while exhaling the breath to the word *Chayyim,* repeating this breathing rhythm for all six directions. From the lower direction, you should now draw up the lower plane of your body of Limitless Light, sealing it to the lower point of your octahedron body with the letter Aleph. From the forward direction, the forward plane of your Neshamah body should be drawn so that it fills the extent between your upper and lower planes, and it should be sealed to the forward point of your octahedron body with the letter Hey. The rear plane of the forming infinite cube should now be drawn forth and sealed to the rear point of your octahedron Ruach body with the letter Mem. Next, the right plane should be drawn forth and sealed to the right point of the octahedron body with the letter Vuv. Finally, the left plane should be drawn forth and sealed to the octahedron's left point with the letter Shin to complete the cubic form of your Neshamah soul body.

With your consciousness now centered within the layered light of your three higher soul bodies and extending out through them to the ends of the universe, you should next draw a beam of light down from the Limitless Light through the uppermost Yod-point and into your crown until it reaches your heart, bringing this light as well into your heart through the forward Hey and chest and through the Vuv and right side. You should let the force of this light build until you feel it shatter your heart, throwing off the shackles of your restrictive ego so that your heart can become a conduit between the transcendent power conveyed through the letters of the divine Name and the cosmic functions channeled by the Mother Letters, through which its purposes may come to pass.

You should now feel the power of the divine unity flowing through you from the Yod above to the Aleph below and providing the force that can unify the feminine power of the Hey with the masculine power of the Vuv, the Hey being similarly transformed through you into the contractive function of the Mem as is the Vuv into the expansive function of the Shin. You should feel and understand that it is only through this higher development of your heart that the transcendent wisdom and power can be translated into cosmic form.

As the infinite power streams through you from the letters of the transcendent Name to the Mother Letters of the cosmic functions, a unification, Yichud, of these letters is accomplished in your heart, the transcendent becoming enclothed in the cosmic, the unspeakable Name in works of the imagination. It is with this new imagination of the heart that the next level of spiritual work should be undertaken. As you begin the process of creative revisualization that marks the higher levels of Ruach spiritual work, you should try to maintain your awareness of this initial geometric work of soul-body construction, of the subtle bodies that enclose and empower you. For though their construction is a mode of training the higher imagination for its later work of manifestation, it also begins to accomplish the very manifestation of the higher soul bodies that is the ultimate purpose of this meditation.

Seated within your complex body of light, you are now ready to begin perhaps the most important phase of meditative work, that of healing. You should begin by drawing another beam of light down through the Yod-point of the Limitless Light and into your crown. As the single beam of light goes down through your head, it should divide into three beams, the right beam going down your right shoulder and arm, the left beam down your left shoulder and arm, and the central beam through your torso, at the base of which it should divide again into two, the right beam going down the right leg and the left beam down the left leg, the passage from unity to duality being mediated though the triplicity that can harmonize the one and the many.

Throughout the whole previous process of visualization and continuing to this point, you should have been repeating the mantra and doing all the imaging to its rhythm. In the present process, it is good to draw the light down through the crown and into your head, while inhaling the breath to the word *Ruach,* holding the light there with the breath to the word *Elohim,* and then sending the light down through your body to the word *Chayyim.* As you continue to do this with successive breaths, your physical body will begin to feel more and more charged with light.

Now send your consciousness down with this light, exploring all aspects of your body and spirit with it to see if there is any evidence of dis-ease and sending back a visual image of your inner condition to your imagination. Your consistent use of the mantra should stop at this point since you must now diagnose this image with your analytic intelligence, recognizing any pattern of disharmony it discloses and tracing it back to its source. Once you have diagnosed the nature and past sources of this self-defeating pattern, you should now enlist the creative capacity of your spirit to search the as yet unrealized future for a model of healing that can prescribe what is required for its cure. You should next direct your imagination to provide a second visualization in which this ideal cure has been adapted to the specific definition of your being with which you can identify. Finally, you should reinforce the power of this revisualization of your self-image in its already cured form with the following silent affirmation:

Let me be transformed into that body of light, radiating the psychic and physical vitality that arises from a willing conformity to the laws of creation, the compassion to love all that is produced by those laws, and the wisdom to understand both the nature and the higher purpose governing the cosmic Law, that I may make my creative contribution to the higher purpose of the cosmos that will fill my own life with meaningfulness while transmuting it into an instrument of divine revelation. VEHAYAH.

You should continue to breathe the light in through your crown and to let your exhalation carry it down throughout your body. Though your use of the mantra to regulate your breathing should not be resumed to allow the verbal center to participate in the higher work of manifestation, it is a good practice to end every affirmation with the manifesting force of the word *vehayah,* and you can, if necessary, repeat this three-syllable word a few times both to reestablish the regularity of your breathing and to direct its psychic energy into manifestation.

The work of inner-directed self-healing that you have just completed marks the first level of Ruach spiritual power, and in the remaining work of this meditation, you will ascend through levels of Ruach power to the final height of the spiritual master. The next higher level of this power is developed as one begins to direct this energy outward. As you have been breathing in the light and directing it down into your body for self-healing, you will begin to feel your body swell with this energy like a balloon, and just at the point at which it feels ready to burst, you should begin to direct the light you breathe in through the crown to go out through your heart at each exhalation, directing it forward through your chest. At the same time, you should also project the image of someone you have chosen to work with in this meditation, directing the light flowing down into you out to that visualized person. You will now repeat the same process with this chosen individual that you earlier used on your self.

First diagnose the image you have projected in terms of any psychic or physical malady it may disclose and then discover the specific cure you can prescribe for this condition. You should now revisualize that person in terms of your image of his or her more perfect realization and repeat the same silent affirmation previously used for yourself though with the substitution of that person's name and the appropriate pronouns for those by which you referred to yourself, such an empowering affirmation ensuring that your outwardly directed healing efforts will only be used for good:

> Let ———— be transformed into that body of light, radiating the psychic and physical vitality that arises from a willing conformity to the laws of creation, the compassion to love all that is produced by those laws, and the wisdom to understand both the nature and the higher purpose governing the cosmic Law, that he (she) may make his (her) creative contribution to the higher purpose of the cosmos that will fill his (her) own life with meaningfulness while transmuting it into an instrument of divine revelation. VEHAYAH.

After you have completed sending these healing and perfecting energies to the other person in your meditation, you should now address the improved image of that person from the level of your own visualized improvement with the invitation:

> Let our souls now embrace, recognizing that you are the other who completes my being as I am the other who completes yours, that together we form a higher unity whose purpose requires both our complementary natures. VEHAYAH.

You should allow yourself to feel that soul embrace with all your heart and soul, so that you can experience the unifying force that binds the two of you together. For anyone who is sufficiently present in your consciousness to become the subject of your meditation is someone with whom you are significantly involved, and it is the significance of this involvement for your life that you will now be meditating upon. You should try to vary the outer-directed subject of your healing meditation, and it is also good to meditate upon something other than a specific person, a problem area associated with your work, family, community, or world and to subject it to the same method of diagnostic visualization and prescriptive revisualization. In this case, the concluding affirmation should, however, be simplified in the following manner:

> Let ——— be transformed into that body of light, radiating the vitality, compassion, and wisdom through which it can make its creative contribution to the higher purpose governing the cosmos. VEHAYAH.

You should then engage in the same embrace with the informing soul of this situation or condition as you would with a single individual and with the same verbal invitation. Whoever or whatever the partner of this soul embrace may be, whether an intimate or a stranger, you should feel the embrace deeply enough to experience the force that binds the two of you into a unity, for it is through this experience that you can rise to the next higher level of Ruach power.

Where up to now you were contemplating only separate individuals, yourself and others, now you begin to see them in their connectedness. The next step is perhaps the most important one of the whole meditation and the most difficult. It requires a shift of consciousness from the individual aspect of yourself as a part of a relationship to the unity of that relationship of which you are a part, a shift from your lower ego consciousness to that larger or higher consciousness from which you can witness your ego self as part of a larger whole. If and when such a shift is truly accomplished, you will also experience a qualitative change that signals the movement into a higher soul body. From the heavier, fluid energies that signified the continuing psychic environment of the Nefesh soul body, you will now move decisively into a lighter element, the more "spaced out," ethereal environment of the true Ruach soul body.

The most immediate work at this third level of Ruach power does not seem to be much different from the work at the lower levels of this power with yourself and another, the work of creative revisualization. Thus again you will project an image of the relationship in which your ego self is involved and diagnose its strengths and weaknesses, those that bind you two together and those that are a source of stress and withdrawal. You will come to understand what function this relationship is serving for both its partners and what can be prescribed to cure its wounds, increase its health, and restore it to that creative purpose for which it was initially contracted. Most importantly, you will determine what energy your single self can contribute to the life of that larger whole of which you are a part to transform it into conformity with your higher vision.

It is such transformative work that most characterizes this level of Ruach power, and its nature supports the old truth that the only thing one can ever really change is oneself. Thus it is only when one's ego heart has so expanded that it can identify itself with such a larger whole that it can know what it needs to contribute to transform this whole. As the heart was earlier visualized as the organ through which transcendent vision can be transformed into the physical products of this cosmos, so can it now be seen to be the organ by which the dualities of this world can be again transformed to reflect their higher source and purpose. And it is only when the heart of an individual becomes as identified with the welfare of a larger whole as it is with its own self that its transformative work will serve the best interests of that whole, as well as of the still larger cosmic whole of which it is also a part. When you have completed this work of understanding and creatively revisualizing your relationship, you should conclude with this silent affirmation:

> Let this relationship be transformed into such a source of mutual empowerment. VEHAYAH.

We come at last to the fourth and final phase of the meditation, that in which your Ruach soul is uplifted still higher through prayer to become a garment for the Neshamah soul in its communion with the source of all, an ascent that can be invoked by the following prayer:

Let me be enlightened by the Ruach Ha-Kodesh, the Holy Spirit, to recognize myself as a centering point of the Limitless Light, with access to all knowledge, and may I rest in that state of blissful being that informs me of all I need to know (especially ————). VEHAYAH.

In this phase you should experience a state of spontaneous meditation and it should, if possible, be without seed, without the aid of any mantra. Whether or not you specify a particular problem you would like to have resolved in this final meditative experience, you should wait in a state of readiness for any answers that may emerge in your conscious-ness. Your previous work during the earlier phases of the meditation may have left a residue of unresolved or imperfectly resolved issues that may now begin to cohere into more instructive patterns. But whether or not this phase affords you any specific insights in answer to an explicit or implicit question, its blissful state is answer enough to the soul's true needs. After five to ten minutes of such wordless meditation, you should start to return to normal consciousness, concluding your meditation with this final prayer:

Let me return transformed by this crowning experience, my indi-vidual will ever enclothing the higher will. Let me draw its wis-dom and power down with me into the world of relationships that I may see and reveal the unifying force within all dualities. And as I reenter the physical plane of my body, let me ever walk in the way that is perfecting me into a body of light, the image of a twice-born, divine personality. VEHAYAH.

Appendix B

THE PRACTICE OF
TRANSFORMATIVE PRAYER

Where appendix A provided a guided meditation as an aid to the basic spiritual practice of meditation discussed in chapters 2 through 4, this appendix will provide a study both of the main stages of the Jewish prayer service and of its hidden meanings, meanings that contain the secret doctrine of salvation that has ever inspired the Jewish mystical tradition from the priests of the Second Temple to the kabbalistic Hasidim and their more modern interpreters. And this study will begin right where we ended our journey through the higher dimensions of the soul, with the Throne vision that chapter 5 has shown to be the central experience of the highest Yechidah level of the soul, a vision in whose very act of perception the union of its lower finite self with its higher infinite self is both accomplished and recognized to fulfill the purpose of creation. We shall now see how this purpose was enshrined in the traditional prayer service that was initiated by the Zadokite priesthood in the Second Temple, refined by the rabbinical sages and the early Merkabah mystics, and finally revealed by the later mystics of the Kabbalah and Hasidism, whose alternative traditions were directly descended from the secret doctrine of the Temple priesthood.[1] In the process we shall also see why the traditional prayer service has always been understood by the Jewish mystical tradition to be the most powerful of spiritual practices, transmitting a power to which one can become sensitized by meditation but that surpasses it as a source of evidential truth. This study will build upon the more detailed consideration of the stages and meaning of the prayer service to which I devoted chapter 4 of *Renewing the Covenant,* but it will also go beyond it.

That the prayer service, particularly on the Sabbath, is understood to be evoking the Throne vision is shown shortly before the Bar'khu (the beginning of the mandated central portion of the service) in the address: "O King who sits upon a lofty and sublime throne."[2] This identification of the object of prayer on the Sabbath as the enthroned deity is continued in the first blessing before the Sh'ma, which draws a connection between the Sabbath and the Throne: "To the Almighty God who rested from all His work, [who] on the Seventh Day was elevated and sat upon His Throne of Glory."[3] The first blessing, that of the heavenly lights, is informed by the understanding of the stars and planets as embodying the heavenly hosts of angels.[4] And it further incorporates the main angelic activity in the Merkabah literature, the singing of the Kedushah before the Throne of Glory, which they all "proclaim in awe."[5]

The Kedushah combines the theophany of Isaiah, "Holy, holy, holy is the Lord of hosts. The whole earth is full of his glory" (6:3), with the portion of Ezekiel's theophany relating to the "glory," "Blessed be the glory of the Lord from his place" (3:12). And its singing culminates the first phase of the service with the ten *oh* sounds of its Hebrew words[6]— *Kad<u>o</u>sh, kad<u>o</u>sh, kad<u>o</u>sh, Adonai tzeva<u>o</u>t. Mel<u>o</u> khal ha-aretz kev<u>o</u>d<u>o</u>. Barukh kev<u>o</u>d Adonai mimek<u>o</u>m<u>o</u>*—which give linguistic expression to the initial stage of awe that must initiate the act of true prayer. This phase may be said to reach its most powerful earlier expression with the beautiful prayer Nishmat, which begins: "The soul of every living being shall bless your Name, Lord our God." In full appreciation of the dependence of all "created things" and "all events" on a power so beyond them who yet "directs His world with kindness and His creatures with compassion," the soul, in true humility, can affirm:

> Even if our mouth were filled with song as the sea [is filled with water], our tongue with melody as the roar of its waves, and our lips with praise as the breadth of the firmament; and our eyes were radiant like the sun and the moon, our hands spread out as the [wings of the] eagles of the sky, and our feet as swift as the deer—we would still be unable to thank You, Lord our God and God of our fathers, and bless your Name for even one of the innumerable myriads of favors, miracles and wonders which You have performed for us and for our fathers before us.[7]

It is only such a sense of the total incommensurability of the praying consciousness with the source of its existence or claim upon it for the grace of continuance that can dislodge the power of the ego from the soul and so create a space for the divine influx, the *shefa,* that can then produce the incomprehensible wonder of their unification. As the process of divine Tzimtzum produces a space within the infinite in which the finite can come into being, so does the complementary human process of ego contraction, of that self-abnegation called *bittul* in Habad Hasidism, produce the space within the finite for the infinite to inhabit.

The principal disciple of the Baal Shem Tov, the founder of Hasidism, was Dov Baer, the Maggid of Mezhirech, and he shows this process to represent the purpose of prayer: "Think yourself as nothing, and totally forget yourself when you pray. Only have in mind that you are praying for the Divine Presence. You can then enter . . . a state that is beyond time. . . . [I]f you consider yourself as 'something,' and ask for your own needs, God cannot clothe Himself in you."[8]

This hasidic understanding of prayer as a process that brings the "Divine Presence," the Shekhinah, into the praying individual was well expressed by a later Hasid, Kalonymus Kalman:

> Once a man attains to humility he becomes automatically stripped of his corporeality to some extent. . . . In proportion to the extent

each man succeeds in humbling himself the more does he become stripped of his corporeality and the more does he remain in his purely spiritual state so that he then attaches himself to the worlds on high and become a chariot to that which he draws down into himself. . . . [W]hen the great *zaddikim* attach themselves to the worlds on high and have the garments of the body stripped off from themselves, the Shekhinah rests upon them. . . . [T]he main way or [*sic*] refining the soul so as to have knowledge of God's divinity and of how to worship Him, blessed be He, is prayer. . . . Now the true *zaddik* proceeds in his prayers through all the upper worlds until he reaches . . . Ein-Sof, the negation of all comprehension. Once he reaches that stage he draws down from there to the children of Israel the influx of grace and blessing.[9]

Becoming, through the mechanism of true prayer, a "chariot" Throne for the Shekhinah through the blessing he "draws down into himself," the Tzaddik can now become a channel of blessing to the worthy of the world.

But prayer's power of blessing goes in both directions. It will be remembered that the Nishmat prayer begins: "The soul of every living being shall bless your Name, Lord our God." Human beings also have the power to bless the Lord, to provide Him with some means to an end that He desires or needs; for as shown by Abraham J. Heschel, "God is in need of man."[10] It is not only the holiest portion of the service, the Amidah, with the originally eighteen and now nineteen blessings of the weekday service, but the whole service whose structure can thus be understood to channel human blessings to God. This, indeed, would seem to have been understood from the beginning to be the primary function of this "service of the heart."

Though Chayyim of Volozhin, like his teacher the Vilna Gaon, was largely an opponent of Hasidism, he did develop an understanding of the Kabbalah that clarifies this power of the human soul upon the higher spiritual realms, a power that forms the basis of kabbalistic theurgy and whose purpose he shows the talmudic sages to have recognized in the biblical source they quote:

> The sages expressed themselves similarly in the Midrash: "Rabbi Azariah said in the name of Rabbi Judah the son of Rabbi Simon. When Israel do the will of the Omnipresent, they add strength to the Divine Power, as it is written, 'We shall add strength to Elohim' (Psalms LX 14).... 'Everyone that is called by My Name I have created for My glory; I have formed him, yea, I have made him'" (Isaiah XLIII 7). Emphasize "for My glory have I created him." The mystery of this verse has been declared: The glory which is under the mystery of the Holy Throne does not become perfected except through the perfection of the sons of the world, when men are pious and pure, and know how to achieve perfection.... Israel pronouncing the sanctification below ascends. For indeed the whole purpose and meaning of the recitation of the Sanctification [the Kedushah] is the elevation of the worlds, their unification—the identification of each world with the world above it in order that their sanctity and the brilliance of their light be increased. Compare the teaching of the Zohar:... "They become joined in sanctity to all those who know how to sanctify their Master in perfect unity.... until they all become one Knot, one Spirit, united with those above them and one with them, identified with them."[11] (My brackets)

The greatest mystery of the cosmic process, what I have termed "the secret doctrine of the son," is here revealed in one sentence: "The glory which is under the mystery of the Holy Throne does not become perfected except through the perfection of the sons of the world, when men are pious and pure, and know how to achieve perfection." The spiritual devotions that perfect the human "sons of the world" also perfect the divine Glory. As the "glory" that fills the whole earth in Isaiah's vision is below the heavenly realm of the enthroned deity, so is this the position of Metatron in the *Shi'ur Komah:*

> And the hand of the Holy One, blessed be He, rests on the head of the lad His servant, whose name is Metatron. . . . [A]nd they say *Qodosh* and *Barukh.* . . . They say after him 'Blessed be the name of the glory of His kingdom forever and ever.' And he enters beneath the throne of glory. . . . And when [the lad] enters beneath the throne of glory, the Holy One, blessed be He, holds him in [the] facial radiance and all the attending angels . . . praise the Holy One, blessed be He, three times every day [led] by the lad.[12]

But since what Metatron is beneath is called "the throne of glory," its hidden meaning is still that it is properly the seat of the Glory, Kavod, the position as well of the antecedents of Metatron,[13] both representing the intermediate category of the divine as the holy Presence, the Shekhinah, who is actually seated on the Throne of Glory in the *Shi'ur Komah:* "And the Shekhinah is on the throne of glory in the center."[14] Metatron's leading of the angelic hosts not only in the Kedushah but in the blessing that appears right after the Sh'ma—"Blessed be the name of the glory of His kingdom forever and ever," in which there is a triple identification of the "name," "glory," and the "kingdom" signifier of Malkhut as the Shekhinah—is further suggestive of Metatron's hidden identification with the Shekhinah.[15] We shall later return to the significance of this triple identification, but it should now be clearer that the "mystery of the Holy Throne" is the further understanding that, in the words of Chayyim of Volozhin, "they all become one Knot," the human and the divine, the finite and the infinite "sons."

So in prayer the Tzaddik "draws down" the blessing of holiness that he may also return it on high, the human personality becoming divinized in the process of personalizing the divine until they "become one knot," the union of still distinguishable threads. The necessity of such mutual interaction for the fulfillment of the cosmic purpose is a common theme of the *Zohar,* as in the following passage:

the Righteous One takes all and inherits all, and all blessings are deposited with him. He first dispenses blessings above, and all the limbs of the body are disposed so as to receive them, and thus is brought into being the 'river which goes forth from Eden.' Why Eden (lit. Delight)? Because whenever all the limbs are knit together in harmony and in mutual delight, from top to bottom, then they pour blessings upon it and it becomes a river which flows forth, literally, from 'delight.' . . . For first the Holy Name must be blessed and then others. . . .[16]

So again the interaction of the Tzaddik, the Righteous One, is not with the highest form of divinity, Ein Sof, but with an intermediate category, before personified in the form of the Glory and now of Adam Kadmon, whose limbs, in the Tikkun being accomplished through the upward blessing of the Tzaddik, become personalized as those upper and lower couples of Partzufim that experience the "delight" of their sexually symbolized unifications, a delight that causes a reciprocal overflow of blessings to the world.

The central portion of the service begins with the words "Bless the Lord who is Blessed"[17] of the Bar'khu. Since in the words "the Lord who is Blessed" there is an acknowledgment of the blessed state of the Lord, the words "Bless the Lord" must signify something else, that the Lord whose blessed state is the source of blessing to us is also in need of the human blessings that, in the words of the Midrash quoted by Chayyim of Volozhin, "add strength to the Divine Power." These two separate meanings of the "blessing" of the Lord are clearly stated in a portion of the following first blessing before the Sh'ma: "Almighty God is the Master over all works, blessed is He, and He is blessed by the mouth of every soul." In the structure of the service, there are two "blessings," those using the formula "Blessed are you Lord," before the Sh'ma. The first, containing the Kedushah, is concerned to arouse that "fear of the Lord" whose more sublime form is the emotion of awe, and it concludes with the formal blessing, which should be understood in the double sense just defined: "Blessed are You Lord, who creates the luminaries."[18]

The second blessing before the Sh'ma, that known as Ahavat Rabbah, is concerned with opening the heart to the second complementary emotion of divine love that can "unite our hearts to love and fear Your Name." This is perhaps the most profound paragraph in the whole service. It is a prayer to be "taught the laws that bring eternal life," ostensibly the laws of Torah but more importantly the "laws" governing the spiritual realm and redeeming it through its mutual interaction with spiritually developed humans. It is of such spiritual laws that Chayyim of Volozhin also speaks:

> "And Enoch walked with Elohim"; "With Elohim did Noah walk"; "The Elohim before whom my fathers did walk." (Gen. V 24; VI 9; XL 15). Now Elohim signifies the Master of all Powers. These verses signify that these men understood the nature of the upper worlds, the laws of heaven and earth and their government, and how their direction, connection with each other and composition are determined by the works of man; hence all their actions in all matters were governed by the knowledge of what they conceived to make for the perfection of the upper worlds....[19]

It is with this understanding of Torah as "the laws of heaven and earth" that we should view the next expression of this prayer: "grant our heart understanding to comprehend and to discern, to perceive . . . and to fulfill all the teachings of Your Torah with love." This is not just the wish to observe all the stipulated laws and statutes with love for such observance, but that all such laws and teachings of their meaning can be fulfilled, as with Sabbath observance, simply through the divine love drawn down into the receptive human heart during mystical prayer.[20] The special insight of Franz Rosensweig, in *The Star of Redemption,* is that such redemptive love is not that of us for God but of God for us: "The relationship between God and the soul ever remains the same. God never ceases to love, nor the soul to be loved."[21] This burning love is understood by the humble and so receptive heart to be an evidential experience of grace, one in which we can already "rejoice and exult in Your salvation." What we so fervently wish in this prayer "to comprehend and to discern" is the law of salvation by which the experience of divine love in our hearts becomes the surety for our eternal proximity to that aspect of the divine figured in His "great Name." As the blessing ends: "For You are God who performs acts of deliverance, and You have chosen us from among all nations and tongues, and have, in love, brought us near, O our King, to Your great Name, that we may praise You, and proclaim Your Oneness and love Your Name. Blessed are you Lord, who chooses His people Israel with love."[22] Perhaps the greatest revelation of the Kabbalah is its central understanding that the divine "Oneness," proclaimed both here and in the immediately following Sh'ma, is not one of unity but of unification. Here it is between Israel, the chosen recipient of the divine love, and the divine hypostasis of the Name, whose love we can now return. In the Sh'ma it is, to begin with, between two different aspects or Partzufim of the divine.

Recitation of the Sh'ma is the high point of the service, its most significant act around which the whole service has been built, since it is this alone that the Bible commands Israel to repeat twice daily (Deut. 6:4). As I have shown at length elsewhere,[23] the Sh'ma, normally translated "Hear, O Israel, the Lord our God, the Lord is One," is esoterically understood to proclaim the unification of the two aspects of the divine that may be related to the transcendent and the immanent. This distinction the *Zohar* sees to be represented most generally by the two main divine names: "'For the Lord God (YHVH ELOHIM) is a sun and a shield' . . . (Ps. LXXXIV, 12). The 'sun,' he said, contains the mystery of the Divine Name YHVH, wherein is the abode of rest of all the grades, whereas 'shield' contains the mystery of the Divine Name ELOHIM."[24] Now, in the Sh'ma, the Tetragrammaton appears twice, the first time modified by the form of Elohim, "Elohaynu," meaning "our God," and the second time without such qualification. Thus the Tetragrammaton can be understood to appear first in its shaded form and the second time in its undiminished brightness, the first representing the personal God apprehensible in this world through His holy Presence and the second the completely incomprehensible form of His transcendent unity. But once the divine has been so distinguished, it is even more important to proclaim the unification of these extremes. Thus the Sh'ma may be read as signifying: "Here, [O] Israel, the Lord our God [and] the [unqualified] Lord [are] one."

But these extremes have also been kabbalistically understood in terms of gender, the former identified with the Sefirah of Malkhut, as that is with the Partzuf of the Nukvah and with the Shekhinah, and the latter with the Sefirah of Tiferet, further identified both with the Partzuf of Ze'ir Anpin and the Holy One, blessed be He. Most importantly, the *Zohar* had earlier shown that in the Sh'ma these two are unified with what can be considered its third element, Israel: "This is the recondite significance of the declaration: 'Hear, O Israel: The Lord our God, the Lord is one' (Deut. VI, 4). . . . 'Israel' here signifies 'Ancient Israel.' . . . 'Ancient Israel' symbolizes the union of the Shekhinah with her Spouse, and in pronouncing that name we have to concentrate our mind on the principle of unity, on the union of the two habitations."[25] But since Israel also signifies the divine son in the significant biblical statement of God, "Israel is my son, even my firstborn" (Exod. 4:22), the suggestion here is that "Israel" unifies "the Shekhinah with her Spouse" in the same way as parents are unified in a son. And if the Shekhinah is here being identified with "the Lord our God" as "her Spouse," the Holy One, blessed be He, can be identified with the unqualified "Lord," then we may finally see the Sh'ma as proclaiming the threefold unification represented in the following reading: "Hear: Israel, the Lord our Lord, [and] the [unqualified] Lord [are] one."

The inclusion of Israel in the unification esoterically understood to be the most hidden truth conveyed by the Sh'ma has also been noted by Tz'vi Hirsch of Zhidachov:

All the words of this pious man [i.e., Bahya] are based upon investigations of the true unity, in fulfillment of the commandment to unify God wholeheartedly, as stated in the portion of Shema Yisrael, and as it was transmitted to us by our venerable patriarch Jacob, who together with his unblemished sons proclaimed the unity of God when his soul was ready to ascend to heaven. . . . Now, my brother, the awesome ways of the unification of God were transmitted to us through the sacred Zohar and by the Ari [R. Isaac Luria] in his book *Peri Etz Hayyim.* According to this doctrine, the unification is effected by proceeding from below to above, through the channels of all the worlds in readiness to offer up one's soul. . . . *This, then, is the true meaning of the commandment to read the Shema: to unify all the worlds, i.e., sefirot, and all souls into the totality of the soul of Israel* [reaching] *unto the Ein-Sof by means of the willingness to offer up one's soul to the Lord.* Thereby we draw down power from the light of His essence . . . to the holy offspring, the people of the Lord, the nation of the God of Jacob. . . . In the unification of Shema Yisrael we elevate the female waters by offering up our souls to the Tetragrammaton, *and we include ourselves with all the souls and worlds for the purpose of ascending to the One.* . . . In this way the name *Elohim,* which denotes specific actions in all the worlds, is unified with the Tetragrammaton, the apex of all levels, and the two are unified with each other and included in each other, until the *ehad,* the First Cause, is reached.[26] (Emphasis added)

In Tz'vi Hirsch's understanding, Israel is recognized not simply as a nation but as "the holy offspring," what must be considered the collective form of the divine son Israel announced by God in Exodus 4:22. This latter is also covertly suggested by the repeated references to Jacob, the Patriarch whose name was divinely changed to Israel, in terms both of his God and "his unblemished sons." But Hirsch's most significant contribution is his further recognition that the unification generally understood in the Kabbalah to involve Partzufim or their correlated Sefirot is also to include Israel.

We now come to a further dimension of the Sh'ma and of the central portion of the service, the understanding that the triple unification of the Sh'ma, in which "we include ourselves" as part of the collective "soul of Israel," is only made possible through love. This is the evident conclusion we can draw from the placement of the Sh'ma between the blessing of the divine love that precedes it and the following commandment to reciprocate this love: "You shall love the Lord your God with all your heart, with all your soul, and with all your might" (Deut. 6:5). The development of such love is again facilitated by the esoteric understanding of the effects of sound, particularly of the vowel sounds productive of the harmonic overtones[27] on the human organism, here the five *ah* sounds, the sound of the relaxed and fulfilled heart, that appear in the Hebrew phrasing of this verse: *Veahavt<u>a</u>/ et Adonai Elohekh<u>a</u> / be knol levavekh<u>a</u> / uh vekhol nafshekh<u>a</u> / uh vekhol meodekh<u>a</u>.* And this *ah* sound, particularly as it appears in the word for the second person singular, *atah,* resounds in the midsection of the service extending from the Sh'ma through the Amidah, God addressing us as "you" in the Sh'ma and we addressing God in the Amidah, the standing prayer, with this same term of close, familiar address, of the face-to-face mystical encounter of love.

The first blessing of the Amidah begins with the forty-two[28] Hebrew words of its first paragraph that reflect the same understanding given in the Ahavat prayer of the receipt of divine love as, itself, effecting redemption. "Blessed are You, Lord our God and God of our fathers, God of Abraham, God of Isaac and God of Jacob, the great, mighty and awesome God, exalted God, who bestows bountiful kindness [*hasidim*], who creates all things, who remembers the piety [*hasday*] of the Patriarchs, and who, in love, brings a redeemer to their children's children, for the sake of His Name"[29] (my brackets). It is not simply that "the great, mighty and awesome God" who yet, like the Patriarchs, is filled with Chesed, loving-kindness, will in the future, because of his sympathetic love for the Patriarchs, bring the Messiah to redeem the Patriarchs' progeny, but that he "brings" the redemptive force of His love to these children in the very moment of their prayer "for the sake of His Name."

We here come to the very heart of Jewish mystical understanding, as it was already epitomized in this very prayer composed by the Great Assembly in the time of the Second Temple. And what it tells us is that the ultimate purpose of the divine-human interaction of love is not for the sake of God's reputation but somehow for the benefit of the divine hypostasis adumbrated in "His Name." The final words of the service, at the conclusion of the Alaynu prayer, clarify the separate character of this Name in its quotation from Zechariah 14:9: "on that day the Lord shall be One and His Name One."[30] As the *Zohar* will later explain:

> At the time when Israel is proclaiming the unity—the mystery contained in the Shema—with a perfect intention . . . the Spouse makes ready likewise to enter the Canopy in order to unite Himself with the Matrona. Therefore we proclaim loudly: "Hear, O Israel; prepare thyself, for thy Husband has come to receive thee." And also we say: "The Lord our God, the Lord is one," which signifies that the two are united as one, in a perfect and glorious union, without any flaw of separation to mar it. As soon as the Israelites say, "The Lord is One," to arouse the six aspects, these six unite each with each and ascend in one ardour of love and desire. The symbol of this is the letter *Vau*. . . . As he united Himself above according to six aspects, so also She unites Herself below according to six other aspects, so that oneness may be completed, both above and below, as it is written: "The Lord will be One, and his Name One (Zech. XIV, 9): Six words above—*Shema Israel YHVH Elohenn YHVH ehad*, corresponding to the six aspects, and six words below—*baruk shem kebod malkuto le'olam waed* (Blessed be the Name, etc.)—corresponding to the six other aspects. The Lord is one above; and His Name is One below.[31]

In this ultimate explanation of the unifications to be accomplished not only in the Sh'ma and that Zechariah prophecy concluding the service but also between their meanings, we learn first of all and again that Israel is to be included in the unification of the Sh'ma, now in its identification with the Shekhinah or Matrona. They are identified insofar as the heart of the praying Israelite is expressing the need of the Shekhinah for Yichud with her Spouse, a subject to which we shall return. This passage also shows that the inclusion of the six words following the Sh'ma—"Blessed be the name of the glory of His kingdom forever and ever,"[32] the word for "kingdom" here being a form of Malkhut and so a reference to the Shekhinah—is meant to encode the secret meaning of the Sh'ma, that the unity proclaimed is really a unification of the transcendent Lord "above" the divine immanence "below," that which embraces and equates the Shekhinah with the "name" and the "glory." So when God is said to act "for the sake of His Name," it is to perfect that variously termed intermediate form of divinity "below." This is the work of Tikkun requiring the collaborative efforts of both God and man, that cosmic fulfillment in which the earth-born son of man and his supernal Partzuf counterpart, both of whom have suffered a Fall and been twice-born,[33] finally become one.

In this development of the heart, prayer is the opposite of such directed meditation as we have seen in chapter 3 to have been practiced by major Kabbalists,[34] the type of meditation also exemplified in appendix A. Where such meditation requires a focusing of the will and so of the mind to be effective, effective prayer involves an abnegation of the will and opening of the heart. We have seen that meditation can be used to further the work of the soul at its lower levels, but to complete this development at its highest level, the meditation-sensitized soul must finally follow the path of Enoch—"And Enoch walked with God: and he was not; for God took him" (Gen. 5:22)—the devotional path of ego-less prayer. It is only such prayer as can draw the divine love down into the human heart that can fulfill the cosmic purpose of producing such a purified specificity as can personalize and clothe the spiritual power preceding and underlying all.

In the prayer of such a humility-opened heart, the words of the liturgy become the conduits for the responsive influx of love that fills such a heart, words that simply require an attention to their meaning. There is an uncanny magic working here reflective of the spiritual "laws of heaven and earth and their government," of which Chayyim of Volozhin has spoken. Something of how such laws could become manifest in the holy potential of prayer can be drawn from an understanding of its history. It is my contention that the secret doctrine the Zadokite priesthood bequeathed to the whole of the Jewish mystical tradition developed from the priestly experience of the holiness the officiating priests were first able to draw into the sacrifices they offered up and then into their own persons through their eating of the sacrifices, a holiness that they then were able to ritually transfer to the prayer service whose core they developed and practiced in the Second Temple.[35]

As further expanded by the spiritually knowledgeable after the destruction of the Temple, the prayer service continued to become an ever more powerful conveyer of spiritual energy as its ritual observance carved ever deeper grooves into the spiritual dimension of reality. It is for this reason that recitation of the service in Hebrew is more powerful than in the vernacular; its two thousand years of repetition have made it a more resonant vehicle of spiritual energy. But as it is even more important that the words be understood, English recitation, though lacking the same spiritual voltage as understood Hebrew, is powerful enough to produce that evidential experience of a higher reality which, for William James, makes prayer the greatest means of access to the existence of something "more":

> religion, wherever it is an active thing, involves a belief in ideal presences, and a belief that in our prayerful communion with them, work is done, and something real comes to pass. . . . [M]an identifies his real being with the germinal higher part of himself;

and does so in the following way. *He becomes conscious that this higher part is conterminous and continuous with a* MORE *of the same quality, which is operative in the universe outside of him, and which he can keep in working touch with.* . . . Disregarding the over-beliefs, and confining ourselves to what is common and generic, we have in *the fact that the conscious person is continuous with a wider self through which saving experiences come,* a positive content of religious experience which, it seems to me, *is literally and objectively true.* . . . The appearance is that in this phenomenon something ideal, which in one sense is part of ourselves and in another sense is not ourselves, actually exerts an influence, raises our centre of personal energy, and produces regenerative effects unattainable in other ways.[36]

The whole process of such evidential prayer as can fill the consciousness with the conviction of a spiritual "more" to reality has been given a knowing expression by Abraham Isaac Kook, the chief rabbi in pre-Israel Palestine, and it conveys the understanding of the entire Jewish mystical tradition:

if the disposition of divine love has begun to vibrate in him . . . and his great thirst remains unquenched. . . . This is in essence the anguish of the *shekinah,* the anguish of the divine Presence. . . . [W]hoever is ready for constant cleaving to God cannot be content with any state below this. . . . But one cannot reach this except through a profound sense of humility, experienced when the spirit expands with great joy in the light of God. . . . As a result of all this the joy of the soul will become more pervasive and the state of cleaving to God will rise to its highest climax, to a point where the grandeur of God will become manifest in the soul. . . . [T]his will not be realized fully until it will be accompanied by sincere prayer. Then will the mighty fountain send forth its flow upon the soul.[37]

True prayer, then, involves that humble sense of dependence whose contraction of ego can leave a space for the influx of divine love. And as the need resulting from this pained comprehension of total dependence can be said to express the anguish of the Shekhinah, so can the influx be understood to be the response of her Spouse, the Holy One, blessed be He, their unification taking place in the heart whose transformation during prayer may also be said to engender that higher self which truly can clothe the divine. The folk identification of the human soul as feminine and the transcendent God as masculine reflects this sexual model of Devekut, that clinging of the receptive heart by which it becomes the vessel for the Holy Spirit drawn into it by its yearning.

Rav Kook not only recognizes that the soul achieves its fullest realization in manifesting "the grandeur of God," but also that the soul has something inestimable to bequeath to its source, its spiritually developed and purified individuality: "However life breaks down into particularization, it continues to draw light from the original divine light, and it needs to return to the higher realm, together with the essence of our souls. Then we shall not ascend devoid of riches and we shall not fail because of feebleness, for we shall not return naked to the higher realm. We shall have with us our multicolored robes we acquired as a result of the proliferation of all life."[38] The return to the spiritual will not be a return to the supposedly perfect realm of the past but to that future realm of all and present realm of many whose perfection has required and profited from the cosmic process precisely in what the perfected human souls, most fully realized in and through prayer, can now give to divinity, "our multicolored robes."

NOTES

NOTES TO CHAPTER 1

1. *The Zohar,* trans. Harry Sperling, Maurice Simon, and Paul P. Levertoff, 5 vols. (London: Soncino Press, 1978), vol. 3, pp. 409–11 (Mantua: 2, 141b–142a).

2. Chayyim Vital, *The Tree of Life: The Palace of Adam Kadmon,* ed. and trans. Donald Wilder Menzi and Zwe Padeh (Northvale, N. J.: Jason Aronson, 1999), p. 32.

3. See Gershom Scholem, *Kabbalah* (New York: New American Library, 1974), p. 229.

4. *Zohar Hadash, Midrash ha-Ne'elam on Ruth,* 82c–82d, trans. David Goldstein, in Isaiah Tishby, *The Wisdom of the Zohar: An Anthology of Texts* (London: Oxford University Press, 1991), vol. 2, pp. 729–31.

5. See Rachel Elior, *The Paradoxical Ascent to God: The Kabbalistic Theosophy of Habad Hasidism,* trans. Jeffrey M. Green (Albany: State University of New York Press, 1993), pp. 103–24, for an excellent treatment of the two aspects of the soul in Habad Hasidism that, though termed the "divine soul" and the "bestial soul," "are not two separate souls but rather two sorts of consciousness or two separate types of interpretive apprehension" (pp. 104–5).

6. As will be shown in the conclusion to this chapter, there is a Lurianic tradition that it was just the six Sefirot identified with the son Partzuf of Ze'ir Anpin that shattered. See also my book *The Secret Doctrine of the Kabbalah: Recovering the Key to Hebraic Sacred Science* (Rochester, Vt.: Inner Traditions, 1999), p. 289.

7. See Aryeh Kaplan, ed. and trans. *Sefer Yetzirah* (York Beach, Maine: Samuel Weiser, 1990), pp. 185–87, as well as his essay on the age of the universe in *Immortality, Resurrection and the Age of the Universe* (New York: Ktav, 1993).

8. Scholem, *Kabbalah,* pp. 132–33.

9. See *The Secret Doctrine of the Kabbalah,* pp. 222–32, which, on p. 226, also contains the diagram I have called "The Hexagram of Creation."

10. *Zohar,* vol. 1, p. 126 (Mantua: 1, 34a).

11. Scholem, *Kabbalah,* p. 108.

12. See *The Secret Doctrine of the Kabbalah,* chapter 3, for my full exposition and comparison of Hellenic and Hebraic sacred science.

13. Vital, *Tree of Life,* p. 14.

14. Kaplan, *Sefer Yetzirah,* p. 261.

15. See *The Secret Doctrine of the Kabbalah,* pp. 390–95, for my attempt to reinterpret the concept of geometric dimension and to extend it beyond the four of space-time to include the upper three dimensions of my cosmological model.

16. Another solution is provided by Cordovero in his *Or Ne'erav* (part 6, chapter 3), where reference is made to "Nezah and Hod, these two testicles of the male." See *Moses Cordovero's Introduction to Kabbalah: An Annotated Translation of His Or Ne'erav,* ed. and trans. Ira Robinson (Hoboken, N.J.: Ktav, 1994), p. 129.

17. See Tishby, *Wisdom of the Zohar,* vol. 2, p. 690.

18. Scholem, *Kabbalah,* p. 120.

19. Ibid., p. 336.

20. Ibid., pp. 121–22.

21. *Zohar,* vol. 1, pp. 83–84 (Mantua: 1, 19b–20a).

22. Vital, *Tree of Life,* p. 24.

23. Ibid., p. 89.

24. Ibid., pp. 33–34.

25. Ibid., p. 10.

26. Ibid., p. 20.

27. Ibid., p. 22.

28. Gershom Scholem, *On the Kabbalah and Its Symbolism,* trans. Ralph Manheim (New York: Schocken Books, 1969), p. 117.

29. Vital, *Tree of Life,* p. 13.

30. See *The Secret Doctrine of the Kabbalah,* chapter 10, which is devoted to this comparison, though lacking the further synthesis of the Lurianic theory with the Zoharic that, as will shortly be pointed out, allows the Tzimtzum model to be still more coherent with the big bang theory of modern cosmology.

31. Max Black, *Models and Metaphors: Studies in Language and Philosophy* (Ithaca,

N.Y.: Cornell University Press, 1962), p. 237. See also my more extended treatment of his analysis in *The Secret Doctrine of the Kabbalah,* pp. 209–10.

32. Scholem, *Kabbalah,* p. 130.

33. Figure 1.4 is the work of Cynthia Ryan Coad of Inner Traditions, and I am most appreciative of her success in giving graphic form to my vision.

34. My next book, still in the process of revision under the working title of *The Star and the Tree,* discusses a new form of experimental geometry that develops a self-similar, enlarging structure derived from the kabbalistic Tree of Life Diagram, a construction of hexagrams whose ever more complex and unpredictable, but repeatable, expansions become the model both for a new understanding of the Kabbalah and a new theory of complexity. In terms of the latter, this model proceeds from an initial condition of chaotic irregularity to a regularity that increases as it grows in complexity until a particular magnitude is reached. It is the magnitude at which the complexity of its components overwhelms the capacity of the system to provide data that are still meaningful, at which point a phase shift occurs through which this data are simplified by a higher level of analysis or programming. In this case it involves the shift from manually constructed geometric expansion to a computer iterative algebraic formula whose three components, one each from the final three geometric expansions, derive from the reduction of all the numerical details of such expansions to a single fraction. This computer program was iterated six thousand times to 1,500 decimal places to reveal a wealth of complex patterning. The development of such intricate patterning from a unique combination of components—from Ilya Prigogine through Humberto Maturana and Francisco Varela to, among others, Stephan Wolfram—has been put down to "self-organization." But this not only violates the vertical hierarchy of rules over components in what I still take to be a viable aspect of general systems theory, that systems contain the dual levels of macrodeterminacy and microindeterminacy; it is also contradicted by the fact that this patterning is a product of a ruling computer program. In what becomes a study of an infinite converging decimal series, periods of one form of patterning suddenly shift to a brief, chaotic transition before a new form of patterning reestablishes itself. It is from this mathematical model that I derive the final "law of complex magnitudes" to which I allude in the text. My present discussion of the program paradigm for cosmic modeling draws, then, from the exhaustively precise analysis of my own scientific model of complexity.

One conclusion that I draw from this culminating "law" is that a "complex" system is one that increases in regularity as it grows in size, as is the case with an organism, while a "simple" system is one dominated by irregular or random instability, as with a storm. These latter systems I consider "simple" because they can never achieve the stable, multifaceted organization of the truly complex systems whose generation of more highly evolved stable forms gives meaning to the cosmic process. This is the opposite of the definitions and consequent conclusions developed by Stephen Wolfram in his recently published, detailed study of cellular automata entitled *A New Kind of Science* (Champaign, Ill.: Wolfram Media, 2002). Wolfram again proves, though with far more systematic exploration and attempted analogies than ever before, that simple programs with simple initial conditions can yield outcomes of remarkably intricate and often beautiful patterning. My book will prove the same. But this choice of significant outcomes reveals the perhaps unfortunate truth that one's most rationally developed scientific or logical proofs are just the fancy dress in which we clothe our personal convictions or prejudices. Thus he dismisses, with the oft-stated words "obviously simple," the majority of uniquely patterned outcomes of slightly different initial components or rules if they show any beauty-generating regularity like nesting and bestows his more honorific term "complex" on the few programs, like rule 110, that produce pure randomness. Further, he takes such production of randomness not only to be the "universal program" that can model the cosmos but derives from this his culminating "Principle of Computational Equivalence" that all such programs have equivalent computational sophistication, that is, that no single such outcome is more meaningful than another. Thus he seems convinced that he has demonstrated that cosmic functioning is essentially random and meaningless. I hope that my book will just as scientifically prove the opposite.

35. "Sifra de-Tzeni'uta" (The Book of Concealment), in *The Zohar*, 3 vols., ed. Reuven Margoliot, Hebrew-Aramaic Edition (Jerusalem: Mossad ha-Rav Kook, 1964), vol. 2, 176b, Parshat Truma; Margoliot, vol. 2, p. 352. My translation.

36. I would like to express my deep indebtedness to Dr. Julian Ungar-Sargon not only for stimulating my interest in and treatment of the "Sifra de-Tzeni'uta" but even more for his seminal role in the inception of this book.

37. See Scholem, *Kabbalah,* p. 142.

38. For my radical thesis that the Hebraic Temple priesthood was the source of

the entire Jewish mystical tradition, see *The Secret Doctrine of the Kabbalah,* chapter 1, especially pp. 2–11.

39. For the relevant Platonic text plus the fine explanation of Plato's musical references by its editor, see *Plato's Cosmology: The Timaeus of Plato,* ed. and trans. Francis MacDonald Cornford (Indianapolis: Bobbs-Merrill, n. d.), 35B–36B; pp. 66–72.

40. See again my discussion of sacred science in chapter 3 of *The Secret Doctrine of the Kabbalah,* particularly pp. 74–86.

41. For a fuller understanding of the three Pythagorean means—harmonic, geometric, and arithmetic—see my discussion of Pythagorean sacred science in *The Secret Doctrine of the Kabbalah,* particularly pp. 77–80; see also the central position of these means in Simone Weil's brilliant study "The Pythagorean Doctrine," in her *Intimations of Christianity,* trans. Elisabeth Chase Geissbuhler (London: Routledge and Kegan Paul, 1957).

42. Chayyim Vital, *Sha'ar ha-Gilgulim,* as trans. and quoted in Gershom Scholem, *Sabbatai Sevi: The Mystical Messiah,* trans. R. J. Zwi Werblowsky, Bollingen Series 93 (Princeton: Princeton University Press, 1973), p. 43.

43. Rabbi Zevi of Zydaczow, *Sur me-Ra va-Aseh Tov,* trans. and quoted in Gershom Scholem, "Redemption through Sin," trans. Hillel Halkin, in *The Messianic Idea in Judaism and Other Essays on Jewish Spirituality* (New York: Schocken Books, 1971), p. 348.

44. Scholem, "Redemption through Sin," pp. 94, 108.

45. Jacob Frank, *The Sayings of the Lord,* trans. and quoted in Scholem, "Redemption through Sin," p. 130.

46. Scholem, *Sabbatai Sevi,* pp. 301–2.

47. C. G. Jung, *On the Nature of the Psyche,* trans. R. F. C. Hull, Bollingen Paperback (Princeton: Princeton University Press, 1969), pp. 116–18.

48. Scholem, "Redemption through Sin," p. 99.

49. For a comprehensive treatment of the "secret doctrine of the son," which has informed the whole of the present chapter, see *The Secret Doctrine of the Kabbalah,* chapter 2.

50. Except where noted, my quotations of the Bible in English translation are always from the King James Version, which I prefer not only for its familiarity but also because its greater literalness often proves a better guide to esoteric meaning than more modern translations.

51. Abraham Abulafia, *The Rose of Mysteries [Shoshan Sodoth],* trans. Aryeh Kaplan, in *Meditation and Kabbalah* (York Beach, Maine: Samuel Weiser, 1982), pp. 109–10.

52. R. H. Charles, ed. and trans., *The Book of Enoch or 1 Enoch* (Oxford: Clarendon Press, 1912), p. 67.

53. *The Ethiopic Book of Enoch,* ed. and trans. Michael A. Knibb (Oxford: Clarendon Press, 1978), vol. 2.

54. *3 Enoch or The Hebrew Book of Enoch,* ed. and trans. Hugo Odeberg, prolegomenon by Jonas C. Greenfield (1928; reprint, New York: Ktav, 1973), pp. 3–5, 8–9, 13, 22, 25, 27, 28–9, 33, 39. My brackets.

55. *Shiur Qoma,* trans. The Work of the Chariot, in *The Secret Garden,* ed. David Meltzer (New York: Seabury Press, 1976), pp. 23, 24, 32.

56. *Shiur Qoma,* in *The Secret Garden,* p. 34.

57. I have preferred the translation by The Work of the Chariot in this instance to that of the more scholarly edition and translation of Martin Samuel Cohen, *The Shi'ur Qomah: Liturgy and Theurgy in Pre-Kabbalistic Jewish Mysticism* (Lanham, Md.: University Press of America, 1983), because it preserves the usage "son of the world to come" that Cohen suppresses but which is true to the original manuscripts. In a private correspondence to me, dated August 8, 1984, Cohen wrote: "The expression to which you refer does indeed contain the Hebrew word *ben* in the expression '*ben ha'olam haba*.' Literally, the words do mean 'a son of the world to come'. . . . The word itself . . . does appear in virtually all of the manuscripts of the *Shiur Komah* known to me." Cohen's preference for a less literal translation of the phrase "*ben ha'olam haba*" follows Scholem (see *Major Trends in Jewish Mysticism* [New York: Schocken Books, 1961], p. 64), but such nonliteral translation obscures the possibility of special esoteric content. Here, as in biblical translation (see note 50 above), literal translation is always to be preferred, and this because central classical texts often preserve esoteric meanings whose significance has become obscured or dulled in more conventional usage of such terminology. In his introduction, Cohen makes the following comment on the translation of this text by The Work of the Chariot: "Their work is literal, but incomplete, and is based solely on the *Sefer Razi'el* recension of the text" (30). I have preferred to use this literal translation when it clarifies meanings.

58. From the "Sh'ar ha-Kelalim" introductory section to the *Eitz Chayyim* of Chayyim Vital (Jerusalem: Kitvei ha-Ari, 1958), *Eitz Chayyim* vol. 1, Hebrew text, chap. 1, p. 2. My translation.

59. Ibid., chap. 4, p. 8.

60. See Eliahu Klein, ed. and trans., *Kabbalah of Creation: Isaac Luria's Earlier*

Mysticism (Northvale, N.J.: Jason Aronson, 2000), pp. 22–23. In this recent translation of the "Sha'ar ha-Kelalim," Klein, following Yossi Avivi and other Kabbalah scholars, attributes this text in whole or part to a direct student of Isaac Luria, Moshe Jonah.

61.   The distinction I have made between the collective and individual aspects of the soul, later to be defined as its "central" and "lateral" aspects, may be compared with the two classes of personality as of religious experience that William James calls "sick," the category with which he identifies himself, or "healthy-minded" in *The Varieties of Religious Experience* (New York: The Modern Library, 1902): "The sanguine and healthy-minded live habitually on the sunny side of their misery-line, and the depressed and melancholy live beyond it, in darkness and apprehension. . . . Does it not appear as if one who lived more habitually on the one side of the pain-threshold might need a different sort of religion from one who habitually lived on the other?" (p. 133).

62.   A similar contrast of the "perennial philosophy" with "enacted" spiritual goals has been drawn by Jorge N. Ferrer in his remarkable new book, *Revisioning Transpersonal Theory: A Participatory Vision of Human Spirituality* (Albany: State University of New York Press, 2002), which, though published too late to be incorporated more integrally into this book, I would now like both to quote and comment upon at length:

> . . . perennialist models typically assume the existence of a universal spiritual reality which is the Ground of all that is, and . . . consistently characterize it as Nondual, the One, or the Absolute. . . . In contrast, what the mystical evidence suggests is that there are a variety of possible spiritual insights and ultimates. . . . [T]he common ocean to which most spiritual traditions lead is not a pregiven spiritual ultimate, but . . . has many spiritual shores, some of which are enacted by the world spiritual traditions. . . . [O]nce a particular spiritual shore has been enacted, it becomes potentially accessible . . . to the entire human species. . . . The various spiritual ultimates accessed during special states of consciousness . . . can be seen as independently valid enactions of a dynamic and indeterminate spiritual power. . . . The idea of a reciprocal relationship between the human and the divine finds precedents in the world mystical literature. Perhaps its most compelling articulation can be found in the writings of ancient Jewish and Kabbalistic theurgical mystics. . . . As Idel puts it, the theurgic mystic "becomes a cooperator not only in the maintenance of the uni-

verse but also in the maintenance or even formation of some aspects of the Deity" (p. 181) [*Kabbalah: New Perspectives* (New Haven: Yale University Press, 1988)]. . . . In a participatory cosmos, human intentional participation creatively channels and modulates the self-disclosure of Spirit through the bringing forth of visionary worlds and spiritual realities . . . ultimately illuminating the mind with a knowing that is both grounded in and coherent with the Mystery. . . . [S]ome spiritual paths and liberations may be more adequate for different psychological and cultural dispositions . . . the indeterminate nature of ultimate reality may be seen to be, legitimately I believe, more in alignment with some spiritual traditions than others. (pp. 89, 146, 149, 150, 153, 157, 169, 170, 179).

Ferrar's understanding of the "spiritual referent as malleable, indeterminate, and open to a multiplicity of disclosures contingent on human creative endeavors" (p. 166) is one I have variously expressed throughout this work, perhaps in most concentrated form in the last sections of chapter 3 detailing the higher workings and powers of the Ruach level of the soul. But though this can best explain the coevolutionary present state of Spirit in the multiplicity of the cosmos, the dialectical opposition Ferrar has noted "between the One and the Many" (p. 191) in spiritual traditions also has the temporal dimension I have discussed above in my text, the One of the perennialists representing the original precosmic source of cosmic emanation and the Many of Ferrar's "spiritual shores" such "enactions" of this "malleable" spiritual substance as, in kabbalistic terms, can provide the garments through which this "Ground of all" can achieve the ever more perfect expression of its Being "coherent with the Mystery." Moshe Idel has rightly focused on the human agency necessary to accomplish such a new "formation of some aspects of the Deity," but the essential salvific gnosis of this tradition is that the mystics engaged in this transformative process *share* in the divine transformation, becoming the androgynous "sons" of the transcendent and immanent forms of the Divine whose unification they have accomplished in and through their mystical practice.

Though I have suggested a way of synthesizing Ferrer's "revisioning" of transpersonal theory with the perennialist perspective he critiques, this not simply in terms of their being the "spiritual shores" enacted by the two major orientations found in the world's great spiritual traditions but also as representing the two necessary stages of any cosmology that would derive a material cosmos from a preexistent and spiritual Ground of Being, his revisioning clearly is "more in alignment with some spiritual traditions than others." And as he has recognized that "perhaps its most compelling articulation can be found in the writings of ancient Jewish and Kabbalistic theurgical mystics," so do his penetrating and original analyses of the philosophical issues that have attended the history of transpersonal theory and his revisioned conceptualization of the workings of spiritual reality provide a new framework for appreciating my similar attempt to revision the tradition of Jewish mysticism.

63. Elliot R. Wolfson, in *Through a Speculum That Shines: Vision and Imagination in Medieval Jewish Mysticism* (Princeton: Princeton University Press, 1994), has demonstrated the central position of the Throne vision in the whole history of Jewish mysticism and shown its core mystery in Hekhalot texts and their later derivatives, particularly those of the German Pietists, to be that epitomized in the transformation of Enoch into Metatron: "It thus makes perfect sense that at some stage in the literary development of Hekhalot mysticism a book such as *3 Enoch* would have been composed, in which Enoch, the prototype of the Merkavah mystic, is transformed into Metatron, the very angel who occupies a throne alongside that of God. . . . The vision of the glory . . . results from the enthronement of the mystic. In that sense, I submit, the enthronement of the mystic should be understood as a form of quasi-deification or angelification, in line with the older tradition expressed in apocalyptic literature concerning the transformation of individuals into angelic beings. . . . [T]he entry to the chariot does culminate in what may be called a deifying vision" (pp. 83–85). In its later development by the German Pietists, "Metatron . . . is the aspect of the glory that is depicted as the measurable anthropos who sits upon the throne and appears in prophetic visions" (p. 224).

64. My application of the diatonic scale to the kabbalistic concept of cosmic worlds was not inspired by a desire to synthesize Hebraic and Hellenic sacred science but rather came from my earlier attempt to derive the Tree of Life Diagram from an underlying diagram composed wholly of hexagrams. As developed in the final section of chapter 6 in *The Secret Doctrine of the Kabbalah,* the spatial relationship of the first four such hexagrams was seen to correspond to the tonal relationship of the first four diatonic tones: Do, Re, Mi, and Fa. And the relationship of the first three of these tones was then taken to correspond further to the concept of cosmic worlds. The development of this correspondence of diatonic tones to kabbalistic worlds in the present chapter, which extends this correspondence to the biblical number

of such worlds that can also be correlated with the octave and is further enriched by the interface of the diatonic and chromatic scales, provides a remarkable tool for piercing the mystery of this multidimensional cosmos.

65. John Milton, "At a Solemn Music," ll. 5–8, 17–22, 25–26. In the remainder of this book I will ordinarily, as here, not give specific references to editions of classical works of literature that appear in many editions, and will not normally footnote literary quotations to such line references unless, again as here, placing such references in the text would overly interfere with the flow of the analysis.

NOTES TO CHAPTER 2

1. *Zohar,* vol. 1, pp. 83–84(Mantua: 1, 196–20a).

2. Tishby, *Wisdom of the Zohar,* vol. 2, pp. 699, 702.

3. See Hans Jenny, *Cymatics,* 2 vols. (Basel: Switzerland, Basilius Presse, 1974), vol. 2, pp. 95–131. See also *The Secret Doctrine of the Kabbalah,* figure 6.1, for a photograph of such a cymatic image.

4. Scholem, *Kabbalah,* pp. 158–59.

5. As quoted in ibid., p. 159.

6. Moshe Chaim Luzzatto, *Derech haShem: The Way of God,* trans. Aryeh Kaplan, 2nd ed. (New York: Feldheim, 1978), pp. 37–41.

7. Ibid., p. 81.

8. For this double etymology of Israel, see the notes in J. H. Hertz, ed. and trans., *The Pentateuch and Haftorahs,* 2nd ed. (London: Soncino Press, 1972), p. 124, and Aryeh Kaplan, ed. and trans., *Living Torah: The Five Books of Moses* (New York: Moznaim, 1981), p. 88.

9. R. A. Schwaller de Lubicz, *The Temple in Man: Sacred Architecture and the Perfect Man,* trans. Robert and Deborah Lawlor (Rochester, Vt.: Inner Traditions, 1977), p. 49.

10. Ibid., pp. 51–53.

11. Ibid., p. 53.

12. Julian Jaynes, *The Origin of Consciousness in the Breakdown of the Bicameral Mind* (Boston: Houghton Mifflin, 1976), p. 84.

13. Ibid., p. 149.

14. Ibid., pp. 104–6.

15. Ibid., pp. 184, 190–91, 297–98.

16. Ibid., pp. 96–99.

17. Schwaller de Lubicz, *The Temple in Man,* p. 51.

18. Aryeh Kaplan, ed. and trans., *The Bahir* (New York: Samuel Weiser, 1979), p. 91. For a similar view of Torah, see note 19 to appendix B.

19. Joseph Conrad, *Heart of Darkness,* in *The Norton Anthology of Short Fiction,* ed. R. V. Cassill and Richard Bausch, 6th ed. (New York: W. W. Norton, 2000), pp. 291, 297.

20. Ibid., p. 298.

21. Ibid., pp. 307, 315.

22. Herman Melville, "Bartleby, the Scrivener," *The Norton Anthology of Short Fiction,* pp. 1193–94.

23. Nathaniel Hawthorne, *The Scarlet Letter* (New York: Penguin Books, 1986), p. 93.

24. Homer, *The Iliad,* trans. E. V. Rieu (Harmondsworth, U.K.: Penguin Books, 1950), chap. 12, p. 229.

25. Ibid., chap. 16, p. 305.

26. Ibid., chap. 9, p. 172.

27. Ibid., chap. 1, p. 34.

28. For this understanding of the love-death as a "flight forward," see Theodore Reik's penetrating psychoanalytic study *Masochism in Modern Man* (New York: Farrar, Strauss, 1941), pp. 115–24. For my full treatment of the theory and the Elizabethan literary tragedies of courtly love, most importantly of *Romeo and Juliet,* as well as such a treatment of the contrasting form that I have named "worldly love" and that now can be considered the form of "lateral" love, see Leonora Leet Brodwin, *Elizabethan Love Tragedy* (New York: New York University Press, 1971).

29. In his great work, *The Varieties of Religious Experience,* William James distinguished the same two religious sensibilities, as will be shown particularly in chapter 5, note 41.

30. Hawthorne, p. 145.

31. For my study of such religious practices, particularly those of kabbalistic meditation, Sabbath observance, and ritual prayer, a study derived from both the esoteric and exoteric traditions of Judaism and focused on suggestions as to effective methods of performing these levels of spiritual practice that can aid the process of spiritual development, see *Renewing the Covenant: A Kabbalistic Guide to Jewish Spirituality* (Rochester, Vt.: Inner Traditions, 1999).

32. As quoted in Zalman M. Schachter-Shalomi, "Gazing into God's Mirror," in *Opening the Inner Gates: New Paths in Kabbalah and Psychology,* ed. Edward Hoffman (Boston: Shambhala, 1995), p. 91.

33. See Scholem, *Kabbalah,* pp. 155–56; see also Luzzatto, *Derech ha-Shem,* pp. 97–99, which states that immortality is the reward only of the righteous: "The wicked, on the other hand, are cast aside and annihilated. . . ."

34. See P. D. Ouspensky, *In Search of the Miraculous* (New York: Harcourt Brace Jovanovich, 1949), pp. 31–33; and *The Secret of the Golden Flower,* trans. Richard Wilhelm with an intro. by Carl Jung (New York: Harcourt Brace Jovanovich, 1962), p. 31f. For my earlier discussion of the forms of immortality of these higher soul levels as related to quantum cosmology, see *The Secret Doctrine of the Kabbalah,* pp. 407–8.

35. Aristotle, "Metaphysics," *The Basic Works of Aristotle,* ed. and trans. Richard McKeon (New York: Random House, 1941), p. 693.

36. These are the closing lines of *A Defence of Poetry* by Percy Bysshe Shelley.

37. Pierre Teilhard de Chardin, *The Future of Man,* trans. Norman Denny (New York: Harper & Row, 1969), pp. 127, 245.

38. Robert Lawlor, "Ancient Temple Architecture," *Lindisfarne Letter 10: Geometry and Architecture* (W. Stockbridge, Mass.: Lindisfarne Press, 1980), p. 58.

39. Ibid., pp. 62–63; see also Robert Lawlor, *Sacred Geometry: Philosophy and Practice* (New York: Crossroad, 1982), pp. 65–73.

`NOTES TO CHAPTER 3

1. C. G. Jung, Foreword, *The I Ching,* trans. Richard Wilhelm and Cary F. Baynes, Bollingen Series XIX (Princeton: Princeton University Press, 1978), p. xxiv.

2. Joseph Klausner, *The Messianic Idea in Israel,* trans. W. F. Stinespring (New York: Macmillan, 1955), pp. 384–85.

3. Ibid., p. 418.

4. Ibid., pp. 455–56, 498.

5. Ibid., p. 278.

6. Ibid., p. 238.

7. See my lengthy discussion of the biblical meanings of the shofar in *Renewing the Covenant,* pp. 10–19.

8. Klausner, *Messianic Idea,* p. 471.

9. Ibid., pp. 401, 497.

10. Ibid., pp. 470–71.

11. Ibid., pp. 504–5, 512.

12. As Gershom Scholem has shown, in *Kabbalah,* p. 335, the millennium was understood to involve a slowing of time: "The messianic age will last approximately a thousand years, but many believed that these years would not be identical with human years, for the planets and the stars would move more slowly, so that time would be prolonged (this view was particular [*sic*] current in the circle of the *Sefer Ha-Temunah,* and it has origins in the Apocryphal books)."

13. Moshe Idel, *Messianic Mystics* (New Haven: Yale University Press, 1998), has shown, "the deep bonds that exist between certain forms of messianism and messianic personalities and certain kinds of mystical experiences" (pp. 1–2), particularly in the case of Abulafia and Hasidism, but he has not shown the mystical testimonies he has discussed to have defined the individual path to spiritual redemption in terms of the traditional stages of the Messianic Age, as I am now to do. I also wish to note his important treatment of the constellation of Enochian topics, involving Metatron, the son of man, and the Messiah, in his treatment of Abulafia in this book (pp. 85–94), evidence that strongly supports what I have called "the secret doctrine of the son." Where Idel finds this mystical internalization primarily in Abulafia and the hasidic Tzaddikim, Yehuda Liebes does the same for the *Zohar* in "The Messiah of the Zohar: on R. Simeon bar Yohai as a Messianic Figure," trans. Arnold Schwartz, in *Studies in the Zohar* (Albany: State University of New York Press, 1993). Liebes does connect this process with the recognized stages of the Messianic Age but only with that stage I have defined as its second stage: "The notion that it is the task of R. Simeon and his circle to uphold the world through the evil times that precede the coming of the Messiah—the period of the 'birth pangs of the Messiah'—is only one step away from the idea that his generation must take measures to induce the Messiah's coming" (p. 11). In his final assessment—"R. Simeon of the *Zohar* is a messianic figure who embodies the fate of the entire cosmos, its flaw, and its redemption" (p. 73)—he shows this central Zoharic figure to contain the same history that the Lurianic tradition will attribute to the Partzuf of the son, Ze'ir Anpin, as I have shown in the concluding section of chapter 1.

14. Though this passage was written some years ago, the third path I then envisioned is one that Michael Lerner has more recently championed both in the pages of his quarterly *Tikkun* and in the Tikkun Community deriving from it, a new political action movement that aims to combine traditional Jewish liberalism with Jewish spiritual development.

15. Edgar in Shakespeare's *King Lear,* 4.6.226–27.

16. From *Elegiac Stanzas,* ll. 15-16.

17. For a fuller discussion of power as a spiritual path, see the section in chapter 5 entitled "The Power Path of the Eagle."

18. Ouspensky, *In Search of the Miraculous,* pp. 42–43.

19. It is a major thesis of my book *The Secret Doctrine of the Kabbalah* that the secret doctrine informing the whole of the Jewish mystical tradition culminating in the Kabbalah derives from the Zadokite priesthood, whose lineage goes back to the time of King David; see particularly its first chapter. See also *Renewing the Covenant,* chapter 4, where I show the influence of the Zadokite priesthood of the Second Temple period in formulating the liturgy for the prayer services practiced in the Temple that provided the nucleus of the later prayer service. This discussion of the prayer service is reviewed and expanded in appendix B of the present book.

20. Henri Bergson, "Laughter," in *Comedy,* ed. Wylie Sypher (Garden City, N.Y.: Doubleday, 1956), pp. 72–73.

21. Homer, *The Iliad,* pp. 38–39.

22. See *Renewing the Covenant,* chapter 2, for a fuller treatment of the classical texts of kabbalistic meditation in the context of my full development of a form of kabbalistic meditation, one beginning with an extended attunement process and concluding with a fuller version of the guided meditation presented in appendix A.

23. Abulafia, *Chayah ha-Olam ha-Ba,* trans. Aryeh Kaplan, *Meditation and Kabbalah,* pp. 96–97.

24. In writing that the meditatively received symbolic image be interpreted as one would a dream, Abulafia was undoubtedly assuming in his readers a knowledge of the midrashic discussion of dreams *(Berakhot,* 55b). The Midrash tells us that in Jerusalem there were twenty-four schools of dream interpretation and that all the interpretations were fulfilled, whatever the school. Its summary statement, "all dreams follow the mouth," contains the surprising understanding that a dream means whatever one says it does, that the dream will become a reality in accordance with the interpretation given to it, whether for good or ill, and that, therefore, the interpreter has a certain power. It might be pointed out that the talmudic understanding of dreams explains the success that the various schools of psychoanalysis have had with psychic healing through dream interpretation despite their rival interpretations of dream symbolism. But just as a positive construction of

dream symbolism can aid in healing, so a negative construction can be injurious, for the combination of image with idea is very powerful and can effect reality.

25. Azriel of Gerona, *Sha'ar ha-Kavanah,* trans. Aryeh Kaplan in *Meditation and Kabbalah,* pp. 119–20.

26. Ibid., pp. 121–22.

27. Ibid., p. 122.

28. Abulafia, *Otzar,* p. 84.

29. Azriel, *Sha'ar ha-Kavanah,* p. 122.

30. See *The Secret Doctrine of the Kabbalah,* chapter 9, the "Epilogue on Probability."

31. The Hebrew word *vehayah,* normally translated "And it shall come to pass," can also be used as a manifesting power word. Support for such a practice throughout the Bible will be found in the lengthy appendix to *Renewing the Covenant.* That appendix defines the same four levels of the spiritual master shortly to be developed.

32. Ouspensky, *In Search of the Miraculous,* pp. 42–43.

33. Conrad, *Heart of Darkness,* p. 297.

34. Samuel Taylor Coleridge, *Biographia Literaria,* chap. 14, in *The Selected Poetry and Prose,* ed. Donald A. Stauffer, Modern Library College Editions (New York: Random House, 1951), p. 269.

35. Ibid., chap. 13, p. 263.

36. Ibid.

37. Abraham Abulafia, *Sefer ha-Tzeruf,* trans. Aryeh Kaplan, in *Meditation and Kabbalah,* p. 80.

38. Abulafia, *Otzar Eden ha-Ganaz,* trans. Aryeh Kaplan, in *Meditation and Kabbalah,* p. 84.

39. Ibid., p. 85.

40. See Karl H. Pribram and Diane McGuinness, "Arousal, Activation, and Effort in the Control of Attention," *Psychological Review* 82 (1975): 130.

41. In *The Secret Doctrine of the Kabbalah,* chapters 4 and 5, I developed a new understanding of the talmudic concept of the "double heart" as referring not to the conflict within it of the good and bad inclinations (the Yetzer ha-Tov and the Yetzer ha-Ra), but to the harmonizing of the hearts of higher and lower levels of the soul, an understanding of particular significance to the meaning of the Tetragrammaton as derived from a new key I there provide to its pronunciation.

42. Spoken by Flamineo in John Webster's *The White Devil,* act 1, scene 2.

43. Mark Twain, *The Adventures of Huckleberry Finn,* chap. 32, 4th paragraph.

44. As I have shown in chapter 1, the *Sefer Yetzirah* in 1:5 provides the basis for an understanding of seven cosmic "depths" as dimensions. In addition to such dimensions as the three of space and a fourth of time, it also defines a moral fifth dimension built into the structure of reality, "a depth of good, a depth of evil." It is such a dimension, I suggest, that can in part explain the workings of Providence.

45. In this analysis of Synchronicity as the mechanism through which Providence may be thought to operate, I have stressed the positive effects of the capacity to apprehend and join the "flow," a capacity that, when spiritually developed, can finally master and direct that flow, with good effects both to the individual and the whole. But before leaving this discussion, I should offer some comments on the negative effects that can sometime afflict those whose spiritual capacities may be unbalanced, producing a heightened capacity to interpret synchronicities as relating special messages to the self that cannot be integrated into the nature and demands of normal life, and that rather produce fear. If I am right that there are meaningful synchronicities and that they are the means through which Providence operates, then there should be nothing to fear from such coincidences that seem meaningful. Thus such fears are reason to question whether their source is not a subjective projection, especially when they seem to demand some display of power of which one is incapable. Such unfortunate individuals, who clearly do not have the power to master and productively use their visions, would be advised not to pay attention to such "signs," since such hyper-attention itself may, in a vicious cycle, lead to a genuine psychosis, combining grandiosity with paranoia, that can finally leave the individual lost in non-functional visions. Such individuals would be well advised to follow a more modest course of spiritual practice and to monitor their responses so as to heighten their positive feelings and diminish the power of such "Signs and Symbols" of which Nabokov has written so penetratingly in his short story of this title.

46. Dov Baer, *Maggid Devarav le-Yaokov,* trans. Aryeh Kaplan, in *Meditation and Kabbalah,* p. 301.

47. Swami Muktananda Paramahansa, *The Play of Consciousness* (n.c., Calif: Shree Gurudev Siddha Yoga Ashram, 1974), pp. 64–65, 163.

48. Ibid., p. 130.

49. For a discussion of rhythm entrainment, see Itzhak Bentov, *Stalking the Wild Pendulum* (New York: E. P. Dutton, 1977), pp. 21–24; and Michael Hutchison, *Megabrain* (New York: Ballantine Books, 1986), pp. 199–201.

50. Support for this understanding can be found in such classics of economic theory as Max Weber's *The Protestant Ethic and the Spirit of Capitalism* and R. H. Tawney's *Religion and the Rise of Capitalism.*

51. Muktananda, *The Play of Consciousness,* pp. 30–31.

52. In *Renewing the Covenant,* chapters 2 and 4, and *The Secret Doctrine of the Kabbalah,* chapter 2, I have developed a different interpretative translation of the Sh'ma that understands it to be proclaiming the secret doctrine of an esoteric Jewish tradition going back to Ezekiel and the Hebraic priesthood, the doctrine of the divine son Israel (see Exod. 4:22) conveyed through the following translation—"Hear: Israel, YHVH our God, [and the unqualified] YHVH [are] one." This understanding of the Sh'ma will be further developed in appendix B on the prayer service.

53. See *The Secret Doctrine of the Kabbalah,* chapter 4, for my analysis of the probable pronunciation of the Tetragrammaton as well as other esoteric aspects of this most Holy Name.

54. See *Renewing the Covenant,* chapter 3, for a full consideration of the meaning and observance of the Sabbath.

55. Muktananda, *The Play of Consciousness,* pp. 15, 19.

56. For a description of Hari Giri Baba, see ibid., pp. 93–94.

57. See Scholem, *Kabbalah,* p. 351.

58. Abraham J. Heschel, "Toward an Understanding of Halachah," in *Conservative Judaism and Jewish Law,* ed. Seymour Siegel (New York: the Rabbinical Assembly, 1977), pp. 143, 150.

59. Abraham J. Heschel, *The Sabbath: Its Meaning for Modern Man* (New York: Farrar, Straus and Giroux, 1951), pp. 8, 59, 60, 75, 87, 101. My brackets.

60. See *The Secret Doctrine of the Kabbalah,* pp. 222–32, for my decoding of the esoteric keys to Genesis 1 as well as chapter 3 of that book for its study of ancient sacred science, a subject summarized in chapter 1 of the present book.

61. Rudolf Steiner, *The Inner Nature of Music and the Experience of Tone* (Hudson, N.Y.: Anthroposophic Press, 1983), pp. 51, 70, 86. My brackets.

62. Ibid., p. 73.

63. Ibid., p. 55.

NOTES TO CHAPTER 4

1. For full definitions of these Behinot, see Scholem, *Kabbalah,* p. 114; and Harold Bloom, *Kabbalah and Criticism* (New York: Seabury Press, 1975), pp. 64–71.

2. For a fuller discussion of the hexagram in relation to these elements, levels of soul, and shamanic worlds, see *The Secret Doctrine of the Kabbalah,* pp. 212–32.

3. John Milton, *De Doctrina Christiana,* trans. Bishop Charles R. Sumner, in *John Milton: Complete Poems and Major Prose,* ed. Merritt Y. Hughes (New York: The Odyssey Press, 1957), p. 986.

4. For my further analysis of Judah's prayer, as also of Jacob's earlier mentioned magical use of the rods, in relation to my thesis concerning the word *vehayah* as a biblical power word, see the appendix to *Renewing the Covenant,* pp. 211–12, 229–32.

5. For an interesting association of hearing and obedience, as reflected in most languages, that may be relevant here, see the analysis of Julian Jaynes, in chapter 2, note 16.

6. Aryeh Kaplan, *Meditation and the Bible* (New York: Samuel Weiser, 1978), p. 110. On the Sabbath, see also *Renewing the Covenant,* chapter 3.

7. Kaplan, *Meditation and the Bible,* pp. 100–1.

8. Rabbi Aryeh Kaplan, *The Living Torah: The Five Books of Moses* (New York: Moznaim, 1981), p. 64.

9. From William Butler Yeats, "Lapis Lazuli," l. 17.

10. Ibid, ll. 55–56.

11. The positions that Jacob and Joseph occupy on the kabbalistic Tree of Life Diagram reveal this understanding of their associations with the two main streams of Jewish religious life, those deriving from priestly and from rabbinical sources. For as Jacob occupies the Sefirah of Tiferet, the main Sefirah of the Partzuf of the son, so does Joseph occupy the Sefirah of Yesod, as representative Tzaddik. In *The Secret Doctrine of the Kabbalah* I have shown that the six-Sefirot Partzuf of the son, Ze'ir Anpin, represents the culmination of an esoteric tradition going back to the Zadokite priesthood. But I should now like to place this secret doctrine within the larger context of the normative tradition, which rather exalts the figure of the Tzaddik.

Though I have just argued that Abraham and Isaac represent even more perfect Tzaddikim than Joseph, it is Joseph who came to symbolize the special characteristic the rabbinical tradition, culminating in the modern

Hasidim, attribute to the Tzaddik, his concern to save the generality of sinners too morally weak to merit the divine mercy without the virtue or intercession of the Tzaddik. Joseph did come to the saving recognition that "God did send me before you . . . to save your lives by a great deliverance" (Gen. 45:5, 7), that the function of the Tzaddik is to save his weaker brethren, but it was Moses who took the further step that, for the rabbinical tradition, is the true measure of the Tzaddik, his ability to plead directly with God that He mitigate justice with mercy. When, after the golden calf incident, God wished to destroy the Israelites and build from Moses a new people, Moses replied: "Turn from Thy fierce wrath, and repent of this evil against Thy people. . . . Yet now, if Thou wilt forgive their sin—; and if not, blot me, I pray Thee, out of thy book" (Exod. 32:12, 32). On almost every page of Midrash, the Tzaddik's pleading or simply his righteousness is cited as the factor influencing God to bestow historical blessings on the Jews. Indeed, Yehuda Liebes, in *Studies in Jewish Myth and Jewish Messianism* (Albany: State University of New York Press, 1993), has argued that the talmudic "myth" is "essentially God's internal struggle over the fate of Israel" (p. 55), a struggle, according to the Babylonian Talmud, in which "the prayers of the righteous turn the mind of the Holy One, blessed be He, from the attribute of cruelty to that of compassion (Sukkah 14a)" (as quoted in Liebes, p. 29).

In contrast to Joseph's concern to save others, Jacob's great moment of prayer is concerned with his own salvation, and in wrestling with the angel, he overcomes both his own imperfections and its liabilities, to be reborn as the Prince of God, Israel. As Israel, he is most overtly related to the secret doctrine of the son, since its first clear biblical announcement is in God's statement: "Israel is my son, even my first born" (Exod. 4:22). But the name of Jacob is also related to this secret doctrine, since it occupies the central Sefirotic position of the son, Tiferet, and in a tradition going back to the Talmud, which culminates with the medieval German Hasidim, Elliot R. Wolfson, in *Along the Path* (Albany: State University of New York Press, 1995), pp. 1–62, has shown that the image of Jacob is understood to be engraved on the Throne. Where the rabbinical tradition of the Tzaddik is mainly concerned with the historical survival of the earthly community of Israel, the priestly tradition of the son is primarily concerned with the salvific doctrine of personal survival for the spiritually developed souls who form the supernal Community of Israel in the World to Come, as reflected in the phrase *Ben Olam ha-Ba* (son of the World to Come) of the *Shi'ur Qomah,* an early Hekhalot text.

But the doctrine of atonement, so central to the rabbinical tradition's understanding of the Tzaddik's role in Jewish history, would also seem to have had its origin with the Hebraic priesthood, since this is the primary cultic role of the priesthood, its highest form being that of the High Priest on Yom Kippur, the Day of Atonement. The tradition beginning with the Zadokite priest Ezekiel is of a Throne vision in which the seer sees his own higher self seated upon the Throne; it is a vision of the identification of a human figure with his divine higher self, a recognition that lifts him to the level termed the "son of man."

In his study *The Jewish Temple: A Non-Biblical Sourcebook* (London and New York: Routledge, 1996), C. T. R. Hayward has argued: "The probability is overwhelming that the House of Zadok through the centuries evolved a particular understanding of its part in God's dispensation for Israel; of a sense of its own eternal worth as the chosen high priestly dynasty; and of the profound significance of the Temple Service for which it was ultimately responsible before God" (p. 39). In his quotations from Philo's *De Specialibus Legibus* (1.114, 116) we may see a synthesis between the understanding of the High Priest as unifying the finite with the infinite (the role of the son) and as effecting atonement (the role of the Tzaddik): "For he (the high priest) is . . . [of] a better nature than that of human sort, approaching near to the divine, bordering on both, if one must speak the truth; so that men may propitiate God through a certain mediator, and God, making use of an underservant, may extend and supply favours to men" (as quoted in Hayward, p. 110).

Such a double role of the High Priest can also be seen in a most telling passage from the Babylonian Talmud (7a):

> R. Ishmael b. Elisha says: I once entered into the innermost part [of the Sanctuary] to offer incense and saw Akathriel Yah, the Lord of Hosts, seated upon a high and exalted throne. He said to me: Ishmael, My son, bless Me! I replied: May it be Thy will that Thy mercy may suppress Thy anger and Thy mercy may prevail over Thy other attributes, so that Thou mayest deal with Thy children according to the attribute of mercy and mayest, on their behalf, stop short of the limit of strict justice! And he nodded to me his Head. (as quoted in Liebes, p. 10)

It is, then, in the Talmud that we see the clearest evidence of the association of the priesthood, alone allowed to enter "the innermost part" of the Sanctuary, with the secret doctrine of the son and of its further association with the Throne vision. But the interaction here of God and his priestly "son" also reflects the priestly Tzaddik's role of influencing God to deal mercifully with His people. What is also most interesting about this passage is God's request for a human blessing, that, in the words of Abraham J. Heschel, in *Between God and Man*, ed. Fritz A. Rothschild (New York: Free Press, 1959), "God is in need of man" (p. 140). But I would go beyond the talmudic understanding of this need, largely shared by Heschel, that it is to increase the divine mercy, to argue that the reciprocal needs of God and man involve that joint personalizing of God and divinizing of man in which the ultimate purpose of the cosmic process is fulfilled. In my earlier cited book, I have developed this final implication of the Hebraic secret doctrine of the son, and this understanding of the divine need for human blessing is further developed in appendix B on the prayer service.

12.   *Zohar,* vol. 1, pp. 15–17, (Mantua: 1, 4a–4b).

13.   Ibid., p. 17.

14.   For this understanding of the Holy One, Blessed be He, see also Aryeh Kaplan, *Jewish Meditation: A Practical Guide* (New York: Schocken Books, 1985): "when we speak of God as 'the Holy One, blessed be He,' we are saying that he is 'the transcendent One, Who is immanent.'. . . the term 'Holy One, blessed be he' therefore bridges the gap between God's transcendence and His immanence" (pp. 150–51).

15.   For further discussion of these Lurianic concepts with many quotations from the *Sha'ar ha-Kelalim* introductory section to the *Eitz Chayyim* of Chayyim Vital, see *The Secret Doctrine of the Kabbalah,* chapter 7.

16.   Muktananda, *The Play of Consciousness,* pp. 144–48.

NOTES TO CHAPTER 5

1.   See especially *The Secret Doctrine of the Kabbalah,* chapter 2.

2.   *Zohar,* vol. 3, pp. 409–11 (Mantua: 2, 141b–142a).

3.   All biblical quotes are taken from the King James Version.

4.   The major medical text of modern morphology is *Les Artes Divinatoires* by Dr. Jerard Encausse (Paris: Payot, 1946). Other members of the French school are Louis Corman, Prof. M. Martiny, and Prof. Dr. Ermiane. The lead-

ing Israeli practitioner is Mme. Colette Aboulker-Muscat, whose teachings have been brought to this country by Dr. Gerald Epstein, to whom I am indebted for this information. See also Dr. Epstein's book *Healing Visualizations: Creating Health through Imagery* (New York: Bantam Books, 1989).

5. 3 *Enoch* or *The Hebrew Book of Enoch,* pp. 8–9, 13, 22, 25, 27, 28–29, 33, 39. My brackets.

6. *Shiur Qoma,* p. 34.

7. Scholem, *Kabbalah,* p. 380.

8. Ibid., pp. 16–17.

9. Vital, *Eitz Chayyim,* Hebrew, 1.5 (chap. 2). My translation.

10. As quoted in Zalman Schachter-Shalomi with Donald Gropman, *The First Step* (New York: Bantam Books, 1983), p. 116.

11. A. E. Waite, *The Holy Kabbalah* (New Hyde Park, N.Y.: University Books, 1969), p. 383.

12. Edmund Spenser, *The Faerie Queene,* 4.5.1.

13. John Dryden, "Alexander's Feast," ll. 12, 15.

14. See my fuller discussion of Hellenic warfare in chapter 2, pp. 204–5.

15. Alexander Pope, "The Rape of the Lock," 2.28.

16. Marlowe, *Tamburlaine,* part 1, 5.2.98–110.

17. Ibid., 5.2.115–19.

18. Spenser, *The Faerie Queene,* 3.6.46.

19. Thomas Mann, "Death in Venice," *Stories of Three Decades,* trans. H. T. Lowe-Porter (New York: Alfred A. Knopf, 1936), pp. 412, 413, 434.

20. See Tishby, *Wisdom of the Zohar,* vol. 2, pp. 447–546.

21. Mann, "Death in Venice," p. 434.

22. Dobh Baer of Lubavitch, *On Ecstasy,* ed. and trans. Louis Jacobs (Chappaqua, N.Y.: Rossel Books, 1963), p. 127.

23. Stendhal, *On Love* (Garden City, N.Y.: Doubleday Anchor Books, 1957), p. 13.

24. Ibid., p. 190.

25. Ibid., p. 6.

26. Ibid., p.164.

27. Ibid., p. 236.

28. Ortega y Gasset, *On Love: Aspects of a Single Theme,* trans. Toby Talbot (New York: Meridian Books, 1958), pp. 25–26.

29. Ibid., p. 42.

30. Ibid., p. 41.

31. Ibid., p. 51.

32. Ibid., pp. 68, 69, 71, 74.

33. For the full development of my revisionist concept of the double heart, see *The Secret Doctrine of the Kabbalah,* chapters 4 and 5.

34. William James, *The Varieties of Religious Experience,* pp. 147–48.

35. Plato, *The Symposium,* trans. B. Jowett (New York: Greystone Press, n.d.), pp. 271–72.

36. From Geoffrey Chaucer, "The Franklin's Tale" in *The Canterbury Tales,* ll. 92–95.

37. See my *Elizabethan Love Tragedy,* in which I define and trace both the theoretical and historical backgrounds of the two major types of love appearing in Elizabethan love tragedies, the death-oriented type of courtly love, shortly to be more fully discussed, and a life-oriented type I have given the name of "worldly love," the former given its greatest expression in Shakespeare's *Romeo and Juliet* and the latter in Shakespeare's *Antony and Cleopatra.* Where courtly love is characterized by the problems of obstruction, finally transcended in death, worldly love is characterized by the problems of living together in a love devoted to life. And where courtly love can be related to the theory of Plato, the theoretical basis of worldly love can be found in Aristotle and Aquinas.

38. Plato, *Symposium,* pp. 285–86.

39. Ibid., p. 286.

40. James, *Varieties of Religious Experience,* p. 133.

41. Ibid., p. 160.

42. Denis de Rougemont, *Love in the Western World,* trans. Montgomery Belgion (Garden City, N.Y.: Doubleday Anchor Books, 1940), p. 145.

43. John Milton, "Areopagitica," *Complete Poems and Major Prose,* p. 733.

44. For my further analysis of the use of magical rods by Jacob and Moses, see the appendix on *vehayah* as a biblical power word in *Renewing the Covenant,* pp. 229–30, 232–33.

45. Shakespeare, *Macbeth,* 1.5. 39–40.

46. Pope, "The Rape of the Lock," 1.1.42.

47. Vital, *Eitz Chayyim,* 1.1 (chap. 1).

48. See Kaplan, *Sefer Yetzirah,* p. 44.

49. Idel, *Messianic Mystics,* p. 53.

50. Ibid., p. 68.

51. Ibid., p. 77.

52. Louis Jacobs, introduction to Dobh Baer of Lubavitch, *On Ecstasy*, p. 1.

53. For a full analysis of these three main aspects of both Pythagorean and kabbalistic sacred science, see *The Secret Doctrine of the Kabbalah,* chapter 3.

54. Percy Bysshe Shelley, "A Defence of Poetry," last sentence.

55. Scholem, *Sabbatai Sevi,* pp. 301–2.

56. Jung, *On the Nature of the Psyche,* pp. 116–18.

57. J. H. Hertz, ed. and trans., *The Pentateuch and Haftorahs,* 2nd ed. (London: Soncino Press, 1972), p. 126, note to Gen. 33:14.

58. As quoted in Scholem, "Redemption through Sin" p. 138.

59. Ibid.

60. Harold M. Schmeck, Jr., "The Complex Organ Known as Skin Continues to Surprise," *New York Times,* 8 November 1983, sec. C, p. 3.

61. See chapter 3 for a parallel discussion of such early exclusion of evil followed by a later inclusion of what had formerly to be rejected as evil in the discussion of the traditional chronology of the Messianic Age, the former related to the war of Gog and Magog corresponding with the period before the appearance of the Messiah, at the midpoint of the fifth world, and the latter related to the ingathering of Jews and conversion of the Gentiles correlated with the period after the coming of the Messiah and preparing for the final Messianic millennium. This is also related to other treatments of the "Transformative Moment," first treated its chapter 2 as a therapeutic model and finally, in chapter 4, as the essence of Neshamah consciousness.

62. John Milton, *Sonnet XXI,* ll. 11–14.

63. Henry Vaughan, "The Retreat," ll. 19–20.

64. Norman Mailer, *Cannibals and Christians,* p. 280, as quoted in Jessica Gerson, "Norman Mailer: Sex, Creativity, and God," *Mosaic* 4 (June 1982): 5.

65. William Wordsworth, *The Prelude,* 14.235.

66. Adin Steinsaltz, *In the Beginning: Discourses on Chasidic Thought,* ed. and trans. Yehuda Hanegbi (Northvale, N.J.: Jason Aronson, 1995), pp. 10–11.

67. Dobh Baer of Lubavitch, *On Ecstasy,* pp. 64, 66, 67, 138.

68. For a fuller discussion of such miraculous transformations, see the analysis of the third level of the Ruach Master in chapter 3 above.

69. *Sophocles, Oedipus at Colonus,* trans. Robert Fitzgerald, in *The Complete Greek Tragedies,* ed. David Grene and Richmond Lattimore (Chicago: The University of Chicago Press, 1959), vol. 2, pp. 83, 92, 102, 123–24. See also *Sophocles' Philoctetes* for another such holy sufferer who is both unaccountably wounded and finally empowered by the gods to be conqueror of Troy.

70. For a further analysis of this testing of Jacob and especially of Abraham, see chapter 4, "The Patriarchs."
71. As quoted in Steinsaltz, p. 10.
72. This phrase is central to the thought of Rudolf Otto in his important book *The Idea of the Holy: An Inquiry into the Non-Rational Factor in the Idea of the Divine and Its Relation to the Rational,* trans. John W. Harvey (New York: Oxford University Press, 1958). See especially his chapter on "The Numinous in the Old Testament," which includes discussions of Isaiah and Job somewhat different from mine, pp. 72–81.
73. *Zohar,* vol. 3, p. 374 (Mantua: 2, 130b).
74. Ibid., pp. 413–14. (Mantua: 2, 142b)
75. Ibid., pp. 403–4. (Mantua: 2, 140a)

NOTES TO APPENDIX B

1. For my thesis that the whole of the Jewish esoteric tradition derives from the Zadokite priesthood, see *The Secret Doctrine of the Kabbalah,* pp. 2–11, 30–65. For my treatment of the contribution of the Zadokite priesthood to the development of the prayer service and its practice by them in the Second Temple, see *Renewing the Covenant,* pp. 177–78. The whole of chapter 4 of this latter book on the prayer service is recommended to those who want a far more detailed explanation and guide to the practice of Jewish liturgical prayer.
2. *Siddur Tehillat Hashem,* ed. and trans. Rabbi Nissen Mangel (Brooklyn: Merkos L'Inyonei Chinuch, 1982), p.168. This Siddur of the Lubavitcher hasidic movement follows the text of its founder, Rabbi Shneur Zalman of Liadi, which itself is based on that of Isaac Luria, and it is recommended to all for private prayer. Its text for the Sabbath Shacharit (morning) service will be used throughout this discussion.
3. Ibid., p. 172.
4. See Kaplan, *Sefer Yetzirah,* pp. 170–73.
5. *Siddur Tehillat Hashem,* p. 173.
6. For my treatment of the progression of vowel sounds through the service, see *Renewing the Covenant,* pp. 164–76. With reference to the *oh* sounds of the Kedushah, I have not counted the short *o,* or really *uh,* sound of the substitute term Adonai, a substitution for the Tetragrammaton not present in the original forms of these prophetic sentences.

7. *Siddur Tehillat Hashem,* pp. 166–67.

8. Dov Baer, *Magid Devarav Le Yaakov,* 159, in Aryeh Kaplan, ed. and trans., *The Light Beyond: Adventures in Hassidic Thought* (New York: Mosnaim, 1981), pp. 213–14.

9. Kalonymus Kalman Epstein of Cracow, *Ma'or ve-Shemesh,* 50a, 56b, in Louis Jacobs, ed. and trans., *Jewish Mystical Testimonies* (New York: Schocken Books, 1978), pp. 217-19.

10. Abraham J. Heschel, in *Between God and Man,* p. 140. For my further treatment of this divine "need," see chapter 4, note 10, particularly its ending.

11. Hayim of Volozhin, *Nefesh Hahayim,* in Raphael Ben Zion, trans., *An Anthology of Jewish Mysticism,* intro. Gershon Winkler (New York: The Judaica Press, 1981), pp. 136, 148, 163.

12. Cohen, *The Shi'ur Qomah,* section J$_x$, 16–17, 19–20, 27, 30–33; p. 230.

13. For my treatment of the "son of man" antecedents of Metatron in relation to the throne vision of Ezekiel and its derivatives in Daniel and Enoch 1, see the last section of chapter 1, pp.56–64, and *The Secret Doctrine of the Kabbalah,* pp. 30–45.

14. Cohen, *The Shi'ur Qomah,* section L,3; p. 238.

15. See *The Secret Doctrine of the Kabbalah,* p. 48, for the covert identification of Metatron with the Shekhinah based on the statement in both *3 Enoch* and the *Shi'ur Komah* that Metatron is to be identified with the angel of whom God had said "my name is in him" (Exod. 23:21), the angel that is later referred to as the Shekhinah (Exod. 29:45–46).

16. *Zohar,* vol. 2, pp. 383–84, 385 (Mantua: 1, 247b, 248a).

17. *Siddur Tehillat Hashem,* p. 170.

18. Ibid., 174. The first blessing begins on p. 170.

19. Hayim of Volozhin, *Nefesh Hahayim,* p. 198.

20. See *Renewing the Covenant,* pp. 138–60 for my treatment of the process of making the heart into a vessel to receive the divine love.

21. See Franz Rosenzweig, *The Star of Redemption,* trans. William W. Hallo (Boston: Beacon Press, 1972), p. 169.

22. *Siddur Tehillat Hashem,* p. 175. The second blessing begins on p. 174.

23. See *The Secret Doctrine of the Kabbalah,* pp. 68–73, and *Renewing the Covenant,* pp. 62–74, 175–77.

24. *Zohar,* vol. 4, p. 267 (Mantua: 2, 224b).

25. *Zohar,* vol. 4, pp.234–35 (Mantua: 2, 216a–216b).

26. Zevi Hirsch of Zhidachov, *Ketav Yosher Divrei Emet,* in Norman Lamm, ed. and trans., *The Religious Thought of Hasidism: Text and Commentary* (New

York:Yeshiva University Press, 1999), pp. 15–19. I am surprised that nowhere in his extended commentary on this text does Lamm call attention to Hirsch's innovative inclusion of Israel in the unification of the Sh'ma, his publication of this translation coinciding with my own such interpretation appearing in both of my prior books in the same year of 1999 as Lamm's book, though not previously known to me. But if I am not the first to have understood the Sh'ma to contain a triple unification, my inclusion of such an interpretation in all of my Kabbalah books has, I believe, highlighted such an interpretation for our time.

27. See *The Secret Doctrine of the Kabbalah,* pp. 165–90, for my extended treatment of the relationship of the vowel sounds to the harmonics.

28. See *Renewing the Covenant,* pp. 57-62, for my treatment of the significance of the number 42 in terms of the name of 42 letters and its relationship to prayer.

29. *Siddur Tehillat Hashem,* p. 178.

30. Ibid., p. 201.

31. *Zohar,* vol. 3, pp. 380–82 (Mantua: 2, 133b–134a).

32. *Siddur Tehillat Hashem,* p. 175.

33. See the last section of chapter 1.

34. There was also the different type of contemplative meditation practiced by the Habad Hasidim, for which see especially Jacobs, *On Ecstasy,* p. 1 passim.

35. See the references in note 1 above.

36. James, *Varieties of Religious Experience,* pp. 479, 498–99, 505, 513.

37. Abraham Isaac Kook, *The Lights of Penitence* in *The Lights of Penitence, The Moral Principles, Lights of Holiness, Essays, Letters, and Poems,* ed. and trans. Ben Zion Bokser (New York: Paulist Press, 1978), pp. 62, 64, 65, 74, 75, 78.

38. Ibid., p. 87.

BIBLIOGRAPHY

PRIMARY SOURCES

Abulafia, Abraham. "Chayah Olam ha-Ba." In *Meditation and Kabbalah*, trans. Aryeh Kaplan. York Beach, Maine: Samuel Weiser, 1982.

Aristotle. "Metaphysics." In *The Basic Works of Aristotle*, ed. and trans. Richard McKeon. New York: Random House, 1941.

Azriel of Gerona. "Sha'ar ha-Kavanah." In *Meditation and Kabbalah*, trans. Aryeh Kaplan. York Beach, Maine: Samuel Weiser, 1982.

Baer of Lubavitch, Dobh. *On Ecstasy*. Trans. Louis Jacobs. Chappaqua, N.Y.: Rossel Books, 1963.

Bergson, Henri. "Laughter." In *Comedy*, ed. Wylie Sypher. Doubleday Anchor Books. Garden City, N.Y.: Doubleday, 1956.

The Book of Enoch or 1 Enoch. Ed. and trans. R. H. Charles. Oxford: Clarendon Press, 1912.

Coleridge, Samuel Taylor. *Biographia Literaria*. In *The Selected Poetry and Prose*, ed. Donald A. Stauffer. Modern Library College Editions. New York: Random House, 1951.

Cordovero, Moses. "Or Ne'erav." In *Moses Cordovero's Introduction to Kabbalah: An Annotated Translation of His Or Ne'erav*, ed. and trans. Ira Robinson. Hoboken, N.J.: Ktav, 1994.

The Ethiopic Book of Enoch. Ed. and trans. Michael A. Knibb. Vol. 2. Oxford: Clarendon Press, 1978.

Gassset, Ortega y. *On Love: Aspects of a Single Theme*. Trans. Toby Talbot. New York: Meridian Books, 1958.

Homer. *The Iliad*. Trans. E. V. Rieu. Harmondsworth, U.K.: Penguin Books, 1950.

James, William. *The Varieties of Religious Experience*. The Modern Library. New York: Random House, 1902.

Jenny, Hans. *Cymatics*. 2 Vols. Basel: Basilius Presse, 1974.

Jung, C. G. *On the Nature of the Psyche*. Trans. R. F. C. Hull. Bollingen Paperback. Princeton: Princeton University Press, 1969.

————. "Foreword." *The I Ching*, trans. Richard Wilhelm and Cary F. Baynes. Bollingen Series XIX. Princeton: Princeton University Press, 1978.

Kook, Abraham Isaac. "The Lights of Penitence." In *The Lights of Penitence, The Moral Principles, Lights of Holiness, Essays, Letters, and Poems*, ed. and trans. Ben Zion Bokser. New York: Paulist Press, 1978.

Luzzatto, Moshe Chaim. *Derech haShem: The Way of God.* Trans. Aryeh Kaplan. 2nd ed. New York: Feldheim, 1978.

Milton, John. "De Doctrina Christiana." Trans. Bishop Charles R. Sumner. In *John Milton: Complete Poems and Major Prose*, ed. Merritt Y. Hughes. New York: The Odyssey Press, 1957.

Muktananda Paramahansa, Swami. *The Play of Consciousness*. N.c., Calif.: Shree Gurudev Siddha Yoga Ashram, 1974.

Ouspensky, P. D. *In Search of the Miraculous*. New York: Harcourt Brace Jovanovich, 1949.

Plato. *The Symposium.* Trans. B. Jowett. New York: Graystone Press, n.d.

————. *Plato's Cosmology: The Timaeus of Plato*. Ed. and trans. Francis MacDonald Cornford. Indianapolis: Hackett Publishing, 1997.

Otto, Rudolf. *The Idea of the Holy: An Inquiry into the Non-Rational Factor in the Idea of the Divine and Its Relation to the Rational.* Trans. John W. Harvey. New York: Oxford University Press, 1958.

Rosenzweig, Frans. *The Star of Redemption*. Trans. William W. Hallo. Boston: Beacon Press, 1972.

The Secret of the Golden Flower. Trans. Richard Wilhelm with an introduction by Carl Jung. New York: Harcourt Brace Jovanovich, 1962.

Sefer Yetzirah. Ed. and trans. Aryeh Kaplan. York Beach, Maine: Samuel Weiser, 1990.

"Shiur Qoma." Trans. The Work of the Chariot. In *The Secret Garden*, ed. David Meltzer. New York: Seabury Press, 1963.

The Shi'ur Qomah: Liturgy and Theurgy in Pre-Kabbalistic Jewish Mysticism. Ed. and trans. Martin Samuel Cohen. Lanham, Md.: University Press of America, 1983.

Siddur Tehillat Hashem. Ed. and trans. Rabbi Nissen Mangel. Brooklyn: Merkos L'Inyonei Chinuch, 1982.

Stendhal. *On Love.* Trans. H. B. V. under the direction of C. K. Scott-Moncrieff. Doubleday Anchor Books. Garden City, N.Y.: Doubleday, 1957.

Sophocles. *Oedipus at Colonus.* Trans. Robert Fitzgerald. In *The Complete Greek Tragedies*, ed. David Grene and Richmond Lattimore. 4 vols. Chicago: University of Chicago Press, 1959.

Teilhard de Chardin, Pierre. *The Future of Man.* Trans. Norman Denny. New York: Harper & Row, 1969.

3 Enoch or The Hebrew Book of Enoch. Ed. and trans. Hugo Odeberg, prolegomenon by Jonas C. Greenfield. New York: Ktav, 1973.

Vital, Chayyim. *Eitz Chayyim.* Jerusalem: Kitvei ha-Ari, 1958.

———. *The Tree of Life: The Palace of Adam Kadmon.* Ed. and trans. Donald Wilder Menzi and Zwe Padeh. Northvale, N.J.: Jason Aronson, 1999.

Wolfram, Stephen. *A New Kind of Science.* Champaign, Ill.: Wolfram Media, 2002.

The Zohar. Trans. Harry Sperling, Maurice Simon, and Paul P. Levertoff. 5 vols. London: Soncino Press, 1978.

The Zohar. Ed. Reuven Margoliot, Hebrew-Aramaic edition. 3 vols. Jerusalem: Mossad ha-Rav Kook, 1964.

SECONDARY SOURCES

Bentov, Itzhak. *Stalking the Wild Pendulum.* New York: E. P. Dutton, 1977.

Ben Zion, Raphael, ed. and trans. *An Anthology of Jewish Mysticism.* With an introduction by Gershon Winkler. New York: The Judaica Press, 1981.

Black, Max. *Models and Metaphors: Studies in Language and Philosophy.* Ithaca, N.Y.: Cornell University Press, 1962.

Bloom, Harold. *Kabbalah and Criticism.* New York: Seabury Press, 1975.

Elior, Rachel. *The Paradoxical Ascent to God: The Kabbalistic Theosophy of Habad Hasidism.* Trans. Jeffrey M. Green. Albany: State University of New York Press, 1993.

Epstein, Gerald. *Healing Visualizations: Creating Health through Imagery.* New York: Bantam Books, 1989.

Ferrer, Jorge N. *Revisioning Transpersonal Theory: A Participatory Vision of Human Spirituality.* Albany: State Universtiy of New York Press, 2002.

Gerson, Jessica. "Norman Mailer: Sex, Creativity, and God." *Mosaic* 4 (June 1982): 5.

Hayward, C. T. R. *The Jewish Temple: A Non-Biblical Sourcebook.* London: Routledge, 1996.

Hertz, J. H., ed. and trans. *The Pentateuch and Haftorahs.* 2nd ed. London: Soncino Press, 1972.

Heschel, Abraham J. *Between God and Man.* Ed. Fritz A. Rothschild. New York: Free Press, 1959.

———. *The Sabbath: Its Meaning for Modern Man.* New York: Farrar, Straus and Giroux, 1951.

————. "Toward an Understanding of Halachah." In *Conservative Judaism and Jewish Law*, ed. Seymour Siefel. New York: The Rabbinical Assembly, 1977.

Hoffman, Edward, ed. *Opening the Inner Gates: New Paths in Kabbalah and Psychology*. Boston: Shambhala, 1995.

Hutchison, Michael. *Megabrain*. New York: Ballantine Books, 1986.

Idel, Moshe. *Kabbalah: New Perspectives.* New Haven: Yale University Press, 1988.

————. *Messianic Mystics*. New Haven: Yale University Press, 1998.

Jacobs, Louis. *Jewish Mystical Testimonies*. New York: Schocken Books, 1978.

————. "Introduction." *On Ecstasy*, by Dobh Baer of Lubavitch. Chappaqua, N.Y.: Rossel Books, 1963.

Jaynes, Julian. *The Origin of Consciousness in the Breakdown of the Bicameral Mind*. Boston: Houghton Mifflin, 1976.

Kaplan, Aryeh. *Immortality, Resurrection and the Age of the Universe*. New York: Ktav, 1993.

————. *Jewish Meditation: A Practical Guide*. New York: Schocken Books, 1985.

————. *Meditation and Kabbalah*. York Beach, Maine: Samuel Weiser, 1982.

————. *Meditation and the Bible*. New York: Samuel Weiser, 1978.

————. ed. and trans. *The Bahir.* New York: Samuel Weiser, 1979.

————, ed. and trans. *The Light Beyond: Adventures in Hassidic Thought*. New York: Mosnaim, 1981.

————, ed. and trans. *Living Torah: The Five Books of Moses*. New York: Moznaim, 1981.

————, ed. and trans. *Sefer Yetzirah.* York Beach, Maine: Samuel Weiser, 1990.

Klein, Eliahu, ed. and trans. *Kabbalah of Creation: Isaac Luria's Earlier Mysticism*. Northvale, N.J.: Jason Aronson, 2000.

Klausner, Joseph. *The Messianic Idea in Israel*. Trans. W. F. Stinespring. New York: Macmillan, 1955.

Lamm, Norman, ed. and trans. *The Religious Thought of Hasidism: Text and Commentary*. New York: Yeshiva University Press, 1999.

Lawlor, Robert. "Ancient Temple Architecture." In *Lindisfarne Letter 10: Geometry and Architecture*. W. Stockbridge, Mass.: Lindisfarne Press, 1980.

————. *Sacred Geometry: Philosophy and Practice*. New York: Crossroad, 1982.

Leet, Leonora. *Elizabethan Love Tragedy*. New York: New York University Press, 1971. (Published under the name Leonora Leet Brodwin.)

————. *Renewing the Covenant: A Kabbalistic Guide to Jewish Spirituality*. Rochester, Vt.: Inner Traditions, 1999.

————. *The Secret Doctrine of the Kabbalah: Recovering the Key to Hebraic Sacred Science*. Rochester, Vt.: Inner Traditions, 1999.

Liebes, Yehuda. *Studies in Jewish Myth and Jewish Messianism.* Trans. Batya Stein. Albany: State University of New York Press, 1993.

————. *Studies in the Zohar.* Trans. Arnold Schwartz, Stephanie Nakache, and Penina Peli. Albany: State University of New York Press, 1993.

Pribram, Karl H. and Diane McGuinness, "Arousal, Activation, and Effort in the Control of Attention." *Psychological Review* 82 (1975): 130.

Reik, Theodore. *Masochism in Modern Man.* New York: Farrar, Strauss, 1941.

Rougemont, Denis de. *Love in the Western World.* Trans. Montgomery Belgion. Doubleday Anchor Books. Garden City, N.Y.: Doubleday, 1940.

Schmeck, Jr., Harold M. "The Complex Organ Known as Skin Continues to Surprise." *New York Times,* 8 November 1983, sec. C, p. 3.

Schwaller de Lubicz, R. A. *The Temple in Man: Sacred Architecture and the Perfect Man.* Trans. Robert and Deborah Lawlor. Rochester, Vt.: Inner Traditions, 1977.

Scholem, Gershom. *Kabbalah.* New York: New American Library, 1974.

————. *The Messianic Idea in Judaism and Other Essays on Jewish Spirituality.* Trans. Hillel Halkin. New York: Schocken Books, 1971.

————. *On the Kabbalah and Its Symbolism.* Trans. Ralph Manheim. New York: Schocken Books, 1969.

————. *Sabbatai Sevi: The Mystical Messiah.* Trans. R. J. Zwi Werblowsky. Bollingen Series XCIII. Princeton: Princeton University Press, 1973.

Steiner, Rudolf. *The Inner Nature of Music and the Experience of Tone.* Hudson, N.Y.: Anthroposophic Press, 1983.

Steinsaltz, Adin. *In the Beginning: Discourses on Chasidic Thought.* Ed. and trans. Yehuda Hanegbi. Northvale, N.J.: Jason Aronson, 1995.

Tishby, Isaiah. *The Wisdom of the Zohar: An Anthology of Texts.* Trans. David Goldstein. 3 vols. London: Oxford University Press, 1991.

Waite, A. E. *The Holy Kabbalah.* New Hyde Park, N.Y.: University Books, 1969.

Weil, Simone. "The Pythagorean Doctrine." In *Intimations of Christianity,* trans. Elisabeth Chase Geissbuhler. London: Routledge and Kegan Paul, 1957.

Wolfson, Elliot R. *Along the Path.* Albany: State University of New York Press, 1995.

————. *Through a Speculum That Shines: Vision and Imagination in Medieval Jewish Mysticism.* Princeton: Princeton University Press, 1994.

INDEX

AUTHORS

Abulafia, Abraham, 57, 153–56, 158, 165–66, 173, 234, 272, 348–349n
Aquinas, St. Thomas, 358n
Aristotle, 124–25, 148, 204, 272, 358n
Arnold, Matthew, 103
Augustine, St., 26, 169
Azriel of Gerona, 155–56

Baer, Dov of Lubavitch, 250, 287
Baer, Dov, the Maggid, 186, 193, 321
Bentov, Itzhak, 351n
Bergson, Henri, 149–50
Black, Max, 28
Blake, William, 107
Bloom, Harold, 352n

Chaucer, Geoffrey, 256
Chayyim of Volozhin, 322–26, 326, 333
Cohen, Martin Samuel, 341n
Coleridge, Samuel Taylor, 162–65, 167, 178, 186
Conrad, Joseph, 98–99, 162
Cordovero, Moses, 16, 203, 244, 337

Dante, 260
Descartes, Rene, 284

Dryden, John, 245
Elior, Rachel, 336n
Epstein, Gerald, 356n
Epstein, Kalonymus Kalman, 321–22

Ferrer, Jorge N., 342–44n
Fludd, Robert, 46–47
Frank, Jacob, 53, 278
Freud, Sigmund, 106, 204

Gasset, Ortega y, 252–53, 255

Hawthorne, Nathaniel, 104, 109
Haywood, C. T. R., 354–55n
Hesse, Herman, 263
Hero of Alexandria, 126
Hertz, J. H., 278
Heschel, Abraham J., 198–99, 201, 322, 355n
Hirsch, Tz'vi, 328–29, 361n
Homer, 104–5, 110, 150

Idel, Moshe, 272, 342–43n, 348n

Jacobs, Louis, 272, 362n
James, William, 63, 254–55, 258, 333–34, 342n, 346n
Jaynes, Julian, 84–87, 352n
Jenny, Hans, 345n

TITLES

SUBJECTS

BOOKS OF RELATED INTEREST

THE SECRET DOCTRINE OF THE KABBALAH
Recovering the Key to Hebraic Sacred Science
by Leonora Leet, Ph.D.

RENEWING THE COVENANT
A Kabbalistic Guide to Jewish Spirituality
by Leonora Leet, Ph.D.

KABBALISTIC ASTROLOGY
The Sacred Tradition of the Hebrew Sages
by Rabbi Joel C. Dobin, D.D.

THE SECRET DOWRY OF EVE
Woman's Role in the Development of Consciousness
by Glynda-Lee Hoffmann
Foreword by Joseph Chilton Pearce

ART AND SYMBOLS OF THE OCCULT
Images of Power and Wisdom
by James Wasserman

THE TEMPLE IN MAN
Sacred Architecture and the Perfect Man
by R. A. Schwaller de Lubicz

THE GENESIS AND GEOMETRY OF THE LABYRINTH
Architecture, Hidden Language, Myths, and Rituals
by Patrick Conty

CRAFTING THE SOUL
Creating Your Life as a Work of Art
by Rabbi Byron L. Sherwin, Ph.D.

Inner Traditions • Bear & Company
P.O. Box 388
Rochester, VT 05767
1-800-246-8648
www.InnerTraditions.com

Or contact your local bookseller